ROYAL THOROUGHBREDS

For Rosemary and Thomas

ROYAL THOROUGHBREDS

A History of the Royal Studs

ARTHUR FITZGERALD

SIDGWICK & JACKSON

LONDON

First published in Great Britain in 1990 by
Sidgwick & Jackson Limited

Copyright © 1990 by Arthur FitzGerald

ISBN 0-283-99593-9

Photoset by Rowland Phototypesetting Limited
Bury St Edmunds, Suffolk
Printed in Great Britain by
Mackays of Chatham plc, Chatham, Kent
for Sidgwick & Jackson Limited
1 Tavistock Chambers, Bloomsbury Way
London WC1A 2SG

Contents

Preface

The long history of the Royal Studs is closely involved with the evolution of the Thoroughbred from the native English running horse of the sixteenth century to the modern racehorse with its international pedigree. For over 450 years a succession of Kings and Queens of England have shown a love of racing, good horses and skill in breeding them and have made an enormous contribution to the development of the breed. It is with good reason that racing is called 'The sport of Kings'.

Much has already been written on the Monarchy and its involvement with racing but there has been a tendency to focus on certain periods and episodes which has given an inaccurate and distorted picture, repeated by successive authors. Arthur FitzGerald has made a fresh start and the three years of detailed research that lies behind this book has enabled him to fill in some enormous gaps and correct several serious misconceptions.

King Charles II is widely credited with having instigated the importation of stallions and mares from the Middle East to improve the native breed. This process in fact began over 100 years earlier with the purchase by Henry VIII of horses from Italy and Spain and while Charles II achieved much by his patronage of racing and Newmarket in particular, the credit for the most influential importations belongs to Elizabeth I, James I, Charles I and William III.

The author shows William, Duke of Cumberland, to be an unfairly maligned figure in history and the victim of a character assassination. However, his achievement in breeding Eclipse and Herod at his studs in Windsor Great Park is unquestioned. Today some 95 per cent of all Thoroughbreds descend in the male line from Eclipse and a high proportion of the remainder from Herod.

That Queen Victoria bred the winners of eleven Classic races will come as a surprise to many but the author shows how the

Royal Studs at Hampton Court during the nineteenth century became one of the most influential in the world at that time. Queen Victoria not only bred the great racehorses Memoir and La Flèche but their half-sister Maid Marian was dam of Polymelus, sire of Phalaris, founder of the world's greatest twentieth century sire line and whose representatives include Nearco, Nasrullah, Mill Reef, Northern Dancer, Mr Prospector and Nashwan.

There have been few breaks in the history of the Royal Studs; Oliver Cromwell was a disruptive influence although he appreciated a good horse, while the death of Queen Anne marked the start of the longest period of inactivity. The disposal sale of William IV's excellent stud in 1837 was a tragedy, but this was soon to be rectified when the stud at Hampton Court was re-established in 1850, mostly at the instigation of Prince Albert, and stocked with some of the best mares in the country.

The Royal Studs have operated from several locations during the last 500 years; Hampton Court, Tutbury, Malmesbury, Eltham, Oatlands, Windsor Great Park and their present bases at Sandringham, Wolferton and Polhampton. Today a quarter of the Royal mares are kept in Kentucky, which reflects the increasingly international nature of bloodstock breeding.

No Sovereign who has guided the fortunes of the Royal Studs has had more success derived from a thorough understanding and love of good horses than our present Queen. Although dwarfed in scale by their principal competitors, the Royal Studs today still have an international influence. Shirley Heights who stands at Sandringham is one of the most successful stallions in Europe. Bustino, an outstanding sire of broodmares, has stood at Wolferton since 1976. Sheikh Hamdan al Maktoum's superb Classic winner Nashwan is out of a Bustino mare bred by the Queen. Her Majesty has bred the winner of every English Classic race except the Derby, a victory in which is the principal objective of all those who work with the Royal Studs.

Arthur FitzGerald has produced the first comprehensive history of the Royal Studs; it will remain the authority on the subject for many years to come.

Michael Oswald
The Royal Studs
Sandringham

1

The Royal Studs in the Sixteenth

and Seventeenth Centuries

King Athelstan (924–40), the grandson of Alfred the Great, is the
first English Sovereign who is recorded as owning racehorses; his
brother-in-law, Hugh Capet, the founder of the Capetian dynasty
in France, presented him with a gift of some bred in Germany. No
record survives of the races in which they took part.

During the Middle Ages the English nobility and gentry amused
themselves with horse-races, often held at Easter and Pentecost.
Races were held annually at Chester, with prizes of silver bells.
The nobility owned superior running horses, sometimes called
hobbies or Galloways, and tested their ability in these races. A few
months before Richard II came to the throne in 1377, he took part
in a Match against the Earl of Arundel, in which both men rode
their own horses. As early as the reign of King John (1199–1216)
we find expenses incurred by running horses in the Register of
Royal Expenditure. Both Edward II (1307–27) and Edward III
(1327–77) are known to have bred horses. The first recorded
importation of Spanish Barb horses occurred in the latter's reign:
Arnold Garcy, the Keeper of the King's Horses in the south of
England, travelled to Spain to buy some Spanish Barbs for
Edward III. There is, however, no documentary evidence of the
existence or organization of a Royal Stud at this period, though
Henry V (1413–22) reputedly imported horses from the east, while
later in the century Edward IV (1461–83) also certainly bred horses
for racing.

It is likely that the Royal Studs were not organized systematically
until after Henry VIII came to the throne in 1509. During his reign
several statutes were passed with the aim of improving both the
quality and the number of horses in England; there is also evidence

in the Royal archives of Turin and Mantua that a very active trade in Barb horses existed between England and Mantua. Henry VIII imported some Barbs in 1514 and 1515 from Francesco Gonzaga, the Duke of Mantua. The Gonzaga family had originally imported Barb horses from North Africa and kept them at the Marmolata Stud on Lago di Mincio. Portraits by Giulio Romano of their descendants can be seen today at the Palazzo del Te in Mantua. The Marmolata Stud belonged to the Duke of Savoy, whose wife, the Duchess Catherine, was a daughter of King Philip II of Spain. Thus the Duke of Savoy was able to obtain stallions from the Spanish Royal Stud at Cordova, where the famous Andalusian jennet reigned supreme. It is also clear from the surviving correspondence between Henry VIII and Francesco Gonzaga that the King himself actually rode some of the horses imported from Mantua. A certain Carlo Cavriana wrote a very interesting monograph on the influence of the horses imported from Mantua on the evolution of the Thoroughbred.

Throughout his reign Henry VIII's agents were actively searching for the best horses they could buy on the Continent. In 1520 Sir Gregory de Cassalis bought him one 'which had no fellow in Italy'. Shortly afterwards, the Emperor Charles V of Spain sent the King twenty-five Spanish horses. In 1533 the Duke of Mantua gave Henry VIII some mares; he found 'this gift most agreeable; not merely because he delights in horses of that breed, but also because they were sent by His Excellency.' As a reciprocal present the King sent the Duke of Mantua some running horses, some English hounds and a lengthy letter of thanks.

For most of his reign Henry VIII's horses were kept at the stud at Eltham in Kent. An inventory of all the stock at Eltham was made in January 1531; these numbered eighty-five, but included nearly every breed of horse known in England. The fall of Cardinal Wolsey in 1530 meant that Hampton Court Palace came into the Royal possession, but it soon became apparent that neither Eltham nor Hampton Court was sufficiently large to accommodate all the horses the King was importing, and so the Royal Studs were formed.

The principal Royal Stud was established at Tutbury, near Burton-on-Trent in Staffordshire. In 1266 this property had been confiscated by Henry III from Robert de Ferrers, the Earl of Derby, after he had fought on the side of the rebel barons at the battle of Lewes in 1265. Henry III gave Tutbury to his relative, Edmund Plantagenet, soon to become the Earl of Lancaster. When his descendant, Henry Bolingbroke, ousted Richard II in 1399 and became King Henry IV, the association between the Duchy of Lancaster and the Crown commenced. Tutbury Castle, in which Mary Queen of Scots was imprisoned for so long, and its 6,840 acres of woodland and agricultural land, still belongs to the Duchy of Lancaster today.

Another Royal Stud was established at Cole Park, Malmesbury, after the dissolution of the monasteries in 1533–6. The Abbey of Malmesbury had been one of the richest and most important monasteries in England since the Norman Conquest.

During the short reigns of Edward VI (1547–53) and Queen Mary (1553–8) the Royal Studs deteriorated. When Queen Elizabeth I came to the throne in 1558, she soon ordered measures to be taken to restore the condition and prestige of the Royal Studs at Tutbury and Malmesbury, and commanded that the existing statutes for the improvement of the breed of horses be more strictly enforced and that landowners be compelled to maintain the numbers of horses laid down in those statutes. The Queen ordered William Humberson to make a further survey of Tutbury. Humberson did not think that there should be a stud at Tutbury at all; apparently he did not think the nature of the soil compatible with the breeding of good horses. He was wrong, as in fact the land around Tutbury and the River Dove consists of very rich pasture that has produced good horses of many breeds for several centuries. Humberson was much more concerned by his discovery that the Surveyor of the Tutbury Stud had embezzled money from timber after he had illegally felled trees in the Park.

As her first Master of the Horse, Queen Elizabeth I appointed Robert Dudley, Earl of Leicester, who was well aware that the Neapolitans had the reputation of being the greatest experts on the breeding of horses and studs in Europe. Leicester therefore commissioned a renowned authority on stud management, Prospero d'Osma, to come to England from Naples in 1576 to undertake a detailed survey of the Royal Studs at Tutbury and Malmesbury. D'Osma's report is an invaluable account of the state of the Royal Studs of Queen Elizabeth I, and on racehorse breeding in Tudor England.

Malmesbury was the first stud that d'Osma visited. There he found ten courser mares, eleven smaller courser mares and eight jennet mares, all healthy enough to be covered; there were also another five mares not in a condition to be covered and thirty-one three-year-old, two-year-old and yearling colts and fillies. The

3

Royal Stud at Malmesbury was thus of considerable size, but there does not appear to have been a stallion standing there.

At Tutbury d'Osma found twenty courser mares. He reported that as fifteen of them had foaled that year, they would be rested until the following year; the other five were to be covered that season by the grey courser stallion 'Grisone'. It would seem, therefore, that the mares were covered only every other year. The six small courser mares at Tutbury, d'Osma said, would be covered by the stallion 'Abbot', who was so named because of his large body, while the six jennet mares were to be covered in 1576 by the stallion called 'Argentino'. His list of mares not to be covered consists of only one and is probably incomplete. He also found twenty-two colts and fillies aged three, two and one at Tutbury.

After Prospero d'Osma had finished his inventory of the stock at the Royal Studs, he proceeded to make his recommendations. He argued strongly against the practice of allowing mares to foal every year, and suggested that they should be given a year's rest after foaling to achieve perfection in 'agility, strength and disposition'. His advice on stallions was that 'if a stallion is given proper care, he can cover twelve mares (much to his pleasure) without suffering any damage. Calculating twelve mares to each stallion, I reckon six stallions will be enough for Her Majesty's entire stud.' He then recommended that the stallions should reside at the studs, both for the health of the stallion and to decrease the expenses of managing the studs.

Prospero d'Osma laid great stress on the absolute need of sound dry pastures and different varieties of grass for the successful breeding of horses. On account of the wet and fen-like nature of the Malmesbury ground, he advised that all the stock there should be transferred to Tutbury; this recommendation was ignored. He further considered it essential that the stock should not be kept in overcrowded conditions and that they should be moved frequently from one paddock to another; and that proper shelters should be provided for the mares and foals so that they could be kept cool in summer and warm in winter. Such shelters evidently did not exist at Tutbury and Malmesbury in 1576. D'Osma advised that mares and foals should be fed more bran and corn, and that mares should be covered in mid-April so that their foals would be born in mid-March. For astrological reasons, d'Osma believed that stallions should not cover mares when the moon was waning. This advice must have been heeded by several breeders, since Lord D'arcy in 1620 particularly noted that the moon was new when his mare Grey Gorge was covered. In 1658 the Duke of Newcastle felt it necessary to declare that 'the moon's aspect, or that of any other celestial body, is absurd in affairs of this kind, and it matters not whether the moon is increasing or decreasing, for horses are not got by astronomy, or by the almanack.'

In 1588 the Earl of Leicester died, and was succeeded as Master of the Horse by Robert Devereux, Earl of Essex, who retained the post until he was executed in 1601. In 1596 he received from Thomas Eyton, who had had overall control of both studs since 1576, a disturbing report on the condition of the Malmesbury Stud, and the failure of its manager, Thomas Baskerville, to carry out his duties effectively. Eyton found that the fences were in such a bad state of repair that colts broke out and covered other people's mares; that the gates were not kept locked; that inadequate fencing allowed the colts to get into the mares' paddocks and cover them; and that a great many trees had been felled. Baskerville, who was severely reprimanded by the Earl of Essex, made the excuse that he had been 'afflicted with a most deadly malady to the loss of my limbs and perfectness of my speech, whereby I am unable to attend to your commands, and answer the unjust slanders of my most malignant and ancient foes.' A further survey in 1598 reported that there were thirty mares and fillies and twenty-four colts up to three years old at Malmesbury; there were no stallions at either stud.

In the reign of Queen Elizabeth I racing was a very popular pastime; we know that race-meetings were held at Chester, Doncaster, York, Croydon, Richmond in Yorkshire, Lincoln, Carlisle and Salisbury, and in St James's Park in London. Queen Elizabeth I attended race-meetings at Croydon in May 1574, 1585, 1587 and 1588, when she was the guest of Archbishop Parker of Canterbury. On each occasion he had a great deal of difficulty in finding adequate accommodation for the Officers of State, her ladies-in-waiting and all their servants. Races in those days were often matches between two horses, the owners of which had challenged each other with one of their best running horses.

No description of either the actual races at Croydon or the horses taking part survives. The Earl of Essex as Master of the Horse donated a golden snaffle to the Corporation of the City of Salisbury to be run for annually; fifty years after his death, this snaffle was sold to augment the value of the prize of one of the Corporation's races at Salisbury. The races for the Silver Bells at Carlisle commenced in 1559, while in Scotland race-meetings were held at Lanark, Peebles, Dumfries, Haddington and on the Anglo-Scottish border at Berwick. One of the most enthusiastic supporters of horse-racing in the reign of Elizabeth I was the fifth Earl of Rutland, who had quite a few racehorses; we know that one of them won 'the forest race of Galteresse' on 21 February 1596, and that later the same year another of his horses won a Match at Galterley Moor near Richmond.

When Queen Elizabeth I died, Sir Thomas Carey left Richmond Palace in Surrey to take the news to her heir, King James VI of Scotland. Setting off at six o'clock on the morning of 24 March 1603, within minutes of her death, he arrived at Holyrood Palace in Edinburgh on the evening of 26 March to inform the King that he had for two days been King James I of England. This epic ride underlines the quality and speed of the best horses in England at this time.

On King James I's accession, the Royal Studs were in a flourishing condition. At Tutbury Queen Elizabeth I had left thirty brood-mares. Although not as enthusiastic about racing as some of his court, James I set great store by horsemanship. In his famous treatise *Religio Regis or the Faith and Duty of a Prince* he wrote: 'The honourablest and most commendable Games that a King can use are on Horseback, for it becomes a Prince above all men to be a good Horseman.' As a result of his great love of hunting, King James I and his court became frequent visitors to Newmarket, which he first visited on 27 February 1605, going hunting the next day in the fields near Fordham. At first he stayed at an inn called The Griffin; but as it became customary for him to remain there for weeks at a time during the winter months, he built a palace on its site complete with gardens, stables, kennels, brewhouse and a tennis court. James was so often at Newmarket that there was a public outcry 'against too much sport and too little business of state'. Parliament even sent a deputation of twelve Members to Newmarket to petition His Majesty to turn his gracious attention to public affairs, but the King turned a deaf ear to their entreaties and warned them off the Heath.

James I was not a particularly good horseman; it would be accurate to say that his horse carried him rather than that he rode it. On one occasion when out hunting, he had a serious fall, disappearing head first through the ice into a frozen river, so that only his boots remained in view. When rescued, 'much water came out of his mouth and body,' and he had to be put in a warm bed to recover. He also had the eccentric habit when at a kill of plunging his arms and legs into the entrails of the dead animal, apparently on the advice of the Royal Physician who recommended this action for the King's health.

Newmarket became almost the second capital of England; the principal activities of the Court were hare hunting, coursing and falconry, but some of the courtiers spent much of their time horse-racing across the Heath. The King himself did not take part, but certainly attended these meetings; even the Queen's death from dropsy on 1 March 1619 was not allowed to interfere with the spring race-meeting at Newmarket on 19 March. James also attended race-meetings elsewhere; at Lincoln 'on Thursday April 3rd 1617 there was a great Horse race on the Heath for a Cupp, where His Majesty was present, and stood on a scaffold the citie had caused to be set up.' That James I owned racehorses cannot be doubted; in 1604 the Earl of Worcester, his Master of the Horse, received £59 from the Treasury for board wages for four child-riders who were under the supervision of the four riders of the stable. The King continued the policy of importing horses from Spain and Italy for the Royal Studs.

In April 1605 the Archduke Albert gave James I 'twelve mares, all in foal, four horses, and eleven stallions, all of them coursers of Naples'; these were sent to Greenwich Palace, where Queen Elizabeth had maintained a large stud of Barbary horses. On 20 December the King bought an Arabian horse from Gervase Markham for £154; Markham had related in 1599 how a member of his family had owned a horse which had been ridden from a part of Arabia called Angelica to Constantinople, across Europe and finally to England, where he gained a great reputation as a stallion. The Arabian that James I bought was probably sired by this horse, but he was utterly useless on the racecourse. The Duke of Newcastle reported that 'when he came to Run, every Horse beat him', and that he was 'but a Little Horse and no Rarity for shape, for I have seen Many English Horses far Finer'.

Two fortuitous events in James I's reign were to have an immense influence on the evolution of the Thoroughbred: the appointment of George Villiers, Duke of Buckingham, as the Master of the Horse in 1616, and the projected marriage alliance between Charles, the Prince of Wales, and the Infanta of Spain in 1623. Buckingham was passionately interested in breeding, and after 1616 spared no efforts to improve and augment the Royal Studs. In November 1616 Sir Thomas Edmonds, the Treasurer of the Household, returned to England from Italy with six Barbs, which were sent to the Royal paddocks at Newmarket. In 1617 Villiers sent George Digby, the brother of the Ambassador in Madrid, John Digby, later the Earl of Bristol, to Italy to buy horses. Digby returned in the autumn of 1618 with four horses that he had bought in Naples and Genoa. About the same time Queen Anne, James I's wife, informed Buckingham that her father, the King of Denmark, had sent her twelve mares, all of whom were in foal. A little later James I wrote to Buckingham: 'God thanke the maister of the horse for provyding me such a number of faire usefull horses.' Buckingham's friends at the Court of Madrid regularly procured for him some of the famous jennets of Andalusia, which he sent both to the Royal Studs and to his own estates.

In late February 1623 the Duke of Buckingham and Charles, Prince of Wales, travelling incognito, left England to travel across France to Madrid to seek the hand of the Infanta of Spain. Their heavy baggage, and twelve pacing nags, a present from James I to the King of Spain, went by sea to Santander on the *Mary Rose*, whose commander, Captain Wilbraham, was ordered to remain in the port to bring back some horses from Madrid. The captain of another ship, Sir Richard Bingley, had received similar orders that spring when his cargo included a Barbary horse bought by the Ambassador in Madrid, the Earl of Bristol, and a camel. Sir Richard complained, 'My respect to the honour of the King's ships makes me sorry to have them used as transporters of beasts.' Another consignment of approximately thirty-five horses, which had been presented to the Prince of Wales and Buckingham in Madrid, left San Sebastian for England later that summer.

By the autumn of 1623 the negotiations for the marriage had proved unsuccessful, and Buckingham and the Prince of Wales left Madrid. The King of Spain's final present to Charles was twenty-four horses and several mares and foals from his famous stud at Cordova, while Buckingham was given twelve horses. James I commanded the Commissioners of the Navy to arrange for their transportation to England 'with all expedition'. The Cordova stud was famous throughout Europe; the Guzman breed, as it was called, were the descendants of twelve very fine Andalusian mares and a stallion that had belonged to the Ambassador of the King of Morocco to the Court of Charles V of Spain. In 1600 Solomon de Branc, head groom to Henri IV of France, considered these Spanish horses to be the best in Europe. In the inventory of the Hampton Court Stud taken in 1623, it is recorded that all the mares were covered either by jennets or by Barbary horses, a distinction being drawn between the jennet of Andalusia and the Barbary from other parts of Spain or Morocco. There are only two lists extant of the stock at the Hampton Court Stud before its dispersal in 1650, but both illustrate the importance of Spanish horses in the estimation of Buckingham and his contemporaries. The first records the matings ordered by Buckingham in 1620; thirteen mares, most of them Spanish, were covered in May and June. The second details the twenty-three mares covered at Hampton Court in 1623 and the stallions, all of whom were jennets or Barbary horses, that covered them. Few of the mares' pedigrees are given in this inventory, but as many had been presents from diplomats like Sir Francis Cottington, the Earl of Carlisle and Sir Thomas Rich, all of whom had been in Madrid, the likelihood is that most were Spanish jennets or Barbs. After its dispersal under Oliver Cromwell in 1650, the Hampton Court Stud was not used for breeding again until the reigns of William III and Queen Anne.

An inventory of the Malmesbury Stud in 1620, ordered by the Duke of Buckingham, showed that there were thirty-nine mares there. In 1624 at Tutbury there were forty-seven mares, fifty-one youngstock and fourteen foals. When inventories were taken after his death in 1628, there were forty-four mares at Tutbury and thirty-two at Malmesbury.

In May 1620 Buckingham married Lady Katherine Manners, the only child and heiress of the sixth Earl of Rutland, the richest man in England. He thus came into possession of the great estate of Helmsley in Yorkshire, where the Earl had an important stud. The Earl and his forebears had taken a great interest in both racing and breeding since the reign of Henry VIII. It would have been only natural for Buckingham to have sent some of the horses and mares he received from Spain to this stud. It was recognized at the time that the best British horses were bred in the north, especially in Yorkshire, and Helmsley was to play a significant role in the evolution of the Thoroughbred.

Both James I and Buckingham were well known enthusiasts at gambling for high stakes. The King gave a party on Twelfth Night in 1608 to which no one was admitted unless he came with £300 in cash. Throughout England in the reigns of James I and Charles I more and more race-meetings were taking place on a regular basis, attracting large crowds. A contemporary play by James Shirley called *Hyde Park* revolves around a race won by a character called 'Jockey' and held in London's biggest park. Disputes were by no means infrequent, many clearly the result of gambling. At one meeting James I was attending, because of 'foul play or foul words, one Ramsey, a Scottishman, struck Philip Herbert with his riding rod.' The incident was sufficiently grave for the King to intervene. He satisfied Philip Herbert's wounded honour and placated his followers by creating him a knight, a baron, a viscount and an earl on the spot!

King Charles I, who ascended the throne in 1625, was an exceptionally fine horseman, and as devoted to hunting as his father had been. Newmarket remained the second capital of England, and in 1630 the King, the Court, the ministers and the whole government were to be found there. The palace was enlarged, and the hospitality was on a lavish scale. 'There were daily prepared no less than eighty six tables groaning under five hundred dishes at each meal, not to speak of bread, beer and wine. This prodigious plenty in the King's Court caused amazement to foreigners and was much honour for the kingdom.' Among the foreign diplomats at the Court was the painter Rubens, who had been chosen as emissary by the King of Spain to negotiate a treaty with England mainly on account of Charles I's great interest in painting. While at Newmarket Rubens persuaded the King to sit for his portrait, during which he had ample opportunity to advocate a treaty with Spain, which was signed soon afterwards in Madrid. When Rubens was asked if Spain's envoy amused himself with painting occasionally, he replied: 'No, the painter amuses himself with diplomacy.' Rubens was knighted by Charles I before leaving Newmarket, as was another very famous artist at the Court, the Dutchman Van Dyck, who painted the renowned portraits of the King and his family.

The King's problems with Parliament overshadowed all the other events of his reign. Their culmination in the Civil War, Charles's execution in 1649 and the establishment of the 'Commonwealth' under the dictatorship of Oliver Cromwell had profound and severe effects on the Royal Studs. The Studs had continued to thrive during most of the reign, though importations of foreign horses were inevitably on a much smaller scale than in that of James I, given the King's financial and political difficulties.

In July 1649 Oliver Cromwell and Parliament sent four Commissioners, A. Mildemay, N. Lempriere, P. Carteret and R. Grafton, to the Royal Stud at Tutbury to take an inventory. They reported that there was a total of 140 horses at Tutbury, which they valued at £1,982. This document is of immense importance in the history of the evolution of the Thoroughbred since it gives a detailed account of all the horses and broodmares in the possession of Charles I at his death. The stock at Tutbury consisted of fifty-seven mares and fillies, twenty-two horses, thirty-seven colts, thirteen filly foals and eleven colt foals. Although the full pedigree of each of the horses listed is not given, the name of its sire is. The number of stallions that had been used was twenty-one, but six predominate: Black Morocco, Frisell, Newcastle, Lennox, Rupert and Fantus. Newcastle clearly came from Welbeck and had been imported by the Duke of Newcastle, whose wife stated in her husband's biography in 1667 that the Duke thought Spanish and Barb horses much the best. The origin of Black Morocco, the sire of seventeen horses, is self-evident, as is that of The Spaniard and Brown Bay Cottington, who derived his name from that of the English Ambassador in Madrid. It is likely that the majority of the others were descendants of the horses imported by Buckingham and James I.

The Council of State considered this inventory on 31 July 1649, and decided not to break up the Tutbury Stud immediately on account of the huge number of horses killed during the Civil War. Gregory Julian, who had been the Stud manager since about 1618, was dismissed on 8 June 1650, and the entire management of the Stud was passed to Major Edward Downes. On 2 July 1650 Lord Grey, Sir William Armyne and Sir Gilbert Pickering were instructed to choose six of the best horses at the Tutbury Stud for Oliver Cromwell. On 4 July, those horses that Downes had already sent to the former Royal Mews were sold; regrettably no record of that sale has survived. On 17 August 1650 Downes was instructed to sell Major General Harrison as many of the Royal horses as he wanted at reasonable prices. On 14 September the Council of State gave orders that the horses, mares and colts were to be put up for sale before the winter. This sale had still not taken place on 9 December, when Downes was told to let Lord Grey have as many horses as he wanted, at a market price, on condition that it did not prejudice the sale. Two days later Downes, by then promoted to Lieutenant-Colonel, was instructed to give the Parliamentarian General, Sir William Brereton, some mares and colts worth £100. By 4 January 1651 the sale of the stock of the Royal Stud at Tutbury had clearly taken place, as the Council of State ordered on that day that the money received from the sale should be paid to a Mr Frost and that Downes should be paid his expenses.

No particulars of the sale of the Royal Stud at Tutbury have been preserved. Possibly the monies obtained were never accounted for to the Exchequer; or the papers relating to the sales may have been destroyed in the fire at Whitehall Palace in 1693. The dispersal of the stock at Tutbury may not have been such a catastrophe as might appear at first sight, for it meant that breeders all over the country, especially in the north, acquired the foreign blood that had previously been concentrated in the Royal Studs; this can only have benefited their own studs. We know that six of the horses from Tutbury were presented to Colonel Michael Jones, the Commander-in-Chief in Leinster, as a reward for his services in Ireland for the Parliamentarian cause. Five of these 'royal stud barbs' were later acquired by the Earl of Thomond, and accounted for the success of his family on the Irish Turf.

The future Charles II fled the country after the battle of Worcester in 1651. He had loved horses all his life, and on hearing that the Royal Studs were to be dispersed, commissioned his brother James, Duke of York, to see whether the studs could be saved. The Duke of York's pleas, however, fell on deaf ears.

There is no written record of the fate of the other Royal Stud, Malmesbury, in 1649. We can only assume that it was dispersed in similar fashion, as there is no record of the Royal Family breeding horses there after the Restoration in 1660. We know from John Evelyn's diary that Parliamentarian soldiers totally ransacked the smaller Royal Stud at Eltham. He described 'both palace and chapel in miserable ruins, the noble woods and park destroyed' in April 1655.

In 1649 the Council of State banned horse-racing throughout England, for reasons of security. The Council of State in February 1655 felt that since race-meetings attracted immense crowds of people, many of whom were Royalists, they might be used as a cover for plots to be hatched against the Commonwealth. Oliver Cromwell in fact was fond of horses and fully realized the importance of encouraging good breeding, even if his ultimate aim was the improvement of cavalry horses rather than racing stock. In 1655 Cromwell instructed Longland, who was in the diplomatic service in Livorno, to buy some coursers from Naples. He reported on 18 June 1655 that:

I now have advice from my friend at Naples that his Highness' commission for the two horses and four mares is complete, I hope to his Highness' full content . . . I do not know yet whether I shall speed in the commission I gave to Aleppo for a horse; but if I do, I am confident, the world has not better horses than that place affords.

These six horses cost the Lord Protector 2,382 piastres.

Cromwell was also anxious to obtain some Arabian horses, and in September 1657 instructions were sent to Sir Thomas Bendyshe, the Ambassador in Constantinople, telling him to assist in the purchase of two in Aleppo and two others in Constantinople, 'and cause them to be sent to England'. It was still very difficult at that time to obtain horses in the region around Aleppo. It appears that only one, a grey horse, could be acquired, and that was shipped to England aboard the *Dartmouth* in the charge of Nicholas Baxter, Cromwell's Gentleman of Horse, arriving at Gravesend in November 1657. Cromwell died a year later in 1658, about the time Place got possession of a 'White Turk' stallion. It seems very likely that on Cromwell's death Place despatched the horse imported from Aleppo to his home in Dinsdale in Yorkshire, for it is difficult to understand how else he could have obtained a stallion from Turkey. Place is also reported to have concealed one of Cromwell's best mares in a cellar in Fenchurch Street at the time of the Restoration, and to have sent her to Dinsdale, where she was known as the 'Coffin Mare', when matters had quietened down. Cromwell had probably obtained her from Tutbury. She was put to the 'White Turk' and bred The White Turk Mare, the dam of The Coppin Mare by the Selaby Turk, a Barb imported in 1699. The Coppin Mare is the ancestress of several notable horses, including Emilius.

In the Tutbury inventory in 1649 there appears 'One Grisled mare with a half Moone in her forhead, with a horse foale'. She was by the stallion Carlton, and was valued at £25. It is likely that she was acquired by Thomas, the third Lord Fairfax, in 1650, and that she is the mare Old Bald Peg who appears in the Stud Book as the dam of Lord Fairfax's Old Morocco mare, Old Peg, by his Morocco Barb. Old Bald Peg is the ancestress of such eminent stallions as Spanker, Flying Childers, the first Derby winner Diomed, Sansovino and Hyperion.

The second Duke of Buckingham had inherited the estate of Helmsley on the assassination of his father in 1628, and found there several horses and mares imported by the first Duke from Spain and Morocco, which had not gone either to the Royal Studs or to his other private estates. In the Civil War he had espoused the Royalist cause, and after Charles I's execution his Helmsley estate was confiscated by the Parliamentarians; Buckingham himself went into exile. Helmsley was given in 1651 to Lord Fairfax, who had besieged and captured Helmsley for the Roundheads in 1644. Lord Fairfax was well known as a breeder of horses, and the stud at Helmsley must have been a major attraction of his new estate. He later wrote a short treatise on breeding, which unhappily has not survived. He almost certainly purchased other horses, in addition to the 'Grisled mare' by Carlton, at the Tutbury dispersal sale in 1650. Lord Fairfax retained possession of Helmsley until the marriage of his only daughter, Mary, to the second Duke of Buckingham in 1657, by which time the Duke had made his peace with Cromwell and returned to England. Fairfax then restored Helmsley to its original owner, his son-in-law, and Buckingham continued breeding racehorses at Helmsley for the rest of his life. The Old Morocco mare bred the famous Spanker to D'arcy's Yellow Turk there in about 1665. When the Duke of Buckingham died in April 1688, Helmsley was sold to Sir Charles Dunscombe to help meet the ducal debts.

Another Parliamentarian soldier, Sir Arthur Hazlerigg, the Colonel of the cavalry regiment called The Lobsters, was permitted to buy as many of the Tutbury horses as he wanted in 1650. He was also given Woodstock Park, to which he sent the stock he had acquired from Tutbury and some racing galloways he had obtained when Governor of Newcastle upon Tyne. In November 1659, realizing that the Restoration was at hand, he sold off all his horses at Woodstock. Hazlerigg himself died in the Tower of London in 1660.

King Charles II arrived in London after nine years of exile on 29 May 1660. One week later, on 6 June, he appointed James D'arcy his Master of Horse and Master of the Royal Stud at Tutbury. James D'arcy was the sixth son of the seventh Lord D'arcy de Knayth of Hornby Castle, near Beldale, Yorkshire. He was born in 1617, and had married Isabel, daughter and heiress of Sir Marmaduke Wyvill, thus acquiring the Sedbury estate, near Richmond, Yorkshire. Both he, and later his son James D'arcy the younger, became closely associated with the famous stud at Sedbury.

King Charles II's first command to James D'arcy as Master of the Royal Stud was that he should inspect Tutbury as quickly as possible, and report his findings to him. D'arcy informed the King that Tutbury had been totally destroyed during the Commonwealth and that it was useless as a stud. He therefore proposed to

Charles II that he should receive a fee of £200 per annum for his office, and that he should also provide the King with 'twelve extraordinary good colts' each year for £800. He pointed out that the King would not incur any expense for broodmares as he would breed the colts from his own mares and two stallions. Charles II considered this proposal to be in his interest, remembering that the Tutbury stud had cost his father between £1,200 and £1,500 a year to run. He accepted D'arcy's proposal on 4 June 1661 with the following conditions: the twelve colts should be bred from D'arcy's own mares and on his own estates; that they should be twelve choice horses; and that the charge would never exceed £800 annually. Tutbury remained in the possession of the Duchy of Lancaster, but was never again used as a stud for breeding Thoroughbreds.

In 1673, when James D'arcy died, his post was filled by Sutton Oglethorpe. Oglethorpe, whose stud was not as large as the D'arcy family's, did not supply any horses to the Royal stable. James D'arcy the younger was made a Gentleman of His Majesty's Privy Chamber in 1677, and two years later was appointed an Equerry to Charles II. He remained very closely involved with the Sedbury stud; from his correspondence over the next twelve years, it is clear that the King was still obtaining horses from the D'arcy family.

For a great many years it has been held that Charles II imported horses and mares from abroad, and that these foreign imports were the 'Royal Mares' that we find in the first volume of the *General Stud Book*. This traditional view appears to have been first mentioned by John Cheny in his Calendar for 1743:

King Charles the Second sent abroad the Master of the Horse (which some say was the late Sir Christopher Wyvill, others, the late Sir John Fenwick), in order to procure a Number of Foreign Highbred Horses and Mares for Breeding, and the Mares, thus procured by the said King's Interest, and brought to England (as also many of their offspring) have, for that Reason, been called Royal Mares.

In the introductory volume of the *General Stud Book* published in 1791, Mr Weatherby neatly paraphrased what Cheny had written fifty years before: 'ROYAL MARES. King Charles the Second sent abroad the Master of the Horse to procure a number of foreign horses and mares for breeding, and the mares brought over by him (as also many of their produce) have since been called

Royal Mares.' This sentence was repeated in the 1791, 1793, 1803 and 1808 issues of the *General Stud Book* and was in every issue till the publication of the fifth or revised edition in 1891, in which edition the following erroneous information was added to the sentence: 'Charles I had at Tutbury, Staffordshire, in 1643, a number of mares and stallions, described as racehorses, a list of which, from the records, includes three Morocco mares.'

The impression that Mr Weatherby originally gave in 1791 was that foreign mares were virtually unknown in England prior to the Restoration of Charles II. Both the records of the studs at Tutbury and Malmesbury, and the details of the imports from Mantua, Naples, Spain and Morocco from the reign of Henry VIII to the execution of Charles I in 1649 show this to be totally untrue. Much of the information that Weatherby had copied from Cheny's Calendar of 1743 is also highly questionable. Sir John Fenwick, who had been Master of the Horse to Charles I, had owned one of the best studs in the north before the Civil War. He had died in 1658, so it would have been impossible for Charles II to have sent him abroad after the Restoration. It is extremely unlikely that he would have commissioned Sir John Fenwick to buy horses when he was in exile, because he was completely impecunious. There is also no record of Fenwick having imported any mares for Charles I. Charles II would have had little or no reason to import foreign-bred horses or mares since James D'arcy was supplying him with twelve colts a year, and there is no record of his having established a new Royal Stud to replace Tutbury, Malmesbury or the smaller Eltham.

There is one mare in the *General Stud Book* who undoubtedly did belong to Charles II, and who was unquestionably imported in his reign: the Natural Barb Mare. She was almost certainly a present from the King of Morocco, and was imported in foal with Dodsworth from Tangiers in 1673, the year Sutton Oglethorpe became Master of the Royal Studs. At the same time Lord Arlington received a present from the Moroccan ruler which became known as the Arlington Barb Mare. Dodsworth's dam was sold on the death of Charles II in 1685 for 40 gns to a banker, Mr Child. The Arlington Barb was sold in the same year, when Lord Arlington also died, to Mr Wilkinson of Boroughbridge, Yorkshire.

Charles II did receive some horses as gifts from King Louis XIV of France, and also some as part of the dowry of Catherine of Braganza. In March 1675 the King instructed Lord Winchelsea, the English Ambassador in Constantinople, to find him some mares and send them to him in England, but there is no record of whether he was able to carry out this command, nor any of their arrival in England. It seems very likely that Charles II was not an importer of foreign-bred horses on anything like the same scale as James I, the Duke of Buckingham or even his father. He took a lively interest, none the less, in the bloodstock that his subjects acquired from abroad. The diarist John Evelyn described how interested he was in the three Arabs that had been captured at the siege of Vienna and brought to England in December 1684.

When Charles II returned to England in 1660, the Sergeant-at-Arms was ordered to seize all the goods of all the men who had sat as judges on Charles I, and to confiscate the seven horses of Oliver Cromwell and take them to the Royal Mews. They were probably taken to Hampton Court. It may be assumed that the destruction of Tutbury, Malmesbury and Eltham meant that any breeding of horses undertaken by the Master of the Royal Stud was carried out at Cardinal Wolsey's former palace, although it must have been on a very limited scale.

It is possible that the 'Burton Barb Mare' was at the Hampton Court Stud during the reign of Charles II. In Volume I of the Stud Book this mare is styled 'the Burton Barb Mare', but in all the old pedigrees she is called 'a Burton Barb Mare', which would indicate that she was a mare by Mr Burton's Barb horse. If she was at Hampton Court, she would have been owned by Charles II; her foals, a filly by Dodsworth, a filly by Dicky Pierson, a son of Dodsworth and a running horse, St Martin by Spanker, who was bred by the second Duke of Buckingham at Helmsley, would have been born there. Dodsworth, who had been imported *in utero* with the Royal mare from Tangiers in 1675, may have stood as a stallion at Hampton Court, since his dam was probably sent there on her arrival in England. The Burton Barb Mare family is one of the most important in the Stud Book; about 15 per cent of modern mares trace back to her through her two fillies by Dodsworth and Dicky Pierson. Among the stallions that descend from her are Whitelock, Selim, Voltigeur, St Albans, Sundridge, Teddy, Hurry On, Gainsborough, Hyperion, Blenheim and Aureole.

Charles II left an indisputable mark on the development of horse-racing and the Thoroughbred, even if the extent of his influence on breeding is considerably less than that claimed by Cheny in 1743 and Weatherby in 1791. He was an extremely able and talented horseman; his riding tutor had been the Duke of Newcastle, one of the foremost horsemen and breeders in England. The first race-meeting he is said to have attended as King was at

Epsom in 1661, but it is as the great patron of Newmarket that he is best remembered. In 1665 he established the Newmarket Town Plate to be run over the new round course on the second Thursday in October 'for ever'. This race is still run, though in a different form; it is now for hacks regularly stabled in Newmarket, but still over four miles. It has the distinction of being the only race run on the Heath not under the jurisdiction of the Jockey Club. Surprisingly, the King did not visit Newmarket for the first time until 1666, but thereafter it became once again the second capital of England.

Charles II frequently rode in Matches and races himself. In 1673 he rode the winner of The Plate, beating his illegitimate son the Duke of Monmouth, Mr Elliot and Mr Thomas Thynne, the ancestor of the Marquess of Bath. In 1674 he won the race again, according to contemporary account as a result of his good horsemanship. The King regularly watched the training gallops on the Heath mounted on his famous hack 'Old Rowley'. This became his nickname, and he is now commemorated by the 'Rowley Mile', one of Newmarket's two courses. On the summit of Warren Hill he had a shelter built, which became known as the King's Chair, so that he could watch the gallops in bad weather.

Charles II personally adjudicated in all disputes relating to the races. On one occasion there was a dispute over the result of a Match between horses owned by Mr Bellingham and Mr Roe. The King heard the evidence of the jockeys on oath, and decided that Mr Bellingham's horse Traveller had won by a foot and a half. The King also adjudicated on a dispute after a Match between a horse of Sir Robert Carr's and a gelding of Sir Robert Geere's, in which the Starter had so totally mismanaged the start that one horse completed the course while the other remained motionless at the start. Since there had been enormous betting on the Match, the whole matter was referred to the King's judgement. Regrettably, his decision has not reached us.

The palace that James I had built at Newmarket had fallen into a state of disrepair under the Commonwealth. When John Evelyn visited Newmarket during its rebuilding in 1670, he was not impressed. He considered it hardly fit to be even a hunting lodge, and particularly objected to the innovation of placing the fireplaces in the corners of the rooms. Evelyn's description of Charles II's Court at Newmarket in July 1671 – 'Jolly blades racing, dancing, feasting, and revelling, more resembling a luxurious and abandoned rout, than a Christian Court' – was far from complimentary.

His views were echoed by Alexander Pope who believed that 'New-market's Glory rose, as Britain's fell.'

Certainly Newmarket in the reign of Charles II was sure to give offence to puritanically inclined Englishmen. The King had purchased a residence at Audley End, where he was able to leave the Queen and more sober members of his Court while he proceeded to the rebuilt palace with his wilder friends and numerous lady companions. Among the latter were Nell Gwyn, who had a house in Palace Street, and his other famous mistress and political intriguer, Louise de Quérouaille, whom he created Duchess of Portsmouth. It was Louise de Quérouaille who suggested to Louis XIV that he should send his celebrated astrologer, the Abbé Pregnani, to the English Court to try to persuade Charles that England should return to Catholicism. The King, and his brother James, Duke of York, felt that his astrological prowess would be better employed at Newmarket prognosticating the results of the races. However the Abbé Pregnani's skills evidently did not extend to picking winners, and after the King and the Duke of York had both lost their money on his astrological predictions in three consecutive races Pregnani returned to France, his reputation in England ruined by the vicissitudes of the Turf.

Another famous figure at Newmarket at the time was Hortense, Duchess of Mazarin, the niece of Cardinal Mazarin. Having tired of her husband, the Duc de Meilleraye and Mayence, she came to England and soon seduced the King with her charms: her gambling house at Newmarket was recognized as an adjunct of the Court. Another of Charles's mistresses, Barbara Villiers, Lady Castlemaine, later the Duchess of Cleveland, was a fearless gambler. In 1668 Samuel Pepys related: 'I was told tonight that my Lady Castlemaine is so great a gamester as to have won £15,000 in one night, and lost £25,000 in another night, at play; and hath played £1,000 and £1,500 at a cast.' Unfortunately for the King, the gambling debts of his mistresses usually had to be paid by him. Pepys reported that at one time the Duchess of Cleveland's losses were so gigantic, and the Royal Purse so low, that the King's Wardrobe contained only three neckbands and not one handkerchief, because those in charge of it were unable to obtain any more credit! Therein may lie the reason why Charles twice tried to sell the Tutbury property, why he was not an importer of foreign-bred horses on a scale like that of James I, and why the Royal Studs were not re-established in his reign, with the possible exception of a modest though influential operation at Hampton Court. His patronage and enthusiastic support of racing at Newmarket, however, was to make it a national sport enjoyed by people of almost every walk of life.

The reign of James II (1685–8) was too brief and too troubled for him to concern himself with the Royal Studs or racing in any influential way. When the Dutchman William III (1688–1702) came to the throne, with his wife, Mary II (1688–94), he realized, being an astute politician, that he must identify himself with the interests and pastimes of the English, and one of the ways he did so was by becoming an enthusiastic supporter of horse-racing and breeding. He paid his first visit to Newmarket in 1689, and ensured that the palace there was properly maintained.

William III also recommenced the practice of importing foreign horses. He brought Pulleyne's Arabian to England early in his reign; this horse was named after his first Master of the Royal Stud. In 1699 the second man to hold that position, Marshall, imported nine Barbary horses and five mares from Tunis. These imported horses and mares were kept at the Royal Stud at Hampton Court, which was completely revitalized by William III. Among the stock at Hampton Court during his reign were Hutton's Grey Barb, whom Mr Hutton presented to the King, Chillaby, a white Barb, the sire of Old Greyhound and grandsire of Sampson, and Old Greyhound's dam, who had been imported with him *in utero*. Old Greyhound became the sire of many good horses including Othello and Goliath.

The King's horses were frequent runners at Newmarket. In 1698 his Stiff Dick, carrying a feather weight, narrowly beat the Marquess of Wharton's Careless, the best horse in England since his sire, Spanker. This victory must have given the King immense pleasure as Careless was considered invincible, even though he was carrying 9 st. No horse was to achieve a similar reputation or such outstanding victories in England until Flying Childers more than twenty years later. In a Match at the same meeting His Majesty's Turk easily beat Lord Carlisle's Spot.

Such was the reputation of English-bred horses by the end of the seventeenth century that William III made presents of them to the Kings of Prussia and Sweden and the Grand Dukes of Tuscany and Florence. On his orders, the English Ambassador to France, the Earl of Portland, presented Louis XIV with nine racehorses. Despite his involvement in racing and breeding, though, and his frequent heavy gambling, William III always seemed a rather serious-minded King, who never acquired the popularity he sought.

Soon after his accession William had appointed Tregonwell Frampton as his 'Keeper of the Running Horses' at a salary of £1,000 a year. Frampton had been born in Dorset in 1641, and his youth is obscure, but he may have held some minor post in the stable of Charles II. His post would have corresponded to that of a modern trainer–manager to his Royal employer. When Queen Anne came to the throne, he remained as her 'Keeper of the Running Horses', and continued to occupy the post under George I. His unrivalled experience in matters relating to the Turf caused people to turn to him for adjudication in racing disputes and he became known as 'The Father of the Turf'. He was, however, an eccentric, notorious for both his uncouth appearance and his unfashionable clothes, a virulent misogynist and, if the legend of the gelding of his horse, Dragon, is to be believed, unscrupulous and sharp in matters connected with the making of Matches and betting.

Queen Anne, the second daughter of James II, reigned from 1702 to 1714. She had been at Newmarket several times before she became Queen, and was an enthusiastic racegoer. She inherited both William III's stable at Newmarket and the Royal Stud at Hampton Court. The most famous of the mares she had at the Stud during her reign was the Moonah Barb Mare, whose dam had been among the mares Richard Marshall, William III's stud manager, had imported from Tunis in 1699. The Moonah Barb Mare was imported *in utero*, so would have been two years old when Queen Anne came to the throne. She is the ancestress of the sires Charles XII, Sweetmeat and Bachelor's Double.

When Queen Anne decided to visit Newmarket for the first time after her accession, Sir Christopher Wren, the Surveyor-General, was sent ahead to see that the Royal Palace was suitably refurbished and, where necessary, rebuilt in time for her arrival in the town. Queen Anne also spent £1,000 on paving Newmarket's streets. During that visit Queen Anne bought Leedes, the most famous son of the Leedes Arabian, from Mr Holloway for 1,000 gns and presented him to her husband, Prince George of Denmark. The Royal couple shared a great interest in the Turf, and Queen Anne was the first monarch to race her horses at York, to which she presented the Gold Cup. In 1713 Queen Anne attended York races herself, but her horse, Mustard, who had been brought up from Newmarket, was unplaced. Her grey gelding Pepper, however, won three races at York and her bay colt Star won a Sweepstakes of forty guineas there a few days before her death in August 1714. Queen Anne inaugurated the Queen's Plates of one hundred sovereigns, which became such a feature of eighteenth- and nineteenth-century racing in England.

The greatest contribution Queen Anne made to racing, however, was her foundation of the Royal racecourse at Ascot. She was an even more passionate follower of the hounds than racegoer, and when she became so obese that no horse could support her weight, she had a two-wheeled chaise specially constructed in which she drove herself at breakneck speed after her buckhounds. Their kennels were situated on the present Ascot racecourse, and in 1710 Queen Anne ordered the Master of the Buckhounds, the Duke of Somerset, to build a racecourse around the kennels. Racing was first held at Ascot on Saturday 11 August 1711, and was attended by the Queen and her Court, who were also present on the following Monday when racing took place again.

After Queen Anne's death in 1714 and the accession of the Hanoverian George I, the Royal Stud at Hampton Court and stable at Newmarket were dispersed. The next member of the Royal Family to take an influential role in racing and breeding was William Augustus, Duke of Cumberland, George II's third son.

2

The Duke of Cumberland's Stud,

Windsor Great Park, 1750–66

Neither of the first two Hanoverian Kings of England, George I or George II, showed the slightest interest in horse-racing or the breeding of Thoroughbreds. The first member of their family to take an active role in the breeding of racehorses was George II's third son, William Augustus, Duke of Cumberland.

Cumberland was born on 15 April 1721, while his father was still Prince of Wales. He soon became the favourite son of his parents, who hoped that he would pursue a naval career and become Lord High Admiral. The young Duke, however, preferred soldiering. At the age of twenty-two he was appointed Captain-General of the British land forces, both at home and in the field, and in May 1745 commanded the allied armies against the French at the battle of Fontenoy. He was described as an intrepid and inspiring leader.

While the army was away, Prince Charles Edward Stuart decided that the time was ripe for him to launch his invasion of Scotland and attempt to re-establish the Stuarts on the throne of Great Britain. Cumberland returned home and in April 1746 routed the rebel army in thirty minutes at the battle of Culloden. Much of the criticism of the Duke of Cumberland's actions both at and after Culloden, as well as his nickname of 'The Butcher', relate to the harsh treatment of the defeated enemy. The Duke, however, had ample cause to harry the remaining Jacobite rebels as they refused to surrender and waged a guerrilla war against his army in the spring and early summer. Furthermore until the Stuart cause was utterly destroyed, there was a very real danger that the French would invade the south of England. On his return to London in July 1745 Cumberland was appointed Ranger of Windsor Great

Park. The attacks that were directed against Cumberland shortly after his suppression of the Jacobite rebellion were orchestrated by his elder brother, the Prince of Wales, who was jealous of his success. Further criticism followed when he carried out a fierce programme of reform in the army, aimed at removing abuses and improving the army's efficiency and discipline. So great became his unpopularity that when the Prince of Wales died in March 1751, Parliament refused to accept the King's wish that Cumberland should become Regent if he should die before his heir and grandson, the future George III, was of age.

In 1757 Cumberland's army was defeated by the French at Hasten and the King instructed Cumberland to make peace. No sooner had the Duke made a treaty than his father changed his mind. When Cumberland returned to London the King told him that 'he had ruined his country and his army, had spoilt everything and hurt or lost his own reputation'. In face of such public humiliation the Duke had no alternative but to resign all his military appointments. He retired to Windsor and spent the last eight years of his life concentrating his energies on building his stud of Thoroughbreds into the best in the country and going to the races at Newmarket and Ascot to watch his horses run. It was a sad end to an illustrious military career.

Cumberland had begun to build his stud around 1750, but inevitably many of the horses he ran in the first half of the following decade he had bought from other breeders. The first winner that he bred himself appears to have been the colt Muley (Muley Ishmael–Young Ebony by Crab), whose dam he acquired from Lord Portmore. Other notable winners he bred before 1758 included the full-brothers Dapper and Dumplin (Cade–Cypron), each of whom won five races, and Dorimond (Dormouse–White-foot Mare), who was victorious thirteen times. In 1758 Cypron, who was never put into training but had entered the Duke's stud four years earlier, gave birth to a bay colt by Tartar; this was the famous King Herod, commonly called Herod, one of the most influential stallions in the history of the Thoroughbred.

Tartar had been bred by Edward Leedes of North Milforth, Yorkshire in 1743, and was by Mr Croft's Partner. Partner's sire was Jigg, a son of the Byerley Turk. The Byerley Turk had been captured by Captain Robert Byerley when Buda was taken from the Turks by the Duke of Lorraine in 1687; Byerley later rode the horse at the battle of the Boyne in July 1690, when he commanded King William III's Sixth Dragoon Guards.

Herod was born at Oulston in Tartar's paddocks. He did not run until he was five, when, still unnamed, he beat the Duke of Ancaster's Roman in a Match over the Beacon Course at Newmarket in October 1763. The following April Herod defeated Sir John Moore's Tartar by Tartar in a Sweepstakes over the same course, and in June 1764 he beat Lord Rockingham's Tom Tinker in a Match over four miles at Ascot. Herod's next race was again at Newmarket over the Beacon Course in October 1764, when he was opposed by the Duke of Grafton's Antinous, who started favourite at 6–4 on. Herod upset those odds by beating Antinous half a neck. This particular Match had created such enormous interest that more than £100,000 was bet on its outcome. In May 1765 Herod beat Antinous, receiving 9 lb, in another Match for 1,000 gns over the Beacon Course.

After the Duke of Cumberland's death in 1765, Herod was sold to Sir John Moore. He won only one of four races for his new owner and then retired to stud at Sir John Moore's seat, Neather Hall near Bury in Suffolk, at a fee of 10 gns a mare and five shillings to the groom. In 1773 this fee was raised to 25 gns owing to his success as a stallion. Herod died on 12 May 1780 at the age of twenty-two. His stock had won £201,505 in stakes, forty hogsheads of claret, three cups and The Whip. He was champion sire for eight consecutive years from 1777 to 1784. In 1781 his progeny won the remarkable total of 121 races; only Stockwell, in 1866, has surpassed this record, and no other stallion has matched Herod's score since.

The best colt sired by Herod was the unbeaten Highflyer, bred by Sir Charles Bunbury out of Rachel by Blank. Bunbury sold him to Lord Bolingbroke, whom Lady Sarah Lennox described as 'much the same as mad when he is drunk and that he is generally'. Richard Tattersall bought him from Bolingbroke to stand as a stallion at a property he bought near Ely, which he named Highflyer Hall, for a fee of 50 gns. His success as a sire was matched only by that of Eclipse and his father Herod; his stock won £170,500 in stakes. He was champion sire on no fewer than twelve occasions: for nine years consecutively from 1785 to 1793 and then in 1795, 1796 and 1798, and he was second in the intervening years. Three of Highflyer's colts won the Derby: Mr Panton's Noble in 1786, Lord Derby's Sir Peter Teazle in 1787 and the Duke of Bedford's Skyscraper in 1789. The principal stallions descending from Sir Peter Teazle were on the one hand, Walton, Partisan, Gladiator, Sweetmeat and Macaroni, and on the other Sir Paul, Paulowitz,

Cain, Ion, Wild Dayrell, Buccaneer and Kisber. Highflyer also got four St Leger winners: Omphale in 1784, Cowslip in 1785, Spadille in 1787 and Young Flora in 1788, and one Oaks winner, Volante in 1792. Other good colts and sires got by Highflyer included Delpini, Rockingham, Escape and Walnut. Highflyer was also a most influential broodmare sire; he was the maternal grandsire of five Derby winners (Spread Eagle in 1795, Didelot in 1796, the colt by Fidget in 1797, Champion, who also won the St Leger, in 1800, and Pope in 1809), two other St Leger winners (Orville in 1802 and Sancho in 1804) and three Oaks winners (Caelia in 1793, Pelisse in 1804 and Meteora in 1805).

Another extremely influential son of Herod was Woodpecker, bred and raced by Sir C. Davers. He won eleven of his twenty-two races; although beaten twice by Pot-8-Os, Woodpecker took his revenge on the third occasion they met over the Beacon Course at Newmarket. His best son, Buzzard, who was foaled in 1787, won twenty-two of the thirty-nine races and Matches in which he took part. In 1800 Buzzard was mated with the Duke of Queensberry's Alexandra Mare, who was out of a mare by Highflyer; the offspring was Castrel, from whom the following descended: Pantaloon, Thormanby, Le Sancy, Roi Herode, The Tetrarch, Salmon Trout, King Salmon, Tetratema, Bacteriophage and Alizier. The Alexandra Mare was acquired by the Prince Regent in 1801; he again sent her to Buzzard and she foaled Selim in 1802. The winner of six races including the Craven Stakes, Selim founded the Sultan, Bay Middleton, Flying Dutchman, Dollar, Bruleur, Ksar, Tourbillon, Djebel, Le Lavendou, Le Levanstell and Levmoss branch of the Woodpecker male line; from Dollar's son, Upas, descend Omnium II and Elf II, Nimbus, Le Capucin and Le Flambeau. The Prince of Wales also bred the full brother of Selim, Rubens, in 1805; he was champion sire in 1815, 1821 and 1822 and a very influential broodmare sire.

The third son of Herod to achieve great fame as a sire was Florizel, who was foaled from his first crop in 1768. Florizel was mated with a Spectator mare in 1776; the offspring of this union was Diomed, the first winner of the Derby. Florizel got another Derby winner with the Duke of Bedford's Eager in 1791. Thus two of Herod's sons, Highflyer and Florizel, were the sires of five of the first twelve Derby winners. Diomed stood first at Uppark in Hampshire and then at Barton in Suffolk. His offspring included Grey Diomed, who was exported to Russia as a stallion, and the brilliant broodmare Young Giantess, the dam of the 1801 winner of the Derby and Oaks, Eleanor.

Diomed was a relative failure as a sire in England; by 1798 his fee had dropped to 2 gns a mare and his fertility was so poor that Colonel John Hoomes of Bowling Green, Virginia, was able to buy him for 50 gns. He then sold the horse to Colonel Selden, who stood him at Chesterfield, Virginia, in 1800. Amazingly, Diomed's fertility revived; he was champion sire in 1803, the first year when his offspring ran in Virginia. C. E. Trevathan, in his work *The American Thoroughbred*, voiced the opinion that 'without Diomed, the most brilliant pages of our turf story could never have been told . . . Diomed, as a progenitor of the American race-horse, stands alone, towering magnificently above all others.' The most influential stallion got by Diomed in the USA was Sir Archy, who was the undisputed champion racehorse there in 1809. He was the sire of Timoleon, from whom descend Boston and the greatest American Thoroughbred of the nineteenth century, Lexington.

There is almost certainly a direct connection on the maternal side between the Duke of Cumberland's stud in Windsor Great Park and Lexington himself. Lexington's dam, Alice Carneal by Sarpedon, traced back to a mare named either Duchess or Diamond by the Cullen Arabian out of Lady Thigh by Partner. Fairfax Harrison has listed twenty-one English mares that were imported to Virginia before the American Revolution in 1776. Duchess or Diamond, who belonged to John Spotswood of Sportsylvania, is acording to him one of these imported mares. In the first volume of the *General Stud Book*, Lady Thigh, who was foaled in 1731 by Partner out of a Greyhound mare, is listed as having produced five foals, all bred by the Duke of Cumberland: two colts in 1752 and 1753 by the Cullen Arabian, Miss Thigh by Rib in 1750, and two filly foals by the Cullen Arabian, earlier than 1750 but undated. As neither of the two Cullen Arabian mares appeared in the lists of the Duke of Cumberland's broodmares at Windsor Great Park in 1759, 1760 or 1761 – Miss Thigh is on the list of his mares during these years – it is more than probable that the Duke had sold either one or both of the Cullen Arabian mares, and that Duchess or Diamond was not named until she arrived in the USA. In that case the Duke of Cumberland bred the eighth dam of Lexington.

Herod got several other high-class colts who became important sires. Between 1769 and 1774 these included Evergreen, Tele-machus (out of mare by Skim), Justice, the sire of the 1790 and 1794 Derby winners, Rhadamanthus and Daedalus, and the 1785

Oaks heroine, Trifle, and Bourdeaux. From his last six crops foaled between 1775 and 1780 Herod got the following good sires: Weasel, who won thirteen races, Anvil, who won nineteen, Drone, a prolific winner and sire of the 1797 St Leger hero Lounger, and Fortitude, the winner of fourteen races and sire of the 1792 Derby victor, John Bull. Other Herod colts of the same period included Tom Tug and Bagot, both of whom became influential sires in Ireland.

Herod's death in May 1780 precluded him from siring any winners of the Derby, which was first run in the year he died. He did, however, have the distinction of siring the first winner of the Oaks in 1779, Lord Derby's Bridget. He was also the sire of Faith and Maid of Oaks, who won the Oaks for Lord Grosvenor in 1781 and 1783. From his last crop in 1780 Herod also got Sir J. L. Kaye's St Leger winner, Phenomenon, the sire of the 1798 Oaks winner, Bellissima, and the 1790 St Leger victor, Ambidexter.

Herod was also exceptionally influential as a broodmare sire: twelve of his mares produced Classic winners. Serjeant (Derby, 1784), Aimwell by Mark Anthony (Derby, 1785), Paragon (St Leger, 1786), Waxy (Derby, 1793) and Benningbrough (St Leger, 1794) were all out of Herod mares. Aspasia, the dam of Serjeant, also produced the very good racehorse Dungannon, the winner of twenty-six of his twenty-nine races. Paragon's dam Calash also produced Whiskey by Saltram, who became champion sire. Not only did Herod sire three Oaks winners, he was also the broodmare sire of five others: The Yellow Filly (1786), Nightshade (1788), Hyppolyta (1790), Portia (1791) and Platina (1795). The influence on the Stud Book of Herod's filly, Maria, the dam of the 1793 Derby winner Waxy by Pot-8-Os, became all the greater when Waxy himself sired four Derby winners – Pope (1809), Whalebone (1810), Blucher (1814) and Whisker (1815) – and two Oaks winners, Minuet (1815) and Corinne, who had also won the 1,000 Guineas, in 1818. Gohanna by Mercury, the runner-up to Waxy in the Derby, was also out of a Herod mare; he was the sire of the 1805 and 1807 Derby winners, Cardinal Beaufort and Election.

The single most important achievement of Herod's career as a stallion and sire of sires was his transmittal of the male line of the Byerley Turk down to the present-day Thoroughbred. Although all his races were over four miles and his stock were also renowned for their stamina, it is noteworthy that four early winners of the July Stakes, founded in 1786, had Herod as their maternal grandsire. He should, therefore, also be given credit for the way in which his offspring adapted themselves to running over the shorter distances of the Classic and other races that came into being at the end of the eighteenth century.

The extent of the Duke of Cumberland's racing stable and stud is best illustrated by certain documents to be found in the Royal Archives at Windsor. The first, dated 1 May 1759, is a list of his horses in training on that day:

Aged:	Cato, 11, Mauro, 7, Spider, 7.
Six-Year-Olds:	Rib.
Five-Year-Olds:	Jolter, Silvia.
Four-Year-Olds:	Dan, Dapper, Jeroboam, Pam, Madam.
Three-Year-Olds:	Mace, Cinnamon, Nutmeg, Cade, Dormouse, Muley Filly.
Two-Year-Olds:	Chesnut Regulus, Brown Regulus, Changeling, Muley, Muley Ishmael, Brown Childers, Bay Childers.
Yearlings:	Muley, Snip Regulus, Bald Regulus, Grey Crab, Bay Crab, Tartar [later named King Herod].[1]

The total, including the six yearlings, comes to thirty horses. There are also three lists of mares in the Duke of Cumberland's Stud in Windsor Great Park for the years 1760, 1761 and 1762. The first, for 1760, contains a list of the following nineteen mares:

Stallions which covered in 1759.	Names of the Mares.	Stallions which are to cover in 1760.	Foals dropped in 1760.
Regulus	Old Ebony.	Muley Ishmael.	Bay Colt.
Regulus.	Young Ebony.	Maske.	Bay Colt.
Bajazet.	Miss Stamford.	Bajazet.	Bay Colt.
Bajazet.	Miss Western.	Bajazet.	Bay Colt.
Young Cade.	Blaze Mare.	Young Cade.	Bay Colt.
Crab.	Godolphin Filly.	Crab.	Colt.
Babram.	Blind Mare.	Regulus.	
Bajazet.	Miss Thighs.	Muley Ishmael.	Bay Colt.
Crab.	Jenny Mare.	Crab.	Colt.
Crab.	Spilletta.	Maske.	

Babram.	Grey Ball Mare.	Maske.	Bay Filly.
Muley Moloch.	Janus Mare.	Young Cade.	
Crab.	Silvia.	Crab.	
	Grey Barb.	Regulus.	
Bajazet.	Second Mare.	Muley Ishmael.	
Muley Moloch.	Snip Mare.	Matchless.	Gray colt.
Regulus.	Lugs Muley.	Crab.	
	Grey Regulus.	Maske.	
	Bay Regulus.	Crab.[2]	

At the time this list was compiled, nine colts and one filly had been foaled by the Duke's broodmares. That by Bajazet out of Miss Thighs was named Selim and won five times; the one by Bajazet out of Miss Western was called Mahomet and won once. The Godolphin mare who dropped a foal by Crab is better known as Miss Cranbourne; the foal, named Milksop, won eleven races. The Blaze mare who was to be covered in 1760 by Young Cade was also known as Cypron – the dam of Herod. Her 1761 foal by Young Cade, named Drone, won one race.

The corresponding list for 1761 shows that the number of mares in the stud had increased to twenty-one, and that thirteen foals were born that year, six colts and seven fillies. The list for 1762 contains twenty mares, with twelve live foals being born that year, seven colts and five fillies. On 27 February Spiletta gave birth to a bay colt by Skim, who was either born dead or died soon after birth. Had he lived, this Skim colt would have been a half-brother to the most famous horse bred by the Duke of Cumberland and the most influential stallion ever to have been foaled: the great Eclipse.

In 1763 the Duke of Cumberland had Spiletta covered by his stallion Marske, who stood at his stud at Cranbourne Lodge. Marske, a great-grandson of the Darley Arabian, was bred by John Hutton of Marske, near Richmond in Yorkshire. In John Hutton's Stud Book it is recorded, 'In the year 1750 His Royal Highness the Duke of Cumberland gave me (John Hutton) a chestnut Arabian in exchange for a Brown Colt, got by Squirt from the Ruby Mare, and which His Royal Highness afterwards named Marske.' As a racehorse Marske was nothing exceptional, though he did win the Jockey Club Plate over the Round Course at Newmarket and a

Match and walked-over for his Royal owner. He then stood as a private stallion at the Duke's stud at Cranbourne Lodge. He was considered such an indifferent sire that in 1765, at the sale of Cumberland's stud, he was sold to a west country farmer for a trifling sum and for a short time covered mares in Dorset for half a guinea. Mr Wildman then bought him for 20 gns. The scintillating performances of his son Eclipse soon made Marske the most popular stallion in the land, and Wildman made a handsome profit when he sold him to the Earl of Abingdon for 1,000 gns. Marske stood at Lord Abingdon's stud at Rycote in Oxfordshire at a fee of 100 gns until his death in July 1779. The broodmare Spiletta, whom Sir Robert Eden had bred in 1749, was beaten on the only occasion that she ran, but she had the merit of being by Regulus, who was champion sire eight times between 1754 and 1766. She was bought from Sir Robert Eden, along with her dam, Miss Western by Sedbury, by the Duke of Cumberland and both mares entered his stud at Cranbourne Lodge. In 1759 Spiletta foaled a bay filly by Crab; in 1760 she was covered by Marske but proved barren in 1761, as she was in 1762 to Skim. Marske managed to get her in foal in 1763, and on 1 April 1764 Spiletta gave birth to a dark chestnut colt foal with a white blaze and a white stocking which almost reached the hock on his off-hind leg. Since a total eclipse of the sun had taken place on All Fools' Day 1765, the foal was named Eclipse.

After the Duke of Cumberland died on 31 October 1765 his entire stud was put up for sale by auction, including Eclipse. Good reports of this foal had reached William Wildman, an important grazier and meat salesman at Smithfield Market, who for many years owned a considerable stable of racehorses at Mickleham, near Epsom Downs. When Mr Wildman arrived at the sale he found that it had already commenced and that Eclipse had been sold for 70 gns. Wildman insisted that the sale had started before the time announced for it, and demanded that the auctioneer, Mr Richard Tattersall, should put up the sold lots again. Much time was lost while Tattersall remonstrated with Wildman; eventually the purchasers of the lots sold asked the meat salesman which of them he had wanted to buy, so that the progress of the sale would not be further delayed. Eclipse was the only one Wildman wanted, so that horse alone was put up for sale again; he fell to Wildman, who briefly owned the famous Gimcrack in 1765, for 75 gns.

Eclipse's temperament was so fiery that he was almost impossible to handle; it is said that Wildman even considered gelding him to make him more manageable. There is a legend that the young horse was put in the hands of a rough-rider near Epsom, who rode him around the countryside all day and often kept him out all night on his poaching excursions. This treatment, the legend alleges, helped subdue Eclipse's indomitable spirit. Little credence can be placed on this story, but the fact that it arose certainly illustrates that Eclipse was a very difficult horse to control and train. It is significant that during his entire career on the racecourse neither of his jockeys, John Oakley and Merriot, ever attempted to restrain or hold him, but always let him have his head and were content to steer him.

Prior to Eclipse's first race on 3 May 1769, the Noblemen's and Gentlemen's Plate run in four-mile heats at Epsom, he was given a secret trial on Banstead Downs. The touts, who came from London, arrived too late to see the trial, but learned from an old woman that 'she had just seen a horse with a white leg running away at a monstrous rate, and another horse behind, trying to run after him; but she was sure that he would never catch the white-legged horse if he ran to the world's end.' Eclipse, who faced four opponents, started at odds of 4–1 on and totally outclassed his rivals. The odds for the second heat were so prohibitive that the Irish gambler Dennis O'Kelly announced that he would place the horses in the correct order. He was able to put some large sums, at evens, 5–4 on and 6–4 on, on his famous prognostication, 'Eclipse first, the rest nowhere.' By nowhere he meant that the other horses would be distanced by Eclipse and the Judge would be unable to place them. A distance was 240 yards from the winning post, the spot being marked by another post, and it was thought that that was the limit of a Judge's vision. A horse distanced in a heat was disqualified from taking part in any later heat. In the second heat the five horses were racing in a bunch at the three-mile post, but then Eclipse's jockey merely touched the favourite with his whip; Eclipse immediately sprinted clear of his rivals and won by more than a distance, thus winning the most famous gamble in the history of betting for Captain O'Kelly.

O'Kelly had come to London from County Carlow in Ireland. His first attempts to make his fortune had not been rewarded with much success; initially he had been compelled to carry a sedan-chair and had even been thrown into the Fleet Prison for debt. By 1769, however, he had become well known as a reasonably successful gambler in the racing world. His title of Captain came from his rank in the Westminster Regiment of the Middlesex Militia, of which he eventually became the Colonel. Eclipse won eight more races in 1769. Some time during that summer O'Kelly gave William Wildman 650 gns for a half-share in the unbeaten colt; the exact timing of this transaction is uncertain as Eclipse ran in Wildman's name for all his outings in 1769. On 29 May 1769 Eclipse won the Noblemen's and Gentlemen's Plate at Ascot, and then the King's Plate at Winchester on 13 June. He then went on to receive two walk-overs, in a £50 Plate at Winchester on 15 June and in the King's Plate at Salisbury on 28 June, win the City Free Plate at Salisbury on 29 June, receive another walk-over on 25 July in the King's Plate at Canterbury and, two days later, win the King's Plate at Lewes. Eclipse's final race in 1769 was on 19 September when he won the King's Plate at Lichfield.

None of the horses that Eclipse had beaten in 1769 was considered top-class by contemporaries, and despite his having treated his rivals with the utmost disdain, there were still some who doubted his claim to be the best horse in England. As he was owned by Wildman and O'Kelly, Eclipse was ineligible for races confined to members of the Jockey Club, in which the best-bred horses in the kingdom usually ran. On 12 April 1770 Wildman made a Match for Eclipse against Mr Peregrine Wentworth's Bucephalus over the Beacon Course at Newmarket. Mr Wentworth, who was renowned for his sartorial elegance, had a fine racing stable and stud at Bramham Moor in Yorkshire. Bucephalus by Regulus, who had never been beaten prior to this Match, was considered a champion, and certainly was the strongest rival that Eclipse had yet faced. Nevertheless, Wildman staked 600 gns to 400 gns on his horse. Bucephalus matched strides with Eclipse for a while, but the effort proved too much for him and Eclipse ran out an extremely easy winner. On 19 April O'Kelly purchased Wildman's share in Eclipse for 1,100 gns, and it was in the Irish adventurer's colours that he trounced three rivals in the King's Plate over the Round Course at Newmarket. Such was his reputation that he received three walk-overs in the King's Plates at Guildford on 5 June, at Nottingham on 3 July and at York on 20 August. In the Great Subscription Plate over four miles at York on 23 August, his rivals included Mr Wentworth's Tortoise, who had been runner-up to Chatsworth in the same race in 1769, and Sir Charles Bunbury's Bellario. Odds of 20–1 were laid on Eclipse, who again distanced his rivals. He received two more walk-overs in the King's Plates at Lincoln on 3 September and at Newmarket on 4 October. The day before the latter he had beaten Sir Charles Bunbury's Corsican in a race for 150 gns over the Beacon Course. O'Kelly now retired his champion to his stud at Clay Hill in Epsom. He had won all his ten races and received eight walk-overs and £2,078 in stakes. At no time had he ever been in danger of defeat, and at the end of 1770 it was felt that he was the best horse to have been seen on the Turf since Flying Childers, half a century before.

Eclipse's fee in his first season as a stallion was 50 gns, but thereafter, till his death at Canons, O'Kelly's estate in Edgware, on 26 February 1789, was 25 gns a mare. O'Kelly alleged that he had earned £25,000 in stud fees from his champion. Initially Eclipse's influence as a stallion was not as pronounced as that of Herod or his son, Highflyer. Surprisingly he never became champion sire, though he was second to Herod or Highflyer on eleven occasions. He sired three Derby winners: Young Eclipse, out of Juno by Spectator, in 1781, Saltram, out of Virago by Regulus, in 1783 and Serjeant, out of Aspasia by Herod, in 1784. He also sired four runners-up in the Epsom Classic: Dungannon in 1783, Meteor in 1786, Gunpowder in 1787 and Aurelius in 1788, while his son, Spitfire, was third to Diomed in 1780. None of these colts was to establish a lasting direct male line that was to carry the blood of Eclipse to the present-day Thoroughbred, 90 per cent of whom trace back to him. The offspring of Eclipse that have that distinction were Pot-8-Os, King Fergus and, for a shorter period until the end of the nineteenth century, Joe Andrews. Besides his Derby winners, Eclipse sired only one other Classic victor: the 1780 Oaks winner, Annette, a full-sister to Saltram.

Pot-8-Os was bred by the Earl of Abingdon out of Sportsmistress by Sportsman in 1773. The horse was known to the stable-lads as Potato before he was named; when Lord Abingdon asked the lad who looked after him to spell out his name, he wrote 'Potooooooo' with a piece of chalk on the top of a corn bin. This was later amended to Pot-8-Os, and the horse went on to win thirty-four races before retiring to the Oxcroft Stud at Balsham in Cambridgeshire, the property of Lord Grosvenor, who had paid Lord Abingdon 1,500 gns for him after his first victory in the 1,200 Guineas Subscription Plate at Newmarket. Pot-8-Os' most significant son was Waxy, out of the Herod mare Maria. Bred by Sir Frederick Poole in Sussex in 1790, Waxy not merely won the 1793 Derby on his racecourse debut, but bred the full-brothers Whalebone and Whisker out of the mare Penelope for the Duke of Grafton; these two colts won the Derby in 1810 and 1815 respectively. Penelope was by Trumpator out of the brilliant Highflyer mare, Prunella, one of the most influential broodmares in the Stud Book. She was the dam of the Derby winner Pope and the Oaks winner Pelisse; she was also the grandam of the champion sire Partisan and nine other Classic winners including the Derby winner Tiresias. Prunella's career as a broodmare is but one striking illustration of how the crosses between Eclipse and his male descendants and mares by Herod and his son Highflyer determined the course of development of the Thoroughbred racehorse.

Three male lines trace back to Waxy's son Whalebone, those of Sir Hercules, Camel and Defence. Some of the most noteworthy sires tracing back to these three horses include Stockwell, Touchstone, Birdcatcher, Ormonde, Blandford, Phalaris, Fairway, Pharos, Hyperion, Nearco, Bold Ruler, Mr Prospector, Northern Dancer, Nijinsky and Danzig. The male line of Whalebone's brother, Whisker, lasted only until King Tom and the 1900 Ascot Gold Cup winner, Merman, who was bred in Australia and traced back to Whisker's son The Colonel.

The second Eclipse stallion to establish an enduring male line was King Fergus, who was foaled in 1775. Bought from her breeder Mr Carver as a yearling by Dennis O'Kelly, for whom he won eight races, he was sent to stand at the Curragh from 1782 to 1784. He was then bought by John Hutchinson of Shipton, near York, and advertised to stand at a fee of 10 gns a mare. He proceeded to sire three winners of the St Leger: Young Traveller (1791), Benningbrough, who was out of a Herod mare, in 1794, and Hambletonian in 1795. Benningbrough sired Orville, the 1802 St Leger winner and sire of Octavius (Derby, 1811), Emilius (Derby, 1823) and Ebor (St Leger, 1817). No son of Benningbrough or Orville, however, founded a lasting male line. That was left to Hambletonian.

Hambletonian raced first for his breeder, John Hutchinson, then for Sir Charles Turner, and lastly for Sir Henry Vane-Tempest. Hutchinson had been found work by his father, a farmer, in the stables of Sir Robert Eden. In 1751, at the age of fifteen, he had been convinced that Miss Western, a half-sister to Eclipse's dam Spiletta, would win the Hambleton Guineas, and put every penny he could muster on her. After her victory he never wanted money; such was his reputation as an excellent judge of horseflesh that he attracted the patronage of leading Turf personalities and his stable and stud at Shipton were renowned throughout England. John Hutchinson was one of those who strongly favoured two-year-old racing, but he bided his time with Hambletonian and did not race him until he was three; that year the horse won all his six starts,

35

including the St Leger and the following day the Doncaster Cup, then run over four miles. Between 1796 and 1800 he won all but one of his other thirteen races, including the Doncaster Cup as a four-year-old, the Craven Stakes at Newmarket the next spring, the Doncaster Stakes in 1797 and 1799 and a four-mile subscription race at York when he beat Benningbrough. As a seven-year-old in 1799, he won the famous 3,000 gns match over the Beacon Course at Newmarket against Mr Joseph Cookson's Diamond. Hambletonian retired to stud at Hornsey Stables, Middlethorpe, York at 10 gns a mare.

Through his son Whitelock and grandson Blacklock, Hambletonian established the other great male line of Eclipse. Among the stallions who descend from them are Voltigeur, Vedette and Galopin, the sire of St Simon, whose descendants have had such a noteworthy influence on the twentieth-century Thoroughbred and who include such prepotent stallions as Persimmon, Prince Rose, Princequillo, Ribot, Tom Rolfe, Graustark and Alleged.

The third, but now less significant, male line established by Eclipse was that of Joe Andrews, foaled in 1778 out of Amaranda by Omnium. His fame rests on the fact that he sired Dick Andrews, who again was out of a Highflyer mare, in 1797. The winner of twenty-six races between 1780 and 1802, Dick Andrews sired three Classic winners: Cwrw (2,000 Guineas, 1812), and the full-sisters Manuella (Oaks, 1812) and Altisidora (St Leger, 1813). It was his son Tramp, foaled in 1810, who was destined to carry on his line. An excellent stayer, whose nine victories included the Doncaster Cup, Tramp sired two Derby winners, Sir Giles (1832) and Dangerous (1833), three other Classic winners and the 1829 Ascot Gold Cup winner, Zinganee. The best son of Tramp as a stallion was Lottery; his twelve victories included the Doncaster Cup, but he is best known as the sire of Sheet Anchor, who continued the Joe Andrews male line through his son Weatherbit, the sire of the 1858 Derby winner Beadsman, himself the sire of Blue Gown (Derby, 1868), Pero Gomez (St Leger, 1869) and Rosicrucian, said by John Porter to have been 10 lbs better than the Derby winner, Blue Gown. Rosicrucian was so ill in his third year that he totally lost his form as a three-year-old, though at six he won both the Ascot Stakes and the Alexandra Plate, and Porter always regarded him when fit as the best colt that he ever trained with the exception of Ormonde. An enormously successful broodmare sire, Rosicrucian's son Beauclerc and grandson Tyrant were the last stallions in the Joe Andrews male line of Eclipse.

The portrait of the Duke of Cumberland that has come down to us from the letters of Horace Wapole as 'proud and unforgiving, fond of war for its own sake; he despised money, fame and politics, loved gaming, women and his own favourites, and yet had not one social virtue,' is as injust as his nickname 'The Butcher'. Certainly he was a compulsive gambler; he was once reported to have been seen playing cards under a tree during a break when the hounds lost the scent while he was out hunting. On another occasion when a half-pay officer returned his pocket book, which he had lost at Newmarket, the Duke allowed him to keep it, although it contained several hundred pounds, saying, 'I am only glad that it has fallen into such good hands, for if I had not lost it as I did, its contents would now have been scattered among the blacklegs of Newmarket.' What cannot be disputed, however, is that by breeding the two great stallions, Eclipse and Herod, the Duke of Cumberland had more influence on the development of the Thoroughbred racehorse than any other breeder before or since. The cross between Eclipse stallions and Herod and Highflyer mares was largely instrumental in producing the middle-distance Classic horse.

3

The Royal Studs of Henry Frederick,

Duke of Cumberland, and the Prince

of Wales, 1766–99

The only member of the Royal Family to continue breeding and racing thoroughbreds after the death of William Augustus, Duke of Cumberland was his nephew Henry Frederick, a younger brother of George III, who was created Duke of Cumberland in 1766. His stud at Windsor was smaller than his uncle's, but between 1767 and 1781 he bred 26 winners of 94 races including Dido (Eclipse – Miss Rose) who won five races and was runner-up to Faith in the 1781 Oaks. Notorious for his dissipated and debauched lifestyle, the Duke's liaison with the Earl of Grosvenor's wife resulted in the offended husband taking Cumberland to court and winning £10,000 damages. In 1771 the Duke married a commoner, the twenty-four-year-old widow Anne Luttrell, whom Horace Walpole described as "extremely pretty, not handsome, very well made, with the most amorous eyes in the world and eyelashes a yard long. Coquette beyond measure, artful as Cleopatra and complete mistress of all her passions and projects." This marriage so infuriated George III that he immediately had the Royal Marriage Act passed by which virtually all the descendants of George II were forbidden to marry a commoner without the Sovereign's consent.

The greatest significance of this Duke of Cumberland in the history of the Royal Studs is the influence he had over the Prince of Wales, born in 1762. He deliberately set out to cultivate the young Prince, both when he was a teenager and after he reached his majority. It can never be proved that this was designed to anger his elder brother, King George III, but certainly relations between the two brothers continued frosty in the extreme after Cumberland's marriage.

When the Prince of Wales was twelve years old, his father complained to the Earl of Holderness, who was in charge of his and his brother's education, of his eldest son's duplicity and sly evasion and of 'his bad habit of not speaking the truth'. George III expected the Prince to be a paragon, and when it was clear to him that his son would not live up to the impossible hopes he cherished, he took to insulting him in front of his courtiers. As he approached the age of eighteen, the Prince, bored with the stifling routine of a humdrum court which provided no outlet for his vivacious energy, forsook even the pretence of living up to his father's standards. This period was coincidental with his growing friendship with his uncle, the amoral Duke of Cumberland.

In the autumn of 1779 the Prince fell in love with a remarkably beautiful 21-year-old actress, Mrs Mary Robinson, who was playing Perdita in Garrick's production of *The Winter's Tale*. She was one of the sensations of the London season, and the Prince became totally infatuated with her. They met secretly in the garden of Kew, and the Prince gave her a locket containing his portrait in miniature. Love-letters to this new object of his adoration flowed from his pen. This tempestuous affair lasted until the spring of 1781 when the Prince tired of Perdita Robinson. But she still had in her possession the Prince's bond of £20,000 to be paid in the autumn of 1783, after he came of age, and all his letters. George III, shocked by the entire episode, instructed Lord North to find £5,000 from the secret service funds to redeem his son's reckless amatory epistles.

Between 1780 and 1783 relations between the monarch and his eldest son became even more acrimonious. No doubt the Prince's wild behaviour and drinking bouts as well as his affairs of the heart played their part, but the principal cause was political. For the first two decades of his reign, the King had been able to exercise almost total patronage in government appointments. His ministers had been literally servants of his choice, like his old tutor, Bute, and Lord North. But the loss of the American War of Independence in 1783 was exploited to the full by the Whig Opposition, frustrated by nearly thirty years starved of power. Given the combination of this new adversarial ferocity in party politics and the already established hostility between George III and his son, it was hardly surprising that the Prince of Wales became associated with the

Whigs and friendly with such men as Charles James Fox and the playwright Richard Brinsley Sheridan.

It was also in 1783 that the Prince of Wales came of age. Clearly it was inappropriate for the heir to the throne to continue living in Buckingham House under the suspicious gaze of his estranged father; but the Cabinet's proposals in June 1783 concerning the settlements to be made on the Prince outraged his father, who considered them 'a shameful squandering of public money in order to gratify the passions of an ill-advised young man'. Eventually a compromise was reached, but though this included provision for the furbishment of Carlton House as the Prince's residence, as well as the settlement of his debts and an independent income, the latter was quite obviously insufficient: George III was expecting his son to live on about half what Charles II's heir had received a century earlier. By controlling the purse-strings, the King hoped to direct his son's life; but in the event the sole effects of his meanness were to ensure that the Prince of Wales soon fell into debt again, and to preclude any prospect of reconciliation between father and son.

In 1784, after various highly visible romances, the Prince of Wales met Mrs Maria FitzHerbert, a respectable and amiable widow aged twenty-eight. Such was his infatuation with her that he determined to marry her within a few weeks of their first acquaintance. Not merely had this woman been born a commoner, Maria Smythe, but she was a practising Roman Catholic. Despite protests from Charles James Fox and the King, the couple were secretly married in December 1785.

The Prince of Wales's name first appears in the *General Stud Book* in 1782 when he is listed as the owner or breeder of Miss Kitty (Highflyer–Squirrel Mare), who ran third to Lord Clermont's Trifle in the 1785 Oaks, and of Figaro (Florizel–Sultana), winner of a Match at Newmarket in 1785. The General Stud Book, the first edition of which was published by Mr. J. Weatherby in 1791, records the birth of every foal born to a Thoroughbred broodmare. Unless a foal is entered in the General Stud Book, it is ineligible to be considered a Thoroughbred. All countries, where thoroughbred racing takes place, have their own Stud Books, and foals entered in them can trace their ancestry back to mares in the English General Stud Book.

The first six volumes of the *General Stud Book* present a problem for those trying to ascertain the actual breeder of a horse, because the entry since used to denote the breeder, in those days referred to the person who first nominated the horse for a race in the *Racing*

Calendar. Entries for races were usually made when a horse was a foal, or sometimes when it was a yearling. Frequently the same person was both owner and breeder, but on occasion the foal or yearling was sold by the breeder prior to its first entry being made in the *Racing Calendar.* Unfortunately, all the records of Tattersalls' sales before 1900 were destroyed in the Blitz of 1940, and sales of horses and mares in the late eighteenth century were not recorded in such detail in the newspapers as in the specialized sporting press that came into existence in the first decades of the nineteenth. Records of foals, yearlings and mares sold privately by breeders, excepting those who attained fame, are even more scarce. Consequently, ascertaining the actual breeder of a foal in this period is often a matter of deduction or inspired guesswork; in the final analysis we are sometimes left with the possibility that a foal was bred by either Mr X or Lord Y, and no way of determining which.

A great friend of the Prince of Wales and his main political ally, Charles James Fox, bred and raced Thoroughbreds in a modest way during the 1780s, frequently going straight from Parliament to attend and bet on the races at Newmarket. Fox almost certainly helped persuade the Prince of Wales that the Turf could be both amusing and rewarding. But the man who wielded the most influence in encouraging his nephew to take up racing and breeding on a large scale was undoubtedly the rakish Duke of Cumberland. A few months after their first visit to Brighton in September 1783, the Duke sold the Prince of Wales thirteen horses. Among these was Braganza (Justice–Firetail) who ran fourth to Noble in the 1786 Derby. After the sale of the Prince of Wales's horses and stud later that summer, Braganza won a Match for Charles James Fox at Newmarket in 1788.

Inevitably, the first horses that ran in the colours of the Prince of Wales, 'crimson waistcoat with purple sleeves black cap', were not bred by him. These colours were first carried to victory at Newmarket in 1784 by Anvil (Herod–Feather Mare), who had been bred by Mr Thomas Panton in 1777, then sold to the Hon. J. Parker, later Lord Boringdon, and acquired from him by the Prince. Parker, who was another good friend of the heir to the throne, won the 1783 Derby with Saltram (Eclipse–Virago), who was bought by the Prince of Wales in 1785. Saltram ran twice in the Royal colours, winning a Sweepstakes at Newmarket on 2 April 1785 after running second in the Claret Stakes to Dungannon a week earlier. He then retired to stud, where his best offspring for his Royal owner was the champion sire Whiskey. Saltram was later exported, though whether to North America or Russia is not altogether certain. No doubt exists about the sale of his dam, Virago, to the Prince by Mr Parker as her produce for 1783 in the *General Stud Book*, Maria by Eclipse, is in the name of the Prince of Wales, for whom she ran third twice in 1785 and 1786; in the latter year she was also unplaced in the Oaks behind The Yellow Filly. Virago's foal in 1784, Annette by Eclipse, is ascribed to the Hon. Richard Vernon in the *General Stud Book*, but her first race entry, in a race for two-year-old fillies at Newmarket on 2 October 1786, which she won, was made in the 1785 *Racing Calendar* in the name of the Prince of Wales. On 25 May 1787 Annette won the Oaks from Augusta for Richard Vernon. Since Virago's next two foals are also listed under the name of the Prince of Wales in the *General Stud Book*, it is reasonable to assume that she was bred by him, but sold at the enforced disposal of most of his horses and stud to pay off his debts in July 1786. Annette, therefore, has the distinction of being the first Classic winner bred by any member of the Royal Family. It is also very likely that the Prince of Wales had bred Augusta (Eclipse–Herod Mare), who ran in the colours of Colonel O'Kelly. Her dam, the Herod Mare out of a Bajazet mare, had been bought by the Prince from Lord Boringdon. Her produce in 1783, Confederate by Prophet, had been bred by the Prince of Wales, and ran twice for him in 1786 before being sold to Mr T. Clayton, for whom he won three races in the north in 1787. Her next three foals, all by Saltram, Caroline (1787), St David (1788) and Queen of Sheba (1789) were all bred by the Prince. O'Kelly must have bought Augusta at the sale of the Prince's horses in July 1786. To have bred the first two in the Oaks so soon after starting his career on the Turf was a notable achievement; the shame was that the Prince was compelled to sell the two fillies before they ever ran.

The best colt bred by the Prince of Wales in 1783 was unquestionably Mufti (FitzHerod–Infant Mare). He never raced for the heir to the throne, for he too was sold, to the Hon. Richard Vernon, in the summer of 1786. Mufti won fourteen races between 1786 and 1792, including the important Craven Stakes at Newmarket twice, in 1788 and 1791.

The inevitable result of the Prince's inadequate financial provision and his tendency to extravagance was that by the summer of 1786 he was deep in debt. George III had tried to control his son's life and choice of wife by limiting his income to £62,000 a year; this ensured that his heir would fall into debt. The love affair with and secret marriage to Maria FitzHerbert meant that in 1786 marriage to a German princess was not a viable method of solving the Prince's chronic financial embarrassments. At the end of April he wrote to his father for assistance. George III, displeased and most uncooperative, first demanded a full written statement of his son's liabilities and a firm assurance that he would mend his ways, and then refused to help. On 9 July the Prince wrote to him saying that his failure to meet the bills of many indigent and deserving creditors laid him open to the risk 'of legal insults, as humiliating to me as I am persuaded that they would be offensive to Your Majesty'. He then announced his intention of reducing all his expenses, 'even the use to which my birth and rank entitle me', within a few days. The pruning of his expenses was drastic. The Prince retained only four gentlemen in his household; they were to manage those funds set apart for the payment of the debts, and included his personal Equerry, Colonel Gerald Lake. Carlton House was closed, apart from two small apartments, the servants were dismissed and instructions were sent to Richard Tattersall to organize the sale of the Prince's stud, horses and carriages as soon as possible. The issue of the *St James's Chronicle* for 11–13 July 1786 reported as follows: 'Yesterday morning about Five o'clock, His Royal Highness, the Prince of Wales, set out for Brighton from Carleton House.' He travelled in a hired chaise with Mrs FitzHerbert. The newspaper was most sympathetic to the plight of the Prince, for it continued,

> The Prince of Wales has done more service to the Manufacturers and Arts of this country than it is possible to estimate. His Table, and his alone, has entertained all the Foreigners of Distinction who visited London. In his house they saw the exquisite Perfection of English Artists and they acquired a Relish for English manufactures. They carryed them back to the foreign courts; and it is to his countenance that we owe the celebrity of English Goods at this day in Europe.

In the same issue of the *St James's Chronicle* there appeared the following advertisement: 'To be sold by AUCTION by Messrs Tattersalls, near Hyde Park Corner Turnpike on Monday 24th and Tuesday 25th instant at Twelve o'clock: The Stud of His Royal Highness the Prince of Wales, consisting of Stallions, Horses in training, Brood Mares, Colts, Fillies, Hunters, Coach-horses,

Hacks, etc. etc.' Regrettably the report on this sale that appeared on 25 July was not detailed, and only mentioned that the 'famous horse Rockingham, 1781, by Highflyer–Purity by Matchem, that cost the Prince of Wales, 2,000 guineas, was bought yesterday at Tattersalls for 800 guineas by an eminent brewer'. Rockingham had been bought from Mr Wentworth after his victory in the Jockey Club Plate in 1785; he won four races for his Royal owner before he was sold to Mr Bullock, the aforementioned brewer. On 27 July the *St James's Chronicle* carried this brief comment on the sale: 'The Stud of His Royal Highness the Prince of Wales was not sold but given away, the two days sale not having amounted to half the sum that was justly expected. The Dealers and Speculators who were the principal purchasers are likely to be the great Gainers by their bargains, as some Horses were disposed of a few Hours after the sale for fifty and a Hundred Guineas more than they were knocked down for.'

Many felt that the King had been harsh in his treatment of his prodigal son, but he showed no sign of relenting. Charles James Fox and his Whig friends advised the importunate Prince to appeal to Parliament. On 27 April a City merchant, Alderman Newman, informed the House of Commons that he intended to move a humble address to be presented to the King praying him to take into His Royal Consideration the present embarrassed state of affairs of the Prince of Wales. In May a compromise was reached which avoided a full-scale debate on the parlous financial state of the heir to the throne. George III allowed the Prince an extra £10,000 a year from the Civil List; Parliament voted him £160,000 to pay off his creditors and an extra £60,000 to complete the renovation of Carlton House. The Prince of Wales gave his father an undertaking 'never to incur future debts, which must be as disagreeable to the King as painful to himself'. Carlton House was reopened and the Prince's Household reinstated, and he was able to buy back much of the Thoroughbred stock that had been sold by Tattersalls the previous July. Thus began the Prince of Wales's second involvement with the Turf.

Among the Prince of Wales's horses that had been sold on 25 July 1786 was a yearling by Highflyer out of Squirrel Mare, a full-brother to Miss Kitty, third in the 1785 Oaks. He was bought for 95 gns by Mr Franco. Soon after his purchase this yearling kicked out in his loose-box and embedded his fetlock in its wood-work. When his groom told Mr Franco about the accident and how his yearling had been extricated, the astonished owner exclaimed, 'Oh, what an escape!' and promptly named the colt Escape.

Escape ran five times for Mr Franco in 1788 and 1789. On his debut in a Match over the Rowley Mile at Newmarket on 29 September 1788, he upset the odds of 5–2 laid on Lord Barrymore's Feenow, who had run third to the Prince of Wales's Sir Thomas in the Derby. Two days later Escape won the Town Plate, beating Minos and Clown, the useful winner of four races. On 28 April 1789 he was beaten in a Match at Newmarket by Harpator, but only four days later he won a Match against the Prince of Wales's Canto Baboo, the winner of six races. Escape received forfeit from Alexander and Clown in a Sweepstakes at Newmarket on 16 May and was then repurchased by the Prince of Wales from Mr Franco for £1,500. He ran once for the heir to the throne in 1789, beating Nimble at Newmarket on 28 September.

When the Prince of Wales bought Escape back, the colt had already proved himself to be one of the best of his generation. The Prince's trainer at that time was Francis Neale at Newmarket, and his racing and stud manager Mr Warwick Lake, the younger brother of Colonel Gerald Lake. Neale found Escape a difficult horse to train; he seldom kept his condition for more than a few days and his work on the gallops and in trials was very erratic.

The Prince was now an active buyer of horses in training. One of the first colts he bought was Sir Thomas (Pontac–Sports-mistress), who had been bred by Mr Dawson, for whom he won a two-year-old race at Newmarket in 1787. He turned out to be an absolute bargain, winning five of his seven races as a three-year-old, most notably the Derby, when he started favourite at 6–5 on, from Aurelius, Feenow and Grey Diomed. The Prince drove to Epsom from Carlton House, his carriage's four horses mounted by pos-tilions and preceded by outriders, and arrived just in time to see the first race. Epsom was inundated with visitors, and one man who wished to rent a house for the week was asked to pay the equivalent of two years' rent. The Prince was delighted by the victory of Sir Thomas, but it cannot be counted as one for the Royal Studs as he was not his breeder. Sir Thomas won seven more races for the Prince from eleven outings in 1789 and 1790, including the Jockey Club Stakes at Newmarket and a Sweepstakes at York.

Another good horse in training that the Prince of Wales acquired in 1789 was Traveller (Highflyer–Henricus mare), bought for 1,500 gns during his visit to York races in the company of his brother, Frederick, Duke of York. Traveller had been bred by Mr Hutchinson, for whom he won eight races in the north as a three-and four-year-old. He won four races for his new Royal owner between 1789 and 1791. A previous acquisition, the useful Eclipse colt Don Quixote, bought by the Prince in 1787, won ten races for him between 1788 and 1791. Sir Thomas apart, the most successful of the horses in training that the Prince of Wales bought at this period was Baronet, whom he got from his breeder, Sir William Vavasour, at the end of 1789. Baronet had won five races for Vavasour as a three- and four-year-old at York, New Malton and Catterick Bridge. He only ran once in 1790 when unplaced to Coriander at Newmarket, but in 1791 he won three races – the richest and most competitive race in the *Calendar*, the Oatlands Handicap Stakes at Ascot, and two King's Plates at Lewes and Newmarket – besides receiving two walk-overs in two other King's Plates at Winchester and Canterbury.

The Prince of Wales entered four horses in the 1791 Oatlands Stakes: Escape, Baronet, Smoaker and Pegasus. Both Smoaker (Pilot–Heron) and Pegasus (Eclipse–Bosphorus Mare) are listed in the *General Stud Book* as being bred and/or owned by the Prince of Wales. Pegasus had won ten races, including the Macaroni Stakes at Newmarket, between 1788 and June 1791; Smoaker's five victories for the heir to the throne included the valuable Conflans Stakes over a mile at Brighton in 1790. Five days prior to the Oatlands Stakes, these four took part in a trial at Epsom under the supervision of Neale and Warwick Lake over the distance of, and carrying the same weights allotted for, the race. Much to his surprise, Sam Chifney, whom the Prince had appointed his stable jockey in July 1790, was ordered by Warwick Lake to ride Pegasus. Escape won the trial by only a neck from Baronet and the other two; Chifney thought that the distance could have been greater, as he felt Escape had been sent to the front too soon, and a row ensued between him and Lake. In 1790 Escape had won two of his four races, a Match against Grey Diomed over the Beacon Course at Newmarket on 10 April and the Great Subscription Stakes over four miles at York from Actaeon in August. He had, however, been beaten into second place by Seagull in the two-mile Oatlands Stakes, and by Skyscraper, the 1789 Derby winner, in a Subscription Stakes over the Beacon Course at Newmarket on 6 October. His only outing prior to the Oatlands in 1790 saw him beat Skylark over the Beacon Course at Newmarket on 26 April.

On the morning of the Oatlands Stakes the Prince of Wales, Lake, Neale and Chifney met to look over the four horses. The moment the sheets were removed from Escape, Chifney asked permission from his Royal employer to ride Baronet instead, maintaining that Escape seemed listless and had so completely lost his condition since the trial that he would never win. Lake and Neale protested that Escape had never been better. The Prince, however, was convinced by Chifney's assessment of the situation, and not merely permitted Chifney to ride Baronet, but added, 'Whenever I have two horses in a race, I wish you, Sam, to ride whichever you fancy most on that day without consulting me.' Unquestionably this was a very wise decision, for Baronet narrowly beat Express and Chanticleer at the remunerative odds of 20–1, with Escape, who was not even quoted in the betting, finishing in the rear. Escape's jockey did not punish him in the final stages of the race when he realized how well Baronet was going and that his mount was unlikely to win under the welter burden of 9 st 10 lbs. Lake's contention that he could have finished second had he not been eased was probably intended to vindicate his opinion that the horse was fit. George III and Queen Charlotte attended the race and were delighted by their son's success; the King afterwards remarked, 'Your Baronets are more productive than mine. I made fourteen last week, but got nothing by them. Your single Baronet is worth all mine put together.' The prize money to the winner of the Oatlands Stakes was 3,800 gns, a huge sum in those days, and the race had generated so much public interest in the country that it was estimated that more than £1 million was bet upon its result.

This was not the first occasion when there had been disputes between Chifney and the Prince's racing manager, Lake, and trainer, Neale. Chifney, one of the most accomplished jockeys of the time, considered that Lake knew little or nothing about racing; Lake, an old Etonian, who was to be appointed Commissioner of Stamps and Gentleman of the Privy Chamber, regarded Chifney as an ambitious upstart whose principal object was to make money by betting on horses, even if it meant cheating on those that he rode. While both views were exaggerated to the extreme, the animosity between the Prince's racing manager and his jockey must be taken into account when considering the scandal that was to occur over the running of Escape in two races at Newmarket on 20 and 21 October 1791. Chifney had also been frequently very critical of Neale's training methods, and had several times complained that the Prince's horses had arrived on the racecourse in a piteous condition and quite unfit to run. On all these occasions Warwick Lake had taken Neale's side. The Prince of Wales's decision that Chifney should be permitted to ride Baronet instead of Escape seems to suggest that he had a little more confidence in his jockey's opinions.

In the autumn of 1791 Escape was engaged in a Match against Grey Diomed for 1,000 gns at Newmarket on 3 October, which he comfortably won. Two days later, he defeated the same horse in a Subscription Stakes over the Beacon Course. On 20 October Escape faced four opponents in a race over the Ditch In course at Newmarket: Grey Diomed, Skylark, Pipator and Coriander: he started favourite at odds of 2–1 on. His jockey Chifney, however, was very doubtful that the horse was fit to run, for he had had neither a sweat nor a strong gallop since his victory on 5 October. The distance of the race was also nearly two miles less than those of his victories earlier that month, being virtually the same as that of the Oatlands, in which he had been well beaten. Escape ran as his jockey feared, and finished last. Neale and Lake, who had not heeded Chifney's warnings, were furious as they had greatly fancied the horse and had wagered accordingly. The Prince of Wales, who had not had a bet, was displeased at Escape's poor running; Chifney, however, persuaded him to let him run again the next day in the Subscription Stakes over the two miles longer Beacon Course, maintaining that his defeat that afternoon was the equivalent of a strong gallop, and thus Escape would be much fitter the following day. On 21 October Escape faced five rivals, including Skylark, who had finished in front of him the previous day, Grey Diomed and Chanticleer, who had been third to Baronet in the Oatlands. Chanticleer was 11 lbs and Skylark 9 lbs worse off at the weights than when they had met Escape in the Oatlands Stakes at Ascot, yet they started first and second favourite at 7–4 and 11–5 respectively: Escape was permitted to start at 5–1. The going had changed radically overnight. The previous day it had been good to firm after a fortnight's fine weather; late that afternoon there was a heavy thunderstorm and it continued to pour with rain all that evening and night. The softened going would have been beneficial to the Prince's horse, whose career up to that time suggested that stamina was his strongest suit. There were thus many indicators that Escape's chances were much greater on 21 October than on 20 October; but the vast majority of the Turf's followers have notoriously short memories.

When Escape easily beat Chanticleer, with Skylark third and

Grey Diomed fourth, the crowd's reaction was very hostile. War- wick Lake, furious at being proved wrong by Chifney, told the Prince, 'I give your Royal Highness joy, but I am sorry the horse has won.' On 26 October, *The Times* felt the discontent caused by Escape's victory justified a long report implying that his jockey had been responsible for some foul play the day before when the horse was beaten. The members of the Jockey Club were not all satisfied with the improved running of Escape on 21 October, and ordered Chifney to appear before the Stewards, Sir Charles Bunbury, Ralph Dutton and Thomas Panton. Ralph Dutton was the younger brother of Lord Sherborne and a friend of the Duke of Bedford; Thomas Panton, who knew the Prince very well and had sold him several horses and mares, had won the Derby with Noble in 1786. Sir Charles Bunbury, the breeder of Highflyer and owner of Diomed, was the pre-eminent figure in the Jockey Club and its Senior Steward frm 1768 to his death in 1821.

Having interviewed Chifney, the Stewards, under the influence of Bunbury, decided not to accept the Royal jockey's explanation of Escape's improved form on 21 October. Sir Charles Bunbury therefore informed the Prince of Wales that no gentleman would match their horses against his if Sam Chifney were engaged to ride them. The heir to the throne was livid, and determined to give up racing entirely; it is to his credit that he stood by his jockey and gave him a pension of £200 a year for life. The reasons for Bunbury's ultimatum to the Prince are not totally clear. Some ascribe it to rank jealousy on the part of his Turf rivals of the popularity the Prince had acquired on the racecourse and of the success of his stable. It is argued that they used Escape's victory as an excuse to make a dead set against him and drive him from Newmarket. Another theory is that the Prime Minister, William Pitt, used the furore to bring pressure to bear on Sir Charles Bunbury, who had been the Member of Parliament for Suffolk from 1760 to 1784, to send the Prince the ultimatum, Pitt's object being to force the heir to the throne to renounce the world of the Turf and its many disreputable followers. An even more bizarre theory is that Sir Charles Bunbury held a grudge against the Prince of Wales concerning the desertion of his wife, the former Lady Sarah Lennox, who ran off with Lord William Gordon in 1768. George III had as a young man been in love with Lady Sarah, and prior to his marriage to Princess Charlotte of Mecklenburg, gossip at the Court suggested that she might be the future Queen. Her link with the Prince of Wales was thus tenuous in the extreme;

Bunbury would hardly have blamed the Prince for a failed marriage which ended when the heir to the throne was but six years old.

What is indisputable is that the Prince of Wales's debts had again reached gigantic proportions. At the beginning of 1792 they came to over £400,000: £127,000 for improvements to Carlton House, almost the same for the Royal Pavilion at Brighton, and more for what the Lord Chancellor called 'Newmarket and other extravagances more referable to profusion than essential to dignity'. In fact only £30,000 of these debts were attributable to his stud and racehorses. Shortly after the Escape affair and his decision to withdraw from racing, the Prince once again announced that he would economize, drastically reduce his establishment, and pay off his most pressing debts by a loan negotiated in the Netherlands. He also postponed transforming the Royal Pavilion into a palace as remarkable as Carlton House and stated that he would withdraw into 'complete retirement'. This new avowal to mend his ways led to a reconciliation with the King and Queen, which made it more likely that assistance would be forthcoming to settle his debts.

The Escape affair has tended to mask the achievements of the other Thoroughbreds bred by the Prince of Wales between 1786 and 1791. Whiskey, a bay colt by Saltram out of Calash foaled in 1789, was to have considerably more influence on the Stud Book than Escape. The Duke of York, writing to his brother on 9 April 1792 from Newmarket, recounts Whiskey's first race in the Great Produce Stakes:

> Whisky, upon whom we had founded all our hopes, for the Great Stakes, was beat very easily indeed. Grosvenor's [John Bull, by] Fortitude out of Zantippe won in the manner of a canter. We were such favourites till the moment of starting that I was not able to bett a half-penny for you, which so far was lucky enough. As soon as the horses came out to start, there was a general cry for Grosvenor. Little Whisky did all he could but he was obliged to yield to superior powers. He was likewise beat by Wentworth's horse.[1]

In his next race, the Derby, Whiskey started at 8–1, but again was outclassed by the favourite, John Bull, finishing only sixth. Yet he then proceeded to win six of his seven remaining races in 1792, among which were the Post Sweepstakes and the Subscription Stakes, both run over the Ditch In Course at Newmarket on consecutive days. Whiskey was sold to Mr Durand at the end of

1792. He won four out of five starts for his new owner, including the Jockey Club Stakes over the Beacon Course at Newmarket on 15 April 1793.

As a stallion Whiskey was even more successful. The best of his colts was Orlando, who ran third to Tyrant in the 1802 Derby; another useful offspring was Fair Star, out of Young Giantess by Diomed; he won thirteen races, was third to Wizard in the 1809 2,000 Guineas and fourth to Pope in the Derby. But Whiskey's colts were far outshone by his fillies. The most celebrated of these was Fair Star's full-sister, Eleanor, owned and bred by Sir Charles Bunbury. She achieved immortality by winning the Derby and the Oaks on 21 and 22 May 1801. Only three other fillies, Blink Bonny in 1857, Signorinetta in 1908 and Fifinella in 1916, have emulated Eleanor's great double. In five seasons' racing from 1801 to 1805, this outstanding filly won twenty-six races, was second eleven times, third four times and unplaced only twice. The best of her foals was Muley, sire of Marpessa, the dam of the best broodmare bred by William IV, the renowned Pocahontas. Another of Whiskey's famous fillies, the Duke of Grafton's Pelisse, who was out of the peerless broodmare Prunella, won the 1804 Oaks and five other races. Eleanor's full-sister, Julia, won fifteen races and was the dam of Phantom by Walton, the 1811 Derby winner and an outstanding sire. Lydia, also a full-sister to Eleanor, won thirteen races, including the Newmarket Stakes. Cressida, who was also by Whiskey out of Young Giantess, won five races, and was the dam of the 1830 Derby winner, Priam by Emilius, who was owned by Sam Chifney's son William. Priam also won thirteen other races from fifteen starts, including the Goodwood Cup in both 1831 and 1832. Although Priam only stood four seasons at stud in England, he got three Oaks winners, Miss Letty (1837), Industry (1838) and Lord George Bentinck's superb filly, Crucifix (1840). Sold to the United States for 3,500 gns by his owner, Lord Chesterfield, who had acquired him from Chifney for 3,000 gns in 1831, Priam headed the sires' list in America four times, in 1842 and from 1844 to 1846. Cressida was also the dam of the 1819 2,000 Guineas winner, Antar. Two other Classic winners, Rhoda (Asparagus—Rosabella), the winner of the 1816 1,000 Guineas, and Nectar (Walton–L'Huile de Venus), who won the 2,000 Guineas the same year, had Whiskey as their broodmare sire.

Although the Prince of Wales never bred a Derby winner before his second retirement from the Turf in 1792, colts bred by him finished fourth for three consecutive years from 1789 to 1791.

Soujah ul Dowlah (Eclipse–Duchess) was fourth to Skyscraper in 1789; Cambooe (Mambrino–Tabitha), who won three races in 1790 and 1791, filled the same position behind Rhadamanthus in 1790; and St David (Saltram–Herod Mare), the winner of two races including the Prince's Stakes at Newmarket's First Spring Meeting in 1791, finished fourth to Florizel that year.

The Prince of Wales's brother, Frederick, Duke of York, had also begun breeding Thoroughbreds at the end of the 1780s, albeit on a smaller scale than George. It was a brief, maiden flirtation with the Turf, as he also sold his racehorses and mares after the Escape scandal. Cymbeline, (Anvil–Mrs Siddons), foaled in 1790, was the best produce of his stud at that time. Cymbeline actually ran both in his colours and in those of the Prince of Wales in his six outings as a two-year-old, when he won three races including the July Stakes at Newmarket and the Orleans Stakes at Brighton. Cymbeline was sold at the end of 1792, and in five more seasons' racing won ten races, including the valuable Prince's Stakes over a mile at Brighton in 1793.

It is also possible that the Prince of Wales bred Eliza (High-flyer–Augusta) in 1791. He had bred her dam, Augusta, and probably bought her back from Colonel O'Kelly after she finished second to Annette in the Oaks. Eliza won nine races including the Newmarket Town Plate for Mr Wilson in 1794, the year she ran second to Hermione in the Oaks. In 1795 Eliza came in third behind Hambletonian in the Doncaster Cup, and the next season her three victories included the Doncaster Stakes.

The break-up of the Royal Studs after the Escape scandal was directed by the Duke of York, and took nearly a year to effect. He sold Escape to Mr Tattersall in April 1792, and the horse never ran again. Amelia (Highflyer–Miss Timms), who had won four races including the Prince's Stakes over a mile at Ascot on the same day as Baronet's victory in the Oatlands, was sold to Sir Charles Bunbury in April 1792; in that and the next year she managed only two wins from fifteen outings. The vast majority of the Royal horses were, however, sold at Tattersalls on Monday 10 December 1792. Saltram and Anvil, the Prince of Wales's two stallions at his Aston Clinton and Newmarket studs, which had been under the management of Warwick Lake, each made 700 gns. Eleven brood-mares fetched 1,728 gns, and the fourteen horses in training were knocked down for 2,671 gns. The stock of the Duke of York was sold for 1,218 gns. It appeared that the two eldest sons of George III had renounced the world of the Turf for ever.

4

The Stud of Frederick, Duke of York,

Oatlands Park, Weybridge,

1801–27

Frederick, Duke of York, was born almost exactly one year after the Prince of Wales on 16 August 1763. Although he was the favourite son of George III, he was also the Prince of Wales's greatest friend. As a young man he was charming, generous and popular. In 1791 he married Princess Frederica Charlotte, the eldest daughter of King Frederick William II of Prussia. The marriage was not a success, and the couple soon separated, the Duchess retiring to Oatlands Park, where she amused herself with her pet dogs till her death in 1820.

The outbreak of war with France in 1793 saw the Duke of York taking command of the English army sent to assist the Austrians in Flanders. Though brave in the field, Frederick lacked the experience and other qualities vital to a general leading troops into battle. Despite this, George III promoted him to the post of Commmander-in-Chief of the British army. The Duke of York's greatest achievements as Commander-in-Chief were in fact not in action but in the valuable reforms in the organization and discipline of the army that were carried out on his direction. Had these reforms not been planned and implemented when they were, it is inconceivable that England could have withstood Napoleon; no such comprehensive review was again made until that of Haldane in the first decade of the twentieth century.

In 1809 Frederick was implicated in a scandal concerning the alleged sale of army commissions by his mistress, Mrs Anne Clarke. A Select Committee of the House of Commons investigated these charges and cleared the Duke of anything worse than reprehensible carelessness in his dealings with Mrs Clarke, but none the less the Duke felt he had no alternative but to resign his post. He was, however, reinstated as Commander-in-Chief by the Prince Regent in 1811, a very popular move, and continued to hold the office even as heir to the throne after 1820.

The Duke of York resumed breeding Thoroughbreds at the stud attached to his estate at Oatlands Park, Weybridge, in Surrey at the turn of the century; and during the next twenty-five years he bred more foals and won more races than his elder brother. The paddocks at Oatlands were sound, dry and the right size; they abounded in short sweet herbage, which at that time was considered the best on which to rear Thoroughbreds. The Duke appointed Warwick Lake, who had served as racing manager to the Prince of Wales, as his racing and stud manager, a position Lake retained until his death in 1820. His first trainer was Thomas Smith; he was succeeded by Bird, for many years Lord Egremont's groom. He had two more trainers, both of whom had been in the service of Lord Egremont, first Cooper and then Butler. His favourite jockeys were W. Wheatley, Sam Chifney, Thomas Goodisson and Sam Day, all among the best riding in the first half of the nineteenth century.

The first winner foaled in the Duke of York's stud after he resumed breeding was Lynceus (Buzzard–Rose), whose dam had been bred by his uncle the Duke of Cumberland. Lynceus ran in the name of Mr Lake when fifth to Lord Egremont's Hannibal in the 1804 Derby; in 1805 he won a Sweepstakes at Newmarket and the following year a Handicap Plate over four miles at Ascot. The best horse the Duke had in training in 1805 was Giles (Trumpator–Mercury Mare), who had won twelve races in 1802 and 1803 before the Duke bought him in 1804. He beat Parasol in the Oatlands Stakes over the Ditch In Course at Newmarket in 1805. Two years later he took up duties as a stallion at Oatlands Park at a fee of 5 gns a mare, increased to 10 gns in 1810. There he replaced Gouty (Sir Peter Teazle–The Yellow Filly), who had won a Sweepstakes at Ascot in 1800 before breaking down a few weeks later at the July meeting at Newmarket. In 1806 Sorcerer (Trumpator–Young Giantess), the winner of fifteen races and leading sire three times, stood for one season at Oatlands at 10 gns a mare; he was replaced by his half-brother, Young Whiskey by Whiskey, in 1807. The latter had failed to win a race, and though beautifully bred, was not to make the grade as a sire either.

The Duke of York's stud soon produced some useful horses. Rosabella (Whiskey–Diomed Mare) won a two-year-old Sweepstakes at Epsom in 1804, and returning to the same course ran third to Bronze in the 1805 Oaks; her contemporary, Humility (Gouty–Estifania), won the prestigious Swinley Stakes over twelve furlongs at Ascot as a four-year-old. Nymphina (Gouty–Mademoiselle), foaled in 1804, won twelve races between 1807 and 1810; in 1808 she won the Oatlands Stakes, beating the 1805 Derby winner, Cardinal Beaufort, and the Jockey Club Plate when she defeated the 1804 Oaks heroine Pelisse. In 1809 she won a Handicap Subscription Stakes at the Newmarket Houghton Meeting from the 1808 Derby winner, Pan, and the 1805 Oaks winner, Meteora; she was also runner-up to the 1807 Derby hero, Election, in the Petworth Stakes at Brighton. The Duke of York sold Nymphina at the end of 1809.

In 1807 the Duke of York had eleven horses in training. The best was Nymphina's contemporary, Coriolanus (Gohanna–Skysweeper), who ran third to Election in the Derby on his racecourse debut. It is recorded that Coriolanus started an outsider at very high odds; these did not deter him from taking the lead at the distance, only to be passed close home by Election and Giles Scroggins. At the same meeting the Duke of York's Marybella (Walnut–Maria) won the Woodcote Stakes. In August 1807 Coriolanus beat some good opposition in the Pavilion Stakes over a mile at Brighton; in 1810 he was standing as a stallion at Oatlands Park at a fee of 3 gns a mare, but he was not a success at stud. Another good horse the Duke of York had in training in 1807 and 1808 was Tim (Whiskey–Grey Duchess), whom he bought in 1806; his four victories for his Royal owner included the Petworth Stakes at Brighton in 1808.

No colts bred at Oatlands ran in the 1808 Derby won by Pan, but the stud was represented by Oberea (Sorcerer–Deceit) in the Oaks. Prior to finishing fourth to Morel in the fillies' classic at Epsom, Oberea was second to the Derby runner-up, Vandyke, in a Sweepstakes at Newmarket's First Spring Meeting, when she also received forfeit in a Stakes. Oberea was eventually sold to Germany in 1816. In 1809 the Duke of York was the owner and breeder of the favourite for the Oaks, Britannia (Gouty–Lady Mayoress), but she was unplaced behind Maid of Orleans. Britannia redeemed her reputation when she floored the odds of 10–1 on laid on Spaniard in the Claret Stakes at Newmarket in May 1810, and ran third to Loiterer a few weeks later in the Ascot Gold Cup. The day after the Claret Stakes, Spaniard died from the effects of poison in his water. The man who administered the fatal dose, a certain Dawson, ended his life on the gallows for this crime. Britannia looked the assured winner of the Oatlands at Ascot in 1811 until she fell, but she won a Match at Newmarket in October.

In 1809 the Oatland Park Stud had been represented by Tumbler (Trumpator–Watlnut Mare) in the Ascot Gold Cup; he had run second to Anderida. He won three races for the Duke of York in 1809, twice at Newmarket and a Sweepstakes at Ascot; his failure to take the Gold Cup may have been influenced by his having bolted twice before the race. At the end of 1809 the Duke sold him to Mr Shakespear, for whom he won thirteen races, including a victory over Pan in a Match at Newmarket in the spring of 1810. He was sold to the East India Company at the end of the 1812 season and exported to India.

The Duke of York's Breslaw (Sorcerer–Maria) won the Produce Stakes over the Ditch Mile at the Newmarket Craven Meeting in April 1810, and a Sweepstakes at the First Spring Meeting, ridden both times by W. Wheatley. In that year's Derby he was no match for the Duke of Grafton's Whalebone, who led from start to finish, but in June 1811 he won the Swinley Stakes at Ascot. Sagana (Sorcerer–Woodpecker Mare), who was also owned and bred by the Duke, finished unplaced behind Oriana on her racecourse debut in the 1810 Oaks; but she was never beaten again. She won the Swinley Stakes and a mile Sweepstakes at Ascot on consecutive days, and then walked over for the Magna Charta Stakes over a mile at Egham. After those three victories she was retired to the paddocks at Oatlands Park.

The year of the Clarke scandal, 1809, saw two very good colts bred by the Duke at Oatlands. These were Pointers (Giles–Woodpecker Mare 1798) and Venture (Haphazard–Woodpecker Mare 1799), who won fourteen and eight races respectively. In the spring of 1812 Pointers won the Newmarket Stakes, but was unplaced behind Octavius in the Derby. In the Magna Charta Stakes over a mile at Egham Pointers got his revenge, beating Octavius into second place. Pointers probably had not stayed the distance at Epsom, for one of his four victories in 1813 was in the inaugural running of the Wokingham Stakes at Ascot over six furlongs. He won a Sweepstakes at Newmarket in the spring of 1814, and was then sold. Pointers won six more times before he was exported to the Cape after his final victory in 1816; unfortunately he died during the passage. Venture won a Match at Egham as a two-year-

arles II attending his last horse race at Dorsett Ferry near Windsor Castle, August 1684. From a drawing by ncis Barlow. Reproduced by kind permission of Arthur Ackermann.

ando, winner of the 1844 Derby Stakes and sire at Hampton Court Stud. Painting by J. F. Herring Snr. produced by kind permission of Arthur Ackermann.

Above: FitzRoland, bred by Queen Victoria and winner of the 1858 2,000 Guineas. Painting by Harry Hall. Reproduced by kind permission of Arthur Ackermann. Below: The Earl, bred by Queen Victoria, winner of the 1868 Grand Prix de Paris and St James's Palace Stakes. Painting by Harry Hall. Reproduced by kind permission of Arthur Ackermann.

Above: Springfield, bred by Queen Victoria, winner of Champion Stakes, July Cup, Gimcrack Stakes and leading sire of winners in 1890. Painting by Harry Hall. Reproduced by kind permission of Arthur Ackermann. Below: Polymelus whose dam Maid Marian was bred by Queen Victoria, was the sire of Phalaris and champion sire five times.

Above: Perdita II, dam of Persimmon, Diamond Jubilee and Florizel II. Below: Persimmon (J. Watts) with the Prince of Wales and Richard Marsh at Egerton House Stables.

Friar Marcus, bred by King George VI, winner of the 1914 Middle Park Stakes. Reproduced by kind permission of HM the Queen.

Scuttle, bred by King George V and winner of the 1,000 Guineas in 1928.

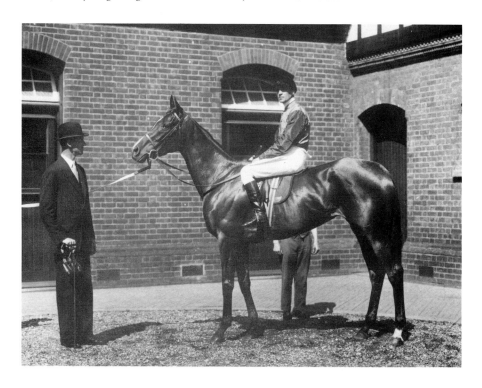

Above: Captain Charles Moore, Stud Manager to King George VI and the Queen, inspects the Queen's Mereworth at the Yearling Sales 1960. Photograph by Sport & General.
Below: Captain Cecil Boyd-Rochfort, trainer to King George V, King George VI and the Queen, on the gallops at Newmarket. Photograph by Graphic Photo Union.

Above: Knight's Daughter, bred by King George VI and dam of American champion racehorse and sire, Round Table. Photograph by W. W. Rouch & Co. Below: Round Table, Horse of the Year and leading sire in the USA. Photograph by Thoroughbred Record.

Above: Aureole, bred by King George VI, at Wolferton Stud. Photograph by R. Anscomb. Below: Aureole being welcomed into the winner's enclosure at Ascot by the Queen and Captain Boyd-Rochfort after his victory in the King George VI and Queen Elizabeth Stakes, July 1954. Photograph by Fox Photos.

old and the first class of the Oatlands Stakes at Newmarket the following season, when he was also runner-up in the Swinley Stakes at Ascot. He showed even better form in 1813: at the Craven Meeting he beat Sorcery, the 1811 Oaks winner, in the Oatlands Stakes, won a Sweepstakes over two and a half miles at Ascot and the Gold Cup at Egham over four miles. The Duke then sold him to Sir W. Roberts, for whom he won the Gold Cup over four miles at Stockbridge in 1814.

The Duke of York bred another very useful colt at Oatlands in 1810: Aladdin (Giles–Walnut Mare), who won fifteen races between 1813 and 1816, and was beaten only once as a three-year-old when unplaced to Smolensko in the 1813 Derby. Aladdin's seven wins that season included the Oatlands Handicap at Newmarket's Second October Meeting and four other races over a mile. He reserved his best two performances for Ascot; ridden by Chifney, Aladdin beat Caterpillar, the runner-up to Smolensko at Epsom, in a mile Sweepstakes, and then beat the 1812 Derby hero, Octavius, in a run-off after they had dead-heated for the Swinley Stakes. His sole win in 1814 was also at the Berkshire course, where he won the Oatlands Stakes over two and a half miles. He was not placed in the 1815 running of the same race, but two days later beat Grey Marquis in the Gold Cup. The day after that Aladdin completed a truly remarkable double when he beat twelve rivals in the six-furlong Wokingham Stakes. In 1816 Aladdin won three more races at Newmarket, where he was also second of fifteen to Bourbon, who had run third to Blucher in the 1814 Derby, in the Craven Stakes. His attempt to win the Ascot Gold Cup in consecutive years was thwarted by the excellent stayer Anticipation, who also won Ascot's most prestigious race in 1819. In 1817 Aladdin retired to stud at Oatlands Park, but he proved a disappointing sire.

Oatlands produced two more noteworthy colts for the Duke in 1812: Castanet (Granicus–Gohanna Mare) and Scrapall (Granicus–Young Whiskey Mare). Castanet ran second in the Woodcote Stakes at Epsom and then won the Two-Year-Old Sweepstakes at Ascot when ridden by Chifney. He was second to Tigris in the 1815 2,000 Guineas, but unplaced to Whisker in the Derby. He received a walk-over at Newmarket's First October Meeting, and at the Houghton Meeting beat Mouse, the runner-up to Minuet in the Oaks, in a Match. His Royal owner then sold him to Mr Goddard, for whom he won four races in the west country in 1816. He was then sold to Ireland where he won five races in 1817 and

1818, eventually being exported to Russia as a stallion. Scrapall's debut on the racecourse was when unplaced in Whisker's Derby, but not much time elapsed before he gained his first victory, in the Swinley Stakes at Ascot. In 1815 he also won a Match and received a walk-over at Newmarket. He began his 1816 campaign by finishing second in the Claret Stakes, winning two matches and receiving one walk-over in the spring at Newmarket. Scrapall then won the Swinley Stakes for the second year running, after which he was sold by the Duke of York. He won three more times, including the Oatlands Stakes at Newmarket's Second October Meeting in 1816; he was finally exported in 1817.

The 1813 crop of foals bred at Oatlands Park is one of the most significant, for it contained a bay colt by Hedley out of Gramarie by Sorcerer named Prince Leopold, who was to become the first colt bred by a Royal Stud to win the Derby Stakes. Gramarie had been bred by the Duke in 1807 and ran only twice, unplaced, once in 1810 and once the following year; Prince Leopold was her second foal.

Prince Leopold made his first appearance on a racecourse in the 1816 Derby. Although he started at odds of 20–1, he was well thought of at home, and the Duke of York had backed him to win several thousand pounds. The favourite was Lord George Cavendish's Nectar, who had earlier won the 2,000 Guineas and Riddlesworth Stakes at Newmarket. The crowd assembled on the Downs that afternoon was reportedly the largest hitherto seen on a Derby day. At the winning-post Prince Leopold, ridden by W. Wheatley, had half a length to spare over Nectar with Pandour third.

The 1816 Derby winner had a vile temper and was most difficult to train. He did not reappear on the racecourse till the Newmarket St Leger on 1 October, for which he was favourite at 5–4. Prince Leopold ran abysmally and was beaten into third place by the 50–1 outsider, Sovereign, whom he had very comprehensively defeated in the Derby. The next day Prince Leopold walked-over. His final race as a three-year-old was in the Oatlands Stakes over the Rowley Mile at Newmarket's Second October Meeting. He was again favourite, at 2–1, but could only manage fourth place.

Prince Leopold began his four-year-old campaign in great style by beating both the 11–10 favourite Nectar and Sovereign in the Port Stakes over 15 furlongs and 125 yards at the Newmarket Craven Meeting. His waywardness and ill-temper soon reasserted themselves, however, and declining to show his best form he was defeated in a Match over the Rowley Mile at Newmarket's First Spring Meeting by Skim, whom he had decisively beaten in the Derby. Prince Leopold's reputation ensured that Nectar was favourite at 2–1 on in a Match over the Rowley Mile a fortnight later, and Lord George Cavendish's 2,000 Guineas winner easily landed the odds as Prince Leopold's temper once more got the better of him. The 1816 Derby winner's final race, in a Sweepstakes over a mile at Newmarket in the autumn of 1817, was equally disappointing: he finished third and last. He had by this time become so unmanageable that the only solution was to geld him, but unfortunately he died following the operation in 1818. When the Duke of York's first Derby winner consented to show his best form, he was a more than useful colt; his victories over the consistent Nectar are proof of that. Still, the 1816 Derby does not rank very highly; the 1813 crop of colts was probably below the normal standard. This evil-tempered horse does have his place in Turf history, however, as the first Derby winner bred at a Royal stud.

The Duke of York had three runners in the 1817 Derby won by Azor: Gazelle (Sorcerer–Jerboa), Doctor Busby (Dick Andrews–Waxy Mare) and Roller (Quiz–Paleface), but none was placed. Roller had beaten Doctor Busby in the Craven Stakes at Newmarket on 7 April, but did not win again that season and was sold to Lord Sligo, for whom he won the Kildare Stakes at the Curragh in April 1818. Doctor Busby's best effort after the Derby was to finish second in the Oatlands at Ascot. The Duke of York then sold him to Mr Page, for whom he won a two-mile Sweepstakes at Epsom in May 1818. Gazelle had won three races prior to the Derby: a Sweepstakes at the Craven Meeting, the Newmarket Stakes at the First Spring Meeting (where his beaten rivals included the 2,000 Guineas winner, Manfred, and Sylvanus, who was to run third to Azor at Epsom) and a walk-over at the Second Spring Meeting. At Ascot Gazelle won a Sweepstakes over the New Mile Course; his two victories at Newmarket in the autumn of 1817 brought his season's total to six. As a four-year-old Gazelle beat Manfred again in the Port Stakes and ran second to Belville in the Ascot Gold Cup; the following year the same race saw him come in second again, this time to Anticipation. The Duke of York then sold him to the East India Company.

The 1814 crop of foals at Oatlands also included Amabel (Election–Young Whiskey Mare) and Vignette (Rubens–Sagana). Amabel, who walked-over at Ascot in 1817, was second to Neva in the Oaks on her racecourse debut. Neva had earlier won the 1,000 Guineas; in 1818 the two fillies met in a Match at Newmarket's Second Spring Meeting, and Amabel, receiving 9 lbs, took her revenge. Later that autumn she won two other races at Newmarket, in the latter beating Manfred, the 1817 2,000 Guineas winner. The Duke of York then sold her and she was exported to India. Two of Vignette's three victories came in the Wokingham Stakes at Ascot, which he won in 1817 and 1818; the other was in a Match at Newmarket in October 1817.

The Duke of York was represented in the 1818 Derby by FitzCloddy (Seymour or Election–Lady of the Lake) and Cockatoo (Seymour–Rosalina), but both colts ran without distinction behind Sam. There were ten false starts to the Epsom Classic that year; on five occasions Prince Paul, who finally finished third, took the lead, and many felt he would have won had he not exerted himself so much beforehand. FitzCloddy met Sam again in a Match at Newmarket's First October Meeting. The Derby winner was conceding 8 lbs to the Duke of York's colt; FitzCloddy took full advantage of the weight differential and had his revenge on his Epsom conqueror. Earlier in the summer he was far from disgraced when runner-up in a mile Sweepstakes at Ascot to Interpreter, whose six wins had included the 2,000 Guineas. FitzCloddy's only other victory had been in a Subscription Plate over the Two-Year-Old Course at Newmarket's Craven Meeting, when he beat Filagree, who had just won the Produce Sweepstakes. Filagree was to become the dam of the 1824 Oaks winner, Cobweb, and grandam of the 1836 Derby and 2,000 Guineas winner, Bay Middleton. Cockatoo won three minor races at Yarmouth (twice) and Epsom in 1819. The Duke of York ran an unnamed sister to Scrapall in the 1818 Oaks, but she ran unplaced to Corinne, and was a maiden when sold to Baron Biel for export to Germany. The only other noteworthy foal of the Duke's 1815 crop was Jeremy Gradus (Eaton–Buzzard Mare), who won the Woodcote Stakes at Epsom in 1817.

The Duke of York won the Woodcote Stakes the next year with Funny (Seymour or Granicus–Young Whiskey Mare), who also won the Two-Year-Old Sweepstakes at Ascot and another race at Newmarket in the autumn of 1818. The most successful of the foals bred by the Duke of York in 1816 was Banker (Smolensko–Quail), who first set foot on a racecourse in the 1819 Derby, when he ran unplaced to Tiresias and Sultan, who was to become leading sire for six consecutive seasons from 1832 to 1837. Banker went on to win a Sweepstakes and walked-over for the Swinley Stakes at Ascot, and ran second to Tiresias in the Newmarket St Leger. Banker began his four-year-old campaign in tremendous style; ridden by Sam Day he won both the Claret Stakes and the Oatlands Stakes on the same day. In the latter his beaten rivals included the 1816 1,000 Guineas heroine Rhoda. Goodisson had the mount on Banker when he received 8 lbs from Tiresias, who had also won the 1819 St Leger, in a Sweepstakes at Newmarket's First Spring Meeting: a race Banker won so easily that the weight he got from the Derby winner probably made no difference to the result. In the Ascot Gold Cup the Duke's much improved colt ran second to Champignon. In the autumn Banker won four races at Newmarket: the Trial Stakes and the Oatlands, both over a mile, a Subscription Stakes over the Ditch In Course and a 50 gns Plate over the Beacon Course. In the latter he met the 1818 Oaks and 1,000 Guineas winner, Corinne, and in a desperate finish got home by a neck. These victories at distances ranging from a mile to over four miles bore eloquent testimony to Banker's versatility.

Banker was opposed by Antar, who had won the 1819 2,000 Guineas, in a Sweepstakes at the Craven Meeting in 1821. Banker ran out an easy winner; very large sums were apparently won and lost on this race. He won three more races at Newmarket in the spring of 1821, but then failed to give Strephon 16 lbs in the Oatlands Stakes at Ascot. His reputation was such that none dared oppose him in the Ascot Gold Cup and he walked-over, the only occasion in the history of the race that this has happened. At Newmarket's Second October Meeting the Duke of York matched Banker against Abjer, the runner-up to Sailor in the Derby. This match was one of the heaviest betting races of the year; 7–4 was laid on Abjer, who won easily. Later that autumn Banker met Sultan in a Match at Newmarket, and here the future leading sire proved too good for him. In 1822 Banker ran second in the Craven Stakes at Newmarket, after which the Duke of York sold him. He won four more races, the Cups at Winchester and Abingdon and a race at Shrewsbury in 1822, and a small race at Buxton in 1823. He then retired to stud at Witherwin Farm, Appleton, Cheshire, at a fee of 5 gns a mare, but was a disappointing sire.

A quite successful filly bred by the Duke of York in 1816 was Soota (Election or Seymour–Young Whiskey Mare). The Duke had two Young Whiskey mares, both foaled in 1808, at the Oatlands Stud; one out of a Walnut mare, Soota's grandam, the other out of Funny's grandam Duchess, a grey Arabian mare brought to

England by Sir Charles Cockerell and presented to the Duke. Soota won the Magna Charta Stakes at Egham and two races at the Newmarket Houghton Meeting in 1819, and ran third in 1819 and second in 1820 in the Wokingham Stakes at Ascot. Her two victories in 1820 were both at Newmarket: the first was a walk-over in the spring, the second in a Handicap over the Two-Year-Old course at the Second October Meeting. Ridden by Goodisson, and an outsider at 16–1, she beat the redoubtable Sultan, four of whose victories were achieved over the 5 furlongs and 136 yards course at Newmarket. Prince Leopold's half-sister, Bella Donna by Seymour, Gramarie's fourth foal and second winner, also came from the 1816 crop. She only made one appearance on the racecourse at Ascot in 1819, when she won a mile Sweepstakes. In 1820 she foaled Jane Shore by Woful for the Duke of York, and this filly won three Matches and received a walk-over at Newmarket in 1823 as well as being runner-up three times, once in the Windsor Forest Stakes at Ascot. Jane Shore was an excellent broodmare and achieved fame when she produced Amato, the 1838 Derby winner. Bella Donna, after foaling Jane Shore, was sold.

The foals bred by the Duke of York in 1817 were moderate. Prodigious (Zodiac–Rosalina), who was unplaced to Sailor in the Derby, won two races for the Duke, one at Ascot in 1820 and a Match at Newmarket the next spring, after which he was sold. He later won two minor Sweepstakes at Winchester and Exeter. Punt (Seymour–Young Whiskey Mare) won twice as a two-year-old at Egham and Newmarket, and in 1820 walked-over for the Windsor Forest Stakes. The 1818 crop was even more disappointing, producing only two winners. The better of the two was Louison (Aladdin–Rubens Mare), who only raced in 1820; she was second in the Woodcote Stakes, and won the Two-Year-Old Sweepstakes at Ascot over six furlongs and a four-furlong Sweepstakes at Hampton.

After these two bad years, however, Oaklands Park in 1819 produced one of its best ever crop of foals, the most significant of which was the bay colt by Whalebone or Seymour out of Gohanna Mare 1807, who was named Moses. His dam, Gohanna Mare, was bred by Lord Egremont, as was his grandam Grey Skim; but all Gohanna Mare's foals prior to Moses had been bred by the Duke of York. Moses' half-brother, Roger Bacon by Sorcerer, had won one race, the valuable Newmarket Stakes, in 1818, and had been runner-up in the Oatlands Stakes at Newmarket's Second October Meeting in 1819. Both Moses and Roger Bacon were half-brothers to Castanet by Granicus, so even before Moses set foot on a racecourse, his dam had proved a very wise acquisition for the Duke's stud.

Moses started at 2–1 on for his first race on 22 April 1822, a Subscription Sweepstakes over 5 furlongs and 136 yards at Newmarket, which he won easily. He was third favourite for the Derby at 6–1; the 3–1 favourite was the Duke of Grafton's Hampden, who had done an excellent trial with the Duke's Pastille and Whizgig; the former had won the 2,000 Guineas and was to win the Oaks, the latter was the winner of the 1,000 Guineas. The crowd at Epsom on Thursday 23 May 1822, a fine, sunny day, was again vast. The Duke of York was accompanied to the Downs by his first cousin, the Duke of Gloucester; regrettably his finances were in such a parlous state, following astronomic losses at cards, that he was unable to have as large a bet on his colt Moses as he would have liked. Other notable personalities to witness the race that afternoon included the Duke of Wellington, Lords Derby, Sefton and Stewart, the French Ambassador and, in the words of a journalist covering the day's festivities, 'as great a show of beauty and fashion as we ever before witnessed, on any similar occasion'.

A few lengths covered the twelve runners, headed by Wanton, until they came near Tattenham Corner, at which point Moses, Figaro and the favourite, Hampden, took a clear advantage, racing almost in line abreast. It was reported that the three jockeys brought their whips and spurs into action unsparingly. Goodisson must have used his to best effect on Moses, as in a thrilling finish, the Duke's colt, who always had a slight lead over his two rivals, held on to win by a head from Figaro, who was just in front of Hampden.

On 5 June Moses ran again in the Albany Stakes over a mile at Ascot. Starting at 10–6 on, he beat Samford and Angelica easily. He was due to run over a mile at Newmarket's Second October Meeting, but gave forfeit. On 17 April 1823 Moses beat Morisco in the Claret Stakes at Newmarket, and eleven days later received a walk-over. His final race was a Match at Newmarket on 1 May 1823, when he failed to concede 10 lb to MacDuff. Moses then retired to the Hampton Court Stud, where he joined Waterloo and Rainbow, at a fee of 10 gns a mare. He did get several winners, but none of particular distinction. He certainly was a very run-of-the-mill Derby winner, but that should not detract from the Duke of York's achievement in having bred two winners of the Blue Riband of the Turf in seven years.

Warwick Lake, the Duke of York's long-serving racing and stud manager, died in 1820 and so did not live to see Moses' victory in the Derby. He was succeeded by the 27-year-old Charles Greville, the famous diarist, who on 23 February 1820 recorded, 'Yesterday the Duke of York proposed to me to take the management of his horses, which I accepted. Nothing could have been more kind than the manner in which he proposed it.' Greville, educated at Eton and Christ Church, Oxford, was a nephew of the Duke of Portland, whose influence had obtained for him the sinecure appointment of the Secretaryship of Jamaica, the duties of which office were performed by a deputy. It was certainly from his mother and uncle that Greville inherited his love of racing and breeding. He was to be an influential member of the Jockey Club between 1830 and his death in 1865. When the Royal Stud at Hampton Court was disbanded in 1837, he kept his broodmares there, and he was also responsible for the excellent sire, Orlando, standing there most of his life as a stallion. In 1824 Greville was appointed Clerk of the Privy Council, a position he continued to hold under George IV's successor, William IV.

Greville's diary has given us an excellent description of life at the Duke of York's country seat at Oatlands Park. Writing in 1818, he describes the weekend parties thus:

> We dine at eight and sit at table till eleven. In about a quarter of an hour after we leave the table, the Duke sits down to play at whist and never stirs from the table as long as anybody will play with him. He is equally well amused whether the play is high or low, but the stakes he prefers is five and ponies on the rubber. The Duke always gets up early whatever time he goes to bed. On August 4th, when the party included Warwick and Page, we played till four in the morning.

In the same entry in his diary, Greville criticizes the running of the house, saying, 'Oatlands is the worst managed establishment in England; there are a great many servants and nobody waits on you; a vast number of horses and none to ride.'

Charles Greville recorded his assessment of his future employer, the Duke of York, in his diary on 18 August 1818, after another visit to Oatlands Park:

> The Duke of York is not clever, but he has the justness of understanding, which enables him to avoid the errors into which

most of his brothers have fallen, and which have made them so contemptible and unpopular. Although his talents are not rated highly, and in public life he has never been honourably distinguished, the Duke of York is loved and respected. He is the only one of the Princes who has the feelings of an English gentleman; his amiable disposition and excellent temper have conciliated for him the esteem and regard of men of all parties, and he has endeared himself to his friends by the warmth and steadiness of his attachments, and from the implicit confidence they all have in his truth, straightforwardness and sincerity.

When Charles Greville became the racing and stud manager to the Duke of York, he set about weeding out the useless stock in the stud. In this task he was greatly aided by the father of Frank Butler, who rode John Bowes's 1852 and 1853 Derby winners, Daniel O'Rourke and West Australian. While Warwick Lake had been a most conscientious and loyal stud manager to the Duke, he had developed prejudices as he aged; he persisted in breeding from such stallions as Young Whiskey, Aladdin and Granicus, who, though well-bred themselves, soon showed signs that they were unlikely to get high-class racehorses. The culling and restocking of a stud takes time, however, and the hoped-for results had not been achieved by the time of the Duke's death on 5 January 1827.

After the Duke of York's death Greville first helped manage the horses of his uncle, the Duke of Portland, and then those of Lord Chesterfield, whose horses included Priam, Zinganee and Glaucus. Greville then formed a partnership with his cousin, Lord George Bentinck, the future autocrat of the Turf. At that time, however, Lord George was unable to run his horses in his own name as a result of his father's hostility to racing. The best horse he owned at this time, the filly Preserve, ran in the colours of Charles Greville; she won the Clearwell and Criterion Stakes in 1834 and the 1,000 Guineas in 1835, when she was also second to Queen of Trumps in the Oaks. The cousins, who had the reputation of being the shrewdest placers of bets, fell out over the propriety of running Preserve in the Goodwood Stakes, and the partnership was dissolved. The two men were, however, later reconciled.

Greville then bought Preserve's full-brother, Mango, from Mr Thornhill. Mango was beaten in the 1837 Derby, apparently as he had had to walk all the way from Newmarket to Epsom. However, he then won three races in two days at Ascot, including the Ascot Derby. When he won the St Leger at Doncaster, both Greville and

Lord George Bentinck landed some hefty wagers. Another good horse owned by Greville was Alarm, who lost his chance in the Derby, for which he was much fancied, by bolting before the race when The Libel charged him at the start and his jockey was thrown. Alarm, however, won the Cambridgeshire in 1845, and the following year the Ascot Gold Cup. He also became a stallion at Hampton Court. Other good winners owned and bred by Greville included Adine, who won the 1853 Goodwood Cup, Yorkshire Oaks and Ebor Handicap, Quince, the winner of the Goodwood Cup in 1855 and Muscovite, who won the 1854 Cesarewitch. The final paragraph of his obituary in *Baily's Magazine* ran: 'No man so high or low, we believe, ever sought his advice and assistance in vain; and to no individual probably have so many and such various difficulties been submitted. Beloved by his friends and feared by his opponents, Mr Greville will ever be considered one of the most remarkable men that lent lustre to the English Turf.'

During Charles Greville's tenure of office as stud manager at Oatlands, the Duke of York won no Classics, though the number of successes increased. Orion (Phantom–Hedley Mare), who was second favourite for the 1824 2,000 Guineas but ran unplaced to Schahriar, won three races for the Duke, including the Wokingham Stakes at Ascot. He was sold in 1825 to Lord Orford, for whom he won seven times. Frogmore (Phantom–Rubens Mare), unplaced to Bay Middleton in the 1825 Derby, won four races including the Albany Stakes at Ascot, where he was second in the Wokingham Stakes in 1825 and 1826. Don Carlos (Election–Miss Wasp) ran in the colours of Charles Greville; he won the Prendergast Stakes at Newmarket in 1823 and ten other races in the next two seasons.

In July 1826 the Duke of York contracted dropsy. Knowing that his illness was fatal, he began the dispersal of his stud and horses in training on 11 December 1826, when six of his broodmares and six horses in training were sold by Messrs Tattersalls. One month after his death, on 5 February 1827, all the Duke's Thoroughbred stock was sold by Messrs Tattersalls. The sale was attended by noblemen and gentlemen from every part of the Kingdom, among them the Duke of Richmond, the Marquess of Graham, the Earl of MountCharles, who was attending for King George IV, the Earls of Chesterfield and Bruce, Lords Southampton, FitzRoy, Orford, Harborough and Pembroke, General Grosvenor, Colonels Leigh, Russell and Udney and Messrs Greville, Payne and Charlton. A total of thirty-two Thoroughbred horses came under the hammer, and fetched a total of 7,632 guineas. The highest price of the sale,

1,100 gns, was given by the Duke of Richmond for the Derby winner, Moses, who then left the Hampton Court Stud where he had been standing, and spent the rest of his life at Richmond's stud at Goodwood. George IV bought Moses' dam, Gohanna Mare, then twenty years old, for 230 gns, Orion's dam, Hedley Mare, a ten-year-old, for 320 gns, and the four-year-old mare, Rachel (Whalebone–Gohanna Mare) for 560 gns. Rachel, who had been unplaced in the 1826 Oaks behind Lilias, had won six races that season for the Duke of York; in 1827 she remained in training and ran in the colours of the King's racing manager, Mr Delmé Radcliffe, though the best she achieved in three outings for him was a fourth in the Oatlands Stakes at Newmarket in the autumn, and a distant fifth to Memnon in the Ascot Gold Cup. Mr Payne gave the highest price for a broodmare when Quadrille by Sorcerer was knocked down to him with her yearling filly foal by Moses, Pauline, for 530 gns. Pauline was the last good filly bred by the Duke of York, for she won six races including the Grand Duke Michael Stakes at Newmarket and was third to Lord George Cavendish's Young Mouse and Lord Exeter's Green Mantle, who was later to win the Oaks, in the 1829 1,000 Guineas. Mr Angerstein paid 120 gns for Prince Leopold's dam, Gramarie, then twenty years old.

At the same sale, all the Duke's carriages, his hacks and his dogs, Pointers and Spaniels were sold (the Duke had been very fond of shooting, as the breeds of his dogs demonstrated). While his stud at Oatlands Park had not been as extensive as those of the Duke of Grafton or Lord Egremont, nor had he achieved such success as they had with their runners, yet the Duke of York had had the distinction of breeding two Derby winners in twenty-five years as well as numerous other high-class horses.

5

The Royal Studs of the Prince Regent

and King George IV,

1800–30

The Prince of Wales had been very much in love with Mrs Fitz-Herbert when they were married. By the winter of 1793–4, how-ever, their relationship had become strained. One of the problems was his enormous debts. It was generally believed that they were the result of extravagant living, but in fact the majority were due to his collection of artistic treasures which would be both a sound financial investment and part of the cultural heritage of the nation. One solution to the debt problem would be marriage to a suitable foreign princess and the birth of an heir to the throne, which might induce Parliament to give him an extra allowance and to settle his outstanding liabilities. The Duke of York had sent favourable reports from Germany of Princess Caroline of Brunswick, the youngest daughter of George III's elder sister, Augusta. Although the Prince of Wales had never met his first cousin, she became his choice of wife. His future bride arrived at St James's Palace on 5 April 1795. The Prince was horrified when he was introduced to her and immediately said, 'I am not well, pray get me a glass of brandy.' Caroline was fat, vulgar, coarse and unwashed. Neverthe-less, on the evening of 8 April they were married in the Chapel Royal at St James's Palace. The Royal bridegroom was able to go through with the ceremony only by becoming completely drunk beforehand.

The Prince of Wales consummated the marriage with as much ardour as that of Henry VIII for Anne of Cleves, and on 7 January 1796 Princess Charlotte was born. Within three months the Prince

68

and Princess had virtually separated, maintaining two households and seldom seeing each other.

Even the payments of the Prince of Wales's debts, one of the principal reasons for his marriage, did not come about as he had hoped. His liabilities amounted to £630,000 in 1795; the House of Commons insisted on setting aside £65,000 a year and the revenues from the Duchy of Cornwall for the following twenty-five years in debt redemption. This left the Prince with an annual income of only £60,000.

In February 1793 the French Republic declared war on Great Britain. The Prince of Wales was commissioned as Colonel of the Tenth Light Dragoons, and a few days later he rode beside his father to Horse Guards to inspect the advance party of the British army that was leaving for Holland under the command of the Duke of York. The Prince of Wales, who longed for action, declared that he would be willing to serve under his brother, but the King forbade him to leave England. It was one of the great disappointments of his life that he was never to join an army in the field in the twenty years of war against the French.

From 1796 onwards the Prince attempted to effect a reconciliation with his secret wife; even his mother Queen Charlotte had written to Maria FitzHerbert personally, asking her to accept a new arrangement that would make her eldest son happy. Finally in June 1800 a reconciliation was effected when on the 16th Mrs FitzHerbert invited her London friends to a grand breakfast at her home in Tilney Street 'to meet His Royal Highness'. Few who saw them during the next six years, especially at Brighton, could doubt their mutual happiness.

At this time the Prince of Wales returned to breeding Thoroughbred horses. He bought the mare Trumpetta (Trumpator–Peggy by Herod) from Lord Clermont in 1796, and all her nine foals from 1797 to 1807 were bred by the heir to the throne at his stud at Six Mile Bottom near Newmarket. Albion by John Bull, Trumpetta's fourth foal born in 1800, was the first winner bred by the Prince after his return to the Turf; he won six races between 1803 and 1806, including the first running of the Pavilion Stakes run over a mile at Brighton in 1803 and worth the then large sum of 1,900 gns to the winner. (Ditto only received 1,700 gns when he won the Derby earlier that summer.) Despite the Prince's refusal to attend racing at Newmarket after the Escape affair, some of the horses he had in training continued to take part in races there. Albion, for example, won a Match and received a walk-over and

Mitre, bought by the Prince from Lord Egremont, won four times for him at Newmarket in 1804. The horses he had running at Newmarket, however, ran not in his own colours but in those of his new racing manager, Mr Delmé Radcliffe. When the Prince first returned to the Turf, all his horses were trained by a man called Smallman, who was a brother-in-law of Sam Chifney, at Albury Grange near Winchester. After a couple of seasons Smallman moved the horses in training to the stables attached to the Royal Pavilion. Neither of these venues was very satisfactory, and after a short time the Prince's horses in training were moved to Perren's stables in Newmarket, remaining under Smallman's control.

The Prince of Wales's absence from Newmarket caused Sir Charles Bunbury and Lord Darlington to write to him on 30 July 1805, when they were attending the races at Brighton, the following letter:

Sir,

We humbly beg leave to represent to Your Royal Highness that we are deputed in our official Situations as Stewards of Newmarket to convey to you the unanimous wish of all Gentlemen of the Turf now present at Brighton, which we respectfully submit for your consideration.

From various Misconceptions or Differences of Opinion which arose relative to a race, in which Your Royal Highness was concerned, we greatly regret, that we have never been honoured with Your Presence there since that Period. But experiencing as we constantly do, the singular Marks of Your Condescension and Favour, and considering the essential benefit not only that the Turf will generally derive, but also the great satisfaction that we all must individually feel from the Honor of Your Presence, we humbly request that Your Royal Highness will bury in oblivion any past unfortunate Occurences at Newmarket and that You will again be pleased to honor us there with Your Countenance and Support.[1]

This letter fell on deaf ears; George IV never attended races at Newmarket in person again after the Escape episode.

The Prince of Wales's stud in the first decade of the nineteenth century was relatively modest, even smaller than that of his brother, the Duke of York. Nevertheless, he acquired some exceptional broodmares, none better than the Alexander Mare (1790) he bought from the Duke of Queensberry after she had foaled Castrel by Buzzard in 1801. Castrel, the winner of three races, became a very important stallion for his son, Pantaloon, was the male-line ancestor of Roi Herode and The Tetrarch. The first colt bred by the Prince of Wales out of the Alexander Mare was Selim by Buzzard, who was foaled in 1802. He won six of his eight races between 1806 and 1808; in October 1806 he won the October Oatlands Stakes over the Rowley Mile on only his second appearance on the racecourse. On 30 March 1807 he beat Walton in the Craven Stakes over ten furlongs at Newmarket. At stud he sired six Classic winners: Medora (1814 Oaks), an unnamed filly (1815 1,000 Guineas), Azor (1817 Derby), Nicolo (1823 2,000 Guineas), Turcoman (1827 2,000 Guineas) and Turquoise (1828 Oaks). His most influential colt, however, was Sultan out of the Ditto mare Bacchante, who was beaten a head by Tiresias in the 1819 Derby. Sultan was almost unbeatable over a mile and ten furlongs between 1819 and 1824, but it was at stud that he was to achieve his greatest fame, being champion sire on six occasions. When he got Lord Jersey's 1836 2,000 Guineas and Derby winner, Bay Middleton, he ensured that the Herod–Woodpecker–Buzzard male line was transmitted to the present day, not only through the Castrel branch, but also through the descendants of Selim. Bay Middleton was the sire of The Flying Dutchman, who was the male-line ancestor of the great French sires Dollar, Chouberski, Bruleur, Ksar, Tourbillon and Djebel. Selim was also a most influential broodmare sire: Camel by Whalebone was out of a Selim mare. Camel won five of his seven races, but as he frequently suffered from lameness his real worth as a racehorse was never really apparent. Though champion sire only once, in 1838, he was the sire of Touchstone, the winner of the 1834 St Leger and of the Ascot Gold Cup in 1836 and 1837. Touchstone was the male-line ancestor of such important sires as Orlando, Hermit, Bay Ronald, Bayardo, Gainsborough, Hyperion, Aureole, Tudor Minstrel, Forli and Star Kingdom, to mention but a few.

The Alexander Mare's foal of 1803 was the filly Bronze by Buzzard, ascribed by the *General Stud Book* to the Hon. B. Craven as breeder or owner. It is almost certain that Craven was the owner and that he bought the filly from the Prince of Wales as a two-year-old, for in the 1805 *Racing Calendar* Bronze was entered for the 1806 Oaks by the Prince's racing manager, Delmé Radcliffe. It was not unusual at that time for the leading owners to sell horses to each other, and the Prince of Wales was no exception. Bronze won three races from five starts for Craven in 1806; the most important was her victory in the Oaks from Jerboa and the Duke of York's Rosabella, a success that must have caused the Prince to rue his decision to sell her. As a four-year-old Bronze only managed one victory from nine outings; she did, however, finish second in the Audley End Stakes to the 1805 Oaks winner Meteora. In 1808 Bronze won the Kingscote Stakes over three miles at Cheltenham. The slightly disappointing performances of Bronze after her Oaks victory were more than compensated for by her achievements as a broodmare. She was the maternal ancestress of such illustrious horses as The Ranger (Grand Prix de Paris), Skirmisher (Ascot Gold Cup), Cremorne (Derby, Ascot Gold Cup), Jongleur (Prix du Jockey-Club), Briar Root (1,000 Guineas), Peter Pan (Belmont Stakes), Rosedrop (Oaks), Teddy (Prix du Jockey-Club, Grand Prix de Paris), The Tetrarch and, above all, Gainsborough, the 1918 Triple Crown winner and sire of Hyperion. There is insufficient space here to enumerate all the other Classic winners the world over who trace back to Bronze.

In 1804 the Prince of Wales bred an unnamed Buzzard filly from the Alexander Mare who ran behind Briseis in the Oaks, and then received four walk-overs in her remaining races. The following year the Alexander Mare threw a colt foal by Buzzard: named Rubens for her Royal breeder, he made his debut in the 1808 Derby, starting second favourite at 100–30 with only Vandyke being preferred in the market at 9–4. Vandyke and Clinker took the lead shortly after Tattenham Corner, and for a while the race seemed to be between them. At the distance, however, Rubens loomed up beside them, passed them and appeared to have the race at his mercy, until in the final hundred yards the Royal colt began to shorten his stride, possibly as he did not truly stay the mile and a half, and he was overtaken by the previously unraced Pan, from whom his jockey, Frank Collinson, had conjured up a scintillating burst of acceleration. Rubens was also repassed by Vandyke, who was half a length behind Pan at the line, and by Chester. Rubens again faced Vandyke in his next race, the very valuable Pavilion Stakes over a mile at Brighton. Before this race the Prince of Wales for some reason thought that Rubens was lame and offered to sell him to the Earl of Darlington for 1,000 gns. Darlington agreed, on condition that Sam Chifney should give him a gallop, and that he would decide finally on hearing the jockey's opinion. Chifney pronounced Rubens to be sound so the sale went ahead. Over the shorter distance of the Pavilion Stakes,

Rubens, splendidly ridden by Chifney, easily gained his revenge on Vandyke, much to the delight of his new owner, who reportedly won £12,000 on him. Sam Chifney is also reported to have had a considerable wager on the colt. Darlington was immediately offered £3,000 for Rubens, but refused. Rubens then received four walk-overs and did not have to contest a race again until the spring of 1809, when he defeated Chester over a mile at Newmarket. That May he was beaten, unsurprisingly, in a Match over the Beacon Course at Newmarket by his old rival Vandyke. Rubens made two more appearances on the racecourse in the spring of 1810. He won the Craven Stakes from Plover on 23 April, but found the concession of 16 lbs to Spaniard too much in the Free Handicap Sweepstakes a month later, and was only able to finish third. The Earl of Darlington then sold Rubens to General Leveson Gower; he was retired to stud at 20 gns a mare and 1 gn to the groom at Bill Hill near Wokingham, Berkshire. From 1814 to 1816 he stood at Barton Court between Newbury and Hungerford; he was then moved to Six Mile Bottom, near Newmarket, where his fee was raised to 25 gns a mare.

Like his full-brothers, Castrel and Selim, Rubens gained even greater renown as a sire than as a racehorse. He was champion sire on three occasions, in 1815, 1821 and 1822, and got three Classic winners: Landscape (Oaks, 1816), Pastille (2,000 Guineas and Oaks, 1822) and Whizgig (1,000 Guineas, 1822). None of his colts, however, managed to win a Classic, though Raphael was second to Whisker in the 1815 Derby, Hampden third to Moses at Epsom in 1822 and Hogarth third to Middleton in 1825. Other useful colts sired by Rubens included Bobadil, the winner of nine races including the Claret Stakes, Sir Joshua, who won the Riddlesworth Stakes, the October Oatlands and four other races, Peter Leley, winner of thirteen races, and Crockery, whose six victories included the Newmarket Stakes. None of them, though, was to make any mark as a stallion. As a broodmare sire, on the other hand, Rubens was quite exceptional: seven of his mares were to produce Classic winners. An unnamed Rubens mare who finished second to Pastille in the 1822 Oaks was the dam of Phosphorus (Derby, 1837), May-Day (1,000 Guineas, 1834), Firebrand (1,000 Guineas, 1842) and Camarine (Ascot Gold Cup, 1832). The 1833 Derby winner, Dangerous, was out of the Rubens mare Defiance, and another of his mares, Ruby, produced the 1841 winner of the Epsom Classic, Coronation. Whizgig was the dam of the 1831 Oaks winner, Oxygen, and Augusta, who won the

Oaks in 1821, was out of an unnamed Rubens mare who was also the dam of Patron, the hero of the 1829 2,000 Guineas. Miniature, the dam of Enamel, who won the colts' classic at Newmarket in 1825, was also by Rubens, as was Chapeau de Paille, who produced the 1837 1,000 Guineas winner Chapeau d'Espagne. The Prince of Wales's sale of Rubens to the Earl of Darlington before he won the Pavilion Stakes, under the misapprehension that his colt was lame, was an enormous loss to the Royal Stud: nevertheless, no one could have foreseen that Rubens, who had finished only fourth behind an unconsidered outsider in the Derby, would turn out to be such an influential sire and broodmare sire.

Inevitably, the Prince of Wales's first runners in and after 1800 were not bred by him, but bought from their owners and breeders. Knowsley (Sir Peter Teazle–Capella), who won five times for the Prince in 1800 at Guildford, Winchester, Lewes (twice) and Lichfield, was bought from Mr Walker; Rebel (Trumpator–Fancy), whom the Prince acquired in 1801, won fourteen races including the October Oatlands in 1802 and 1804 and the Petworth Stakes at Brighton in 1803. One of the Prince's best acquisitions at this time was Orville (Benningbrough–Evelina), who had been bred by Lord Fitzwilliam in 1799 and had won the 1802 St Leger. He won twelve races for his Royal owner in 1806 and 1807 at Newmarket, Lewes and Brighton (the Somerset Stakes). Orville was a very successful stallion, siring two Derby winners, Octavius in 1812 and Emilius in 1823, three other Classic winners and two Ascot Gold Cup winners. In 1805 the Prince bought Haphazard (Sir Peter Teazle–Miss Hervey) from Lord Darlington; he was one of the best four-mile horses of the time. He too was a successful stallion, siring four Classic winners, the most famous of which was the 1815 St Leger hero Filho da Puta.

In 1802 the Prince of Wales bred Barbarossa (Sir Peter Teazle–Mulespinner), who was unplaced behind Cardinal Beaufort in the 1805 Derby. Barbarossa turned out to be a very versatile racehorse, his eleven wins in three seasons including the Egremont Stakes over twelve furlongs in 1805 and the Somerset Stakes over four miles in 1806, both at Brighton. The Prince had two runners in Election's Derby in 1807, Lewes (Gohanna–Trumpetta) and Mungo (Sir Peter Teazle–Alexina), but both were unplaced. Lewes later won the Town Plate at Lewes and ran third to Coriolanus in the Pavilion Stakes; Mungo won two races, one of them a King's Plate at Ascot in 1809, after the Prince had sold him, and was eventually exported to Prussia. In 1807 the Prince of Wales bred Miss Wasp (Waxy

–Trumpetta), who won her only race, a Sweepstakes at Egham in 1809, when she ran in the colours of Mr Ladbroke, to whom she had presumably been sold. The Prince must have bought her back as a broodmare soon afterwards, for 'The Druid' (the pseudonym of Henry Hall Dixon) states that the Prince was the breeder of her first foal in 1814, Manfred by Election, who won the 1817 2,000 Guineas. On 13 May 1822 Miss Wasp was among thirteen brood-mares owned by King George IV to be sold by Tattersalls; covered by Rubens, she made 150 gns. That proved to be a bargain for the foal she produced in 1830 was Vespa, who won the Oaks three years later.

After 1808 it seems that the Prince of Wales ceased to have any horses in training, either home-bred or purchased. The reason for this withdrawal from ownership is not altogether clear. According to 'The Druid': 'The running of Selim in 1808 when Sam Chifney was not riding was so suspicious that the Prince sent a peremptory message to his trainer to the effect that the whole of his horses were to be sold or given away immediately.' On 7 November 1808 six of his youngstock were sold at Tattersalls: three foals, including Merry-Go-Round (Trumpator–Highflyer Mare), bought by Lord G. Cavendish, two two-year-olds and one three-year-old, Renishaw (Coriander–Skypeeper) fetched a total of 1,680 gns. Merry-Go-Round turned out to be a useul racehorse, winning two races in 1811, including the Pavilion Stakes at Brighton, and four, including the Port Stakes at Newmarket, the following season.

It is possible that there were other reasons behind the Prince's decision to sell his racehorses in 1808. Among these was his extreme depression after the death in September 1806 of his friend and political ally, Charles James Fox, which caused the Prince to sit strangely silent at dinner, sometimes even crying. He was certainly in extremely low spirits in 1807; England had been at war with France for a decade and a half and Russia had become an ally of Napoleon. Most of the continental ports were closed to British trade, and this blockade was causing privation among the English population. The Tory governments of the Duke of Portland and, later, Spencer Perceval were weak and incompetent, lacking any clear direction. Inevitably a disaffected public turned its con-tempt on the Prince of Wales.

During this period Maria FitzHerbert was replaced in the Prince's favour by the Marchioness of Hertford, a haughty, matriarchal grandmother from one of the strongest Tory dynasties in the land. Maria FitzHerbert lived on in her house on the Steyne in Brighton with an allowance of £6,000 a year. Within three years she and the Prince of Wales were little more than acquaintances, and the secret marriage became a separation.

The death from consumption in November 1810 of George III's youngest daughter, Princess Amelia, following the scandal of the Duke of York's resignation as Commander-in-Chief of the army the year before, greatly distressed the King. These were his two favourite children, and one's disgrace and the other's death caused him to lapse once more into the delusions of madness. The malady persisted, with the result that on 5 February 1811 the Prince of Wales was sworn in as Regent of the United Kingdom. He was to remain Regent until his father's death in 1820.

Although the Prince Regent had given up owning horses in training himself and had virtually ceased breeding Thoroughbreds after 1808, he commanded in 1812 that the paddocks at Hampton Court be turned into a stud under the direction of Mr Goodwin, whose son was subsequently inspector and veterinary surgeon to the stud for thirty-seven years. The paddocks were divided by brick walls and a spacious hovel was allotted to each. The first stallion to stand at the newly established stud was Election (Gohanna–Chestnut Skim), winner of the 1807 Derby. Election, who had remained in training until 1811 and had won many races, though minor ones, after his triumph at Epsom, stood at a fee of 10 gns at Hampton Court for the rest of the decade. Among the mares who took up residence were Miss Wasp, the Alexander Mare and the Mercury Mare 1790, who was a sister to Silver. This mare, who had been driven in a gig and used as a saddle-horse for several years before she went to stud in 1805, was bought by the Prince Regent from Mr Vansittart in 1812. The produce of the stud was sold at an annual sale in the summer, and not retained by the Prince Regent to race himself. Since certain fillies returned to the stud after their racing careers, it is probable that they were only leased for the period they remained in training or else were repurchased by the stud on their retirement.

Among the foals bred at the Royal Stud at Hampton Court in 1813 was Belvoirina (Stamford–Mercury Mare), named in compliment to the Duke of Rutland, in whose colours she ran throughout her racing career. She made her debut on the racecourse in the July Stakes on 10 July 1815; as she had been suffering from a sore back for some days prior to the race and had done no 'regular work', she was allowed to start at 7–1. These setbacks, however, did not stop her from defeating Lord Foley's filly by Sir David. Belvoirina did not reappear until the Riddlesworth Stakes at Newmarket on 15 April 1816, when she was unplaced to Nectar, who was to win the 2,000 Guineas and finish second to Prince Leopold in the Derby later that year. On 2 May Belvoirina won a Sweepstakes over a mile at Newmarket; she won two more Matches that season, both at Newmarket, and received one walk-over. She was then retired to stud, and proved a most influential broodmare. She was the ancestress of the 1873 Derby and 1875 Ascot Gold Cup winner, Doncaster; among other Classic winners who trace back to her are Refraction (Oaks, 1845), Thor (Prix du Jockey-Club, 1933), Corteira (Prix de Diane, 1948), Masaka (Oaks and Irish Oaks, 1948) and Needles (Kentucky Derby and Belmont Stakes, 1955).

The 1814 crop of yearlings at Hampton Court included Manfred (Election–Miss Wasp), who was bought by Mr Stonehewer. Manfred won the 2,000 Guineas and three other races at Newmarket in 1817, though he was unplaced behind Azor in the Derby and behind Waterloo in the St Leger. He was slightly disappointing at four and five, winning only once in 1818 and three times in 1819 from eighteen outings. Another foal from the same crop as Manfred was an unnamed filly by Election out of the Alexander Mare. This filly, purchased by Mr Blake, ran third to Neva and Amabel in the Oaks, was third again in the Oatlands Stakes at Ascot and won a Sweepstakes at Newmarket. Canvas, a filly by Rubens out of a Gohanna mare 1803, who won ten races, was also foaled at Hampton Court in 1814.

Although the Prince Regent had no horses in training at this period, this did not stop him from frequently attending race-meetings – with the exception, of course, of Newmarket. One of the most colourful of these occasions was at Ascot after the abdication of the Emperor Napoleon I, when the Prince Regent entertained the Russian Tsar Alexander I, the King of Prussia, General Blucher and General Platoff. The travelling arrangements went slightly awry, with the Royal host arriving on the course after his guests; but still the crowd gave the conquerors of Napoleon such a rapturous and prolonged reception that the start of racing had to be delayed.

Throughout the first two decades of the nineteenth century, when the Prince of Wales made the Royal Pavilion and Brighton the centre of society, it was inevitable that racing on the Downs, both there and at Lewes, came almost to rival Ascot and Newmarket in importance. The Pavilion Stakes, Petworth Stakes, Smoaker Stakes and Somerset Stakes, all run at the seaside course, and the

Gold Cup at Lewes, were among the most important races of the season. 'The Druid' quotes Tom Raikes's diary to paint a picture of life at Brighton at that time:

> The Prince made Brighton and Lewes races the gayest scene of the year in England. The Pavilion was full of guests and the Steyne was crowded with all rank and fashion from London. The 'legs' and betters, who had arrived in shoals, used to assemble on the Steyne at an early hour to commence their operations on the first day, and the buzz was tremendous till Lord Foley and Mr Mellish, the two great confederates of the day would approach the ring, and then a sudden silence would ensue to await the opening of their books... About half an hour before the departure for the hill, the Prince himself would make his appearance in the crowd, in a green jacket, white hat and light nankeen pantaloons and shoes. He was generally accompanied by the late Duke of Bedford, Lord Jersey, Charles Wyndham, Shelley, Brummell, Churchill... The Downs were soon covered with every species of conveyance and the Prince's German waggon and six bay horses... issued out of the gates of the Pavilion and, gliding up the green ascent, was stationed close to the Grandstand where it remained the centre of attraction for the day. At dinner-time the Pavilion was resplendent with lights and a sumptuous banquet was furnished to a large party.

None the less, 'Nimrod' (the pen-name of Charles Apperley) records: 'Bibury was his [the Prince's] favourite track, where divesting himself of the shackles of state, he appeared as a private gentleman, for several years in succession an intimate of Lord Shelbourne's family, and with the Duke of Dorset, then Lord Sackville for his jockey.' There were many races run at Bibury at that time confined to amateur jockeys, among whom the Prince's racing manager, Delmé Radcliffe, was held in high esteem.

The full-brothers Regent and Plumper (Election–Stamford Mare) were the best two foals of the 1816 and 1817 crops bred at Hampton Court. Regent was second to Tiresias in the Palace Stakes in the spring of 1819 at Newmarket; that form came to look much better when the Duke of Portland's colt won the Derby. Regent won a Handicap Sweepstakes at Newmarket later that year and was then exported to Ireland, where he was successful in ten races in 1819 and 1820, including the Wellington Stakes three times and the Kirwan Stakes. Returning to England in 1822, he won once at

Edinburgh and received a walk-over at Newmarket. Plumper won eight races in 1821 and 1822, on one occasion beating his brother, Regent, in a Match at Newmarket.

It was in 1818 that a grey colt by Election out of Lady Grey by Stamford was foaled either at Hampton Court or at the Six Mile Bottom Stud, which belonged to the Prince Regent until it was bought by Colonel Leigh. It is more likely that the foal, named Gustavus, was born at the stud by the Thames as that was where his sire, Election, was standing.

Gustavus was bought at the annual sale at Hampton Court for 25 gns by Mr J. Hunter, a member of the Jockey Club and a famous tilter in the ring. Gustavus was extremely small and Hunter was so dissatisfied with him after he had had him some months that he offered to resell him for 15 gns; but even at that low price he found no takers and so was obliged to keep him. 'The shabby little grey', as 'The Druid' described Gustavus, made his first appearance on the racecourse on 10 July 1820 in the July Stakes; his lack of reputation meant that he started one of the outsiders at 100–6. To the surprise not only of his owner but of all others present, he won easily from Lord Jersey's unnamed colt by Soothsayer. On 11 May 1821 Gustavus beat Tressilian in the Newmarket Stakes, on the strength of which victory he was made 2–1 favourite for the Derby on 7 June. His principal rival at Epsom was Reginald by Haphazard, who had earlier that year won the 2,000 Guineas, and sure enough Reginald led the field until the distance – when the only colt in a position to challenge him was Gustavus, ridden by Sam Day. Running on more strongly in the final furlong than the Guineas winner, Gustavus had half a length to spare over Reginald at the line.

At that time the Derby was run at half past one; during the short interval before the next race, members of the Royal Family present were entertained to lunch at Mr Ladbroke's house at Headley. The crowd, meanwhile, took their lunch and much liquid refreshment in the town or at booths on the course. When racing resumed, the public was sometimes a little unruly under the influence of the wine and beer consumed. In 1821 the trouble commenced during the Derby itself: the groundkeepers, who were paid one shilling and sixpence a day, found themselves overwhelmed and the boisterous crowd surged on to the course. Sam Day recalled that 'Buckle [Reginald's jockey] and I wound in and out all the way from Tattenham Corner like a dog at a fair.' This cannot have been to Buckle's advantage as that great rider's dash and confidence were diminishing by this stage in his career.

After this memorable Derby, Gustavus was unplaced behind Jack Spiggot in the St Leger and beaten into second place in the Gascoigne Stakes on the same course by My Lady, who had finished third in the Oaks. He returned to form and ended his three-year-old career by winning two Matches at Newmarket's Houghton Meeting, and began his four-year-old campaign by beating Ibla and Augusta, respectively second and first in the 1821 Oaks, in the Claret Stakes at Newmarket. Gustavus managed only one more victory in six subsequent outings: a Match against Black and All Black. Sultan beat him in a Match over the Rowley Mile, Augusta beat him in the Post Sweepstakes in October and in his final race he was unplaced in the Oatlands Stakes to the 1822 1,000 Guineas winner, Whizgig. Gustavus was then retired to stud, where he proved a total failure. Almost certainly he was a below average Derby winner; nevertheless that should not detract from the Prince Regent's achievement in breeding the winner of that great race from his relatively small stud of broodmares at Hampton Court.

The best foal bred by the Prince Regent in 1819 was Electress (Election–Stamford Mare). Her five victories included the Windsor Forest Stakes at Ascot and the Oatlands Stakes at Newmarket in 1822; she also ran second to the 2,000 Guineas and Oaks winner Pastille in a Subscription Stakes at Newmarket.

Soon after George IV ascended the throne on 29 January 1820, he cut down the number of broodmares at Hampton Court. Belvoirina was one of those he retained; he also kept Waterloo, who had replaced Election as the chief stallion. It was not until 1823 that another noteworthy foal was born in the Royal paddocks: Elizabeth (Rainbow–Belvoirina), unbeaten in three races at Ascot, Newmarket and Brighton as a two-year-old and winner of three of her seven starts in 1826. These included the Frogmore Stakes at Newmarket, when she beat Problem, the 1,000 Guineas winner and runner-up in the Oaks to Lilias. Elizabeth had also run in Lilias's Oaks, but had failed to reach the frame. She was a small mare, dark chestnut in colour and described by a contemporary as having 'great beauty and elegance of form'.

In 1824 Belvoirina produced another chestnut filly by Whalebone, who was named Maria as a compliment to the last great love of George IV, the Marchioness of Conyngham, whose Christian name was Maria. She became the King's favourite soon after his accession, and her dislike of the Royal Pavilion, which was finally completed in 1822, was one of the principal causes of the King spending much of his reign at Royal Lodge, Windsor, where

Cumberland Lodge was used as an annexe. Although he knew she was an opportunist with little real affection for him, he tolerated her presence as he was accustomed to it and by then was too indolent to change. He was, moreover, able to find relief from her trivial mind and greater intellectual satisfaction from the waspish tongue of Dorothea Lieven, the highly intelligent wife of the Russian ambassador Count Lieven, and Emily Cowper, the daughter of his old friend Lady Melbourne, who was to marry Lord Palmerston and become the greatest political hostess of the 1850s. From 1824 onwards George IV was often in pain, both from gout and bladder trouble, to relieve which he took ever larger doses of laudanum. Frequently his ministers journeyed from London to Windsor only to find that the laudanum had made the King too drowsy to give them an audience. It has been suggested that one of the reasons why the King cut himself off from his own friends, especially Maria FitzHerbert, was that he did not wish them to see him in such a sorry state.

The filly Maria ran in Charles Greville's colours in 1826 and was one of the best two-year-olds of her generation, winning all her four races. Her most significant victory came in the Prendergast Stakes at Newmarket, when she beat Atticus. On the death of the Duke of York, the King purchased several of his brother's broodmares and re-entered the ranks of the owners, with Delmé Radcliffe once more appointed his racing manager and the training of his horses under the supervision of William Edwards. Maria ran in the Royal colours, therefore, in 1827 when she won four of her six races; her two most important victories were at Ascot in the Windsor Forest Stakes over a mile and the Swinley Stakes over twelve furlongs. When she won the latter by a length to great cheering from the crowd, the King was congratulated by all the nobility around him and he expressed himself highly gratified by the result. In 1828 Maria won four of her seven races including the Somersetshire Stakes over fifteen furlongs at Bath, two races at Egham and the Windsor Oatlands at the second Ascot meeting which George IV had instructed to be instituted that year. The same day Maria ran in the King's Plate but fell on the second circuit, the groundsmen at the lower end of the course having forgotten to lower the rope. She was not injured but her jockey, Robinson, was quite seriously bruised. At the principal Ascot meeting two weeks earlier she had finished second to Belzoni in the Oatlands Stakes. Maria ran once in 1829 when she met Lord Sefton's Souvenir in a Match at Ascot. It was reported that 'the

King watched the progress of the race with great anxiety sweeping the entire course with his glass.' When Maria won the King was highly delighted; the crowd gave him three cheers and the monarch acknowledged this acclamation with repeated bows. After the race he is said to have watched Maria being groomed with close attention and concentration. A contemporary described Maria as 'a chestnut mare of exquisite form, showing a great deal of blood, and is remarkable for the beauty of her Eye, that has the prominence and expression of good temper so characteristic of the Mercury blood'. She was a notable addition to the Royal band of brood-mares at Hampton Court when she retired there in 1829.

In 1825, only two years before his final return to the Turf, the King had inaugurated the Royal Procession at Ascot. The first Procession was led by Lord Marlborough, dressed in the green uniform of his position of Master of the Royal Buckhounds, followed by a carriage containing George IV with the Duke of Wellington on his right and the Lords-in-Waiting opposite; this carriage was flanked by liveried outriders and was followed by the other carriages of the Royal party. Entering the racecourse at the start of the Straight Mile, the procession made its way up the course to the Royal Stand. In subsequent years it became traditional for the Royal Procession to take place every Tuesday and Thursday of the meeting.

After his return to the ranks of the owners, one of the King's principal ambitions was to win the Ascot Gold Cup. In pursuit of this aim, he bought three horses between 1828 and 1830: The Colonel, Fleur-de-Lis and, finally, Zinganee. The Colonel (Whisker–Delpini Mare), who had dead-heated with Cadland for the 1827 Derby in the colours of his breeder, the Hon. E. Petre, but had lost the run-off, had gone on to win the St Leger; the King gave his owner 4,000 gns for him. In a letter written by Delmé Radcliffe to Sir William Knighton, Keeper of the Privy Purse, the racing manager admits that 'some purchases have certainly occurred at enormous prices. I did not recommend such a sum to be given for The Colonel, but when His Majesty commands me positively to buy a horse, I must obey.'[2] The Colonel was never to win the Ascot Gold Cup for the King, but is significant in the history of the Hampton Court Stud as he stood there on his retirement from racing.

George IV bought Fleur-de-Lis (Bourbon–Lady Rachel) from Sir Matthew White Ridley for 1,500 gns at the end of 1827. In the previous three seasons she had won twelve races, including the

Gold Cup at York, beating Actaeon, and the Doncaster Cup in 1826 when she beat Mulatto, the runner-up to Tarare in that year's St Leger and winner of the Doncaster Cup in 1827, and Humphrey Clinker. Both he and Mulatto were to make their mark as sires. In 1828 Fleur-de-Lis was unplaced to Bobadilla in the Ascot Gold Cup, but won three races for the King, including the Oatlands at Newmarket on 2 October. The best of her three victories in 1829 was in the Goodwood Cup when she beat the 1827 Derby winner, Mameluke. After her second consecutive win in the Goodwood Cup, when she beat The Colonel and Zinganee, she became another valuable addition to the broodmare band at Hampton Court, though she was not as successful a mare as she had been on the track.

The King bought Zinganee from Lord Chesterfield after he won the Ascot Gold Cup in 1829 from the Derby winners Mameluke and Cadland, with The Colonel finishing only fourth. Chesterfield had paid 2,500 gns to purchase him from William Chifney shortly before the race. The King ran both Zinganee and The Colonel in the Gold Cup of 1830, but both were beaten by Lucetta, The Colonel finishing second and Zinganee unplaced.

In 1827 the King also owned the runner-up in the Ascot Gold Cup, his colt Mortgage, whom he had bought from the Duke of Portland, finishing second to Memnon, the 1825 St Leger winner. A fortnight before he died, in June 1830, he gave instructions that the result of each race at Ascot should be immediately brought to him on his sick-bed by messenger from the course, but he never achieved his ambition of winning the premier race.

The last three years of George IV's reign had witnessed a gradual build-up of the Royal Stud at Hampton Court; while the real fruits of this were to be seen in the reign of his brother and successor, King William IV, nevertheless some useful horses were bred by George IV in these last years. Young Orion (Master Henry–Hedley Mare), the 1829 Royal Stakes winnner at Ascot, was the last colt bred by King George IV to carry his colours to victory during his lifetime. By January 1829 there were eighteen broodmares at the stud and nine yearlings, in those days still considered foals until 1 May. In addition, the Royal stable at Newmarket housed nine horses in training, including two-year-olds. Walter (Whalebone–Electress) ran at Ascot as a two-year-old in 1830 for the King, but was unplaced. He was sold to Mr Rogers, for whom he won ten races between 1831 and 1833. Landgravine (Waterloo or Smolensko–Electress) was bought by Charles Greville after

George IV's death and won three races, including the Lavant Stakes at Goodwood in 1831. He was exported to Prussia, but died on the road to Berlin. Posthumus (Woful–Posthuma) won two races and was second in the 1832 2,000 Guineas to Archibald. Shylock (Waterloo–Gohanna Mare) won eight races, including the Wokingham Stakes, and was the last major winner bred by George IV. He was foaled exactly forty-eight years after the young Prince of Wales had bred his first winner, Miss Kitty.

Among the broodmares that William IV inherited at the Hampton Court Stud were Belvoirina, Maria, Elizabeth, Sultana (Selim–Bacchante), a sister to Sultan, Electress, Rachel, and Spermacetti (Whalebone–Kate), who had won the Riddlesworth Stakes at Newmarket in 1823 and the Wokingham Stakes at Ascot in 1825 before being acquired by the Royal Stud in 1827. It was a fine nucleus of mares on which to build one of the best studs in England, and a worthy legacy of a King who found the racing and breeding of Thoroughbreds one of his chief pleasures.

6

William IV,

1830–37

William IV was the classic example of a man, who, through unexpected circumstances, finds himself elevated to a position that requires intelligence, vision and abilities with which he has not been blessed. As Duke of Clarence he had taken little part in the life of the Court. In the correspondence between his mother, Queen Charlotte, and his eldest brother, there are many jokes at the expense of his bluff character and unsophisticated lifestyle. Contemporary opinion thought of him as a comical, harmless but affable buffoon. Prior to the death of Princess Charlotte, in 1817, which had made him second in line to the throne, 'Sailor Bill' had lived in contented poverty with the actress Mrs Jordan, by whom he had fathered ten children, who bore the name of FitzClarence. In 1818, in his fifty-fourth year, he was married to Princess Adelaide of Saxe-Meiningen. When George IV died in the early hours of 26 June 1830, the Duke of Clarence was informed immediately, and to the surprise of most people returned to bed. When asked why he had done so, he replied that he wished to discover what it was like to sleep with a Queen.

The government and establishment had great misgivings at this buffoon, however affable, now occupying the throne of England. The spirit of reform was in the air; the Reform Bill itself was passed two years after William IV's accession. 'Sailor Bill' at first tried to act the role of a democratic sovereign, which he thought meant spitting out of the window of his state coach and walking around the streets unattended to be shoved and jostled by the crowds. The failure of the 1832 Reform Act to satisfy the now widespread calls for greater freedom and equality, however, soon extinguished the barely lit flames of his democratic ideals. An incident at Ascot in

1832 may have assisted his change in attitude: a sailor who had lost a leg in action and who had been thrown out of a naval veterans' hospital earlier that year made his way on one leg from London to Ascot and gave vent to his fury at his expulsion by hurling two stones at the King in the Royal Box. The King's fears that similar incidents and disturbances would lead to a bloody revolution transformed him within two years into a panic-stricken reactionary, who bombarded his ministers with unsound advice and unjustified complaints.

As Duke of Clarence the new King had shown not one iota of interest in either the racing or breeding of Thoroughbreds. His ignorance was manifested when his trainer asked which of the Royal horses should run in the Goodwood Cup in July 1830. He replied, 'Let the whole Squadron sail.' Accordingly three Royal stayers, Fleur-de-Lis, Zinganee and The Colonel fought out the finish ahead of the Oaks winner Green Mantle, with victory going to Fleur-de-Lis. Fears that William IV's lack of interest in racing might cause the links between the Turf and the Crown to be considerably diminished seemed justified when on 15 November 1830 six horses in training, two yearlings, one foal and two broodmares from Hampton Court went under the hammer at Tattersalls. Since the draft included The Colonel, Zinganee and Young Orion, the sale caused quite a stir and the *Sporting Magazine* reported that 'a great number of Nobility, Gentry and other influential members of the Turf were attracted to the Yard.' Zinganee was bought by Lord Chesterfield, who also purchased the half-brother to the 1824 Wokingham Stakes winner, Orion, Young Orion by Master Henry, who had won the Royal Stakes at Ascot just a few days before the death of George IV. Charles Greville purchased a yearling filly by Waterloo or Smolensko out of Electress; she was named Landgravine and won the Lavant Stakes at Goodwood in 1831. Electress herself, a sister to Regent, and covered by Waterloo, was also sold. The Colonel was offered for sale; fortuitously there was no bidder and he was led out unsold to return to the Hampton Court Stud to stand as a stallion. The ten lots realized 2,378 gns, and their disposal seemed to indicate that William IV had decided on a much reduced role in racing and breeding for the Crown.

In early 1832 the death occurred of Mr Delmé Radcliffe; racing manager to George IV as both Prince Regent and King, he had remained in that position under William IV. Since practically all the King's horses ran in his racing manager's name, they lost all their engagements: this gave William IV the opportunity to divest himself of his ten remaining horses in training. At their sale by Tattersalls at the 1832 Newmarket Craven Meeting, it was officially announced that William IV would no longer have any horses in training. In May the King granted his trainer, William Edwards, a pension and use of the stables and apartments in the Palace in Newmarket in recognition of his past services to both himself and George IV. On his jockey, George Nelson, he settled an annuity. The future of the Royal Stud at Hampton Court looked bleak indeed.

In spite of the eccentric and vacillating views that William IV held regarding the correct comportment and duties of a sovereign, and notwithstanding his total lack of interest in racing, he nevertheless believed it right and to the public advantage that he should continue breeding Thoroughbred horses. Accordingly, almost as soon as he had sold all his horses in training, it was announced that the Royal Stud at Hampton Court would be maintained as it had been prior to his accession, and that the Royal yearlings would be sold without reserve by Tattersalls every May at Hyde Park Corner. On 14 May 1832 the first of these annual sales took place: nine yearlings, one two-year-old filly and one three-year-old filly were sold. Lord Orford bought the highest-priced yearling, Paris (Waterloo–Posthuma), who won four races. Six of the nine yearlings went on to win twenty races; the best was Intriguer (Reveller–Scandal), whose nine wins included the Magna Charta Stakes at Egham and the Mostyn Stakes at Holywell Hunt, when he beat the St Leger winner, Touchstone. Both he and Paris had been considered good enough to take part in the 1834 Derby behind Plenipotentiary.

At the time of William IV's accession to the throne, the Royal Stud at Hampton Court principally housed broodmares that had been bred by George IV or the Duke of York. The most notable of those bred by the late King were Belvoirina (Stamford–Mercury Mare 1790), her two daughters, Maria (Waterloo–Belvoirina) and Elizabeth (Rainbow–Belvoirina) and Posthuma (Orville–Medora); of those bred by the Duke of York, Xarifa (Moses–Rubens Mare 1814) and Moses' dam (Gohanna Mare 1807 out of Grey Skim) were the most significant. Other good mares that George IV had bought included Spermacetti 1820 (Whalebone–Kate 1809 by Gohanna), winner of the 1825 Wokingham Stakes, and Scandal 1822 by Selim. These broodmares were joined at Hampton Court by the brilliant Fleur-de-Lis 1822 (Bourbon–Lady Rachel 1805 by

Stamford), sold to George IV by Sir Matthew White Ridley for 1,500 gns in October 1827. She had won nineteen races between 1825 and 1830, including the Goodwood Cup in 1829 and 1830, the Doncaster Cup and the Yorkshire Cup in 1826, the Doncaster Stakes in 1826 and 1827, and the Oatlands Stakes at Newmarket in 1828. She had fallen in the St Leger on the turn into the straight, so impeding The Alderman that Sam Chifney had been forced to stop riding him to prevent his mount falling over her. Since The Alderman finished second to Memnon, many felt that, had she kept her feet, Fleur-de-Lis would have beaten both of them. The principal stallion standing at Hampton Court in 1830 was Waterloo (Walton–Penelope 1798 by Trumpator), a half-brother to the Waxy colts Whalebone and Whisker who won the Derby in 1810 and 1815 respectively. In 1831 he was joined at Hampton Court by The Colonel (Whisker–Delpini Mare 1802), the winner of the St Leger and runner-up to Cadland in the Derby in 1828 and to Lucetta in the 1830 Ascot Gold Cup. The Colonel had dead-heated with Cadland in the Derby, and only lost the race in the subsequent run-off. William IV had, therefore, inherited the nucleus of a potentially most influential stud.

During the reign of William IV the Hampton Court Stud was under the supervision of Colonel Wemyss, whose brother was an Equerry to the King and Member of Parliament for Fife. He was most ably assisted by Mr Worley, who for many years had been the stud groom to the Duke of York at Oatlands. Colonel Wemyss's goal was to make the Royal Stud one of the best in England. In 1833 he bought Actaeon (Scud–Diana by Stamford), who had finished third to Memnon in the 1825 St Leger, as a extra stallion for the Stud. Wemyss's intention to improve the stud to the highest standard becomes more evident from the quality of the broodmares he purchased during his tenure of office. He bought the 1829 1,000 Guineas winner, Young Mouse (Godolphin–Mouse) from Lord Cavendish in 1833, the 1827 Oaks winner, Gulnare (Smolensko–Medora), from the Duke of Richmond in 1835, the 1825 Oaks winner, Wings (The Flyer – Oleander) from General Grosvenor in 1833, and Nanine (Selim–Bizarre), the dam of the 1834 Ascot Gold Cup winner, Glaucus, in 1835. Other notable broodmares acquired by Wemyss for the Royal Stud were Marpessa (Muley–Clara by Marmion), who had beaten the 1833 Oaks winner, Vespa, in a Match at the Second October Meeting at Newmarket four months after Vespa had won the Epsom Classic, Miss Craven (Mr Lowe–Soothsayer Mare 1815), whose victories included the

Goodwood Cup in 1828 and the Goodwood Stakes the previous year, and La Danseuse (Blacklock–Madam Saqui 1814), who was to become an ancestress of both Pharos and Fairway. It is clear that Colonel Wemyss could not have embarked upon this expansion of the Royal Stud during the reign of William IV without the latter's express sanction and approval. The success of the annual sales of the Royal yearlings may have played a decisive contribution in raising sufficient funds for the Colonel to embark on his policy of improvement.

Eleven yearlings bred by William IV at Hampton Court were sold at Hyde Park Corner on 29 April 1833; six of these won eleven races, but none reached Classic standard. As a result of the expansion of the stud, eighteen yearlings from Hampton Court were offered for sale on 26 May 1834; seven of these yearlings won twenty-four races, the best of them undoubtedly Recruit (The Colonel–Galatea) who ran behind Plenipotentiary in the Derby and won four races including the Craven Stakes at Epsom.

In 1835 there were thirty-one broodmares in the paddocks at Hampton Court; that year twenty-seven yearlings were sold on 1 June at Hyde Park Corner. Only seven of these yearlings turned out to be winners, but between them they won forty-two races. The best was Caravan (Camel–Wings), whom Lord Suffield bought. He won nineteen races between 1837 and 1841. One of the best three-year-olds in 1837, he started second favourite for the Derby and ran second to Phosphorus, after which he won the Craven Stakes at Goodwood. In 1838 he was victorious five times and was third in the Ascot Gold Cup to Grey Momus, whom he later beat in a Match at Newmarket, and third to Rat-trap and Epirus in the Port Stakes. Caravan's greatest success came in 1839 when he beat St Francis in the Ascot Gold Cup; St Francis emphasized the merit of Caravan's victory when he won the Ascot Gold Cup in 1840 and ran third to Lancercost in 1841 and to Beeswing in 1842. Another yearling sold at Hyde Park Corner in 1835 who became a high-class performer was Rat-trap (Bizarre–Young Mouse), a great bargain for Mr Sloane Stanley at only 25 gns. On his first appearance on a racecourse Rat-trap beat Phosphorus in the New-market Stakes on 26 April 1837, as a result of which he started 7–4 favourite for the Derby in which he was unplaced. In 1838 he won six of his eight races including the Port Stakes at Newmarket. Another Royal yearling from the 1834 crop who turned out to be quite useful was Benedict (Peter Lely–Phantasima), whose three successes included the Magna Charta Stakes at Egham, and who had been considered good enough to run in the 1837 Derby.

Nineteen yearlings bred by William IV were sold at Tattersalls on 16 May 1836; six became winners of seventeen races, but none was in the highest class. Volunteer (Tranby or The Colonel–Galatea) won three races including the Champagne Stakes at Bibury Club in 1837, but the next season was unplaced to Amato in the Derby.

The 1836 crop of foals from Hampton Court was as good as that of 1834; twenty-three yearlings were submitted for sale on 22 May 1837. The highest-priced colt, a chestnut by Rowton out of Nanine, was exported to the USA, as was a bay colt by Emilius out of Fleur-de-Lis; Lord Litchfield purchased The Corsair (Sir Hercules–Gulnare) for 500 gns, a sum not to be considered excessive in view of his victory over Lord Jersey's Caesar in the 1839 2,000 Guineas. The Corsair won four other races in a career lasting until 1843, though he never really fulfilled his early promise. Six of the 1836 crop from Hampton Court won twenty-three races in England. Besides The Corsair, Camellino (Camel–Maria) gained eight victories including the Prendergast Stakes at Newmarket in 1838; Reel (Camel–La Danseuse) won five times including the Clearwell Stakes at Newmarket in 1838, though she was unplaced to Deception in the Oaks the next season. Prism (Camel–Elizabeth) won once at Newmarket in 1838 for the Duke of Rutland before he sold her to the Duke of Richmond, for whom she produced the 1845 Oaks winner, Refraction by Glaucus.

The thirty-one foals born at the Royal Stud at Hampton Court in 1837 were the last bred by William IV, who died in July that year. This crop was sold as foals, and ten of them won forty races in England. Lord Albemarle bought Spangle (Croesus–Variella) for only 71 gns; in 1840 she won two races, including the Coronation Stakes at Ascot, from only three starts, and ran third to the brilliant Crucifix in the 1,000 Guineas. In 1841 Spangle was runner-up in the Wokingham Stakes. Captain Gardnor bought Monops (Actaeon–Wings) for only 46 gns; he made his racecourse debut when unplaced behind Little Wonder in the 1840 Derby, and won five times, including the Wokingham Stakes at Ascot in 1842. Lord Albemarle also purchased Iris (Cain–Elizabeth) for 81 gns; another bargain, for she won the Woodcote Stakes at Epsom and the Pavilion Stakes at Brighton in 1839, and in addition was second to Crucifix in the Chesterfield Stakes at Newmarket and third to her in the Molecomb Stakes at Goodwood.

The foal that was to have more influence than any other bred at

Hampton Court during William IV's reign was sold to Mr Greatrex for a paltry 62 gns. Pocahontas (Glencoe–Marpessa) was to make her mark as a broodmare rather than on the racecourse, for she certainly cost her owner a huge amount in bets.

Pocahontas was raced once as a two-year-old; she ran with such promise when finishing a close third in the Criterion Stakes to Lord George Bentinck's unbeaten filly Crucifix, whose nine victories included the July Stakes, Lavant Stakes, Molecomb Stakes, Clearwell Stakes and Prendergast Stakes, that she was installed as third favourite for the 1840 Oaks at 13–1 in November 1839, Crucifix being at that time the 4–1 favourite. Her owner John Greatrex backed to win a small fortune at these odds. Pocahontas did not run again before the Oaks, when she started third favourite at 11–1; Crucifix in the meantime had easily won the 1,000 Guineas and so started hot favourite. One observer at Epsom remarked that Pocahontas was a very fine animal. Crucifix duly won the Oaks, but Pocahontas was not disgraced, finishing close on the heels of the placed horses. Considering that it was only her second appearance on the racecourse, this performance inspired Greatrex to launch another substantial gamble on her in the Goodwood Cup. Pocahontas took the lead after a mile and was still ahead till nearing the distance where the Duke of Orleans's Beggarman took up the running. He resisted the late challenges of Lanercost and Hetman Platoff by half a length and the same; Charles XII was a neck behind in fourth place having beaten Pocahontas in the last strides by a head. The remainder of the field were beaten out of sight. The quality of this field merely emphasizes how good a racemare Pocahontas was as a three-year-old. Lanercost had been third in the 1839 St Leger, had won the Cambridgeshire from Hetman Platoff in 1839 and was to win the Ascot Gold Cup in 1841. Hetman Platoff had numbered the Northumberland Plate at Newcastle among his six victories; Charles XII had won the 1839 St Leger. Had Pocahontas not been owned by such a massive gambler as John Greatrex, it seems certain that she would have run more than twice in 1839 and not against such tough opposition; it is unlikely, too, that she would have still been a maiden. Greatrex did not run Pocahontas again till the Goodwood Cup in 1842 when she was unplaced to Charles XII. He then sold her to the breeder, Mr Theobald, for whom she ran unplaced in the Cesarewitch behind Lord Palmerston's Illiona, who was getting 15 lbs from her. In 1842 Mr Theobald ran her three times in minor events at Goodwood, Brighton and Rochester, but she could only manage second place on each occasion. Maybe the severity of her tasks as a three-year-old had taken their toll, and she had lost heart.

Pocahontas retired to stud in 1842. Her first four foals won only one race between them, but in 1849 she produced a foal by The Baron, who was named Stockwell after Mr Theobald's stud, to which The Baron had retired after winning the St Leger and Cesarewitch in 1845. Stockwell was bought as a yearling by the Marquis of Exeter. On Mr Theobald's death in 1851, Pocahontas was bought by Captain Thelluson for 260 gns, but in the summer of 1852 he resold her to Lord Exeter. Stockwell proved himself the best colt of his generation, winning ten of his twelve races in 1852; after winning the 2,000 Guineas and the Newmarket Stakes, he went wrong shortly before the Derby when he was unplaced to Daniel O'Rourke. He then proceeded to win his next eight races; his victory over Harbinger and Daniel O'Rourke by ten lengths in the St Leger demonstrated that he would have won the Derby had he been right on the day. Although he was beaten by Teddington in the Gold Cup at Ascot in 1853, he was unquestionably an outstanding colt.

Stockwell was to win even greater renown as a stallion. He was champion sire in 1860, 1861, 1862, 1864, 1865, 1866 and 1867, and second on the list of sires in 1863, 1868, 1872 and 1873. He got three winners of the Derby: Blair Athol (1864), Lord Lyon (1868) and Doncaster (1873); six winners of the St Leger: St Albans (1860), Caller Ou (1861), The Marquis (1862), Blair Athol (1864), Lord Lyon (1866) and Achievement (1867); and four winners of the 2,000 Guineas: The Marquis (1862), Lord Lyon (1866), Bothwell (1871) and Gang Forward (1873). His fillies were not quite so good as his colts, for he only got one Oaks winner – Regalia (1865) – and three 1,000 Guineas winners: Lady Augusta (1863), Repulse (1865) and Achievement (1866). He was, however, an important sire of sires; Doncaster was the sire of the 1880 Derby winner, Bend Or, who was himself the sire of the 1886 Derby victor, Ormonde, and the grandsire of Cyllene, who got four Derby winners: Cicero (1905), Minoru (1909), Lemberg (1910) and Tagalie (1911).

Pocahontas's foal in 1850, a chestnut colt by The Baron named Rataplan, was another prolific winner. His forty-two victories between 1852 and his retirement to stud in 1856 included the Doncaster Cup, the Queen's Vase at Ascot and the Manchester Cup. A useful rather than an outstanding stallion, Rataplan nevertheless sired Kettledrum, winner of the 1861 Derby and runner-up in the 2,000 Guineas and St Leger.

Pocahontas's foal of 1851 was the lightly raced colt, King Tom by Harkaway. He won twice as a two-year-old at Brighton and Newmarket from three starts, but injury prevented him running in 1854. As a four-year-old he ran twice, winning once over two miles at Newmarket. At stud, however, he was a most successful sire, heading the list of stallions in 1870 and 1871, finishing second on the list in 1864 to his half-brother, Stockwell, and third in 1866 and 1867. He got one Derby winner, Kingcraft (1870), and one St Leger winner, Hannah, who also won the 1871 Oaks and 1,000 Guineas. His fillies were probably better than his colts, for in addition to Hannah, he was the sire of Tomato (1863 1,000 Guineas) and of Tormentor and Hippia, who won the Oaks in 1866 and 1867. As a broodmare sire, King Tom has a special place in Turf history as the sire of St Angela, the dam of the other great stallion of the nineteenth century, the Duke of Portland's St Simon.

None of Pocahontas's other four colts was of the same class as Stockwell, King Tom or Rataplan, though Knight of St Patrick 1858 by Knight of St George, who won four races in 1861, sired one Classic winner, Moslem, who dead-heated for the 2,000 Guineas with Formosa in 1868.

Pocahontas's filly foals never achieved such distinction on the racecourse as her colts, but five out of six were winners. Ayacanora by Birdcatcher won four races including the Ham Stakes at Goodwood in 1856, and she was third to Imperieuse in the 1857 1,000 Guineas. In 1860 she was bought by Colonel Maude from Lord Portsmouth for the Royal Stud at Hampton Court, where she bred four winners: Chatanooga by Orlando, who won the Criterion Stakes in 1864, St Amyas by Trumpeter, the 1871 July Stakes victor, Nike by Orlando and Cestus by Newminster. Nike was exported to Germany in 1881 where she foaled Narrin by Chamant or Whitebait, who won the Preis von Diana in 1887; she was also an ancestress of Moucheron, the 1928 Irish 1,000 Guineas winner. Cestus was the fourth dam of Belfonds by Isard II, who won the 1925 Prix du Jockey-Club, Prix Hocquart and Prix Greffulhe.

Pocahontas's last foal, Araucaria by Ambrose, won a minor race at Stamford as a three-year-old in 1865, but became a most influential broodmare. She bred six winners, of whom three won Classics. Camelia by Macaroni won both the 1,000 Guineas and the Oaks in 1876; Chamant by Mortemer won the 2,000 Guineas in 1877 after successes in the Middle Park Plate and Dewhurst

Stakes the previous year; and Rayon d'Or by Flageolet won the 1879 St Leger and the Champion Stakes in 1880. These three were all owned by the Comte de Lagrange, on whose behalf Araucaria had been bought by Monsieur Lefèvre in 1872. Other Classic winners who trace back to Araucaria were Sans Souci II, winner of the 1907 Grand Prix de Paris, Sayajirao, who won the St Leger and Irish Derby, and the Derby winner, Dante.

One of the great French families belonging to Monsieur Edmond Blanc, that of Kazah, the Prix de Diane winner in 1892, her daughter, Kizil Kourgan, who also won the fillies' Classic at Chantilly and the Grand Prix de Paris in 1902, and her son, the great champion Ksar, the sire of Tourbillon and grandsire of Djebel, also traced back on the maternal side to Pocahontas, as did Lord Derby's Prix de l'Arc de Triomphe winner, Kantar.

Contemporaries may have sneered at William IV's gauche behaviour. Charles Greville may have lamented that the parties during Ascot week lacked the style, splendour and colour of those of the previous reign. The nobility may have been affronted by Queen Adelaide sewing between the races at Ascot. No one, however, could or can dispute the prestige that William IV and the Royal Stud earned by breeding Pocahontas, a broodmare as influential as the Duke of Grafton's Penelope or the Prince of Wales's Perdita II, and probably with no comparable rival in the nineteenth century.

7

Dispersal of the Royal Stud

at Hampton Court and Interregnum,

1837–50

On the day of her accession to the throne at the age of eighteen Queen Victoria wrote the following in her diary:

> Since it has pleased providence to place me in this situation, I shall do my utmost to fulfill my duty towards my country: I am very young and perhaps in many, though not all things, inexperienced. But I am sure that very few have more real good will and more real desire to do what is fit and right than I have.

This desire to do what was fit and right is the key to many of her actions throughout her reign. She sought the advice of her Prime Minister and mentor, Lord Melbourne, on what plays were suitable for her to see, if she should waltz at balls, if she should permit the fashionable novelist, Mrs Gore, to dedicate a book to her; and if she ought to receive people with bad moral characters at Court. On all such questions Melbourne advised the Queen never to do anything that might compromise the dignity of the Crown or tarnish her own reputation for virtue, while at the same time never to be so censorious that she became disliked. The young Victoria, who had always inclined towards strictness, had no difficulty in following this counsel. The etiquette of the Court was stiffened; Maids of Honour were not permitted to walk unchaperoned on the terrace of Windsor Castle. The Queen was alert for deviations from this tighter protocol, and would display her displeasure to any offender with a sharp, irate glance.

It was almost certainly this firmly held belief in the necessity of keeping up the right kind of appearance that led to the Queen's endorsement of the government's decision that the Royal Stud at Hampton Court should be dispersed. In King William IV's will the following provisions were made for the Royal Stud at Hampton Court: it was first to be offered to the country, having been independently valued; if it was not accepted by the government, it was to be disposed of by public auction, the proceeds to go in discharge of various other bequests. Lord Melbourne had never been a great lover of the Turf, as had Charles James Fox or Charles Greville; when he went to Ascot with Queen Victoria in 1838, it was his first visit to a racecourse since his time at Eton more than forty years earlier. While he had spent many a night gaming in the clubs around St James's Street over the previous forty years, and so had no puritanical scruples about gambling, the racing and breeding of Thoroughbred horses held no fascination for him. He is unlikely to have realized what an original idea was the first provision in William IV's will, namely to use the Royal Stud at Hampton Court to establish a National Stud. Similarly, he had no conception of the importance of the blood-lines that had been built up at the Stud, nor of the deleterious effect on breeding in England that would ensue if much of the stock were to be bought by foreign bidders.

In 1837 no respectable woman was connected with racing and breeding; there were, indeed, many very unsavoury characters in the world of the Turf with whom no lady, let alone a Queen, would ever think of being associated. So a combination of Victoria's own concern to do what was right, and the Prime Minister's insistence that she should do nothing that might tarnish her reputation made it inevitable not only that the Stud would be disbanded, but that none of its stock would be acquired by the young Queen.

The fear that the new reign might see the closure of the Royal Stud at Hampton Court was clearly in the mind of Colonel Wemyss, the Stud's manager, when he got his cousin, the Duke of Sutherland, to write to the Prime Minister on 26 June 1837, just six days after the death of William IV:

Dear Lord Melbourne,
    My cousin, Colonel Wemyss, wishes me to give him a letter of introduction to you in order that he may have the satisfaction of laying before you a statement of the stud at Hampton Court, which His Late Majesty had kindly placed under his management. It would gratify him if you would have the goodness to

allow him to place this in your hands hoping that if the Stud should be continued by Her Majesty, his management of it may be found such as to give him the hope that he may have the Honour of continuing to take charge of it. I understand he has hitherto had no salary, but has been allowed to occupy the Stud House.

> Yours very Faithfully,
> Sutherland.[1]

Despite the balance sheet from January 1835 to June 1837 showing a profit of £1,899, and payments of £4,331 10s made by Colonel Wemyss out of the Stud's receipts, which the manager considered as a profit as they did not relate to the purchase of horses or other stud expenses, but to separate expenditure necessary for the Park at Hampton Court, the Duke of Sutherland's intercession on behalf of his cousin fell on deaf ears. On 14 August 1837, a local doctor, F. H. Holbertson, was sent the following letter from an official of the Master of the Horse:

Sir,
    In reply to your application to be allowed to continue to attend Her Majesty's servants at the Stud, I am directed by the Master of the Horse to inform you that His Lordship is unable to comply with your request; the Stud is to be broken up and the Establishment entirely reduced. Therefore the attendance of a Medical Practitioner will not be required.

> I am etc,
> R. W. Spearman[2].

The decision to disband the Royal Stud by sale at public auction must have been taken in the very first weeks of Queen Victoria's reign. That the Dowager Queen Adelaide, as Ranger of Bushey Park, had to receive a rent of £800 per annum for the paddocks, and that there may have been a disagreement between her and Lord Errol, the Master of the Horse, could only have had a peripheral, if any, bearing on that decision.

The racing world was totally shocked by the imminent dissolution of the Royal Stud. In an attempt to avert the sale many influential members of the Jockey Club sent a petition to Lord Melbourne:

We, the undersigned, have heard with great concern of the probability of the dissolution of the Royal Stud at Hampton Court. We think that the great and permanent attraction of the annual stud sale, by producing competition, enhances the value of thoroughbred horses, and thus promotes the improvement of the breed throughout the kingdom. We trust therefore that Her Majesty's Government may be induced to advise the Queen to retain the establishment; and we have less scruple in expressing this hope because we are persuaded that, under judicious management, the proceeds of the sale would be found, upon an average, to cover all the expenses of maintaining the stud.
Signed by:

Beaufort	Richmond	G. Anson	W. Powlett
G. Bentinck	Suffield	S. Batson	G. Rush
Chesterfield	Tavistock	H. Biggs	J. R. Udney
Clarendon	Uxbridge	G. Byng	H. S. Waddington
Dorset	Wilton	C. G. Greville	C. Wilson
Orford		W. Hallett	

This petition did not move the recipient to change his mind; neither did a six page attack by the editor of the *Sporting Magazine* in September 1837. Describing the Royal Stud as 'superior to any other in the world', he bitterly attacked the decision to disperse it. He concluded by exhorting the government

> to save an Establishment, which years of care and munificence has brought almost to perfection, from becoming the spoil of the stranger. Let it be preserved whole and untouched; and if I know anything of the spirit of Englishmen, it will be a proud moment for that Minister of the Crown who shall rise and say to the Representatives, 'in your name we have done a great good: we have saved for you that which in future is the National Stud of England'.

None of these impassioned and eloquent pleas served their purpose, and the sale of the Royal Stud went ahead as originally planned at Hampton Court paddocks on Wednesday 25 October 1837. Although the weather was unfavourable in the early part of the day, the *Sporting Magazine* reported that the sale 'drew an immense concourse of people, including many influential Noble-

98

men and Gentlemen connected with the Turf, a vast number of breeders and agents from France, Germany, Russia and Prussia, and an immense collection of breeders, trainers, grooms and others interested in the Sale'. Eighty-one lots were on offer: thirty-one foals, forty-three broodmares, five stallions and two half-bred two-year-olds. The mare that fetched the highest price was Nanine, the dam of Glaucus, who was sold for 970 gns. Other mares that fetched large sums included Oscar Mare (670 gns), Wings (600 gns), Fleur-de-Lis (550 gns), Scandal (400 gns) and Gulnare, winner of the 1827 Oaks (395 gns). Twenty-one of the forty-three mares sold were exported: ten went to France, six to Germany, two to the USA and Belgium and one to Denmark. The most famous old mares bred by George IV were all exported: Belvoirina to Belgium, Rachel to France and Maria to Germany. Lord Stradbroke obtained a bargain in Marpessa for only 230 gns, for she became the dam of Idas, the winner of the 1845 2,000 Guineas. Xarifa, bought for the French government, became the third dam of Souvenir, the Prix du Jockey-Club and Prix Royal-Oak winner in 1862. In total, the sale of the broodmares realized 9,568 gns; the export of so many was a tragic loss for English breeding.

The two stallions that excited most interest were The Colonel and Actaeon. The former, who had been bought from the Hon. E. Petre by George IV for 4,000 gns after winning the St Leger, fetched 1,550 gns, about 500 gns less than expected. He was bought by Mr Tattersall, who stood him at his stud at Dawley near Uxbridge. The Colonel was later sold to Brunswick for £1,900 by Tattersalls, and in 1843 was repurchased by them for the 1844 covering season. The reason for the relatively low sum paid for him in 1837 was that there existed then a prejudice against him among breeders, as he had only got four winners in 1835 and twelve in 1836. Actaeon, who had been bought from Lord Kelburne for 1,000 gns, fetched 920 gns and was exported to Russia. The thirty-one foals had only just been weaned when the sale took place; some of them, who had been severely affected by influenza only a short time previously, did not look well. The foal by Actaeon out of Wings, who had been expected to make 300 or 400 gns, was bought by Captain Gardnor for only 46 gns, as the illness had made him temporarily blind. Recovering his sight and named Monops, he won five races including the Wokingham Stakes at Ascot. The greatest bargain of the entire sale was unquestionably Marpessa's filly-foal, to be named Pocahontas, who was bought by Mr Greatrex for a mere 62 gns. The future Coronation Stakes winner,

Spangle (Croesus–Variella), was purchased for only 71 gns, while Iris, who won the Woodcote Stakes in 1839, cost only 10 gns more. In all, the foals realized a total of 2,583 gns, and the total receipts from the whole sale came to 15,692 gns. The great shame was that Lord Melbourne and the government had not been prepared to spend a similar sum of money to buy the Royal Stud for the country.

The paddocks at the Hampton Court Stud did not fall into disuse after the dispersal sale. The Dowager Queen Adelaide leased them to Mr Charles Greville and to General Peel, the younger brother of the Tory leader and Prime Minister Sir Robert Peel. General Peel was the owner of Orlando, who had been awarded the 1844 Derby on the disqualification of Running Rein, when it transpired that he was a four-year-old. Other stallions standing at Hampton Court between 1838 and 1850 included Ion, the runner-up to Amato in the Derby and to Don John in the St Leger in 1838, and himself the sire of the 1855 Derby winner Wild Dayrell; Slane, runner-up to Touchstone in the 1837 Ascot Gold Cup, and sire of The Princess (Oaks, 1844), Merry Monarch (Derby, 1845), and Conyngham (2,000 Guineas, 1847); and Bey of Algiers, winner of the Chester Cup in 1840.

The fate of the twelve employees of the Royal Stud after its dispersal, thrown out of work without any resources save the poorhouse, was not initially a very happy one. The Master of the Horse, Lord Albemarle, at first relieved their pressing necessities by advancing them small sums of money in weekly payments. The Head Groom, William Worley, had fifty-seven years' service, and the Helpers, Thomas Towndley, Thomas Goodall and George Carter, fifty, thirty-five and thirty-four years' service respectively. Thomas Towndley died in 1838 and the Master of the Horse eventually procured employment or pensions for all the others.

8

The Royal Stud

Re-established by Queen Victoria,

1850–67

Queen Victoria had always enjoyed riding and was known to be a good judge of a horse. When Lord Melbourne visited Windsor Castle he accompanied the young monarch on her daily ride in the Park. Her reputation as a horsewoman extended as far away as Russia, where the ladies of the Tsar's court copied her fashions and rode 'à la mode de la Reine Victoria' in the late 1830s and 1840s. In spite of her secluded childhood, she had been taken to the 1831 Derby won by Spaniel and had witnessed the victory of Queen of Trumps in the 1835 St Leger. After her first visit to Ascot, when she rode in the same carriage as King William IV and Queen Adelaide, she recorded in her diary how good the races were. On 14 June 1838 the young Queen, accompanied by Lord Melbourne, attended her first Ascot as Sovereign. In her diary she records the results of the five races she stayed for, although it rained continually from the second race onwards. She commented that the St James's Palace Stakes won by the Duke of Portland's Boeotian was 'a most interesting race; the 4th (for the Cup), also very interesting, by Lord George Bentinck's Grey Momus . . . I was much amused.'

In 1839 this enthusiastic, vivacious young girl fell ecstatically in love with Prince Albert of Saxe-Coburg. On the very evening of his arrival in her diary she wrote, 'It was with some emotion that I beheld Albert – who is beautiful.' The subsequent entries in the diary catalogue his perfections: 'His beautiful blue eyes and exquisite nose and such a pretty mouth with delicate moustaches and slight, very slight, whiskers.' In a few days Queen Victoria was completely enraptured, and decided to marry him.

Prince Albert was thoroughly, almost alarmingly, respectable; not at all like the typical pleasure-seeking, casual, ironical and sports-loving English aristocrats. A stiff, serious-minded and utterly conscientious man, Prince Albert was the quintessence of earnestness. The Queen told Lord Melbourne that 'The Prince is much severer than me,' and that he considered that she should not receive anyone at Court whose reputation was in any way tainted. Even during their engagement it was clear that the priggish Prince Albert was taking over the role of mentor and guide to the Queen, certainly in relation to etiquette and social behaviour. Thus from the very beginning Albert's influence set the tone for the Victorian Age. Nearly all of the puritanical spirit of the era can be attributed to Queen Victoria's Prince Consort.

The marriage took place on 11 February 1840. In the summer of that year Queen Victoria and Prince Albert attended the Derby at Epsom. A special lawn was laid out for the occasion, where the Queen walked around with her crinolined ladies-in-waiting, sheltered from the brilliant sun by a small sarsenet parasol with a long ivory handle. The normal paddock having been turned into the Queen's promenade, the horses were saddled in an open space near Langley Bottom. The Prince Consort rode his cob over there to see the runners prepare for the race, which was won by Mr Robertson's outsider Little Wonder. After the race the Queen sent for the young boy, Macdonald, who had ridden the winner, and asked him what his weight was. 'If you please, Your Majesty,' the youthful jockey replied, 'my master says I must not tell anyone my weight.' Both the Queen and Prince Albert laughed, and the latter complimented Macdonald for obeying his orders so strictly. Three years later the Queen and Prince Albert went to watch one of the gallops of the Derby favourite, Cotherstone, who had earlier won the 2,000 Guineas. Owned by the Earl of Strathmore's son, Mr John Bowes, Cotherstone was trained by John Scott at his stables at Mickleham near Leatherhead. All the colts from Scott's stable that were entered in the Derby took part in the gallop on the Downs, and it was reported that the Queen thought Cotherstone the best of the lot, making flattering remarks about his splendid condition. He duly justified his position as favourite for the Derby by winning easily.

The Queen continued the tradition of attending Ascot every Tuesday and Thursday until the death of the Prince Consort in 1861. While watching the New Stakes in 1854, she became so excited as the runners approached the Royal Stand that she failed to notice that a window had been closed and broke a pane of glass as her head struck it. When the 1857 Derby and Oaks winner, Blink Bonny, received a walk-over at Ascot, Queen Victoria gave specific orders for the renowned filly to be brought round to the Royal Stand so that she could inspect her more closely.

That Prince Albert did not share the aristocracy's love of racing and fox hunting need not be emphasized. He considered such activities as no more than the pursuit of idle pleasure. Even when he accompanied his wife riding in the Great Park at Windsor, he made a carriage follow them in case it should rain. Ironically, his criterion that sovereigns should act in the correct manner befitting their rank may have been one of the reasons why the Royal Stud at Hampton Court was re-established at the end of 1849. He would have been aware that the King of Prussia and several of the lesser German sovereigns had Thoroughbred studs. He would have thought that it was the correct thing for a monarch to have, and would not have liked his wife to lack this normal Royal possession. The owning of a stud would therefore have fitted in with his notions of behaviour desirable in a sovereign; but not actually racing the animals bred, for that might bring the sovereign too close to the pernicious evil of betting. It was therefore decided that all the produce of the Royal Stud at Hampton Court would be sold as yearlings at public auction.

The care of the re-established Royal Stud at Hampton Court was put in the hands of John Ransom, who had been in the service of Lord Jersey for many years, and on the death of Jersey's trainer, Edwards, had taken charge of the training of his horses. Ransom proved a most trustworthy and able stud groom, and must take much of the credit for the success of the Hampton Court Stud in the 1850s and 1860s. The stud's manager initially was the Clerk of the Stables, Mr Lewis, but within a few years the Crown Equerry, Colonel Maude, took over the supervision of the stud. In the first few years Mr W. Goodwin was consulted on the purchase of the broodmares, but his age and ill-health unfortunately curtailed his activities to merely the giving of advice.

General Peel had decided in 1850 to cut right back on his Turf activities and had relinquished his lease on certain of the paddocks at Bushey Park. Despite the leases held by Mr Charles Greville, his sometime Turf partner, Mr Payne and General Peel on some of the paddocks at the stud, the lack of Royal tenants had meant that the unused paddocks had deteriorated and several of the hovels had fallen into disrepair. In a letter to the Clerk of the Works on 5

December 1850, George Lewis wrote that there were nine brood-mares and four foals at Hampton Court, and added that it could not be stated 'how many broodmare and bloodstock hovels will be required at the Bushey Paddocks as we are making additions whenever opportunities offer. The hovels and paddocks which it will be most convenient to have restored are those in the immediate vicinity of the house of the Stud Groom.'[1] It also appeared that the herbage, which had been celebrated for its goodness, had become rank and sour. Although cattle of the Polled Scots breed had been kept on the paddocks to consume the long grass, appar-ently they had not done the job efficiently. It was suggested that the size of the paddocks, of which there were forty, should be reduced, so that the grass should be more closely eaten and worn down, thus improving the quality of the herbage.

The most urgent task facing George Lewis and John Ransom in rebuilding the Royal Stud was the acquisition of high-class broodmares. Although some mares were acquired privately, a great many were bought at public auction. The policy was to buy the highest quality available. At Tattersalls' Sale on 3 July 1850, the Earl of Chesterfield's mare Distaffina (Don John–Industry), who had won the Ascot Derby Stakes and was a sister to Lady Evelyn, the 1849 Oaks and Park Hill Stakes winner, was bought by the Royal Stud. On 15 July 1850, at the dispersal sale of the late Earl of Albemarle, the Royal Stud acquired Flight (Jereed–Elopement) and Spangle (Croesus–Variella), who had been bred by King Wil-liam IV and had won the Coronation Stakes and come third to Crucifix in the 1840 1,000 Guineas. Other well-bred mares who were acquired by the Royal Stud in 1850 and 1851 included the 1849 1,000 Guineas winner, The Flea (Coronation–Puce), Mr Charles Greville's Despatch (Defence–Nanette), whose grandam Nanine was the dam of the 1834 Ascot Gold Cup winner Glaucus, and the same owner's Jamaica (Liverpool–Preserve), whose dam had won the 1,000 Guineas and been second in the 1835 Oaks. At the dispersal sale of General Peel's stud on 25 August 1851 the Royal Stud bought a broodmare by Sir Hercules out of Electress for 310 gns; Electress had been bred in 1819 at Hampton Court by the Prince Regent and had won seven races. The Sir Hercules mare was a half-sister to Miss Twickenham by Rockingham, the dam of the 1851 Derby winner Teddington by Orlando, and also a half-sister to Splitvote, the grandam of St Albans, winner of the 1870 St Leger. At the same sale the Royal Stud purchased Hersey (Glaucus–Hester).

In March 1852 the Royal Stud bought the broodmare Stamp (Emilius–Receipt) from Mr Lily for 170 gns. Receipt was the grandam of Dollar by Flying Dutchman, the winner of the Prix Lupin and Goodwood Cup and an exceptional sire in France. In September that year at Doncaster Mr Goodwin bought two very important additions to the Royal Stud at the dispersal sale of Mr Robert Stephenson's stud: Martha Lynn (Mulatto–Leda), the dam of the 1850 Derby winner Voltigeur, whose famous Match with The Flying Dutchman had so excited the world of the Turf in 1850, and Martha Lynn's daughter Eulogy by Euclid. Another mare bred by Stephenson, Volley (Voltaire–Martha Lynn), was bought by Goodwin for the Royal Stud the same year. In January 1853 Lord Exeter sold the Royal Stud the exceptionally well-bred mare Equation (Emilus–Maria by Whisker), in foal to Birdcatcher; Equation was a full-sister to both Extempore, the 1843 Oaks and July Stakes winner, and Euclid, who had won the St James's Palace Stakes.

The Royal Stud's policy of buying the best-bred mares that came on to the market continued in 1854 and 1855. In the early part of 1854 the Royal Stud acquired Bay Celia (Orlando–Hersey) privately. Nun Appleton (Bay Middleton–Miss Milner), who had been bred by Lord George Bentinck, was bought by the Royal Stud on 12 June 1854. The Arrow (Slane–Southdown), who was a half-sister to Alarm, the winner of the 1845 Cambridgeshire and 1846 Ascot Gold Cup, was also bought privately by the Royal Stud in 1854. All of these broodmares were to have a great influence on the development of the Royal Stud, and their descendants include many notable winners. The benefits of the policy of purchasing such high-class mares became apparent almost immediately.

The principal stallions standing at Hampton Court when the Royal Stud was re-established were Orlando, Alarm, Lanercost and Slane. Charles Greville bought Orlando and Slane at General Peel's dispersal sale in August 1851, and he was to remain at Hampton Court for the rest of his life, making an enormous contribution to the success of the Stud. Lanercost, the winner of the first Cambridgeshire in 1839 and the 1841 Ascot Gold Cup, only remained at Hampton Court until 1852 when he went to stand in Yorkshire, but Alarm remained at Bushey Park until 1857 when he too left, this time for Newmarket. Voltigeur, the 1850 Derby winner, was leased to stand one season at Hampton Court in 1853, but was then transferred to Mr Smallwood's stud at

Middlethorpe. His place was taken by his older full-brother, Barnton, but he proved most disappointing as a sire. Slane, who was seventeen in 1850, was virtually at the end of his career as a stallion, but had got The Princess, the 1844 Oaks winner, Conyngham, the 2,000 Guineas victor, and Lady Orford, the heroine of the 1850 1,000 Guineas.

Three yearlings were submitted by the Royal Stud at Hampton Court to Tattersalls' Sales at Hyde Park Corner in 1851. The next year seven yearlings from the Royal Paddocks were sold on Monday 5 July at Hyde Park Corner, of which three won thirteen races; the best, Spinaway (Orlando–Distaffina), won five races, including the Chesterfield Stakes at Newmarket in 1854. The following year the sale disposed of thirteen yearlings from the Royal Stud, and four of these won twenty races; Redemption (Orlando–Stamp) was victorious on seven occasions, and by winning the Ascot Stakes in 1856 became the first horse bred by Queen Victoria to be successful at the Berkshire course. The same afternoon Mr J. A. Hind purchased The Slave (Melbourne–Volley), for only 70 gns; she was placed once at Radcliffe from three runs as a two-year-old and then retired to the paddocks. Only two of her four foals ever ran: one was Lord Clifden by Newminster, whose seven victories included the 1863 St Leger, the 1862 Champagne Stakes at Doncaster and the Woodcote Stakes; he was beaten a head by Macaroni in the Derby, but many spectators at Epsom felt he had won outright. The distances between the first four were a head, a neck and a head, and several of those qualified to comment thought that the Judge, Mr Clarke, had overlooked Lord Clifden, who was the sire of four Classic winners including Petrarch and Wenlock. The Slave's other winning foal was Lady Clifden by Surplice, who won twenty-one races including the Stewards' Cup at Goodwood. Thus from its very commencement the Royal Stud under Queen Victoria began to have a significant influence on the Stud Book.

The fourteen yearlings sent up from Hampton Court to Tattersalls in June 1854 fetched the then astronomical sum of 6,199 gns. The *Sporting Magazine* reported that 'bidders ran up against each other with spirit and gusto. Certainly a fairish looking lot of well-made-up young ones never sold at such extraordinary prices. How many of them will be worth what was given for them a year hence?' Mr Howard bought the two most expensive, Yellow Jack (Birdcatcher–Jamaica) and Queen's Head (Bay Middleton–Stamp). Yellow Jack certainly repaid Howard handsomely for he won a

Sweepstakes at Newmarket in 1855, and as a three-year-old was runner-up to Fazzoletto in the 2,000 Guineas, to Ellington in the Derby, to Rogerthorpe in the Goodwood Cup and in the Ascot Derby Stakes and Chester Cup. The total place money he won was in excess of £11,000, at a time when the Derby was worth only half that sum to the winner. Queen's Head only won two races, but was third to Manganese and Mincepie in the 1856 1,000 Guineas. She was the dam of four winners and fourth dam of Aboyeur by Desmond, who won the 1913 Derby on the controversial disqualification of Craganour. In all, eight of the fourteen Royal yearlings sold in 1854 won thirty-nine races between them. Flyaway (Orlando–Flight), one of the cheapest at 155 gns, won the 1855 Chesterfield Stakes and nine other races, and ran third to Malacca in the 1856 Cambridgeshire; Spindle (Orlando–Distaffina) numbered the July Stakes among her three victories and she was runner-up in the Woodcote Stakes, St James's Palace Stakes, Coronation Stakes and Molecomb Stakes. Not merely were these remarkable results for a stud that had only produced thirty-seven foals since its re-establishment, but it was a great tribute to those who had bought the broodmares to restock it.

The first Classic winner bred by Queen Victoria came from the seventeen yearlings sold by Tattersalls on Monday 11 June 1855. At 480 gns, Imperieuse (Orlando–Eulogy) was the highest-priced; a rich bay filly, she won three of her six starts as a juvenile, twice at Stamford and the Lavant Stakes at Goodwood, and ran third in the Molecomb Stakes and fourth in the Champagne Stakes at Doncaster, after which she was bought by her trainer John Scott for 900 gns. On her reappearance in the 1,000 Guineas at Newmarket, Imperieuse beat her Champagne Stakes conqueress, Tasmania, half a length, with the odds-on favourite Blink Bonny unplaced. When the latter slaughtered her rivals in the Oaks, in which Imperieuse was only fourth, she was completing a memorable double, as she had won the Derby earlier that week. After winning a Free Handicap at Newcastle, Imperieuse was twice unplaced at York and was allowed to start at 100–6 for the St Leger, for which Blink Bonny was again hot favourite. Imperieuse gave the best performance of her career, winning very easily by two lengths from Commotion with Blink Bonny only fourth. She thus became the first filly to achieve the 1,000 Guineas and St Leger double, a feat only accomplished since by Achievement (1867), Tranquil (1923), Meld (1955) and Oh So Sharp (1985). In 1859 Imperieuse, covered by Warlock, was sold to Monsieur Lupin and sent to France, where she became the ancestress of one of the most important French broodmare families. Imperieuse was the dam of the 1865 Prix de Diane heroine, Deliane, and grandam of two other Diane winners, Enguerrande (1876) and La Jonchere (1877). Among notable colts that traced back to her was Filibert de Savoie (Isard II–Yolande), who won the 1923 Grand Prix de Paris, Prix Royal-Oak and Prix du Cadran; his dam, Yolande, was bought by the Sandringham Stud in 1923 and imported to England, but she never produced a foal of the quality of Filibert de Savoie for King George V.

The other noteworthy yearling sold at Tattersalls in 1855 by the Royal Stud was Claude Lorraine (Orlando–Sir Hercules Mare), who won the Ascot Stakes in 1857. Eight of the seventeen Royal yearlings sold that year won a total of thirty-two races.

Seventeen yearlings from Hampton Court were sold on 17 June 1856. Imperieuse's full-sister, Eurydice, made only 76 gns, but won three races including the Cambridgeshire in 1858. Unfortunately she died later that autumn. She was one of the ten winners from that crop, who were successful in thirty-nine races. The highest-priced, FitzRoland (Orlando–Stamp), whom Sir Joseph Hawley bought, became the second Classic winner bred by Queen Victoria. FitzRoland ran once as a juvenile when sixth in the Woodcote Stakes. On his second appearance on a racecourse in the 2,000 Guineas, he beat The Happy Land a length and a half, but he failed to stay when unplaced to Beadsman in the Derby. When he reverted to a mile, he easily won the St James's Palace Stakes and, a fortnight later, the Stockbridge Derby, which was also over eight furlongs. FitzRoland only ran once more, as a five-year-old when unplaced to the juvenile, Queen of the Vale, in the Queen's Stand Plate at Ascot. FitzRoland stood briefly as a stallion at Hampton Court, but was soon sent to the north, where he did not distinguish himself as a sire. One other colt of the 1855 Royal crop of yearlings, Gin, a full-brother to Claude Lorraine, won five races, including the July Stakes at Newmarket.

Sixteen Royal yearlings came under Tattersalls' hammer on Monday 15 June 1857 at Hyde Park Corner. That the sale of the Hampton Court Stud's yearlings had become a very important occasion in the Turf's calendar is demonstrated by those who attended. Admiral Rous, Lords Scarborough, Althorp, Villiers and Galway, Sir W. Wynne, Sir Tatton Sykes and Sir George Strickland, and Messrs Foljambe, Payne, Cooper, Sutton and Merry MP were some of the personalities present. The trainers and agents included

Joe and Mat Dawson, John Day's son and Mr Harry Hill, who bought four yearlings for the Danebury stable, Stevens, Reeves and Stephenson. One trainer, John Scott, was a notable absentee, but his powerful stable was under a cloud, having not won a single race in 1857 at either Epsom or Ascot. Eight of the yearlings sold in 1857 won thirty-three races; the best of them was unquestionably Trumpeter (Orlando–Cavatina) who was knocked down to Harry Hill for 290 gns, a price the correspondent of the *Sporting Magazine* thought 'a dear one'. Trumpeter, however, proved a real bargain; unplaced on his only run as a two-year-old at Bath, at three he won both his starts, at Newmarket over a mile and at Bath over twelve furlongs, before starting third favourite at 4–1 for the Derby. At Epsom he was only beaten half a length and a neck by Musjid and Marionette; his third place made him the first colt bred by Queen Victoria to be placed in the premier Classic. Unfortunately one of Trumpeter's legs went after the Derby and he had to be retired to stud. A light chestnut horse with three white heels and a bald face, contemporaries described him as being 'full of quality'. He stood first at Althorp Park and later at Hampton Court; although he never got a champion, he was by no means a total failure as a stallion, for most of his crops included several smart handicappers.

The other very interesting yearling sold by Queen Victoria in 1857 was Queen of Prussia (Orlando–Hersey), who was described by an observer at the sale as 'small but clever'. She fetched 220 gns and won four races at the Curragh, including the Madrid Stakes Handicap. She was considered good enough to come over and challenge for the Coronation Stakes at Ascot, but could only manage fifth place. The dam of three winners, Queen of Prussia was the ancestress of Oppressor (Irish Derby, 1899), Judea (Irish Oaks, 1918), Zionist (Dewhurst Stakes, 1924; Irish Derby, 1925) and Money Maker (Dewhurst Stakes, 1926). Judea's descendants were even more illustrious and included Stroma, the dam of the Eclipse Stakes winner, Canisbay, and of Strathcona, the dam of probably the best racemare ever bred so far by Her Majesty the Queen, the Oaks and St Leger winner, Dunfermline. It is a remarkable coincidence that the only Thoroughbred to defeat the dual Prix de l'Arc de Triomphe winner, Alleged, whom she beat in the St Leger, should trace back to a mare bred by her Royal owner's great-great-grandmother at Hampton Court.

In 1858 the venue for the sale of the Royal yearlings, nineteen in this year, moved from Hyde Park Corner to Hampton Court itself, the sale taking place on 29 May. Hecate (Loup-Garou–Vanity), who made 780 gns, was the highest-priced yearling sold at public auction that year. She was an immense disappointment, never even setting foot on a racecourse. Although there were eight winners of sixteen races in this batch, none was outstanding. Admiral Rous paid 610 gns for Montenegro (Melbourne–Tarella), which caused the correspondent of the *Sporting Magazine* to remark that it was 'the first time for many a long day that the purple stripes will have been carried by such an expensive yearling'. In fact Montenegro never did carry those famous silks, for the Admiral sold him to the Duke of Bedford, for whom he won one solitary Match at Newmarket in October 1860. Other notables of the Turf who attended this first sale at Hampton Court included the Duke of Beaufort, the Marquess of Stamford, Earl Vane, Lords Strathmore, Clifden and Chesterfield, Messrs Payne, Hill, Cooper and Gully, and the trainers John Scott, John Day, Sam Rogers and Robert Peck. It was a raging hot day, made more endurable by the cool lobster salad that the Stud Groom provided in his parlour before the sale commenced.

It was during 1857 that Colonel Maude was appointed Manager of the Royal Stud at Hampton Court, a position he held till its dissolution in 1894. Colonel Sir George Maude had served with distinction in the Crimean War. At the battle of Balaclava he had commanded a battery of artillery, but had the misfortune to be severely wounded by a shell that burst under his horse. The poor man found it no easy matter to explain to ladies for a long time afterwards that he was unable either to sit down or to ride a horse without extreme discomfort. He therefore used a specially designed wagonette with a hood to transport himself around the paddocks at Bushey Park. He also made much hospitable use of this conveyance, especially for his charming lady friends of whom, one of his contemporaries remarked, 'he seemed to possess a great many'. Colonel Maude, who was appointed Crown Equerry and Secretary to the Master of the Horse on his return from the Crimea, lived in the Lodge at the Royal Mews. As he became older, he went very deaf, which made it almost impossible for him to have interviews with Queen Victoria. Most of their communication therefore took place by letter.

The seventeen yearlings sold by the Hampton Court Stud on 10 June 1859 proved to be of much higher quality than those of the previous year; ten of them won seventy-four races during their careers. The outstanding colt was Diophantus (Orlando–

Equation), who was bought by Lord Stamford. Diophantus won three of his five starts as a juvenile including the Molecomb Stakes at Goodwood, but was well beaten in the Chesterfield Stakes and Prendergast Stakes. He was therefore allowed to start at 25–1 for the 2,000 Guineas on 30 April 1861, when he proceeded to trounce Kettledrum by three lengths, with his stable-companion Imaus (Newminster–Himalaya), whom Lord Stamford had also bought at Hampton Court, only fourth. Diophantus probably found the trip of the Derby a shade too far for him when beaten a length and a head by Kettledrum and Dundee on 29 May, for when he reverted to a mile in the Midsummer Stakes at Newmarket in July, he won easily. A walk-over in the Post Stakes at Goodwood concluded Diophantus's racing career; at stud he produced nothing of any great account. Imaus was far from a total disappointment, for he won six races including the Newmarket St Leger and the Scarborough Stakes at Doncaster. Lord Stamford bought another yearling, whom one observer described as 'a racer to the core', at Hampton Court that afternoon: Walloon (The Flying Dutchman–Nina) fully justified the description, for he won fifteen times between 1860 and 1864, including the Champagne Stakes at Doncaster as a juvenile when he beat Kettledrum a neck, the St James's Palace Stakes the next year and the Wokingham Stakes in 1864. Little Lady (Orlando–Volley), who was sold for only 70 gns as she seemed very awkward in the sale ring, was an even more prolific scorer, winning sixteen minor races. Her first success was in the Anglesey Stakes for yearlings over two furlongs at Shrewsbury on 15 November 1859. Her greatest claim to Turf fame was that she became the dam of the 1875 2,000 Guineas winner, Camballo.

Eight of the twenty Royal yearlings sold at Hampton Court on Saturday 2 June 1860 won forty-four races. The most outstanding was the full-sister to Imperieuse, Imperatrice, who was bought by Colonel Towneley. The winner of two races, Hopeful Stakes at Doncaster in April and Hopeful Stakes at Newmarket in October as a two-year-old, Imperatrice also ran The Marquis, who won the St Leger the next year, to a head in the Champagne Stakes. She was unplaced to Hurricane when favourite for the 1,000 Guineas, but in the Oaks was runner-up by two lengths to Feu de Joie, to whom, after winning a Sweepstakes at Goodwood in the meantime, she ran third in the Yorkshire Oaks. Imperatrice gained her revenge on Hurricane when beating her a head in the Park Hill Stakes at Doncaster two days after running unplaced in the St Leger. As a broodmare Imperatrice was even more influential. The highest-priced yearling at the 1860 Hampton Court sale, and the second highest of the entire year, was Exchequer (Stockwell–Stamp), for whom Lord Coventry paid 810 gns. His eight victories included the Wokingham Stakes in 1863.

The following year's group of twenty-five yearlings, sold at Hampton Court on 8 June 1861, on the whole achieved disappointing results. There were eight individual winners of thirty-eight races, but all of these were relatively minor events. The most expensive purchase, Oenopides (The Cure–Equation), who fell to Lord Stamford for 1,000 gns, failed to win on either of his two outings, and was a bitter disappointment. The 1861 yearling who was to have the most significant influence on the Stud Book, Fidget (The Fallow Back–Flight), bought by Colonel Towneley, never ran but became the dam of four winners. Fidget was the third dam of Trayles, winner of the Ascot Gold Cup, Alexandra Plate and Goodwood Cup in 1889. An even more important descendant of Fidget was Maypole by Silvio, who won the 1888 Grand Criterium and 1889 Poule d'Essai des Pouliches. She was the dam of Rose de Mai, the winner of the Prix de Diane and Poule d'Essai des Pouliches in 1903. Among the renowned colts and fillies who descend from Rose de Mai are Algae Grace (Prix de Diane, 1950), Rose Prince (Queen Alexandra Stakes and Cesarewitch, 1923, and sire of Prince Rose), Soltikoff (Prix de l'Arc de Triomphe, 1962), Gris Perle (Prix du Cadran, 1933) and Glenjade (Poule d'Essai des Pouliches, 1919).

Voltigeur returned to stand at Hampton Court for the 1860 covering season, and twelve of the twenty-five Royal yearlings sold on Saturday 14 June 1862 were sired by him. This crop produced fourteen winners of fifty-seven races among the horses sold. None of the Voltigeur stock was particularly distinguished; indeed, the best was probably the maiden Lord Zetland (Voltigeur–Lady Gough), who was third in the 1864 Ascot Gold Cup. The best of the crop, Cambuscan (Newminster–The Arrow), won nine races including the 1863 July Stakes and finished third to Blair Athol and General Peel in the St Leger, fifth to Blair Athol in the Derby and runner-up to Ely in the 1865 Goodwood Cup. He was also quite successful as a sire; among his progeny were Camballo, the winner of the 1875 2,000 Guineas, and the remarkable Austrian mare, Kincsem, who was bred in Hungary by Herr Blascovitz. Kincsem won the Goodwood Cup in 1878 on her only appearance in England and was unbeaten in all her fifty-three other races in

Austria, Hungary, France and Germany. An excellent traveller, Kincsem apparently lay down on the straw as soon as she entered her horse-box and, sharing her bed with her Hungarian stable-boy, kept perfectly still throughout the journey.

Sunday 30 May 1863 saw twenty-eight yearlings up for sale by the Crown at Hampton Court; eleven became winners of sixty-four races. Archimedes (Newminster–Equation) was bought by Lord Stamford for 720 gns. He came on the market again at the dispersal sale of Lord Stamford's Thoroughbred stock on 3 December 1863, when he was sold to Captain White for the then gigantic sum, for an unraced colt, of 3,000 gns. It seems that the free-spending peer's financial difficulties were only temporary, for he had repurchased Archimedes when he made his racecourse debut in April 1865 in the 2,000 Guineas. It was a sensational first outing; Archimedes was beaten only a neck by the Comte de Lagrange's greatest champion, Gladiateur. Archimedes was unplaced in Gladiateur's Derby, but ran third to the famous French colt in the St Leger. Archimedes won six races in all, including the valuable Post Sweep-stakes at Goodwood. As a four-year-old he lost his form, and even when cut never regained it. A more prolific winner, and one of the favourites of the Stud Groom, John Ransom, was The Duke (Stockwell–Bay Celia), whom Mr Padwick bought at the Hampton Court sale. Padwick later sold him to the young Marquess of Hastings, whose fateful Turf career had commenced in 1863 when he first registered his colours and was elected a member of the Jockey Club. The Duke won eighteen races including the Good-wood Cup in 1866, besides finishing fourth to Gladiateur in the St Leger and fourth to Gardevisure in the Cambridgeshire in 1865. Another useful colt of the 1862 crop was Chattanooga (Orlando–Ayacanora), who won the Criterion Stakes at Newmar-ket. His dam, Ayacanora, who was out of the brilliant Pocahontas, had won three races including the Ham Stakes, Goodwood, and had run third to Imperieuse in the 1857 1,000 Guineas. She had been bought by the Royal Stud with her filly foal, Cachuca by Voltigeur, from Lord Portsmouth in 1861.

Twenty-four Royal yearlings were sold at Hampton Court on 4 June 1864. These included La Dauphine (Stockwell–Braxey), for whom Mr W. Morris gave the immense sum of 1,250 gns, the highest price up to that time ever given for a Hampton Court yearling. La Dauphine never fulfilled the high hopes held of her, only winning three minor races, at Newmarket in 1866 and 1867 and at Egham in 1867. Although the 1863 crop from Hampton

Court produced twelve winners of fifty-five races, none won any noteworthy races.

La Dauphine's half-sister, Ruthven by Newminster, fell to the bid of Mr Henry Chaplin, costing him 1,500 gns at the 1865 Hampton Court sale. He was to stagger the racing world that year when he gave 11,000 gns for two three-year-old colts, Breadalbane (Stockwell–Blink Bonny) and Broomielaw (Stockwell–Queen Mary). Ruthven was a total failure on the racecourse, running only twice, without success, as a two-year-old. The twenty-five Royal yearlings sold on 10 June included thirteen individual winners of seventy-six races. Undoubtedly the best colt was Julius (St Albans–Julie); he won fourteen races in three seasons, including the Cesarewitch Stakes in 1867, when he also ran a very close third to Achievement and Hermit, the winners of the 1,000 Guineas and the Derby, in the St Leger, and fourth to Vauban in the 2,000 Guineas. As a four-year-old Julius twice beat Hermit at Newmarket, defeated Achievement fifteen lengths in the Beaufort Cup at Stockbridge and was runner-up in the Doncaster Cup. He retired to the Clumber Stud at Worksop at 20 gns a mare.

Julius's sire, St Albans, had arrived at Hampton Court in 1862 to stand at a fee of 50 gns. In 1866 Queen Victoria had ten nominations to him; of the other thirty nominations Mr Blenkiron, the owner of the Midle Park Stud at Eltham, the only other in England that rivalled Hampton Court at that time, had four, the Marquess of Hastings and Duke of Beaufort two each, and the Earl of Chesterfield one. St Albans (Stockwell–Bribery), whose third dam, Electress, was bred by the Prince Regent and whose sire's dam was Pocahontas, was thus already intimately connected with the Royal Stud. He had won the St Leger, the Chester Cup and the Great Metropolitan Handicap in 1860 in the colours of Lord Ailesbury. Although he was not to prove so prepotent a sire as Orlando, he was still to get many very important winners for the Royal Stud in the next thirteen years. Another very useful Royal foal got by St Albans in 1864 was a half-sister to The Duke, The Duchess, whom the Marquess of Hastings bought. Her seven victories included the Nassau Stakes at Goodwood. Pericles (Newminster–Peri) turned into a very good sprinter, winning fourteen races including the Prendergast Stakes at Newmarket as a juvenile, when he was also third in the Molecomb Stakes and Clearwell Stakes. Misfortune (aft. Nike) (Orlando–Ayacanora) won ten races; she was exported to Germany in 1881, where she became the dam of Narrin, the winner of the Preis von Diana in 1887.

Moucheron, who won the Irish 1,000 Guineas in 1928, also traced back to Nike.

It had been the custom, since the sale of the Royal yearlings moved to Hampton Court in 1858, for the yearlings belonging to Charles Greville to be sold one hour after those of Queen Victoria. Greville had died earlier in the spring of 1865, and on 10 June that year a dispersal sale of all his stock was held at Hampton Court. Colonel Maude bought three of the mares: Catwaba (Cowl–Miami), with a filly foal by North Lincoln, Lady Blanche (Stockwell–Clementine) and Doralice (Alarm or Orlando–Preserve), with a colt foal by Vedette. Catwaba, whose dam Miami won the Oaks in 1847 and the July Stakes, had won the Revival Stakes at Doncaster and been third in the St James's Palace Stakes in 1860. Her filly foal by North Lincoln, Minnie Warren, who was sold to Mr Y. King at the Hampton Court sale in May 1866, won six minor races at Doncaster, Weymouth, Plymouth and Kelso, but it was as a broodmare that she achieved lasting fame: she was the third dam of the enormously influential mare Ballantrae by Ayrshire, who won the 1901 Criterion Stakes and 1902 Cambridgeshire Stakes. Exported to the USA in 1904, Ballantrae became the ancestress of the American champions Equipoise, Balancoire and Seabiscuit, while her filly Mendiant returned to England to win the 1909 Stewards' Cup at Goodwood. In 1919 Ballantrae was bought by textile magnate Marcel Boussac, and in 1921 she foaled Coeur à Coeur by Teddy, one of the most important foundation mares in Boussac's stud. Coeur à Coeur was the grandam of his outstanding colt, Djebel by Tourbillon, whose victories included the 2,000 Guineas, Prix de l'Arc de Triomphe and Grand Prix de Saint-Cloud and who became one of the most prepotent sires in England and France in the late 1940s and 1950s as well as a notable sire of sires. Lady Blanche was also the ancestress of one of Marcel Boussac's great foundation mares: Hélène de Troie by Helicon, who was the dam of Adargatis, the winner of the Prix de Diane in 1934 and dam of Ardan, whose victories included the Prix du Jockey-Club, Prix de l'Arc de Triomphe, Coronation Cup and Grand Prix de Saint-Cloud. Another of Hélène de Troie's daughters, La Troienne, was exported to the USA by Boussac, where the great Buckpasser was among her illustrious descendants. The mare to whom all these champions trace, Lady Caroline (Orlando–Lady Blanche), was bred in 1861 by Charles Greville at Hampton Court, four years before Lady Blanche was bought by Colonel Maude for Queen Victoria.

The third of Charles Greville's mares bought by Colonel Maude, Doralice, was out of the 1835 1,000 Guineas winner Preserve, who was a full-sister to the 1837 St Leger victor Mango. Her colt foal by Vedette, Speculum, was sold to the Duke of Newcastle at Hampton Court in May 1866. Speculum turned out to be a real bargain, for he won sixteen races including the Goodwood Cup and the City and Suburban Handicap and was a successful sire; among his progeny was the 1878 Derby winner, Sefton.

Thirteen of the twenty-two yearlings bred by Queen Victoria that were sold at Hampton Court on 20 May 1866 were winners of eighty-five races. Speculum and Minnie Warren, who had been bred by Charles Greville, were sold on the same day. This crop included possibly the best colt bred up to then by Queen Victoria: The Earl (Young Melbourne–Bay Celia), sold to the Marquess of Hastings.

Henry Weysford Charles Plantagenet was born in 1842 and succeeded his brother, the third Marquess of Hastings, in 1851. After a brief and disastrous stay at Oxford, the profligate young nobleman embarked on his notorious downward path to ruin. In the summer of 1864, Lady Florence Paget, the only daughter of the second Marquess of Anglesey, one of the beauties of that season and nicknamed the 'Pocket Venus' on account of her tiny figure, became engaged to Henry Chaplin. Hastings, who was jealous of Chaplin's popularity, began making overtures to her. Nothing was allowed to interfere with his fanatical determination to win her from her fiancé; and a few days before the marriage he succeeded. Lady Florence left her father's house alone in his brougham on the excuse of making some purchases at Marshall and Snelgrove. She walked straight through the shop to Oxford Street, was met by Hastings, and drove with him to Euston in a cab. They married immediately. This sensational elopement evoked huge sympathy for Henry Chaplin among his friends and society in general. The 'Pocket Venus' soon realized the error of her choice, for she found herself married to the archetypal irresponsible rake, who, having won her in such an unscrupulous manner, soon tired of her company. Despite having won his rival's bride-to-be, his implacable jealousy of Henry Chaplin was not assauged. In the months following his purchase of The Earl at Hampton Court, Hastings laid Chaplin's good colt Hermit to thousands of pounds against his chance in the 1867 Derby. When Hermit won the Derby on 22 May 1867, Lord Hastings lost more than £120,000 and he retired to Paris, 'as I am sick of being pointed out as a man who has lost such a sum'. By September 1867 Chaplin still had not been paid. Hastings, in reply to a reminder that the money was still owing, answered from Baden: 'It is not my fault, but my cursed lawyer who takes such an infernal time getting the money.'

The Earl, meanwhile, had developed into a very useful two-year-old, winning five of his twelve starts including the Gimcrack Stakes at York. The Marquess of Hastings had an even better juvenile filly, Lady Elizabeth. Unbeaten in eleven races before overconfidence by her jockey led to her defeat in the Middle Park Plate, she redeemed her reputation in a Match over the Bretby Stakes course two days later against Julius, who, despite having only to give her 9 lb, was still beaten a short head by the juvenile prodigy. Julius had won the Cesarewitch three days before and had been third in the St Leger and fourth in the 2,000 Guineas earlier in the year. Lady Elizabeth's performance was all the more remarkable as she was receiving 12 lb less than dictated by the official weight-for-age scale. Convinced that Lady Elizabeth was a certainty for the Derby in 1868, Hastings backed her to win huge sums for the Epsom Classic, at the same time laying The Earl to lose thousands of pounds. Lady Elizabeth never recovered from her exertions against Julius, wintered badly and by the spring was a shadow of herself. Hastings and the Danebury stable kept her condition a closely guarded secret, and two days before the Derby she was still 5–4 favourite for the race, though on the day her price went out to 7–4.

Meanwhile, The Earl had wintered well and when he beat Sir Joseph Hawley's Blue Gown a neck at the Newmarket Craven Meeting, he staked his claim to be the best three-year-old colt in England. Blue Gown's victory in the Spring Stakes at Newmarket in May meant that he started second favourite at 7–2 for the Derby. Hastings could not afford to run The Earl in the Derby as he had backed him to lose too much money; indeed, his entire financial future depended on Lady Elizabeth winning. The Earl was therefore scratched the day before the Derby and ran instead in the Grand Prix de Paris on 7 June, when he beat the Prix du Jockey-Club winner, Suzerain, by a length. Admiral Rous was so furious about the late scratching of The Earl that he wrote a letter to *The Times* suggesting that Hastings had been made a dupe by Mr Padwick and his trainer John Day. It was true that most of his horses had been assigned to Padwick as security for a loan to meet pressing debts; in April, when he had beaten Blue Gown and walked over for the Newmarket Stakes on 1 May, The Earl had run in Padwick's name. Both Hastings and Padwick sent replies to the newspaper: Padwick stated that he had tried to dissuade the Marquess from scratching The Earl; Hastings said that 'The Earl was scratched by my express desire and authority, and no one either prompted me or suggested to me to adopt that course.' When John Day instituted legal proceedings against the Admiral, Rous formally withdrew the accusing letter, stating that on the day he wrote it, he sent a second letter to the editor of *The Times* asking him not to publish the first one.

When the 1868 Derby took place, Blue Gown beat King Alfred half a length, with Speculum third and Lady Elizabeth trailing in at the end of the field. Had The Earl been permitted to take his chance, it is more than likely that Queen Victoria would have seen a colt of her breeding win the Derby for the first time. On 10 June, only three days after his triumph in Paris, The Earl won the Ascot Derby Stakes; the next day he beat Suffolk, in the Biennial Stakes over a mile. On 12 June he rounded off a truly amazing six days by winning the St James's Palace Stakes. It is probable that such a string of victories in such important races in so short a time, which also included a journey to Paris and back, has never, before or since, been equalled. The Earl then retired to stud, but was not a success. Hastings, totally ruined, died of phthisis the following November at the age of twenty-six.

None of the other Royal yearlings sold at Hampton Court in 1866 achieved such eminence on the racecourse as The Earl, though Our Mary Ann (Voltigeur–Garnish) won the Chester Cup. Two of the fillies, Clemence (Newminster–Eulogy) and Thrift (Stockwell–Braxey) were to become illustrious broodmares. Thrift, whose dam, Braxey, was a half-sister to Blink Bonny, Blinkhoolie and Broomielaw, received a walk-over in the Glasgow Stakes at York in 1867, and was the dam of three winners in England, including the remarkable Tristan by Hermit and Pursebearer by Scottish Chief. Tristan won twenty-five races including both the Champion Stakes and Hardwicke Stakes for three consecutive years in 1882, 1883 and 1884, and the Ascot Gold Cup in 1883; Pursebearer won the Gimcrack Stakes. Tristan was also the sire of Lord Derby's brilliant Oaks winner Canterbury Pilgrim, who was the dam of Swynford, the winner of the 1910 St Leger and 1911 Eclipse Stakes; she was to become one of the most important foundation mares in Derby's stud. Thrift was exported to France in 1881, where she bore Thomery, who won the Prix Daru. She was the grandam of MacDonald, the winner of the Deutsches Derby and Grosser Hanser Preis in 1902. Clemence won four races and was the dam of five winners including Sandiway, the winner of the Coronation Stakes, Prendergast Stakes and Liverpool Cup. She was the grandam of the greatest Australian champion of the nineteenth century, Carbine, whose thirty-three victories in the Antipodes included the Melbourne Cup. Such was Carbine's reputation that the Duke of Portland bought him and brought him to stand as a stallion in England, where he sired the 1906 Epsom Derby and Grand Prix de Paris winner, Spearmint. Clemence was the grandam of the very useful French colt and stallion, Le Samaritain, and the 1893 Derby Italiano winner, Festuca.

Clemence's half-brother, Martyrdom by St Albans, was the most successful of the twenty-four yearlings bred by Queen Victoria and sold at Hampton Court on 1 June 1867. Bought by Captain Machell for Lord Calthorpe, Martyrdom won seven races, including the Prince of Wales's Stakes at Ascot when he beat Pero Gomez, who later beat him only a neck in the St Leger. Earlier that spring Martyrdom had finished fourth to Pretender in the 2,000 Guineas. Among the spectators at the sale that afternoon were the Prince of Wales, his friend Henry Chaplin, Lord Poulett and Captain Machell. Admiral Rous, after the acrimonious correspondence in *The Times* that morning about The Earl, did not put in an appearance, but the crowd was so large that, had they all stood around the ring, they would have been five or six deep. Captain Machell also bought Wamba (Orlando–Trickstress) for only 100 gns; the correspondent of the *Sporting Magazine*, who liked this yearling a lot, thought Machell had got him 'dirt cheap, for his compactness and quality made up for his lack of size'. Both proved right: Wamba won sixteen races.

The death of John Ransom, the Stud Groom at Hampton Court, on 11 December 1867, was ascribed to his having attended a sale at Danebury on a cold bitter day a short time before. He, possibly more than anyone, had been responsible for the Royal Stud's immense success since its re-establishment in 1850. In his period of stewardship four fillies sold at the annual sale were the most expensive yearling fillies ever bought at public auction: Queen's Head (1854), Hecate (1858), Yamuna (1862) and La Dauphine (1864); Ruthven in 1865 was the most expensive colt yearling. In a tribute to him in the *Sporting Magazine* in January 1868, the editor remarked that

Hampton Court will hardly look itself on a sale day without 'Old Ransome' on his pony, directing the parade. He had a courteous word and pleasant smile for all ... Never had a Sovereign such a model servant on the Turf ... A fine old man, proud of his Crown charges, and alway doing his duty. His pride when he heard any of the youngsters knocked down for a thousand and upwards was only exceeded when he saw them pass the post first. When he was 75 he paid his last visit to Doncaster to see The Duke (a great pet of his) run for the St Leger; and a nice sight it was, as the old man passed down the High Street, leaning on the arm of his youngest daughter. He always thought he would have outlived Orlando, and he watched with sorrow the bay's failing eyesight and muscle ... Whenever asked how the old horse was, his eye brightened up when he told how many foals he had had that season and how many were expected the next.

The death of the Royal Stud's best stallion, Orlando, shortly after that of its first Stud Groom marked the end of a period that had been crowned with great success, much credit for which was due to both the prepotent sire and the model stud groom. On 1 January 1868 Ransom's wife, Charlotte, was placed on the Queen's Bounty List for widows and received £40 per annum for life.

9

The Royal Stud at Hampton Court,

1868–94

The death of Prince Albert in December 1861 so shocked and distressed Queen Victoria that she almost withdrew from the world for the rest of her reign. The Queen, always dressed in black, led a life of virtual seclusion from society and she never set foot on a racecourse again. Fortunately this forty-year period of mourning did not mean that the Royal Stud at Hampton Court was disbanded.

The death of John Ransom in 1867 meant that a new Stud Groom had to be found for Hampton Court. The man selected was William Scott, the Stud Groom to the Duke of Newcastle at the Clumber Stud, Worksop. On 16 January 1868 Colonel Maude wrote Scott the following letter:

Sir,

It is perhaps rather premature to think that you have been selected for the vacant office of Stud Groom to the Queen at Bushy; but nevertheless I hope that after due enquiries have been made the appointment may be given to you.

My first business was to enquire whether the place suited you, and whether the Duke of Newcastle, your present employer, had any objection to your becoming a candidate for it.

On these two points I have got satisfactory answers, and I make no doubt that as far as the Duke is concerned, he will testify as to your ability and good conduct while in His Grace's service.

But it will be necessary before engaging you for the Queen's service that I should be made a little more acquainted with your antecedents, as the appointment does not rest with me, but with

Sir Thomas Biddulph, the Keeper of Her Majesty's Privy Purse, and I shall have to satisfy him that you are in every way qualified and fit for the post.

Pray therefore let me know the names of any noblemen or gentlemen, besides the Duke of Newcastle, to whom you can refer for a character.

I should like to know whether there is any chance of your being in London shortly, because there are many things which can be explained verbally which cannot be put in a letter.

It is probable also that Sir Thomas Biddulph may wish to see you, but do not come up without letting me know, as Sir Thomas is at present at the Isle of Wight with the Queen, and I might be out of town too, if you come by chance.

Yours truly,
G. A. Maude
(Crown Equerry).[1]

On 30 January 1868 Colonel Maude wrote again to William Scott:

My dear Sir,

I have heard from Sir Thomas Biddulph and he approves of my engaging you as Stud Groom to Her Majesty at Hampton Court at the salary and emoluments which I mentioned in a former letter but which I think it better to recapitulate, viz: Salary, £200 per annum. Fees on mares sent to stallions by private individuals say £60. Coals and candles, soap and linen or an allowance in lieu thereof. Keep for a pony and a cow and the house partially furnished.

Should it be convenient to the Duke of Newcastle that you come up as proposed on the 12th February, we shall give you an allowance for lodging as Mrs Ransom will not turn out of the house before the end of February.

Yours truly,
G. A. Maude.[2]

William Scott was to remain in charge of the Royal Stud until he retired on 11 February 1878.

The ten years of William Scott's tenure as Stud Groom at Hampton Court were not as successful as the period of his predecessor. Twenty-nine Royal yearlings were sold at Hampton Court on 6 June 1868. The Baron (King Tom–Bay Celia), who cost Mr John Day 1,350 gns, was the most expensive yearling sold at public auction in 1868, but he never raced. Mr Sherwood bought Temple (Orlando–Lady Palmerston); he was ridden by Richard Marsh when he won the New Stakes at Ascot, the sole noteworthy race won by any of the 1867 crop, fourteen of whom won seventy-five races. The most prolific was Lincoln (Ely–Orlando Mare), who won twenty-eight events in seven seasons' racing. There were no notable performers among the twenty-seven Royal yearlings sold at Hampton Court on 5 June 1869; of these, eight won just eighteen races. Only nine winners of thirty races emerged from the 1869 crop of twenty-four yearlings; Sir Amyas (Trumpeter–Ayacanora), who was bought by Lord Anglesey for 950 gns, turned out to be the best, winning the July Stakes at Newmarket after an initial success in the Troy Stakes at Stockbridge; but then injury ended his career. The twenty-three yearlings sold at Hampton Court on 3 June 1871 did not include any high-class performers, but twelve of them won eighty-seven races. The two principal contributors to this large total of races won were Templar (Adventurer–Lady Palmerston), bought by Mr J. Barnard for 150 gns, and Middle Temple (Lord Clifden–Lady Gough). Templar ran 166 times between 1872 and 1882 and won thirty-five minor races; his two best performances were in 1872 when he was runner-up in both the New Stakes at Ascot and the Woodcote Stakes at Epsom, but most of his victories were in selling events. Middle Temple won twenty-four flat races between 1872 and 1879, when he was killed on 29 November in a hurdle race at Kempton Park. The best of the 1870 crop, Cambuslang (Cambuscan–Hepatica), won two races, the Manchester Tradesmen's Cup and the Northumberland Autumn Plate at Newcastle and he was second in the Goodwood Stakes. He was to become a minor sire, and it is interesting to note that, when the Prince of Wales founded the Sandringham Stud in 1886, Cambuslang stood there for two seasons. The highest-priced yearling of the 1871 Hampton Court sale, Bushranger (Young Melbourne–Orlando Mare), never ran on the flat, but as a five-year-old was a faller when second favourite for the 1875 Grand National won by Pathfinder. Again, the twenty-eight Royal year-lings sold at Hampton Court on 8 June 1872 were nothing out of the ordinary, only nine being winners of fifty-six races. The best, Mr Winkle (St Albans–Peri), won nineteen sprint races and became a useful sire of sprinters. The most expensive, Kidbrooke (Young Melbourne–Orlando Mare), won eleven times and was runner-up in the Woodcote Stakes and New Stakes as a juvenile. Only five of the twenty-three yearlings sold by Queen Victoria in 1872 were winners of a paltry sixteen races; the most expensive, Inglemere (Young Melbourne–Orlando Mare), only won three small handicaps at Pontefract and Newmarket.

Much of the lack of success of the yearlings bred at the Royal Stud at Hampton Court during this period was due to the absence of a really high-class stallion such as Orlando had been. Although St Albans was to get Springfield in 1873, he never produced quality foals with the same consistency as the 1844 Derby winner. Of the other three stallions at Hampton Court, Trumpeter seldom got a foal better than a handicapper; Mentmore had only been a moderate racehorse and was a worse sire; and Young Melbourne had neither won a single race nor inherited the qualities of his sire as a stallion. Ely, who had stood at Hampton Court in the late 1860s, had also turned out to be a failure as a sire.

The year 1873 saw a brief revival of the Royal Stud's fortunes, for that year's crop threw up two really high-class horses: Springfield (St Albans–Viridis) and Julius Caesar (St Albans–Julie). These two colts were among the twenty-one yearlings bred by Queen Victoria in the 1874 sale. Julius Caesar cost Captain Machell the very large sum of 1,600 gns, nearly half of the sale's receipts. He won the Westminster Stakes at Epsom from five outings as a juvenile. On 2 May 1876 Julius Caesar ran second to Petrarch in the 2,000 Guineas, and four weeks later was third to Kisber and Forerunner in the Derby. He again took the minor honours behind Petrarch and Wild Tommy in the St Leger on 13 September. Although he never won as a three-year-old, by being placed in all the Classics open to him, Julius Caesar had proved himself to be a top-class colt. Overdue success came to him when he ran out a six-length winner of the City and Suburban Handicap at Epsom on 24 April 1877, giving 24 lbs to Touchet, who was to win the Lincolnshire Handicap and finish third to Isonomy in the Ascot Gold Cup two years later. Julius Caesar won eight races as a five-year-old, his victory in the Royal Hunt Cup being arguably the finest of his career: carrying top weight he gave Belphoebe 8 lbs and a three-length thrashing. Belphoebe's victories the previous season had included the 1,000 Guineas and Coronation Stakes, and she had been runner-up to Placida in the Oaks; in 1878 she won the Manchester November Handicap under top weight and the Liverpool Autumn Cup. Julius Caesar retired to stud in 1879, but had only very limited success as a stallion.

Springfield was bought by Mr J. H. Houldsworth, and was to prove even more valuable than Julius Caesar. As a juvenile he won three of his five races, including the Gimcrack Stakes, and was second in the other two, the Criterion Stakes and the Dewhurst Plate. In 1876 he was unbeaten in all his nine starts, winning the July Cup by twelve lengths from Crann Tair, later bought for the Royal Stud as a broodmare by Colonel Maude, and the Stockbridge Cup over six furlongs by three lengths from Lowlander. Some idea of the quality of Springfield's victory over Lowlander can be seen from the latter's previous record: he had won the same race by twelve lengths and the Royal Hunt Cup in 1875, and in 1876 his six victories included the Queen's Stand Plate at Ascot, the Lennox Stakes at Goodwood and the FitzWilliam Stakes at Doncaster. He was generally judged to be the best sprinter in England for two seasons before he met Springfield. Mr Houldsworth's champion remained unbeaten in 1877, extending his sequence to fourteen consecutive victories. He began his four-year-old career by slamming the very useful Ecossais by four lengths in the Queen's Stand Plate, and two days later took the New Biennial Stakes over a mile. He then won the July Cup for the second consecutive year. Springfield's greatest triumph came in the Champion Stakes at Newmarket, where he was opposed by Silvio. Silvio had won the Derby, St Leger and Ascot Derby before meeting Springfield, and he had been third to Chamant in the 2,000 Guineas. When he beat the champion three-year-old by a length at Newmarket, Springfield proved himself to be an outstanding racehorse with excellent prospects of becoming a great sire. His final victory was in the All-Aged Stakes at Newmarket on 26 October, when he trounced Ecossais by fifteen lengths. Ecossais won twenty-four races in his career including the July Stakes and Chesterfield Stakes as a juvenile, and he had run third to Atlantic in the 1874 2,000 Guineas. Springfield was responsible for many of the winners bred by Queen Victoria at Hampton Court after he retired to stud in 1878. He became champion sire in 1890 when his son, Sainfoin, became the first colt bred by Her Majesty to win the Epsom Derby. Earlier, Springfield had sired Briar Root, the winner of the 1888 1,000 Guineas and Yorkshire Oaks.

Unfortunately, Springfield and Julius Caesar could arrest the decline of the Royal Stud at Hampton Court only temporarily. Only fourteen yearlings were offered for sale on 5 June 1875, plus three two-year-olds and one six-year-old. This crop produced only two winners of five races, the worst record for the Royal Stud since 1850. In an attempt to improve the situation two new stallions were brought to stand at Hampton Court in 1875: Prince Charlie

(Blair Athol–Eastern Princess), who had won twenty-five races in four seasons, including the 1872 2,000 Guineas, the Middle Park Plate and the Criterion Stakes, and had also been second in the St Leger to Cremorne; and Pell Mell (Young Melbourne–Makeshift), who only ever ran twice, and without success, in 1872. Nevertheless, on one of these outings, he finished runner-up to Cremorne in the Derby. Regrettably, neither of these two horses was to make the grade as a sire.

These poor results must have cast doubts in the mind of Queen Victoria concerning the viability of the Royal Stud, for any loss had to be borne out of her own money. It was possibly to allay those doubts that the Master of the Horse reported to Her Majesty on 14 March 1876 that in the twenty-four years since the re-establishment of the Stud at Bushey Park, 'Your Majesty was a gainer of more than £24,000 or about £1,000 a year.'[3] He further added that there was a loss of £1,414 for 1874 and that the accounts for 1875 had not yet been made up.

The results of the sale of the Queen's fifteen yearlings put up on 10 June 1876 were even more disappointing than those of the previous year. The highest-priced foal, Alfred the Good (Mentmore–Doralice), only won five minor races; the total realized was a measly 1,480 gns. Only one of this crop, the sprinter Financier (Mentmore–Lady Ann) was of any note, winning ten small races. The 1876 crop sold for much better prices on 23 June 1877; these fourteen yearlings made 4,230 gns. This improvement was not reflected, however, in their racecourse performances; only five were winnners, and took no more than eleven races. Two, none the less, became useful broodmares. Blue Mountain (Young Melbourne–Gunga Jee) won the Great Whiteley Stakes at Worcester in 1878 and was exported to Germany in 1884, where she produced Hardenberg by Kisber, who won the 1893 Deutsches Derby and Grosser Preis von Berlin. Albania (St Albans–Lady of the Manor) was sent to France in 1881 after running twice unplaced; she bore Le Hardy by St Louis, who won the Poule d'Essai des Poulains in 1891, and was grandam of the Prix du Conseil Municipal winner, Luzerne by Simonian.

The eighteen Royal yearlings sold at Hampton Court on 29 June 1878 included Wokingham (St Albans–Viridis). He was bought by Mr Robert Jardine for 2,200 gns, which made him the second most expensive yearling sold at public auction that year. Although he only won three races, two of those successes were gained in the Wokingham Stakes, appropriately enough, in consecutive years,

1881 and 1882. There were, however, only six winners of seventeen races from the 1877 crop. In the summer of 1878 both Prince Charlie and Pell Mell left Hampton Court. On 24 July that year Colonel Maude wrote to Mr H. Jones the following letter:

Dear Sir,
Now that the covering season is over and we shall not require Prince Charlie for another season at Her Majesty's Stud, I shall be much obliged if you will find another home for him and remove him at your convenience. I have every confidence that the horse will get racehorses but the Public have not faith in him, and although his stock are very good looking, buyers are loth to invest in them.
Yours truly,
G. A. Maude.[4]

On the same day he wrote a similar letter to Mr J. M. Astley:

Dear Sir,
Now that the covering season is over and we shall no longer require the services of Pell Mell, we shall be glad if you will remove him at your convenience. The Horse is looking very well and is in excellent health and covers the mares capitally, but his stock are not taking to look at at present.
Yours truly,
G. A. Maude.[5]

For the 1879 covering season the following stallions stood at Hampton Court: Springfield, at 100 gns a mare, the winner of the 2,000 Guineas and St Leger in 1876 and Ascot Gold Cup in 1877; Petrarch (Lord Clifden–Laura), at a fee of 100 gns; Winslow (Lord Clifden–Creslow), who had been bought by Colonel Maude for the Stud in 1874, at 30 gns a mare; and General Peel (Young Melbourne–Orlando Mare 1853), the winner of the 1864 2,000 Guineas and Doncaster Cup, and runner-up to Blair Athol in the Derby and St Leger, at 25 gns a mare. Neither of the latter two was to improve the quality of the foals bred by Queen Victoria. In retrospect, the purchase of Winslow for more than 2,000 gns was an error of judgement by Colonel Maude.

In the late 1870s and early 1880s Colonel Maude bought several broodmares to improve and replenish those at Hampton Court; he obtained Croisade (Monarque–Vivid), in a private transaction in July 1878. Two years earlier he had acquired Wallflower (Rata-plan–Chaperon) from Mr T. Lant, who himself had bought her for only 55 gns in May 1874. Her foal in 1876, Eye-pleaser by Brown Bread, the last of the two bred by Lant, was to become the third dam of the great racemare and broodmare, Pretty Polly, whose twenty-two victories included the 1,000 Guineas, Oaks and St Leger in 1904. Many still regard her as one of the best fillies to have raced this century. Had Colonel Maude bought Wallflower but a few months earlier, Pretty Polly's third dam Eye-pleaser would have been born at Hampton Court. On 21 June 1879 Colonel Maude paid 410 gns for General Peel's eight-year-old mare Quiver (Toxophilite–Young Melbourne mare); she was to become exceptionally important in restoring the fortunes of the Royal Stud and worth a hundred times the sum given for her; certainly she was a much better buy than Modena (Parmesan–Arch-eress), who had cost the Royal Stud 800 gns at Newmarket about three weeks earlier. Some of the Royal Stud's yearling fillies in the 1870s were only leased at the Hampton Court Sale for their racing careers, after which they were to return to the paddocks at Bushey Park. One of these, Simplex (Young Melbourne–Ayacanora), was bought by Mr R. H. Long at the 1874 Hampton Court sale and put into training with Joseph Dawson at Newmarket. She never ran, and it seems she was spirited off to the Emerald Isle. Colonel Maude's two letters to Long on 1 and 28 February went un-answered, so one was sent to Dawson and another to Michael Hartigan, who had conducted a sale of some of Long's bloodstock at Limerick in the autumn of 1876.[6] Mr Long was employed by the Irish Turf Club as a handicapper, and on 18 June 1877, Simplex's whereabouts still not having been ascertained, Colonel Maude let the Stewards know that legal proceedings for the recovery of the filly were being instituted against one of their em-ployees, 'in case he may have any explanation to offer'.[7] Eventually Simplex was returned to Hampton Court. The outcome of this episode for Long himself is unclear, but at the Hampton Court sale in 1879 he bought a filly by Lord Gough out of Simplex named Miss Gough for 40 gns, who was exported to Buenos Aires in 1882.

By 1878 the increased number of mares at Hampton Court was causing problems for Colonel Maude, as the following letter to N. M. Mitford at the Office of Works, Whitehall Palace, demon-strates:

My dear Mitford,

We are very much pressed for room for our foaling mares in the paddocks at Hampton Court this spring. As they must be taken in to shelter if rain comes on, we cannot turn them out in the Park as it is so large that we cannot easily catch them.

We want therefore to hurdle off the three cornered piece of the Park between the Stud House, the Canal and the Paddock Wall ... Will you be good enough to let me hear whether the first commissioners have any objections. It would only be temporary and the hurdles could be removed in the autumn.

Yours truly,

G. A. Maude.[8]

These efforts to restore the fortunes of the Royal Stud of course did not have an immediate effect, though they were to bear fruit in the 1880s. The sale of twenty-five yearlings at Hampton Court on 21 June 1879 yielded only six winners of seventeen races. Voluptuary (Cremorne–Miss Evelyn) turned out to be the most successful, winning four races on the flat including the Dee Stakes at Chester. His chief claim to fame rests with his victory in the Grand National at Aintree at the age of six in 1884, though few people would associate Queen Victoria with being the breeder of a winner of the world's greatest steeplechase. One of the fillies bred at Hampton Court in 1878, Rose Garden (Kingcraft–Eglentyne), was to become an influential broodmare; she was bought by Sir J. Kelk in 1879 but was unraced: her six foals included two winners, Dornroschen by Prism and Gloire de Dijon by Galopin, who won the Zunfunfts Rennen at Baden-Baden, and the unraced Castania by Hagoiscope, the dam of Vahren by Bona Vista, who won three races, at Pontefract twice over nine furlongs and at Manchester over eleven furlongs. Vahren was mated with Roi Herode in 1910; the grey colt to whom she gave birth in 1911, The Tetrarch, was probably one of the greatest two-year-olds ever to race. He was unbeaten in seven outings, winning the Woodcote Stakes, Coventry Stakes, National Breeders' Stakes, Champagne Stakes (Doncaster), Rous Memorial Stakes (Goodwood), Champion Foal Stakes (Derby) and a maiden race at Newmarket. Injury prevented him being trained as a three-year-old unfortunately. In the opinion of Richard Marsh, trainer to King Edward VII and King George V, The Tetrarch was 'a phenomenal horse ... I never saw a two-year-old win race after race with such ease.' He was anything but a prolific sire, but his daughter Mumtaz Mahal, out of the

Sundridge mare, Lady Josephine, ensured that his speed was transmitted to future generations. Bought by the Hon. George Lambton on behalf of the Aga Khan for the then record sum of 9,100 gns at Doncaster on 14 September 1922, Mumtaz Mahal was the fastest juvenile seen since her sire, showing dazzling speed in her five victories which included the Champagne Stakes, Queen Mary Stakes, National Breeders' Stakes and Molecomb Stakes. The following year she won the Nunthorpe Stakes and King George V Stakes at Goodwood. Mumtaz Mahal became one of the cornerstones of the Aga Khan's Sheshoon Stud at the Curragh. She bred Mah Mahal, the dam of Mahmoud and Migoli, Rustom Mahal, the dam of Abernant, Mumtaz Begum, the dam of Nasrullah, and the useful colt Mirza II. It is noteworthy that her broodmare sire Sundridge was out of another mare bred by Queen Victoria at Hampton Court, Sierra by Springfield. Tetrametra, the winner of the 1920 2,000 Guineas and champion sprinter, was probably The Tetrarch's most influential son.

Twenty-five yearlings bred by Queen Victoria were sold at Hampton Court on 19 June 1880; one, Nimble (Blair Athol or Prince Charlie–Miss Foote) won thirteen minor races; seven others won another sixteen contests. On balance, however, this crop was again disappointing. The Royal Stud put thirty-one yearlings up for sale at Hampton Court on 25 June 1881; the best colt, Deceiver (Wenlock–Boot and Saddle), ran third to Galliard, the 1883 2,000 Guineas winner, in the Chesterfield Stakes as a two-year-old, and was runner-up to the same horse in the St James's Palace Stakes. Although he only won one race, that victory came in the newly instituted and short-lived Epsom Grand Prize. This race over one and a quarter miles, open only to three-year-olds and worth £3,837 to the winner, was run on the day after the Derby. When the Eclipse Stakes was founded in 1886, it lost its importance and was discontinued. Ossian, later to win the St Leger and Sussex Stakes, could only finish a bad third to Deceiver at Epsom that afternoon. Distant Shore (Hermit–Land's End) was sold at the same sale, and she was destined to have a much greater influence on the Stud Book than Deceiver. Although she only ever won once, a maiden plate as a juvenile over five furlongs at Alexandra Park, she became an enormously influential broodmare. Six of her eleven foals were winners, including Gulliver and St Damien, both of whom won the Hardwicke Stakes, in 1889 and 1892 respectively. It was Distant Shore's 1887 foal, Arcadia by Isonomy, who was to become the most significant. The winner of two races, including the Royal

Plate at Windsor as a two-year-old, Arcadia was the dam of Cyllene by Bona Vista. Without question Cyllene was the best three-year-old of 1898, a fact acknowledged by Richard Marsh, the trainer of the Derby winner Jeddah, but he was unfortunately never entered in the Derby. Cyllene had won four of his five races as a juvenile, including the National Breeders' Stakes, and was only narrowly beaten in the Imperial Produce Stakes when conceding 10 lb to Dieudonne. In 1898 he slaughtered his opponents by four lengths in the Newmarket Stakes and won the Jockey Club Stakes and Sandown Foal Stakes. The next season his victory in the Ascot Gold Cup confirmed him as the best colt of his generation. At stud Cyllene was an outstanding success, becoming the sire of four Derby winners – Cicero, Minoru, Lemberg and Tagalie – between 1905 and 1912. His most influential son, however, was the 1905 St Leger runner-up Polymelus, who won ten races including the Princess of Wales's Stakes, Champion Stakes, Cambridgeshire Stakes and Duke of York Stakes in 1906, as well as the 1904 Criterion Stakes. Polymelus was champion sire in 1914, 1915, 1916, 1920 and 1921; in 1917 and 1918 he was second and in 1919 third on the stallion list. He got the Triple Crown victor, Pommern (1915), two other Derby winners, Fifinella (1916), who also won the Oaks, and Humorist (1921), the 1914 St Leger winner, Black Jester, and the 1,000 Guineas victress, Cinna (1920). It was his son Phalaris, who between 1915 and 1918 won fifteen races, including two runnings of the Challenge Stakes, who was to become his most significant stallion, as he sired both Pharos and Fairway, whose enormous worldwide influence need not be re-stated.

In 1881 Clanronald, who had won two races as a two-year-old, including the 1875 Criterion Stakes, came to stand at Hampton Court. He had never raced since that win, so it was rather a surprising choice of stallion. Twenty-eight yearlings were sold at Hampton Court on 17 June 1882. Although eleven won forty-five races, and two, Monotony (See-Saw–Orchestra) and Bagpipe (Strathconan–Crann Tair), both won eleven times, none was top-class. Twenty-nine yearlings were sold by the Royal Stud at Hampton Court on 16 June 1883. The Duke of Portland, encouraged by the initial success of his juvenile St Simon, whom he had bought the previous year for 1,600 gns at the dispersal sale of Prince Battyhany's horses, instructed his trainer, Mat Dawson, to buy him some yearlings at Hampton Court. On his return from the sale, Dawson told Portland, 'I have bought you three yearlings, and you can have them or not, as you like.' Portland said that he would take them without seeing them, such was his confidence in Dawson's judgement. The first, and the most expensive of the sale at 1,150 gns, Langwell (Springfield–Furiosa), turned out to be a very good two-year-old, winning both the Champagne Stakes at Doncaster and the Clearwell Stakes at Newmarket, but he did not train on and only won one other race, a lowly selling plate at Lincoln as a six-year-old. The second, Hurry (Pell Mell–Miss Mary), won six races, including the Park Hill Stakes and the Drawing Room Stakes over ten furlongs at Goodwood when she beat St Helena, the runner-up to Lonely in the Oaks and winner of the Coronation Stakes and Yorkshire Oaks. The third, Satchel (Galopin–Quiver), won the Lavant Stakes in 1884, and the next spring ran third to Farewell in the 1,000 Guineas. She also won the Racing Stakes at Goodwood and the Molyneux Cup at Liverpool in 1885. At stud Satchel was the dam of four winners including The Prize by Bend Or, who won the 1892 Champagne Stakes; she was also the fourth dam of Haintonette, the 1928 Irish Oaks heroine. There were twelve winners of forty races from the 1882 crop of Hampton Court yearlings; one maiden, a filly by Galopin out of Miss Foote, was to turn out to be a very useful broodmare. Unplaced on her only appearance on the racecourse in the Acorn Stakes at Epsom in 1884, her first foal was Surefoot by Wisdom, who won three of his four outings as a juvenile including the New Stakes at Ascot and the Woodcote Stakes at Epsom. In 1890 Surefoot won the 2,000 Guineas and started odds-on favourite for the Derby. An ill-tempered colt, he was so upset before the race that he could only finish fourth to Sainfoin. He won a Biennial at Ascot; two weeks later, he beat the Oaks winner Memoir by two lengths in The Prince of Wales's Stakes over a mile at Leicester. This short-lived race was worth the immense sum of £7,750 to the winner. Surefoot's temperament then got the better of him and he ran badly in the St Leger. On the death of his trainer Jousiffe in the spring of 1891, Surefoot was trained by Garrett Moore. His first appearance as a four-year-old was in the Eclipse Stakes, where he was opposed by Memoir and the first two in the Derby, Common and Gouverneur, who had won the Grand Poule des Produits in May. In the paddock Surefoot seemed so calm and relaxed that Lord Marcus Beresford asked Garrett Moore how he had managed to accomplish this transformation. Moore replied, 'Well, one of us had to be master, and it was not going to be Surefoot.' In the race Surefoot produced the best form he ever showed, stormed past

Common and Gouverneur and won easily by a length. Common went on to win the Triple Crown when he took the St Leger in September; Surefoot was exported to France as a stallion.

Ten of the twenty-seven Royal yearlings sold at Hampton Court on 21 June 1884 were winners of thirty-six races; the best of this rather moderate crop was St Michael (Springfield–Eglentyne). The winner of seven races including the Ebor St Leger, St Michael was runner-up in both the Goodwood and Doncaster Cups and fourth in both the St Leger, to Ormonde, and the following year's Ascot Gold Cup. Twenty-two Royal yearlings were sold at Hampton Court on 27 June 1885; only five were winners of seventeen races. Seven of these were won by St Michael's full-brother, Woodland, including the 1887 Electric Stakes, then a prestigious and valuable sprint over five furlongs at Sandown.

Douglas Baird bought the full-sister to Woodland and St Michael, Briar Root, for 800 gns at the Hampton Court sale on 19 June 1886, when twenty-five yearlings bred by Queen Victoria were sold. Briar Root, who, like Woodland, was the highest-priced yearling of the sale, won once as a juvenile, beating Caerlaverock and Ayrshire a head and a neck in the Whitsuntide Plate over five furlongs at Manchester, at £5,000 to the winner another valuable and prestigious but short-lived race. That was form of the highest class, as the Duke of Portland's Ayrshire won the Derby and the 2,000 Guineas the following season. In the 1,000 Guineas Briar Root defeated Lord Calthorpe's Sea Breeze; she started 5–4 favourite for the Oaks, but was beaten into fifth place by Lord Calthorpe's filly. Sea Breeze later won the St Leger, in which Ayrshire was unplaced, and a week afterwards beat Ayrshire and the good French horse Le Sancy in the Lancashire Plate, worth £10,223 to the winner, over ten furlongs at Manchester. Several very valuable but short-lived races were founded around this time, all offering more prize-money than the Classics. Sea Breeze had only earned £2,950 for her Oaks victory and £4,350 for that in the St Leger; Ayrshire, who received £3,550 in the 2,000 Guineas and £3,680 in the Derby, won £11,165 for his victory in the Eclipse Stakes in 1889. The Eclipse was the only valuable race instituted in the 1880s that was to become a permanent fixture in the *Racing Calendar*. Briar Root won one more race for Douglas Baird, the Yorkshire Oaks, before she was retired to the paddocks. She was the dam of six winners and the grandam of Prunus by Dark Ronald, who won the 1918 Henckel Rennen and Deutsches St Leger. The 1922 Dewhurst Stakes winner, Hurry Off, also traced back to Briar

Root. Her victory in the 1,000 Guineas marked the re-emergence of the Hampton Court Stud as a major influence on the Stud Book. Apart from her, the 1885 crop of Royal yearlings was disappointing, producing only seven winners of fifteen races.

In February 1887 Colonel Maude received a request from an Austrian, Lieutenant Grafsmann, who wanted to write an article on the Royal Stud at Hampton Court for an Encyclopaedia to be published in Vienna.[9] A rough draft of Maude's answers to Grafsmann is in the Royal Archives at Windsor Castle, and it provides an interesting account of the Stud in 1887. Colonel Maude states that the stud is

> about 75 acres, all pasture, good loam soil on gravel subsoil, with a south aspect. There are 26 paddocks containing 96 loose boxes for mares and foals, and 6 loose boxes and yards for stallions; a house for the Stud Groom and cottages for some helpers. The average number of foals born yearly is about thirty. In summer the mares and foals run in the Paddocks during the day and are shut up at night in the Boxes; they are fed three times a day upon oats, bran and hay. In winter they go out in favourable weather and are fed the same as in summer but with a larger quantity of bran. The stallions are always kept in the boxes and yards but are exercised in the Paddock for a certain time during the day. All the mares are not served by the stallions standing in the paddocks, but some are sent to different studs to be served by other stallions. Lean oxen are purchased annually and fed and fatted in the paddocks. They are generally kept a year, and then sold to butchers. These bring in a profit and also improve the pasture.[10]

Colonel Maude also says that he manages the stud and that he is assisted by the Stud Groom and nine helpers, though in the summer it is necessary to employ extra assistance. He further tells Grafsmann that 'the State Cream and Black Horses are bred at Hampton Court. There are 5 Cream mares and 5 Black mares. The stallions are sent down from the Queen's stables in London to cover the mares. The breed of the Cream Horses is Hanoverian and that of the Blacks Mecklenburg.'[11] Colonel Maude also informed the Austrian lieutenant that the Stud had belonged to Her Majesty Queen Victoria since the year 1849, but that it had been carried on for many years previously on a smaller scale by the preceding Sovereign or other member of the Royal Family.

Douglas Baird paid 1,050 gns for Briar Root's half-brother, Roslin by Rosicrucian, at the 1887 Hampton Court sale on 18 June. Roslin was extremely disappointing, winning one minor five-furlong event at Hamilton from twenty-one outings in 1888 and 1889. Of the twenty-eight yearlings sold, a mere seven were winners of twelve races. Mr F. Lawson bought Maid Marian (Hampton–Quiver) that afternoon, but all she could manage on the racecourse was two seconds at Epsom and Manchester and a third at Scarborough as a juvenile. Few would have considered her as potentially one of the most influential broodmares bred by Queen Victoria when she was claimed after running unplaced in her last race, the Bury Selling Plate over five furlongs at Manchester on 21 September 1888. Eventually she found her way into the stud of Lord Crewe, but only three of her first nine foals were winners, though one, Ercildoune by Kendal, was good enough to win the Duke of York Stakes at Kempton in 1899. Maid Marian's 1902 foal, however, was Polymelus by Cyllene, one of the most influential sires of the century, through his son Phalaris, his two grandsons, Pharos and Fairway, and his great-grandsons Nearco, Pharis, Fair Trial and Blue Peter. There is insufficient space here to list all the great stallions and champions who trace back to Polymelus in the male line; Nasrullah, Bold Ruler, Northern Dancer, Nijinsky, Never Bend, Mill Reef, Secretariat, Blushing Groom, Shirley Heights and Nashwan are merely a few who spring immediately to mind. Perhaps the most remarkable thing about Polymelus's pedigree, as far as the Royal Stud at Hampton Court is concerned, is that not merely his dam, but also the grandam of his sire Cyllene, Distant Shore, was bred by Queen Victoria.

The revived fortunes of the Royal Stud at Hampton Court pushed up the prices obtained for the twenty-five yearlings who came under the hammer on 23 June 1888 to a level much higher than the previous year's; they made 11,835 gns, an average of 473 gns, which exceeded the previous best average obtained by the Royal yearlings of 443 gns in 1854. John Porter recalled that

> before the sale began I wandered around and examined the lots that were to come under the hammer. I was particularly struck by a chestnut colt by Springfield out of Sanda. Later I met Sir Robert Jardine, who asked if I had seen anything that I liked. 'Yes,' I replied, 'I have seen a little chestnut by Springfield I am rather fond of.' Sir Robert suggested we should go and look at him together, and when he had seen the colt said he would buy

him. This pronouncement rather took the wind out of my sails. I explained that I had intended buying the colt myself. 'Then we will have him between us,' said Sir Robert, 'and you shall take him to Kingsclere to train.' In due course the colt went into the ring, and I was able to buy him for 550 guineas. We called him Sainfoin. When fully grown he did not measure more than 15.2. He was, however, very cleverly made, and blessed with a most amiable disposition.

Sainfoin won his sole race as a juvenile, the Astley Stakes over five furlongs at Lewes in August 1889, and the next year made his reappearance on 25 April in the mile Esher Stakes Handicap at Sandown, which he won in a canter by four lengths. His victory so impressed Sir John Miller, then a subaltern in the 14th Hussars, that he went to Kingsclere to see if he could buy Sainfoin. Sir Robert Jardine left the decision to his partner in the colt; John Porter came to the conclusion that Sainfoin would not beat Archibald Merry's 2,000 Guineas winner, Surefoot. It was arranged that Sir John Miller should pay £6,000 for Sainfoin, plus half the Derby Stakes if he won the race. John Porter recalled that 'when the deal was completed Sir Robert Jardine expressed himself perfectly satisfied, and at the time I certainly thought we had got the best end of the bargain. Events proved that we had not.'

Sainfoin remained with Porter till the following September, and on 8 May easily beat his solitary opponent in the Dee Stakes at Chester. The weather on the day of the Derby, 4 June, was appalling; it never stopped raining and was really pouring during the race itself, for which only eight runners went to post, so certain was everyone that Surefoot was already past the post. Sainfoin, second at Tattenham Corner, took the lead shortly before the furlong post and withstood the late challenge of the 2,000 Guineas runner-up, Le Nord, with Orwell, also trained by Porter, and Surefoot, a neck and a head back in third and fourth. It was generally felt that Surefoot had failed through lack of stamina, though his evil temperament may also have contributed to his downfall. Sainfoin next ran second in the Hardwicke Stakes at Ascot, where he ran the four-year-old Amphion to a length with Surefoot another four lengths back in third. In the St Leger the Derby winner could only manage fourth place to Memoir, who was also bred by Queen Victoria. He then left Kingsclere to be trained at Newmarket and ran unplaced to St Serf in the Free Handicap over ten furlongs there on 23 October. He only ran twice as a four-year-old in October 1891, finishing unplaced over six furlongs at Newmarket and third in a mile handicap at Hurst Park. At stud Sainfoin was not a tremendous success, though he did sire the 1903 Triple Crown winner Rock Sand. On Sir John Miller's death in 1906, Sainfoin was sold to Lord Carnarvon for 700 gns and stood for four years at the Cloghran Stud near Dublin; he then passed into the hands of Messrs Slocock for a small sum and died in Carlow in 1911. Rock Sand, his best son, was bought by Mr August Belmont of New York in 1906 for £25,000. After some years in the USA he was acquired by a French syndicate of breeders and died in France in 1914. Not merely was he the sire of Tracery, the St Leger and Eclipse winner in 1909, the 1916 Belmont Stakes winner, Friar Rock, and 1912 Prix de Diane heroine Qu'elle est Belle, he was also to become an enormously successful broodmare sire. It was his filly Mahubah who in 1917 produced a chestnut colt named Man O'War, one of the greatest American horses this century and leading sire in 1926. Other notable horses out of Rock Sand mares included Chatterton, who became leading sire in the USA in 1932, and My Play and Mad Hatter, both winners of the Jockey Club Cup.

Thus, although Sainfoin might not rank among the truly great horses to have won the Derby, he was not without influence on the Stud Book, especially in the USA through Rock Sand. He also has the distinction of being the only Derby winner to have been bred by the reigning Sovereign. He was not, however, the only Classic winner sold at Hampton Court in 1888; Memoir (St Simon–Quiver), went to the Duke of Portland for 1,500 gns. Immediately after the sale Portland invited some friends to see her in her box, and one of these wise judges said, 'She is a very nice filly, but no one will ever be able to train her as she has ring bones.' Mat Dawson, who was standing nearby, heard this remark, and, after the friends had left, said to the Duke, 'I have never heard a man talk such nonsense; she has no more got ring bones than he has himself. Yearlings often seem to have bony enlargements on their pasterns; they come from galloping about on the hard ground and disappear when they go into training.' Although she won the last three of her six races as a juvenile, including the Prendergast Stakes at Newmarket, Memoir was totally overshadowed in 1889 by her owner's brilliant but small Semolina. A half-sister by St Simon to the 1889 Derby and St Leger winner, Donovan, Semolina won thirteen of her fifteen races, including the Brocklesby Stakes at Lincoln in March, the Prince of Wales Stakes at Goodwood and a brilliant victory by a head over Surefoot at Ascot. After winning a trial on 12 April from Memoir and St Serf, Semolina, declared to win by Portland, started 2–1 on favourite for the 1,000 Guineas. She won; but only managed to beat Memoir by three quarters of a length. Memoir then won the Newmarket Stakes from the very useful colts Blue-green and Le Nord. It was by now clear to Portland that Memoir was the better prospect for the Oaks, in which both his fillies were opposed by Chevalier Ginistrelli's unbeaten Signorina, whose nine victories as a two-year-old had included the Middle Park Stakes and a length defeat of Memoir in the Harrington Stakes at Derby. Portland regarded Signorina 'as one of the best two-year-olds I have ever seen or known'. Since it was felt that Signorina might not be totally fit, it was decided that Semolina should make the strongest possible running at Epsom. Memoir was thus enabled to wait on Ginistrelli's filly and beat her two lengths with the trail-blazer Semolina back in fourth place. The Royal Stud had therefore achieved the remarkable double of breeding the winners of both the Derby and Oaks. Memoir lost no credit a month later when runner-up to Surefoot in the Prince of Wales's Stakes at Leicester, for a mile was patently too short a trip for her against an opponent who had won the 2,000 Guineas. An easy victory in the Nassau Stakes at Goodwood against lesser opposition preceded her second Classic triumph in the St Leger, when she beat Blue-green two lengths with Sainfoin three lengths away fourth and Surefoot unplaced. In her final two races in 1890, Memoir ran unplaced to Amphion in the Lancashire Plate at Manchester and second to the same horse in the Champion Stakes at Newmarket. Amphion was indubitably the best four-year-old in training and was to become a successful sire.

Memoir never fully recovered her three-year-old form in 1891. Unplaced to Surefoot on her reappearance in the Eclipse Stakes, she won the July Cup against lesser opposition at Newmarket six days later; but she disappointed in her other four outings, finishing a poor fourth in the Goodwood Cup and unplaced in the Cambridgeshire when favourite. She had always run in a hood as it was found that this improved her performance; and her jockey had always been ordered never to be behind the other horses as she greatly disliked having dust or mud kicked up in her face. These idiosyncrasies notwithstanding, Memoir was utterly game and courageous, and was one of the best fillies ever bred by Queen Victoria at Hampton Court. At stud Memoir was the dam of four minor winners and the unraced Miss Gunning II by Carbine, the dam of Silent Lady by Cyllene. She bred Hush, who ultimately went to France to become a very useful broodmare.

One other yearling sold at Hampton Court in 1888 was to run with distinction: FitzHampton (Hampton–Lady Binks) won four races in Italy including the Premio Omnium; he was also second to Fitz Roya in the Grand Prix de Paris.

In 1888 Lord Hastings' 1885 Derby and St Leger winner, Melton, came to stand at Hampton Court at a fee of 50 gns a mare. The Queen was given six nominations to him at the reduced fee of 240 gns. He was to remain at Bushy Paddocks until the end of 1890, when he was exported to Italy.

The twenty-seven Royal yearlings sold on 29 June 1889 were very disappointing; the most expensive, Penzance (Hampton–Land's End) never reached the frame in three appearances on the racecourse. Only three actually managed to win in Great Britain; the best was Golden Garter (Bend Or–Sanda), who won nine races at four and five. He was exported to the USA and there became an influential stallion.

Although only twenty of the Queen's yearlings were sold at Hampton Court on 28 June 1890, this sale was the most successful of any held during the entire existence of the stud. The twenty lots realized the very large sum of 14,295 gns, an average of almost 715 gns. The yearling who contributed most to this total was Memoir's full-sister, La Flèche. The Prince of Wales, the Duke of Portland, Douglas Baird and Colonel North were among the good judges who were most taken with the filly. In 1889 the Prince of Wales had introduced Baron Maurice Hirsch to the Kingsclere stable of John Porter. Hirsch, an enormously rich Austrian-Jewish financier who had enlarged his fortune constructing railways in Germany, Holland, Belgium, Russia and Turkey, had settled in Paris after 1871. He had been introduced into English society in 1887 after the death of his son, who had had many English friends, by the Prince of Wales, who encouraged his friend to bid for La Fleche. It was arranged that the Prince's racing and stud manager, Lord Marcus Beresford, would bid on Baron Hirsch's behalf. The Duke of Portland opened the proceedings with a bid of 3,000 gns; he was opposed by Douglas Baird, Robert Sherwood, acting for Colonel North, and Lord Marcus Beresford. Throughout this spirited rivalry, Hirsch was apparently a careless and disinterested spectator. When Lord Marcus Beresford's bid of 5,500 gns silenced his opponents, however, the auctioneer, Mr Edmund

Tattersall, called for 'three cheers for Baron Hirsch and success to the Royal Stud'. In 1890 this was a staggering sum to be paid out for a yearling; it created a new record that was to stand until the first decade of the twentieth century.

Richard Marsh, who trained La Flèche as a four- and five-year-old, described her in 1893:

> She did not stand more than 15.3 hands, and was a pronounced specimen of the varminty, greyhound and wiry type. She had a beautiful head and shoulders, the best possible legs and feet, and yet she strongly belied her looks. When she looked what you would call well she was not at her best as a racing machine; when she was ragged and thin she could be relied upon to give of her very best form. Sir Arthur Bigge, who had been at the Hampton Court Sale in 1890, wrote the next day to Sir Henry Ponsonby, saying that 'the Queen ought to be pleased with its result. The 5,500 gns filly is a beauty'.[12]

La Flèche went into training with John Porter after the Hampton Court sale. She made her debut in the Chesterfield Stakes at Newmarket on 16 July 1891, easily beating Lady Hermit and Bona Vista. She then ran twice at Goodwood, winning the Lavant Stakes and Molecomb Stakes. Her final race as a two-year-old was in the Champagne Stakes at Doncaster, where she beat Gossoon and Sir Hugo a length and a half and six lengths. Baron Hirsch's filly did so well in the early months of 1892 that Porter did not even think it necessary to subject her to a formal trial before the 1,000 Guineas. Starting at 2–1 on, she readily won the Newmarket fillies' Classic by a length from The Smew. For the Derby on 1 June, although she was opposed by the first and second in the 2,000 Guineas, Bona Vista and St Angelo, and Monsieur Blanc's good colt, Reuil, who was to win the Grand Prix de Paris a few days later, La Flèche started at the very short odds of 11–10. The bare result of the race, that the 40–1 outsider Sir Hugo beat La Flèche three quarters of a length in no way conveys the misfortune suffered by Baron Hirsch's filly. In John Porter's words, this is what happened:

> This Derby was a race the recollection of which always arouses within me a feeling of annoyance. She [La Flèche] would, if properly ridden, have won in a canter. Coming down the hill to Tattenham Corner, she was lying eight to ten lengths behind the

leaders instead of being at their heels. There must have been something wrong with Barrett [La Flèche's jockey] that day. It was sheer madness on his part to allow her to be so far behind at that stage. After entering the straight Barrett undoubtedly did his utmost to repair his mistake by pushing the filly along with all his persuasive powers, but he was asking her to do an impossibility. The long and the short of it is that the jockey rode a shockingly bad race, and thoroughly deserved all the blame he received. I believe he was chatting with some of the other jockeys in the early part of the race instead of concentrating his attention on the business in hand. Knowing as he did what La Flèche's abilities were, he despised her opponents. There were at that time indications that Barrett's brain was slightly affected.

The strenuous but unavailing effort that La Flèche made to catch Sir Hugo did not leave her sufficient time to recover her normal condition before the Oaks on 3 June. Barrett again had the mount, though not without misgivings on the part of Hirsch and Porter. Before the race she was in a very nervous state and sweating freely, so it was not surprising that she only scraped home by a short head from The Smew. She was back on song, however, when she won the Nassau Stakes at Goodwood in a canter on 29 July.

In the St Leger La Flèche was opposed by the Duke of Westminster's Orme, who was also trained by John Porter. Orme had won the Richmond Stakes and Prince of Wales's Stakes at Goodwood, the Dewhurst Stakes and the Middle Park Stakes, and he had been second to Signorina in the Lancashire Plate at Manchester in 1891. A few days before the 2,000 Guineas Orme was poisoned and for several days hovered between life and death. The Duke of Westminster offered a reward of £1,000 for information leading to the apprehension and conviction of the person or persons guilty of the crime. Orme pulled through and in July he won the Eclipse Stakes, beating Orvieto a neck, and a fortnight later took the Sussex Stakes at Goodwood. Orvieto was one of the best colts of his generation, having won seven races in 1890 including the Sussex Stakes and Great Yorkshire Stakes, and finishing second to Common in the 2,000 Guineas. In the St Leger Orme was made favourite at 10–11 with La Flèche at 7–2 and Sir Hugo 10–1. Barrett did not ride the most judicious race on Orme: he sent him to the front after less than half a mile, and a furlong and a half out he had run himself to a standstill. La Flèche then took the lead and easily avenged her Derby defeat by beating Sir Hugo two lengths to record her third Classic victory. Seventeen days later she comprehensively defeated Orvieto three lengths in the Lancashire Plate at Manchester; Orvieto was only giving her 2 lb, 9 lb less than the weight-for-age scale and sex allowance; Orme had received 10 lbs in the Eclipse Stakes. La Flèche then won the Grand Duke Michael Stakes and the Newmarket Oaks. Her final appearance in 1892 was in the Cambridgeshire, for which she was favourite at 7–2 carrying 8 st 10 lb. Only two of her twenty-eight rivals carried more: the Ascot Gold Cup winner, Buccaneer, and the six-year-old Miss Dollar, who had got a 10 lb penalty for winning the Duke of York Stakes at Kempton. La Flèche's length and a half victory over Pensioner, who was receiving 34 lbs, was extremely meritorious, for two days later he came out and won the Old Cambridgeshire.

At the end of the 1892 season Baron Hirsch and the Prince of Wales moved their horses from Porter at Kingsclere to Richard Marsh at Newmarket. The reason given was that the Prince had more opportunity to visit his horses at Newmarket. On her first outing in 1893 La Flèche could only finish third to Orme in the Eclipse Stakes. Richard Marsh said, however, that she was not herself as she was amiss at the time; he added, 'the blacksmith could not plate her and really she should not have run.' When she received 7 lbs and was still beaten a neck by Orme in the Gordon Stakes at Goodwood, Marsh again stated she was not herself. She then ran third to Raeburn and the 1893 Triple Crown winner Isinglass in the Lancashire Plate at Manchester. She was beaten only a length and half a length, giving Raeburn 16 lbs and Isinglass 6 lbs; the weight-for-age-and-sex scale would have required her to give a three-year-old colt only 5 lbs. Strictly, therefore, this performance showed La Flèche to be the equal of Isinglass. Her two victories as a four-year-old came in the Lowther Stakes over ten furlongs at Newmarket in October and the Liverpool Autumn Cup in November. On the day of the latter Marsh recalled that 'she was looking so bad, though I knew I could not make her any better, that, in fact, she was the real La Flèche.' In the Cambridge-shire and Manchester November Handicap, Baron Hirsch's excep-tional mare was unable to cope with the welter burdens of 9 st 7 lbs and 9 st 11 lbs, and ran unplaced in both. La Flèche was victorious in two of her four races as a five-year-old, easily winning the Ascot Gold Cup and the Champion Stakes, her final race. Ravensbury beat her half a length in the Hardwicke Stakes at Ascot, but at that time she had probably not recovered from her exertions over two and a half miles. In her only other run that year she was fourth, carrying 9 st 7 lbs, in the one-mile Prince Edward Handicap at Manchester.

In a career spanning four seasons this brilliant filly had won sixteen races, including three Classics, and £34,703 in winning prize money. Without doubt she was the best of all the colts and fillies to have been bred by Queen Victoria at Hampton Court. Had she won the Derby, as she unquestionably should have done, she would now definitely be regarded as the best filly of the nineteenth century.

Baron Hirsch died in 1896, and La Flèche came up at the Newmarket July Sales; Sir Tatton Sykes asked Lord Marcus Beresford to buy her for his Sledmere Stud, but did not tell him the maximum he was to pay. When Beresford sent him a telegram to announce that he had bought La Flèche for 12,600 gns, the famous Yorkshire breeder was horrified. When La Flèche arrived at Sledmere station, she remained in a railway box for a fortnight before Sir Tatton agreed to take her. During that time she was fed by the stationmaster, who, seeing her almost starving, gave her fodder from his nearby smallholding. La Flèche passed the rest of her life at the Sledmere Stud; she finally died on 22 April 1916, having produced only seven foals between 1895 and 1912. The best two of her offspring were John O'Gaunt and Baroness La Flèche. John O'Gaunt ran seven times, winning once as a two-year-old at Bibury Club; he was, however, also runner-up to St Amant in the 1904 Derby. Mated with Lord Derby's great mare Canterbury Pilgrim in 1906, he got Swynford, whose eight victories included the St Leger in 1910, the Hardwicke Stakes (twice) and the Eclipse Stakes in 1911. Swynford was most successful at stud; he was the sire of Sansovino (Derby, 1924), four 1,000 Guineas winners – Ferry (1918), Bettina (1921), Tranquil (1,000 Guineas and St Leger, 1923), Saucy Sue (1,000 Guineas and Oaks, 1925) – and Keysoe (St Leger, 1919). Baroness La Flèche won the Acorn Stakes at Epsom as a two-year-old, but was to prove a better broodmare than racemare. She was the dam of nine winners, the best of which was Cinna by Polymelus, who won the 1920 1,000 Guineas and Coronation Stakes. Cinna was also the dam of Buckler (New Stakes, 1925) and Belle Mere (Molecomb Stakes, 1926). La Flèche's influence on the Stud Book was not as great, perhaps, as that of Pretty Polly; still it is interesting to note that the 1989 Kentucky Derby and Breeders' Cup winner, Sunday Silence, traces back on his dam side to Baron Hirsch's brilliant filly.

The achievements of the rest of the 1889 crop of Royal yearlings are inevitably overshadowed by La Flèche. In fact there were seven winners of thirty-four races in this group, Haymaker (Springfield –Lady Binks) winning three races including the Dee Stakes at Chester.

In the late 1880s Edward Stevens was succeeded by George Mackrell as Stud Groom at Hampton Court. An interesting sidelight on the terms of his employment is revealed by two letters written to him by Colonel Maude in January 1891. The first was on 28 January:

> Mackrell,
>   I am surprised to find that Dr Roots' account for medical attendance on you and your family for 1890 amounts to £37 5s. Last year it was pointed out to you that £34 3s. – Dr Roots' account for 1889 – was far and above anything that would be sanctioned on that head. Of course Dr Roots must be paid, but I don't feel justified in doing so on the Privy Purse's account, having given you notice last year. Servants of the Royal Household are by the Queen's gracious permission provided with medical attendance gratis, but this must be kept within proper limits and is only intended to cover acute cases of illness, and a Doctor's account for £37 5s. cannot be entertained. I shall be glad if you can give me any explanation of such a charge.
>   Yours truly,
>   G. A. Maude.[13]

Mackrell must have given his explanation to Colonel Maude by return, for on 30 January the Crown Equerry wrote again to the Stud Groom:

> Mackrell,
>   We will pay Dr Roots' amended bill on this occasion, but it must be understood that no charge must be made in future on account of your son. He is a chronic case, and much as I am sympathetic with you in having a son so afflicted, it would not be right that year after year the Privy Purse should be charged with medical attendance on him.
>   Yours truly,
>   G. A. Maude.[14]

We are not told what disease Mackrell's son was suffering from;

this entire episode is, however, illustrative of the social attitudes of the time.

The 1891 Hampton Court sale saw twenty-one yearlings purchased. The most expensive, Louis XIII (St Simon–Eglentyne) never raced. Sainfoin's brother Vetch only won four minor races. Five of the 1890 crop won thirty-two races; Best Man (Ormonde or Melton–Wedlock) was the most successful. Having won eight of his eighteen races in 1892–3, he improved out of all recognition as a four-year-old, winning eight of his nine outings, being undefeated in his last seven. His victories included the Queen's Prize Handicap at Kempton, the Queen's Stand Plate at Ascot and the July Cup. His greatest triumph came in Paris on 7 October when he beat Callistrate and Fripon in the Prix du Conseil Municipal. Callistrate had been runner-up to La Fleche in the Ascot Gold Cup, and had won the Prix d'Hedouville and Prix Dangu earlier in the season; in 1893 he had taken the Prix du Conseil Municipal and he was to win the Jockey Club Cup at the end of 1894. Although Best Man only won one race, the Old Cambridgeshire Handicap, as a five-year-old, he was second in the Rous Memorial Stakes and third in the Queen's Stand Plate at Ascot, and a most praiseworthy runner-up, under the burden of 9 st, to Marco in the Cambridgeshire itself. He was then retired to stud.

The Duke of Portland and Lord Londonderry generally drove down to the Hampton Court sales with a coachload of friends. On 20 June 1891 one of the passengers in the coach was Miss Mildred Sturt, later Lady Charles Montagu. When Portland bought a yearling filly by Melton out of Merino, he asked Miss Sturt if he could name her Miss Mildred. In her three appearances on the racecourse, Miss Sturt's namesake only managed one victory, in a five-furlong Match at Newmarket against the Duke of Westminster's Zebra, whom he had also bought at Hampton Court. Miss Mildred's second foal, La Roche, was the best staying filly of her generation, winning the Oaks, the Manchester Cup, the Yorkshire Oaks and the Newmarket Oaks in 1900. Portland recalled that during the running of the Oaks a friend standing close by said out loud to himself, 'Well, in any case La Roche the favourite does not win.' No sooner had he uttered these words than La Roche lengthened her stride, went to the front and won in a canter. At stud La Roche was the dam of eight winners including Cannobie by Polymelus, who won the 1916 Jockey Club Stakes and became a successful sire in France, and Almissa, who was exported to Australia where his victories included the Australia Cup.

Only five winners of eight minor events emerged from the
seventeen yearlings sold at Hampton Court on 25 June 1892. On
the whole it was a very disappointing crop. Springfield was then
in his twentieth year and clearly had little more to contribute to
the Stud in the future. On 5 December 1892 Sir Henry Ponsonby
wrote the following letter to Queen Victoria:

> Sir George Maude declares that Your Majesty's thorough-
> bred stud at Hampton Court will deteriorate and eventually end
> unless a high-priced horse is purchased.
>
> He believes the cost would be £5,000. But expects the saving
> after this would be considerable. Sir Henry Ponsonby objected
> that the Privy Purse could not conveniently afford to spend
> £5,000 on a horse.
>
> Prince Christian agrees with Sir George Maude and strongly
> advises the purchase of a horse which possibly might be less than
> £5,000.
>
> After a discussion with Mr. Gibson, the Secretary of the
> Privy Purse, Sir George and he suggest that the money might be
> paid in instalments. No doubt this would do if Sir George Maude
> is certain that the whole sum will not be asked for at once.
>
> Would Your Majesty approve of such a horse being pur-
> chased, and arrangements for a gradual payment?
>
> From 1850 to 1891 the Stud has made about £26,000. But
> expenses increase and the proceeds are diminishing. Therefore
> it becomes necessary to consider whether it would be wise to
> continue the Stud or not.[15]

This letter contains the first public mention of the possibility of
the Royal Stud's being closed. The Duke of Portland, who was
Master of the Horse at that time, was much against it, but said
that wiser counsels than his prevailed. Certainly the lack of a
top-class stallion, coupled with the reluctance of Sir Henry Ponsonby to provide sufficient funds to buy another, was a major
cause of its eventual dispersal in 1894. The establishment of the
Stud at Sandringham by the Prince of Wales in 1886 could also
have been a contributory reason, for the retention of Hampton
Court Stud would have meant that when he became King he would
have two separate establishments to maintain.

The poor results of the 1893 sale, when twenty-seven yearlings
from the Royal Stud were sold for only 5,005 gns at Hampton
Court on 24 June, must have added weight to the arguments of

those members of the Royal Household who wished to disband the stud. Of these twenty-seven yearlings only three were winners of a mere twelve races.

On 30 June 1894 the final sale of bloodstock bred by Queen Victoria took place at Hampton Court. The lots consisted of twenty-eight yearlings, forty-five mares and twenty-seven foals sold with their dams. The yearlings made 5,640 gns, an average of 201 gns; the mares and foals realized 16,715 gns. Seven of the yearlings won thirty races; the best was unquestionably Amphora (Amphion –Sierra), who won eight races including the Gimcrack Stakes in 1895 and the Stewards' Cup at Goodwood in 1897. She was then acquired by the Prince of Wales, and retired to stud at Sandringham where she was the dam of six winners, including the useful colt Perrier by Persimmon, who was later a very good sire in Argentina. Amphora's dam, Sierra, was bought by Sir S. Scott for only 410 gns. Mated again with Amphion in 1897, Sierra's 1898 foal, Sundridge, became the best sprinter in England, winning seventeen races between 1901 and 1904, including the July Cup three times as well as the King's Stand Stakes. Sundridge, who was bought by J. B. Joel when still in training, sired the 1911 2,000 Guineas winner Sunstar and the 1913 1,000 Guineas and Oaks winner Jest before he was exported to France in 1911.

Baron Hirsch gave 4,600 gns for the mare Wedlock, the dam of Best Man. This was easily the highest price of the sale, but none of Wedlock's ten foals after 1894 emulated their illustrious half-brother. Sanfoin's dam, Sanda, was the second highest-priced mare in the sale; she was knocked down to Sir James Miller for 2,000 gns. Her final foal, Black Sand by Melannion, won nine races including the Jockey Club Cup and Cesarewitch Stakes in 1902.

Regrettably many of the mares and foals in this final sale were bought by foreign bidders, so the blood was lost to English breeders. Among those mares exported to France was Sagesse (Wisdom–Inez), who was the grandam of 1920 Prix du Jockey-Club hero Sourbier. She was also the ancestress of such good performers as Samos, who won the Prix de l'Arc de Triomphe in 1935, Marveil, the winner of the King George VI Stakes at Ascot in 1947, and Hugh Lupus, who won the Champion Stakes and was the sire of the St Leger winner Hethersett, and grandsire of the Derby victor Blakeney. Lord Annerley bought Milady (Kisber– Alone), whose 1899 foal by Winkfield, Bachelor's Button, won sixteen races including the Ascot Gold Cup, the Gold Vase (twice), the Hardwicke Stakes, the Jockey Club Cup and the Doncaster

Cup. Milady was also the grandam of Bachelor's Double by Tredennis, whose nine victories included the Royal Hunt Cup, the City and Suburban Handicap and the Great Jubilee Handicap; he was also the sire of Comrade, the first winner of the Prix de l'Arc de Triomphe.

Only two of the foals sold at Hampton Court in 1894 were winners in England. Theale (Donovan–Maria), who won a Nursery Handicap at Warwick in 1896, was a more than useful broodmare; she was the dam of seven winners including Throwaway, the winner of the 1904 Ascot Gold Cup.

The Royal Stud at Hampton Court had bred winners of every Classic race during the forty-five years of its existence. The total number of winners that had been bred there by Queen Victoria amounted to 349; between them they had won 1,503 races. It was perhaps even more extraordinary that, with the exception of Amphora, virtually none of the mares or their foals which had been bred at Hampton Court were acquired for the Stud at Sandringham by Lord Marcus Beresford, the Prince of Wales's stud and racing manager. The Stud at Hampton Court had proved one of the most successful in England in the second half of the nineteenth century; its disbandment was a matter for profound regret to those seriously concerned with maintaining the quality of the Thoroughbred in England.

10

The Foundation of the Royal Stud

at Sandringham

The eldest son of Queen Victoria, Albert Edward ('Bertie'), was married to Princess Alexandra, daughter of Prince Christian of Denmark, on 10 March 1863 at St George's Chapel, Windsor. The young Danish princess had captivated Queen Victoria during a visit to Windsor and Osborne the previous November; it is interesting to note that in her entry in her diary on 12 November, the Queen wrote, 'How beloved Albert would have loved her!'[1] Returning from a week's honeymoon at Osborne House, the Prince and Princess of Wales stayed first at Windsor, then spent ten days at Sandringham and finally took up residence at Marlborough House in London. The whole of London society was entertained there at a ball, which launched a season reminiscent of the days of the Prince Regent. Disraeli described it as a Royal honeymoon extended over a period of months. From that moment on, the Prince of Wales reigned supreme in society.

Shortly before the Prince of Wales had reached the age of twenty-one, £220,000 of the capital that had accrued during his childhood from the income of the Duchy of Cornwall had been used to buy the 7,000-acre estate at Sandringham in Norfolk. After his marriage the Prince's income was increased to £100,000 per annum, and taking rents into consideration he probably received about £110,000–£115,000, much less than magnates like the Dukes of Westminster, Portland, Bedford and Devonshire and Lords Derby and Cadogan. Often the Prince's expenditure exceeded his income by £20,000 a year. Shortage of money precluded him from owning any Thoroughbred horses in the years immediately following his marriage. Nevertheless he enjoyed racing at Ascot, Goodwood and Newmarket, and in 1864 was elected a member of the Jockey Club.

While Queen Victoria led her secluded life at Osborne and Balmoral, the Prince of Wales established another set routine for each year. January and February were spent at Sandringham, which he looked upon as his home. It was here that he was able to indulge in his greatest passion in life, shooting. The house parties at the Royal estate during the shooting season were almost continuous. At the beginning of March the Prince of Wales went alone to the Côte d'Azur for a month, usually staying a few days in Paris on both the outward and return journeys. It was during these trips that his friendships with Sarah Bernhardt, Hortense Schneider and the Parisian society beauties, Princesse de Sagan and Duchesse de Mouchy, were formed. Frequently he made his yacht his headquarters, having sent it on ahead of him, and the month was occupied with dinners, balls and parties almost every evening. The heir to the throne then returned to Marlborough House for the London season. Throughout the summer he attended as many race-meetings and theatre performances as possible. When at Newmarket he stayed either at the private quarters kept for him at the Jockey Club or at friends' houses in or near the town; he especially liked staying with Leopold de Rothschild in his palatial house. It was usually in the summer that the Prince undertook the public engagements that were beginning to be expected of the Royal Family. These were much less onerous than they are now: in the 1860s they occupied on average only twenty-seven days a year, and included public dinners, laying foundation stones and visiting institutions.

At the end of July the Prince of Wales went to Cowes to sail for two or three weeks. He then took a holiday, often alone, in one of the spa towns in Germany or Austria, in an attempt to reduce weight, for although he did not drink a lot, the heir to the throne had a prodigious appetite and adored rich food. At the start of October the Prince of Wales went to Abergeldie, near Balmoral, when he enjoyed a month's grouse shooting. He then returned to Sandringham for the remainder of the year.

When the Prince bought the Sandringham estate, the house itself was neither large nor in particularly good condition. It soon became clear that a completely new house would have to be built to cater for the needs of the Prince and Princess of Wales. By 1867 Sir William Knollys, his Comptroller and Treasurer, reckoned that the cost of improvements, alterations and building had already reached £80,000. This lack of money did not stop the Prince from betting on horses in moderate sums. On 27 April 1866 he wrote to Charles Carrington from Paris:

As you will not be back in time to settle my account at Tattersall's, do you mind writing or telegraphing to some friends to do so in your name?

Our account is – I win £300 on Vauban – lose £100 on Plaudit – and win £75 on Plaudit – making a total of £275, I win. This is, I hope, correct.[2]

The Prince of Wales first registered his racing colours – purple, gold braid, scarlet sleeves, black velvet cap with gold fringe – in 1875. Two years later, in July 1877, they were first seen in public at Newmarket, when his Arab horse Alep was matched against Lord Strathnairn's Avowal over four miles. Although favourite at 9–4 on, Alep was beaten thirty lengths. In the next few years the Prince owned a few steeplechasers, which were trained at Epsom by John Jones, the father of the jockey Herbert Jones. Some were moderately successful, but it was not until 1886 that the Prince of Wales made his debut as an owner of Throughbred racehorses racing under Jockey Club Rules.

Early in 1886 Lord Allington informed John Porter that the Prince of Wales had bought two two-year-old fillies, both by Hermit, who had won the 1867 Derby for his friend, Henry Chaplin, and that he would like them to be trained by him at Kingsclere. The brilliant trainer, who sent out seven colts to win the Derby, felt that a great honour had been conferred upon him and immediately accepted the responsibility of training for the heir to the throne. The Prince had travelled to Kingsclere three years earlier to watch the final trial before the Derby of St Blaise, who was owned in partnership by Lord Allington and Sir Frederick Johnstone; afterwards he had taken lunch with Porter at Park Lodge and inspected the stables. St Blaise's victory at Epsom was a second consecutive success for the master of Kingsclere, for the previous year, 1882, he had won the race with Shotover.

The two-year-old fillies the Prince had bought were Counterpane out of Patchwork and Lady Peggy out of Belle Agnes. Counterpane, ridden by Fred Archer, won a maiden plate in a canter at Sandown first time out in June. In the middle of May the Prince had again visited Kingsclere to see Ormonde do his final trial before he won the Derby and to see his two fillies. The Prince was present at Sandown when Counterpane won and told his son, Prince George, that he 'got quite an ovation from the crowd afterwards'.[3] Counterpane was not destined to be one of the foundation mares of the Royal Stud at Sandringham, however; running for the Stockbridge

Cup later that June, she seemed to have beaten her rivals when she dropped down dead as she approached the winning-post. A post-mortem revealed that she had a diseased heart. Since Counterpane was one of the Blakeney yearlings sold by Henry Chaplin at the Newmarket Sales in July 1885, when the Prince of Wales had paid 400 gns for her, her breeder wrote a letter of commiseration to his Royal friend after her untimely death. The reply that the Prince of Wales sent to Chaplin illustrates his sporting and realistic approach to the ownership of Thoroughbreds:

> My dear Harry,
>   I am very much touched by your kindness in writing to condole with me on the sad end of poor little Counterpane who never looked better, and Porter fully expected her to win the Cup. But I must bear it with philosophy as I know what the glorious uncertainties of the Turf are.
>   From yours very sincerely, A.E.[4]

The other filly, Lady Peggy, whom the Prince had purchased from her breeder, Sir Tatton Sykes, was beaten on her racecourse debut in a maiden plate at Newmarket's July Meeting, but then won a 100 gns maiden plate at the Houghton Meeting. She was ridden by Fred Archer, who a few weeks earlier had sent the Prince of Wales a signed photograph of himself in the Royal colours. Lady Peggy was then retired from racing and went to the paddocks at Sandringham.

It was in the autumn of 1886 that the Prince of Wales told John Porter that he intended to found a stud at Sandringham, and asked his trainer to give him advice on the best way of laying out the paddocks. At that time the Prince was breeding Hackneys at Wolferton, but the land so used was eventually turned over to broodmares visiting the stallions at Sandringham. The tragic death of Fred Archer, who shot himself in a fit of depression brought on by his continual wasting in November 1886, meant that his stud manager, Edmund Walker, was without employment. John Porter, therefore, recommended that he be appointed Stud Groom at the new Royal Stud. To quote Porter's words, Walker was to prove 'a skilful, painstaking, reliable servant'. When Archer's broodmares were put up for sale at Newmarket on 17 December 1886, Porter bought the six-year-old mare Hazy (Hermit–Fog by Macaroni) for 440 gns for his Royal patron.

The boxes at Sandringham that had formerly been used for

Preceding page: William Augustus, Duke of Cumberland, inspecting his broodmares in Windsor Great Park. Painting by Gilpin and Marlow. Reproduced by kind permission of H.M. the Queen.

Above: Eclipse, bred by William Augustus, Duke of Cumberland. Painting by George Stubbs, 1770. Reproduced by kind permission of Arthur Ackerman. Photograph by Laurie Morton.

Below: Pocahontas, bred by William IV, was the dam of champion sires Stockwell and King Tom. Reproduced by kind permission of the Jockey Club. Photograph by Laurie Morton.

Queen Victoria in the Royal Box at Ascot Gold Cup in 1839. The winner, Caravan, bred by William IV, is in the centre. Painting by John Herring Senior.

Baron Hirsch's La Flèche bred by Queen Victoria. Painting by Emile Adam 1897. Reproduced by kind permission of the Jockey Club. Photograph by Laurie Morton.

Above: The Prince of Wales's Diamond Jubilee (B. Jones) bred by the Prince of Wales and winner of the Triple Crown. Painting by Emile Adam, 1900. Reproduced by kind permission of the Jockey Club. Photograph by Laurie Morton. Below: The Royal Stud at Sandringham with the statue of Persimmon in front of the main offices. Photograph by Gerry Cranham.

Above: HM the Queen presenting
the Grand Military Gold Cup to
HM the Queen Mother after The
Argonaut's victory at Sandown,
9 March 1990. Photograph by
Ronald Frain. Right: HM the
Queen Mother's Special Cargo,
(Mr G. Oxley) winning the
Whitbread Gold Cup at
Sandown Park in March 1986.
Photograph by Gerry Cranham.

Left: The Queen Mother's Insular
(E. Murphy) bred by the Queen,
winning the Imperial Cup
Handicap Hurdle at Sandown Park
March 1986. Photograph by
Gerry Cranham.

Highclere (J. Mercer) winning the Prix de Diane at Chantilly from Comtesse de Loire, June 1974. Photograph by A. Well.

The Queen inspecting Highclere and her foal by Diesis, Hierarch, at Lane's End Farm, Lexington, Kentucky, May 1989. Photograph by Bill Straus.

Left: Dunfermline (W. Carson) winning the 1977 Oaks Stakes at Epsom from Freeze the Secret. Photograph by Gerry Cranham. Below: Dunfermline (W. Carson) winning the St Leger from dual Prix de l'Arc de Triomphe winner Alleged in 1977. Photograph by Wallis Photographers.

Buttress (W. Carson) is welcomed by the Queen, the Queen Mother, Lord Porchester, Michael Oswald and Major Hern into the winner's enclosure at Royal Ascot after his victory in the 1979 Queen's Vase. Photograph by Gerry Cranham.

Bustino at the Wolferton Stud with the Sandringham Parish Church in the background. Photograph by Gerry Cranham.

shorthorn cattle and Shire horses were transformed into boxes suitable for broodmares. Additional boxes were built for the yearlings. All of these buildings, and the majority of the buildings on the estate, were made of Carr stone, a brown ironstone quarried locally.

Initially it was decided to buy about half a dozen broodmares for the Royal Stud, but Porter was warned that no fancy prices were to be paid. The majority of the mares were purchased at public sales in 1887. At the Newmarket Sales on 4 July 1887 John Porter bought the following mares for the Prince of Wales: Lilian (Wingrave–Lady Blanche by Voltigeur), the winner of forty-six of her 109 races between 1871 and 1876 including twenty-nine Queen's Cups; Fluster (Young Melbourne–Makeshift by Voltigeur), Poetry (Petrarch–Music by Stockwell), a half-sister to the 1883 St Leger winner, Ossian by Salvator. At the sales on the Knavesmire at York on 4 August 1887 Marie Agnes (Macaroni–Belle Agnes by King Tom, together with her bay filly foal by Mark, was purchased for the Sandringham Stud. At the Newmarket Sales on 11 October 1887 the Prince of Wales bought the mare Skelgate Maid (Speculum–Habet by Gladiateur) and her colt foal by Petrarch, later named Shamrock. Shamrock was to win four races for the Prince. The last two purchases of 1887 were made at the Newmarket Sales on 16 December: the mare Fanchette (Speculum––Reticence by Vespasian), for 900 gns, and her colt foal by Energy, later called Gallifet. The reason why Fanchette cost nearly double of any of the other mares acquired was that her dam Reticence was an unraced half-sister to the Derby winner and leading sire, Hermit.

The mare who was to have the greatest influence on the Prince of Wales's racing fortunes was not, however, bought at public auction. While at the 1887 Newmarket December Sale John Porter met Mr David Falconer, a jute broker in Mark Lane, London, who raced under the name of 'Mr Benholm'. Falconer said to Porter, 'I understand you are buying mares for the Prince of Wales. I have one I want to sell. Go and look at her; she is standing at John Dawson's. I want a thousand for her.' Porter went to see the mare in question, Perdita II (Hampton–Hermione by Young Melbourne) and liked the look of her. He described her as 'an angular sort of mare, but I could see that she had good points, and was likely to develop into a nice brood mare.' At that time Perdita II was just out of training, having been runner-up in her final race, the Markeaton Welter Handicap at Derby in November. In July that year she had dead-heated with Mr Leopold de Rothschild's Middle-thorpe for the Liverpool Cup, with The Sailor Prince, who was to win the Cambridgeshire that autumn, back in third place. That performance had impressed the great trainer and contributed to his decision to recommend her as a broodmare to his Royal patron. The morning after he had inspected Perdita II, Porter went to see the Prince in his rooms at the Jockey Club and told him, 'They are asking a thousand for her, sir, but I may be able to get her for less.' The Prince of Wales then asked if Porter thought she was suitable for the Royal Stud. When Porter replied in the affirmative, he said, 'Then you can buy her if you can get her for nine hundred.'

Mr Falconer agreed to sell Perdita II for £900. When the Prince of Wales's Keeper of the Privy Purse, Sir Digton Probyn, gave Porter the money to pay for her he said, 'You will ruin the Prince if you go on buying these thoroughbreds.' Since this exceptional mare was to prove one of the bargains of the century, many people were later quick to take credit for having been associated with her purchase. John Porter, however, stated quite categorically, 'Nobody except Mr Falconer and myself had anything to do with the deal.'

When Perdita II was bred by Lord Cawdor in 1881, few would have anticipated that she was destined to achieve such fame as a broodmare. She was the first of three foals produced by her dam, Hermione, who had run unplaced on her two racecourse appearances in 1877 and 1878. Perdita II's grandam, La Belle Helene by St Albans, five of whose nine foals won minor races, never won in nine outings in 1868 and 1869, and her dam Teter-rima by Voltigeur, only two of whose foals turned out to be winners of moderate races, had managed to win only one small race at Newmarket as a three-year-old. The first really notable mare among Perdita II's maternal ancestors was Teterrima's dam, Ellen Middleton by Bay Middleton, among whose foals was Wild Dayrell by Ion, winner of the 1855 Derby.

Perdita II's racing career also started in humble company. She ran nine times as a two-year-old, winning on three occasions. After her first victory in a selling stakes at Goodwood, Lord Cawdor bought her in. She was then runner-up in the FitzWilliam Stakes at Doncaster and in the Friary Plate at Derby to Henry Chaplin's useful Raffaello. After another victory in a selling sweepstakes at Newmarket over six furlongs, she was bought by Mat Dawson for 560 gns for Mr David Falconer, for whom she won the £1,000 Chesterfield Nursery Stakes over five furlongs at Derby in

November. As a three-year-old, Perdita II won two of her nine races, the Great Cheshire Handicap over ten furlongs in the spring and the Ayr Gold Cup in September. In those days the Ayr Gold Cup was not a valuable sprint; its distance was once round the course and its prize money a paltry £290. As a four-year-old Perdita II was a disappointment, failing to win on any of her eleven outings, though she was runner-up on six occasions. In 1886 she won two of her eight races, the Great Cheshire Handicap and the Liverpool Cup, dead-heating with Middlethorpe. She was quite fancied at 10–1 when unplaced in the Ebor Handicap and she was also unplaced in the Liverpool Autumn Cup, won by Melton under the top weight of 9 st 3 lbs. Perdita II carried only 7 st 5 lbs against Melton at Liverpool, so we can safely assume that the handicapper rated her about 2 st behind Classic form: Melton had the previous year won the Derby and St Leger for Lord Hastings.

Inevitably, victories were few and far between for horses bred by the Prince of Wales at Sandringham, for there were only nine mares in residence in 1889 and eight in 1890. Still, there were two winners from the stud's first crop in 1888: Pierrette (Mask–Poetry), who won three times as a two-year-old in 1890, at Newmarket (twice) and Doncaster, and twice as a three-year-old at Sandown and Portsmouth; and Perdita II's first foal, Derelict by Barcaldine. Derelict had disappointed in five outings at two and three, and it was only after he had been cut that he won a small race over a mile at Yarmouth in 1892. The previous autumn, however, he had shown signs of ability when he finished third to Comedy in the prestigious Cambridgeshire Handicap. Pierrette was retired to the paddocks at Sandringham, but Derelict met with an accident and died in 1893.

In 1890 Henry Chaplin's excellent stallion Hermit died. His owner sent to his friend, the Prince of Wales, one of Hermit's hooves. The Prince replied in the following manner:

Marlborough House,
July 27th 1890.

My dear Harry,

How kind of you to have sent me the hoof of dear old Hermit! so prettily mounted, which I shall always greatly value and constantly use as an inkstand.

I am also very much touched by the kind expressions in your letter wishing me good luck with my racehorses. Though I can never expect to have the good fortune which attended the Dukes of Portland and Westminster, I still hope with patience to win one or more of the classic races with a horse bred by myself.

I sincerely hope that you will be able to come to Goodwood for part of the time, at any rate.

Thanking you again for your kind remembrance of me and giving me so interesting a souvenir of your 'best friend'.

From yours very sincerely, Albert Edward.

P.S.   I shall always take the shoe about with me.[5]

This letter is very interesting, illustrating again the sporting spirit in which the Prince regarded breeding and racing. And as a result of John Porter's most sagacious purchase of Perdita II and, to a lesser extent, Poetry, the Prince's ambition to breed a Classic winner was to be fulfilled sooner than he expected.

Perdita II's second foal, Barracouta, a bay filly by Barcaldine, ran once as a two-year-old in 1891. She won the Champion Breeders' Foal Stakes at Derby, and Porter had high hopes of her. Regrettably these were misplaced; she did not train on as a three-year-old. She was eventually sold for £367 and exported to Austria, where she produced Llubar by Friar Lubin in 1899, the winner of the Österreichisches Derby. Lady Peggy's first foal, County Council, a chestnut colt by Isonomy, was also a promising two-year-old, winning the Ham Produce Stakes at Goodwood for the Prince, but he never ran after 1891. The only other winner bred by the Prince of Wales from the 1889 Sandringham crop was Versailles (Hampton–Fanchette), who won the Dullingham Plate at Newmarket.

The 1890 crop of foals bred by the Prince of Wales was a catastrophe: they included not one winner. Both Perdita II and Lady Peggy were barren and none of the eight living foals was any good at all. It was a year that the Prince of Wales would probably have preferred to have forgone, for it included the famous Baccarat scandal. The damage to the Prince's reputation and that of the monarchy was horrendous, especially when it was learned not merely that had he been involved in a card game that was illegal but that he had supplied the chips for the game. The Church, the Press and high-minded and self-righteous Members of Parliament thundered into the attack on the Prince and his racing friends. The court case was the most sensational in the reign of Queen Victoria. The Prince was forced to write a letter to *The Times* after pressure from the Archbishop of Canterbury, in which he said, 'I consider gambling, like intemperance, one of the greatest curses that a country can be afflicted with.' At the end of this letter, however, he made a strong defence of horse-racing, which, the Prince stated, 'may produce gambling or it may not. I have always looked upon it as a manly sport which is popular with Englishmen of all classes, and there is no reason why it should be looked upon as a gambling transaction.'

The year 1890 was also notable for a very important event in the development of the Royal Stud. Lord Marcus Beresford, the second son of the Marquess of Waterford, was appointed an Extra Equerry and racing manager to the Prince of Wales. As a young man, when he was a successful amateur jockey and a Starter for the Jockey Club, Beresford had been quite hot-tempered and was far from averse to using his fists when aroused. On one occasion, after a race-meeting at Bibury, he and Sir Claude de Crespigny had taken on some hooligans at the Grosvenor Arms at Stockbridge. On another occasion in March 1877 Lord Marcus's pugilistic skills landed him in front of the magistrates at Marlborough Street Police Court: on a visit to a solicitor with whom he had become financially embroiled, Beresford had given him not merely a piece of his mind but a hiding as well. This incident had not interfered with Beresford's riding, for the previous Friday he had won the Veterans' Chase at Sandown's Grand Military meeting, and the day before the case rode Lucy to win a race at the National Hunt meeting at Cottenham.

During the time that the Prince of Wales had his horses in training at Kingsclere, he often paid visits there to see them, generally travelling by the nine o'clock train from Waterloo to Overton, where he was met by a fly. Porter would wait for him at the foot of the Downs on his hack; on arrival there the Prince would mount Porter's old grey cob Jack, and the two would ride over to the gallops. When the work was finished, the party would repair to Park House for a large lunch at noon. Porter remarked that on these visits, 'The Prince took a great interest in his racehorses. He was always most kind and considerate, and very grateful for anything that was done which added to his comfort and enjoyment.' Porter himself was several times invited as his guest on the Royal yacht, and he attended the great Naval Review that was part of the Jubilee Celebrations in 1887. Even after the Prince's horses left Kingsclere for Newmarket in 1892, John Porter was still invited to Sandringham each year, usually in November, and together with his former patron made a tour of the estate and the stud.

At the end of the 1892 flat racing season the horses of both the Prince of Wales and Baron Maurice Hirsch, including the brilliant racemare La Fleche, were taken away from John Porter at Kingsclere and sent to Newmarket to be trained by Richard Marsh. The expressed reason for the move, that it would be easier for the Prince to visit his horses at Newmarket, which was nearer to Sandringham, was clearly only a cover story, for Porter in his autobiography asserts,

> As I have no wish to reopen an old sore I shall not gratify the curiosity of inquisitive mortals by relating the inner history of this separation. I had at the time, however, the comforting assurance that the Prince and the Baron greatly regretted the necessity for severing their association with the stable. That assurance was later, on more than one occasion, reconveyed to me by His Royal Highness.

It is interesting to note that Baron Hirsch asked Porter to train for him again just twelve months later, but the great trainer had to refuse as he had no vacant boxes. Porter suggested that the Baron send his horses to George Blackwell, who had been head lad to Mathew Dawson. Hirsch followed Porter's advice, but Blackwell only had his horses a year before the Baron died.

It cannot have been a coincidence that the Lord Marcus Beresford, in addition to being the Prince's racing manager, occupied the same post for Baron Hirsch in 1892. Clearly there had been a personality clash between the autocratic peer, who expected to make all the decisions concerning his two employers' horses, and the most successful trainer in England, who would have objected to taking the high-handed orders of any mere racing manager. It is interesting to note that the only Classic winners bred at the Royal Stud at Sandringham prior to the death of King Edward VII were out of two mares, Perdita II and Poetry, both of whom had been bought by John Porter in 1887. It is also interesting that not one of the broodmares bought by Lord Marcus Beresford for the Royal Stud at Sandringham ever managed to produce a Classic winner.

11

The Royal Stud at Sandringham,

1892–1910

The Prince of Wales's eldest son, Prince Albert Victor, who was always known by his family as 'Eddy', died of pneumonia in 1892 at the age of twenty-eight. His younger brother George was enormously distressed by his death and fearful that he would not have the qualities needed of a King, for he was now in direct line of succession to the throne. The Prince of Wales became persuaded that an early marriage was the answer, to revive his son's spirits and increase his self-confidence. In the following spring, Prince George, who had been created Duke of York, became engaged to his late brother's fiancée, Princess Mary of Teck, and the couple were married on 6 July 1893.

It was at the end of this year of sorrow and mourning that the Prince of Wales's horses in training were removed from the care of John Porter at Kingsclere to Richard Marsh's stables at Egerton House, Newmarket. Richard Marsh, who had been born in 1851, rode his first winner on 24 August 1866, when partnering Captain Smith's Manrico to victory in the Members' Plate at Dover. He was then attached to the stables of Charles and Henry Bloss, who trained Hermit to win the Derby. When his father moved to Epsom, Marsh left Newmarket and rode for the stables of Sherwood and Reeves. One of his biggest successes on the flat was his victory on Temple, who had been bred by Queen Victoria at Hampton Court, in the New Stakes at Ascot in 1869. Continual weight problems, however, curtailed his career as a jockey on the flat, and Marsh therefore started a new career as a hurdle and steeplechase jockey, riding for the Gloucestershire trainers, T. Golby and Teddy Weever. On his first mount in a steeplechase Marsh won the Sefton Handicap Chase on The Nun on 10 March 1870. He was to ride in eight Grand

Nationals between 1871 and 1881, but the closest he came to winning was when third on Thornfield, which he also trained, in 1881.

Marsh had begun training for Mr Hector Baltazzi at Banstead Manor, Epsom, in the mid-1870s when Golby retired from training. Among the useful steeplechasers produced by Marsh at this period was Jackal, whose victories included the first Grand Hurdle at Auteuil in 1874 and the Craven Steeplechase at Liverpool in both 1877 and 1878, in the latter year in Lord Marcus Beresford's colours, after he had bought Jackal for the Prince of Wales earlier in the year. The next season Jackal ran second to The Liberator in the Grand National.

In 1876 Marsh moved his stables from Epsom to Lordship Farm at Newmarket, where his principal patron became the Duke of Hamilton. According to Marsh, 'The Duke treated me more like a son than a trainer and spared no thought to make my busy life a happy one.' In 1883 Marsh won the St Leger for the Duke with Ossian, whom he had advised his patron to back for the Doncaster Classic in June at Ascot. Hamilton had immediately put £100 on Ossian to win £10,000. Another Classic winner Marsh trained for the Duke was Miss Jummy, who won the 1,000 Guineas and Oaks in 1886. In 1890 Marsh trained Morion to win the Royal Hunt Cup; the next year Morion won the Ascot Gold Cup. Marsh also won the Stewards' Cup three years running, in 1890 and 1892 with Marvel and in the intervening year with Unicorn.

In 1892 the agent for Lord Ellesmere, Mr Percy Heaton, approached Marsh with the idea of creating the best stable in Newmarket at Egerton House and giving the tenancy to him. He told Marsh that the estate had made a profit of £50,000 from the fees of the stallion Hampton, and that this would pay for the building of the new training establishment on a site of 120 acres. Marsh signed a new lease for Lordship Farm, which permitted him to sub-let it to Joseph Cannon; he then proceeded to set about making Egerton the finest training stables in Newmarket. He built the private gallops which circled the grounds and planted the beautiful belts of trees which, growing slowly to maturity, made the place so enchanting. The private gallops were to prove invaluable for the Royal horses in training, particularly the mile-and-a-quarter moss litter gallop. Marsh had first come across a moss litter gallop when, out hunting with the Duc d'Aumale's boarhounds in the forest of Chantilly, he found himself galloping along a 'ride' on which the going seemed like a carpet of velvet. His enquiries revealed that it was the Duke's private moss litter gallop, on which no one was permitted to ride. He was then told how it had been laid out and took the knowledge home. When the racecourse side gallops of Newmarket were hard and caused anxiety to trainers, Marsh was able to work his horses on this private gallop. He relates that it took three years for the Turf to reach nearly perfect condition, and that it still continued to improve every year after that. So famous did it become that the Stewards of the Jockey Club and the custodian of the Heath at Newmarket, Mr Marriott, came to inspect it, after which they gave orders that similar gallops were to be laid out on the Limekilns and on the racecourse side of the town for use in the dry summer months.

It was in the autumn of 1892 that Lord Marcus Beresford met Richard Marsh at Challis's Hotel in London and asked him if he would train the Prince of Wales's horses at Egerton. Marsh recalled that he had known 'this perfect gentleman and splendid sportsman' for some years before this meeting. He also felt that Lord Marcus must have been the prime mover in suggesting him as the trainer to the Prince of Wales. When Beresford asked Marsh to become the Royal trainer, he was a trifle surprised that the offer was not accepted with alacrity; Marsh told him that he felt he had to consult with his principal patron, the Duke of Hamilton, before accepting the appointment. Lord Marcus replied, 'In the old days you would have had your head cut off for hesitating about such a thing.' The same evening Marsh met the Duke of Hamilton, with whom he had arranged to stay. When the Duke heard about the Royal offer, he exclaimed, 'For goodness' sake wire off at once your grateful acceptance. You should not have said what you did.' Later, when the Prince of Wales told his new trainer that he had heard that 'you had to seek the Duke of Hamilton's permission before you accepted my horses,' Richard Marsh reluctantly agreed that the story was true. He was relieved when the Prince commended his action: 'You were quite right, Marsh, in doing what you did. I am glad you had that respect for a good master.'

On 1 January 1893 Marsh and Lord Marcus went to Overton to see the Prince's eight horses in training at Kingsclere loaded on to a special train for Newmarket. They arrived in their boxes at Egerton that evening, to be followed four days later by Baron Hirsch's twenty horses, including La Fleche, whom Marsh described as 'the best mare I ever trained'. When Hirsch's horses left Kingsclere, Porter wrote to Marsh: 'I am glad, as they are leaving me, you get them. They will help fill up and pay the expenses of the new establishment. You and I are not foolish enough to fall out over other people's quarrels.'

Richard Marsh's first season as the Royal trainer was not crowned with success; he won only two minor races. Perdita II's third foal, Florizel II by St Simon, was the only one of the eight from Kingsclere to show his new trainer the faintest glimmer of potential racing quality. He was coarsish, plain and backward with weak forelegs in the summer of 1893, but had the merit of being good-tempered. On his debut in the Breeders' Foal Stakes at Manchester, it was an unsurprised Marsh who watched him trail in nearer last than first. In his second race, the Boscawen Stakes at Newmarket, he ran much better than Marsh expected and finished second. In his two remaining outings as a two-year-old Florizel II competed in two nurseries without troubling the Judge. None of the remainder of the 1891 crop of yearlings bred at Sandringham gave the impression that they might win a race either as two-year-olds or throughout their racing careers.

Florizel II matured well over the winter. His first victory at three was in the St James's Palace Stakes at Ascot, the best race yet won by a Sandringham-bred foal. Florizel II won three more races over a mile that summer at Ascot, Goodwood and Brighton; his fifth win, over ten furlongs at Newmarket in October, was witnessed by the Prince of Wales. He had won prize money of £3,499, thus easily recouping the money Porter had spent on his dam. In 1895 Florizel II won six of his seven races; victories in the Prince of Wales's Plate at Epsom over a mile and the Prince's Handicap at Gatwick over ten furlongs in the spring were followed by four noteworthy successes in the Manchester Cup, the Gold Vase at Ascot, the Goodwood Cup and the Jockey Club Stakes. Florizel II won a total of £4,359 in prize money in 1895, which was only £1,091 less than Sir Visto's prize money in the Derby. Marsh considered the four-year-old Florizel II much better than a handicapper, remarking that 'in addition to having some speed, he was a thoroughly good stayer.' Marsh recalled that the Prince was delighted with Florizel II's success, and never lost an opportunity of coming round the stables with his friends when attending race-meetings at Newmarket. On other occasions the Prince would ride on to the Heath in the early mornings and watch his horses work, asking questions and showing the liveliest interest in their progress and condition. After Florizel II's victory in the Manchester Cup, the Prince sent Marsh a pin as a souvenir of the win. Sir Digton Probyn also wrote the following in a letter to the Royal trainer:

The Prince has always known that Florizel was a good Horse, but His Royal Highness desires me to say he is equally well aware that no man could have done more than you to bring out the horse's good qualities, and His Royal Highness heartily congratulates you on having trained the horse so very success-fully for the big race yesterday. Please let Calder know that the Prince of Wales was much pleased to hear from so many people how well he rode the race.

Florizel II ran only once in 1896, finishing third to Love Wisely in the Ascot Gold Cup. He had by then developed suspensory ligament trouble and it had been impossible for Marsh to train him properly for the race. Florizel II was then retired to the Royal Stud at Sandringham as a stallion, having won a total of £7,858 in his career on the racecourse.

Florizel II turned out to be a more than useful sire, but his success at stud was overshadowed by that of his full-brother, Persimmon. Nevertheless he sired the 1901 Derby winner, Volodyovski, and Doricles, who beat Volodyovski into second place in that year's St Leger and became an important sire in France. His son Consols was the sire of Massine, who won the 1924 Prix de l'Arc de Triomphe and was leading sire in France in 1932 and 1936, when his sons Strip the Willow and Mieuxcé won both the Prix du Jockey-Club and Grand Prix de Paris. Massine was also the grand-sire of Souverain, the winner of the Grand Prix de Paris in 1946 and the Ascot Gold Cup the following year. Florizel II was also the sire of Vedas, who won the 2,000 Guineas in 1905.

In 1892 Perdita II was barren, and only one foal bred by the Prince of Wales, Hamiltrude (Hampton–Fortuna), who won three minor races at Sandown, Leicester and Doncaster, had any ability. She was sold out of the Royal Stud and became the dam of five minor winners. She left her mark on the Stud Book, however, as the grandam of Silvermere, the winner of the 1932 Ascot Gold Vase, and she was the fifth dam of that great sire of chasers, Vulgan, who won the 1948 Queen Alexandra Stakes.

In 1893 the stud groom at Welbeck reported to Lord Marcus Beresford that Perdita II had produced a most beautiful foal by St Simon, who was named Persimmon, on 15 April. The stud groom believed he was the best foal he had ever seen at Welbeck. Richard Marsh first saw Persimmon on his own very first visit to the Royal Stud at Sandringham in the summer of 1893. When the Prince of Wales inquired what he thought of him, his trainer replied that if he grew and developed the right way, he would become a Classic horse. Marsh later wrote,

I must say I have never set eyes on a more beautiful foal. If you ever saw a high-class horse in the foal then here was one. He stood well, and he was so well proportioned all through. What struck me on that first view of him was the absolute straightness of his hocks . . .

In the second week of August 1894 Persimmon arrived at Egerton to go into training. Marsh was most impressed by the progress the young colt had made:

Behind the saddle he was indeed wonderful in the remarkable length from hip to hock. I should be correct in saying that he was a trifle slack in the back ribs, but he girthed rare and well. His shoulders were what may be called strong. I mean that I have seen more perfectly sloped ones. He had a nice clean neck, while his countenance was bold and good. Slightly derogatory to his appearance was a tendency to lop ears, a characteristic undoubtedly derived from the Melbourne blood in his pedigree.

Persimmon, who most of his life was a perfect-tempered horse, gave no trouble when he was broken. In October 1894 the Prince of Wales and Lord Marcus Beresford came to inspect him at the stables; they were assured that he had a bright future, but Marsh warned that he would take time to mature and develop into his big and ample frame. In the second week of May 1895 Marsh gave Persimmon his first serious gallop with a four-year-old mare, Rags, whom he had been using for trials with his two-year-olds. Persimmon, ridden by Jack Watts, who already knew the colt well, was set to give Rags about 2 st. Without Watts even touching Persimmon with his heels, the two-year-old totally outclassed Rags and won the gallop in a canter. A delighted Lord Marcus immediately remarked, 'Well, this is the first time, and it may be the only time, we shall ever have a chance of a Derby horse. All I can say is he must be a high-class horse to have done what he has this morning.'

Hard ground prevented Marsh from giving Persimmon another gallop before his debut in the Coventry Stakes at Ascot. The Prince of Wales, Lord Marcus and several friends made a special visit to the paddock to see his debutant after he had been saddled, and were able to see that he looked a picture. The public noted that the Prince took the then unusual step of inspecting his runner before the race and made him favourite. They were not disappointed, for Jack Watts had no difficulty in steering the Royal colt to an easy three-length victory over Meli Melo. So impressive was the performance that Persimmon was soon talked about as the possible Derby winner.

The Prince of Wales was present at Goodwood when Persimmon gained his second consecutive victory in the Richmond Stakes, since he was staying at Goodwood House with the Duke of Richmond and Gordon. Marsh was a little anxious before the race as Persimmon started sweating after he saddled him and seemed nervous. Knowing that both his sire, St Simon, and grandsire, Galopin, both often sweated before their races, he was not overly worried, but he realized that a Thoroughbred with such nervous energy would have to be treated with care and attention.

A fortnight prior to Persimmon's intended final race in 1895, the Middle Park Stakes at Newmarket, the Royal colt was coughing. Lord Marcus was extremely keen for Persimmon to run, and after seeing him in a rough gallop with some second-class horses three or four days prior to the race, pronounced him to be back to his old form and ordered that he should run. Marsh obeyed, but reluctantly; he felt that Persimmon had not shown his usual fire and dash in the gallop, that he was not at his best and so was unfit to run. Marsh's fears proved more accurate than Beresford's subjective judgement, for Persimmon was beaten half a length and five lengths into third place by St Frusquin and Omladina. Marsh was very upset by this unnecessary defeat, and was very worried that the colt could have been ruined by running in a condition when not fit to do his best. Fortunately Jack Watts eased the Royal Classic prospect when he realized he was not going to win, so no long-term harm was done to his prospects.

Perdita II used to grow a long and dense winter coat and passed this trait on to Persimmon, who took a long time to shed his winter coat in the spring of 1896. Marsh recalled, 'In all my experience of high-class horses I do not think that I have ever had a horse come to hand so sluggishly and slowly as did Persimmon.' During the Craven Meeting at Newmarket Marsh gave him a gallop with two moderate horses owned by the Prince of Wales, Courtier and Chinkara; even taking into account his backwardness, Persimmon ran so abysmally in the trial that his trainer was most disappointed and very worried. When, a few days later, an abscess was discovered under one of his teeth, a discussion was held with the Prince of Wales and Beresford and it was decided to strike him out of the

2,000 Guineas. The Guineas saw Mr Leopold de Rothschild's St Frusquin trounce Love Wisely by three lengths; Love Wisely was to win the Ascot Gold Cup the following year. Inevitably St Frusquin became a firm favourite for the Derby.

Persimmon, meanwhile, began to show the benefit of the patient preparation Marsh was giving him, and by the end of April his progress had begun to please his trainer. Three weeks before the Derby Marsh arranged for him to gallop with, among others, the Prince of Wales's moderate three-year-old, Safety Pin, and Lord Marcus Beresford came specially down from London to witness this test. Both Lord Marcus and Marsh stationed themselves on their hacks opposite the Rowley Mile winning-post; as the horses passed the Bushes, they expected Watts on Persimmon to come away from the rest. To their horror the Royal Derby hope, rolling all over the place with his tongue lolling out, finished four lengths behind Safety Pin. As the horses passed them, Lord Marcus tersely observed to Marsh, 'A nice Derby horse!' Marsh recalled that he had never felt so foolish or depressed in his life as after that fiasco of a trial. In later years, as at the time, he was unable to account for that terrible performance, and it was a very dejected racing manager who returned to London that Tuesday afternoon.

Persimmon, being a big horse who needed a strong preparation, had another gallop the following Saturday with the same horses. This time, to Richard Marsh's intense relief, the big bay colt totally outclassed the rivals that had made him look so moderate a few days before. Marsh wired the good news to Lord Marcus and suggested that another gallop should be held the next week which the Prince of Wales might be invited to attend. Marsh intended to run Persimmon against the Duke of Devonshire's Balsamo, who had run second to St Frusquin's stable-companion Galeazzo in the Newmarket Stakes. The 2,000 Guineas winner had not run in that race in case he jarred his suspect forelegs on the hard ground. Marsh arranged for the trial to take place on the ten-furlong moss litter private gallop at Egerton, and for the Royal Derby hope to give 21 lbs to Balsamo and even more weight to Safety Pin and Courtier. He ordered a special stand to be built so that the Royal party could watch the entire gallop. Safety Pin and Courtier made the running until five furlongs out, when Madden on Balsamo and Watts on Persimmon swept past them. Persimmon toyed with the Duke of Devonshire's useful colt, who was to win the City and Suburban Handicap the next spring, and won going away by over two lengths. The Prince of Wales immediately remarked, 'Well,

Marsh, that should please you very much. Very satisfactory, most satisfactory.' His trainer replied, 'I am delighted, Your Royal Highness. I think we shall win the Derby.' Later Princess Alexandra drew him on one side and asked if he really thought Persimmon would win at Epsom. His answer to her was a little more cautious: 'I think, Your Royal Highness, we must have a tremendous chance if the horse keeps well. The only one I am afraid of is St Frusquin, because I think he must be a really good horse.'

Marsh arranged for Persimmon to be sent to Epsom from Dullingham Station on a horse special the day before the Derby. Some of his dam's occasionally spiteful and obstinate temperament must have taken control of him that afternoon as he stubbornly refused to be boxed. Two horse special trains came and went, and with the last due to leave in fifteen minutes, Marsh was at his wits' end to know what to do. Persimmon lashed out every time his trainer and one of his lads linked hands behind his hindquarters and tried to force him into his box. Finally Marsh called for volunteers from the crowd of onlookers, to whom he promised a sovereign each, and half-a-dozen men on each of his flanks virtually lifted Persimmon into his box. Unconcerned, the colt proceeded to attack his feed of corn with gusto. When he arrived at Epsom, however, he looked terrible; the struggle to get him into his box must have taken its toll. Fortunately, he settled down comfortably in his stable and did not leave a single oat or drop of water all the time he was at Epsom.

Another scare that had begun much earlier concerned his jockey, Jack Watts, who like Fred Archer had severe weight problems. He was frequently depressed and during the previous winter had told Marsh that he was seriously considering retiring from the saddle, saying that, having already won the Derby three times on Merry Hampton, Sainfoin and Ladas, he felt that there were no other goals for him to achieve as a jockey. Eventually Marsh persuaded him of the honour it would be to ride the winner of the Derby for the Prince of Wales. On the Monday of the Derby week Marsh weighed Watts and found him to be over the weight at 9 st 2 lbs. After he had ridden his mount in canter on the course on the morning of the race, Marsh accompanied Watts, with his sweaters on, despite the muggy weather, on a fast walk around Ashtead Park. On their return to Holt's Place, where Watts was staying and Persimmon was stabled, Marsh was much relieved to find that Watts would do the weight.

Lord Derby's trainer, the Hon. George Lambton, who was staying with Lord Rosebery at Durdans for the Epsom meeting, went out on the Downs to see the morning work. One of the first horses he encountered was Persimmon, 'rather irritable, the sweat running off him and not looking in the least like a Derby winner, with Dick Marsh, quite as hot and nearly as irritable'. He then met St Frusquin and his trainer, Alfred Hayhoe, 'the horse looking beautiful, but moving a little short, and Hayhoe in a very bad temper, declaring that the course was beastly'. The public, who had heard of the difficulties in preparing the Royal colt for the race, sent off St Frusquin favourite at 13–8 on with Persimmon second favourite at 5–1.

Neither of the two favourites appeared in the paddock; in those days it was not obligatory for runners to appear there, nor was there a parade before the race. St Frusquin was saddled at Durdans, and Persimmon at Sherwood's stable, which was on the crest of the hill opposite the stands near the mile-and-a-quarter start. The Prince and Princess of Wales travelled to Epsom by special train from London.

After three false starts, the Starter, Mr Arthur Coventry, got the field away. Bay Ronald took the lead from Bradwardine, Tamarind, Earwig and Gulistan, St Frusquin's pacemaker, who had been slowly into his stride, with the favourite and Persimmon the back markers of the field of eleven. With a mile to go Gulistan had taken up the running from Bradwardine, while Loates had moved St Frusquin up to a position just behind the leaders, closely tracked by Watts and Persimmon. Bay Ronald regained the lead as the field swung round Tattenham Corner into the straight with Loates on St Frusquin on his heels and Persimmon about two lengths behind on the outside. Two furlongs out St Frusquin swept into the lead past a beaten Bay Ronald, but Watts on the Royal colt followed him through. From that moment on it became a two-horse race. Tommy Loates on the rails was riding for his life but could not get away from Persimmon. At the distance Watts called on Persimmon to make his effort, and, responding most courageously, the Royal colt gradually closed the gap and drew level with the 2,000 Guineas winner. Persimmon then seemed to falter and Watts had to steady and balance him well inside the final furlong. Gathering the colt again, Watts renewed his challenge and gained a narrow advantage less than one hundred yards out; at the winning-post Persimmon had a neck to spare over his rival. In George Lambton's opinion, 'Watts's quietness and nerve in such a critical moment was one of the greatest feats of jockeyship I ever saw.'

Marsh had not even seen the finish of the race, for he had left the start so late on his hack that he had not been able to reach the stands. Mornington Cannon, who spotted him when pulling up on Knight of the Thistle, told him that Persimmon had won. Fighting his way through the crowd, he reached Jack Watts on Persimmon. The jockey looked so glum that Marsh felt for a moment that he must have been beaten. Only when he roared at him, 'Do you know that you've just won the Derby for the Prince of Wales?' did a faint smile break over the jockey's face. The Prince of Wales, meanwhile, was showered with congratulations. He walked from the balcony of the Club enclosure, where he had watched the race, to the weighing-in enclosure gate with the Duke of York and Marcus Beresford amid a wild tumult of cheering, excitement and enthusiasm. This spontaneous reception demonstrated what a popular victory Persimmon's had been, and indeed how popular a figure the Prince himself had become in the country.

To commemorate Persimmon's famous victory, the Prince of Wales sent Marsh a pin and a cheque for £800; £500 for him 'for the splendid way you trained Persimmon for the Derby in face of so many difficulties',[1] £100 for Persimmon's lad Crisp, £50 each for the head lad, Leach, and travelling head lad, Prince, and £100 for the boys in the stable.

In Persimmon's next race, the Prince of Wales's Stakes at Newmarket, he again met St Frusquin. The concession of 3 lb to Mr Leopold de Rothschild's colt proved too much for him, and he was beaten half a length. There can have been but little between them as three-year-olds; however, this race was then over a mile, which must have suited St Frusquin more. They never met again; after St Frusquin won the Eclipse Stakes, he broke down and was retired to stud. Only six dared oppose the Royal Derby winner in the St Leger at Doncaster, for which he started at 11–2 on and won in a canter from Labrador. In the Jockey Club Stakes at Newmarket, Persimmon was opposed by Sir Visto, who had won the 1895 Derby and St Leger. The Royal champion had no difficulty in winning by two lengths.

'Good as Persimmon was as a three-year-old,' George Lambton wrote later, 'he improved like good wine with age.' His first objective now was the Ascot Gold Cup. That shrewd judge, Captain Machell, was so certain that his runner, Winkfield's Pride, who had won the Cambridgeshire in 1896, would beat Persimmon, that he had a bet of £100 with Marsh; for once his judgement was at fault. George Lambton recalled many years later that 'when Persimmon was stripped for the Ascot Gold Cup, he stands out in my memory as the most perfectly trained horse I ever saw.' Lambton's opinion was upheld by Persimmon as he beat Winkfield's Pride in a canter by eight lengths with Love Wisely, the previous year's winner, another four lengths away third. Persimmon's final race was in the Eclipse Stakes, when he beat the 1897 Derby and 2,000 Guineas runner-up, Velasquez, an easy two lengths with Bay Ronald four lengths away third. Velasquez was to win the Champion Stakes in 1897 and 1898 and the Eclipse Stakes as a four-year-old, thus underlining the merit of Persimmon's last victory.

Persimmon retired to stud at Sandringham at a fee of 300 gns and made his mark as a stallion from the outset. His first crop included the peerless filly Sceptre, who won the 1,000 and 2,000 Guineas, the Oaks and the St Leger in 1902; she probably should have won the Derby as well but for the poor riding of her inexperienced jockey, Randall. Persimmon was also the sire of two other Oaks winners, Keystone II in 1906 and Perola in 1909, and two St Leger winners, Your Majesty in 1908 and Prince Palatine in 1911. The latter won the Ascot Gold Cup in 1912 and 1913; Zinfandel had won Ascot's most important race in 1905 for Lord Howard de Walden. Had Zinfandel's previous owner, Colonel McCalmont, not died before the 1903 Derby, it is likely the colt would have been Persimmon's first Derby winner. Persimmon was champion sire on four occasions, but regrettably for King Edward VII never sired a champion from a Sandringham mare. He was also leading broodmare sire four times, and an important sire of sires: Prince Palatine was the sire of Rose Prince and grandsire of Prince Rose, who was the sire of Princequillo, Prince Chevalier and Prince Bio; these three all became influential stallions, among Princequillo's most famous sons was the great American champion Round Table. Other notable horses descended from them include Doutelle, Sicambre, Baldric II, Stage Door Johnny, Pretendre and Charlottesville.

In 1908 Persimmon slipped in his box at Sandringham and fractured his pelvis. He was hung in slings and every effort was made to save him, but tragically he had to be put down. A statue commissioned by King Edward VII now stands on the lawn in front of the Royal Stud at Sandringham to commemorate its greatest foal.

Thais (St Serf–Poetry), another foal bred by the Prince of Wales in 1893, was also to become a Classic winner. A rather delicate and highly-strung filly, she had won a £1,000 race at Gatwick from three outings as a two-year-old. In the spring of 1896 Thais gave her Royal owner his first Classic success as an owner – breeder when she beat Santa Maura and seventeen others on a very cold and windy afternoon in the 1,000 Guineas. The two fillies had raced on opposite sides of the course and Thais only got the verdict by a short head. Richard Marsh recalled that 'she never looked back after winning the 1,000 Guineas, and I must say that I had rarely seen a three-year-filly, before or since, look as well as she did on the day I left home for Epsom.' The confidence in the stable that Thais would triumph in the Oaks surpassed even the hope that Persimmon would win the Derby. On account of her temperament, she did not travel to Epsom until the day before the race. Marsh's head lad, Felix Leach, was so certain she would win that he wired Marsh for permission to attend the race; but on his arrival at Epsom he did not recognize her! From the moment of her departure from Newmarket, Thais had not touched a morsel of food or a drop of water. Leach found her in her box with her ears back and shivering. Her trainer told the Prince of Wales in consequence that her condition made him think she had no chance, even though she was favourite at 13–8 against. Despite her deplorable condition Thais ran with remarkable courage. Until Rickaby challenged on Lord Derby's Canterbury Pilgrim just below the distance, she looked the winner; but in the final furlong Canterbury Pilgrim took her measure and won by two lengths. The two fillies had come very close, however, and when the Prince of Wales congratulated Lambton he said, 'Tell your jockey from me that he came too close to my mare.' The two fillies met again in the Coronation Stakes at Ascot. Thais showed none of the distress that she had got into at Epsom and finished in front of Lord Derby's filly, but failed to give 7 lbs to Helm. Canterbury Pilgrim was to become one of the great foundation mares of Lord Derby's stud and was the dam, amongst others, of Swynford and Chaucer, the broodmare sire of Hyperion.

The addition of Thais to the broodmares at Sandringham was an exciting prospect in 1897. Disappointingly, she was barren to Isinglass in 1898; she was covered again by him that summer, but then disaster struck when she died from inflammation of the bowels on 22 November. The Royal Stud's vet, Brown, could do nothing to save her; Walker, the Stud Groom, who stayed with her in her agony till she died, was broken-hearted. Her premature death, before she had produced a single foal, was a grievous loss to the Royal Stud. Nevertheless, the foal crop of 1893 was one of the best ever achieved in the history of the Sandringham Stud. Both Safety Pin and Courtier won four races each, so from the six foals bred that year from seven mares, four won seventeen races including three Classics.

Inevitably the crop of 1894 could not rival that of 1893. Three of the foals bred that year won a total of four races; the best was Thais's half-brother by Donovan, Oakdene, whose two wins included the Criterion Stakes at Newmarket; unfortunately he never fulfilled his early juvenile promise. Persimmon's half-brother, Farrant by Donovan, never even set foot on a racecourse. Only three of the foals bred by the Prince of Wales in 1895 were victorious, but the eight races they won between them were of much better quality. The best of this crop was Mousme (St Simon–Fanchette), whose two successes included the July Stakes at Newmarket in 1897. Dunlop (Ayrshire–Fortuna) won four races and was third at 100–1 in the Derby behind Jeddah. He raced in the colours of Mr W. Ward, to whom he had been sold as a foal with his dam. Perdita II's foal by Surefoot, Azeeza, ran once as a juvenile, but was useless; she was finally sold out of the Royal Stud. Only one winner, Eventail (Ayrshire–Fanchette) emerged from the 1896 crop of foals bred at Sandringham. She proved a useful two-year-old, winning three races: the Acorn Plate at Epsom, the Prince of Wales's Stakes at Goodwood and the Royal Two-Year-Old Plate at Kempton. Another foal bred by the Royal Stud in 1896 was Persimmon's full-brother Sandringham. Lacking the strong constitution of his illustrious brothers, he could never be properly trained and so never raced. He was eventually sold to stand as a stallion in the United States.

In 1896 Perdita II was sent back to Welbeck to be covered again by St Simon. On 12 March 1897 she gave birth at Sandringham to a bay colt, which was named Diamond Jubilee in honour of Queen Victoria's sixty years on the throne. When Perdita II had been in training, she had often shown such temper and spitefulness that it had been a difficult task to get her to the Limekilns to do her work. Up to 1897 she had not passed on this waywardness and obstinacy, which she had inherited from her grandsire Galopin, to her offspring in any great measure. Diamond Jubilee, unfortunately, inherited all of these traits. He arrived at Marsh's stables at Egerton House as an unbroken yearling in August 1898. Marsh described him then as 'a beautiful young horse and immensely pleasing to the eye, for he was a bright bay with dark legs and a dark line down the middle of his back to the root of his tail. He had a most intelligent head and a perfect back and loins. What more can I say of a faultless horse. I looked for faults and could not find one.' One day when Henry Chaplin was visiting the stables with the Prince of Wales, Marsh told him that he had a horse with perfect conformation in the yard. Chaplin bet Marsh five pounds that there was no horse who could not be faulted. When the party arrived at Diamond Jubilee's box, Chaplin lingered behind after they departed. When he caught them up, he handed Marsh a five-pound note without a word.

In his early days at Sandringham as a foal, Diamond Jubilee had the habit of walking straight at the grooms, and would have walked over them if they had not given way; nothing at all seemed to frighten him. He was not easy to break, but developed into a lovely two-year-old. After his first serious trial, when he gave 7 lbs and a beating to the Woodcote Stakes runner-up, Simonswood, Marsh decided to run him in the Coventry Stakes at Ascot, the same race in which his brother, Persimmon, had made his racecourse debut. In the paddock, Diamond Jubilee, who was favourite at 6–5, lashed out and kicked a man standing near him. On arrival at the starting-post he seemed to go mad; he reared up, walked about on his hind legs and tried to get the foot of his jockey, Jack Watts, into his mouth. The Starter, Arthur Coventry, later told Marsh that he had never seen a horse behave so badly at the post. Unsurprisingly, Diamond Jubilee finished a distinctly moderate fourth to Democrat. This out-rageous behaviour had taken Richard Marsh quite by surprise. After Ascot the horse behaved so well at home that Marsh hoped his antics would not recur in the July Stakes at Newmarket, for he had made excellent progress. The errant colt had other ideas, however; he threw Watts when they arrived at the start and ran riderless down the course. Caught by one of his stable-lads and returned to the post, he dug his heels in and refused to race when the Starter got them away; he trailed in an inglorious last.

Thinking that Diamond Jubilee might have an intense dislike of Watts, Marsh put Mornington Cannon up on him in the Prince of Wales's Stakes at Goodwood, and he ran a better race, finishing second to the useful Epsom Lad. Cannon again had the mount on Diamond Jubilee when he won his first race, the Boscawen Stakes at Newmarket in the early autumn; on this occasion the colt wore a chifney, which must have curbed any ideas he may have had of playing up. Cannon could not ride Diamond Jubilee in the Middle Park Stakes as he was claimed for the Duke of Westminster's runner, Goblet, so Watts took the mount. Persimmon's brother was on his best behaviour, and put up the finest performance of his two-year-old career. Despite conceding Democrat the gelding allowance of 3 lbs, he ran him to half a length. A fortnight later

Democrat, giving Diamond Jubilee 1 lb, beat the Royal colt three quarters of a length in the Dewhurst Stakes. Democrat, incidentally, did not train on and ended his days as Lord Kitchener's charger in India when he was Commander-in-Chief of the forces there.

Although Diamond Jubilee's career as a juvenile could not be described as anything more than one of modest achievement, he seemed to make steady improvement throughout the autumn. His breeding, size and action all suggested that stamina would be one of his greatest assets, and both his brothers, Florizel II and Persimmon, had made more than normal improvement between two and three. The biggest problem Marsh felt that he would have with the colt would be to stop him from becoming unmanageable.

In the spring of 1900 the Prince of Wales had the pleasure of winning the Grand National with Ambush II, whom he had bought on the advice of an amateur jockey friend of Lord Marcus Beresford, G. W. Lushington. A few days later, while travelling to Copenhagen, the Prince was victim of an assassination attempt by a fifteen-year-old Belgian anarchist student named Spido on Brussels Station. The Prince wrote to his friend Henry Chaplin a week later, from Copenhagen:

My dear Harry,
   I am most grateful to you for your kind letter of sympathy on the occasion of the narrow escape I experienced in Brussels last week. Luckily the individual was a very indifferent shot, as it is inconceivable that he missed me at two yards! ... Many thanks for all you say about the Grand National. It is a race I was very proud to win. Indeed I hope that Diamond Jubilee may run well for the Derby, but it would be almost too good luck to expect to win it.
   Ever Yours sincerely, Albert Edward.[2]

In 1900 Richard Marsh married Grace Darling. On his return from his honeymoon, Marsh found that Diamond Jubilee had made magnificent physical improvement. Although his hot-headed idiosyncrasies had not disappeared, the colt's exceptional merit was plain to his trainer. A few weeks before the 2,000 Guineas the Prince of Wales was due at the stables to see him work. Two days earlier Diamond Jubilee showed he had not lost his unpredictability; Mornington Cannon, who was to partner him in his races, had just finished riding him round the private gallop at Egerton and was leading him by the bridle, when the colt seized him and tried to savage him.

Cannon was rescued immediately, but after another gallop a few days later he asked Marsh to find another jockey for the ill-tempered colt. This request put Marsh in a serious quandary, as the other leading jockeys of the time were already engaged.

Diamond Jubilee was normally ridden in his work by a young jockey attached to Marsh's stable, Herbert Jones, whose father, Jack Jones, had earlier trained chasers for Lord Marcus Beresford and the Prince of Wales. Although Bert Jones was very inexperienced, having only ridden his first winner in 1896 and but two in 1899, Richard Marsh was impressed by the way Jones kept the colt calm and quiet when riding him. It was clear that Diamond Jubilee knew and trusted Jones, whom Marsh knew to be a first-class rider, even if he had not yet proved that in public. Marsh therefore wrote to Lord Marcus Beresford suggesting that Jones should ride the Prince's colt in the 2,000 Guineas, pointing out that he did more for him than any other jockey, and asked him to recommend this plan to the Prince. The Prince of Wales agreed. The confidence Marsh had reposed in young Bert Jones was not misplaced; they won the 2,000 Guineas by four lengths from Sir Ernest Cassel's Bonarosa. In order that the Duke of York could go to Newmarket to see his father's colt run in the Newmarket Stakes on 16 May, the christening of his son, later the Duke of Gloucester, was postponed one day to 17 May. Diamond Jubilee beat Mr John Musker's Chavening, but only by a short head, which caused some to lose confidence in his chances at Epsom.

Despite his two victories at Newmarket, Diamond Jubilee's behaviour on the gallops was far from impeccable. He frequently refused to move and stood stock still or reared up when Marsh wanted him to go down to the end of the gallop; then for no apparent reason he would take it into his head to stop misbehaving and move on. Marsh never listened to those who suggested he should give the colt a good hiding to make him more manageable. In his opinion, 'You must never hide the high-class horse of great courage. It is courage which makes him high-class. Break that and you destroy the whole fabric of the splendid racehorse.'

When Marsh was saddling Diamond Jubilee for the Derby in the paddock, he received a message from the Prince that the Princess of Wales would like to see him in the parade. Parades were not then compulsory and his patient trainer would have preferred to have sent the 2,000 Guineas winner direct to the start, as Epsom, with its vast and vociferous crowd, is a tremendous ordeal for a highly-strung colt of known ill-temper. A compromise was reached whereby Diamond Jubilee was permitted to take part in the parade, but at the first sign of trouble Jones was to go immediately to the start. For once Diamond Jubilee, who was favourite at 6–4, behaved faultlessly. For the first time in the Derby the starting gate was used, but this innovation did not disturb the Royal colt.

Chavening took the lead at the start, and Jones secured a good position for the favourite in the middle of the field. A mile out, the second favourite, Forfarshire, was sent into the lead followed by Tod Sloan on James R. Keene's American-bred Disguise II with Diamond Jubilee close behind. As the leaders swung round Tattenham Corner into the straight, Sloan took Disguise II into the lead, but in doing so interfered badly with Forfarshire, who completely lost his action and dropped back. This incident also caused Diamond Jubilee to become unbalanced, but with commendable composure Jones got the colt on an even keel again and went off in pursuit. A little below the distance Jones gave Diamond Jubilee his head and he quickly overhauled the tiring Disguise II. For a moment it seemed he had his race won, but then Simon Dale came on the scene with a most menacing challenge. Diamond Jubilee never flinched from his task and ran on most gamely to hold Simon Dale off by half a length. The Prince of Wales had bred two winners of the Derby in four years: a remarkable achievement.

The Prince, Diamond Jubilee and Bert Jones were greeted with thunderous applause when they reached the winner's enclosure. At a moment when the British army in South Africa, by then under the command of the very competent Field Marshal Lord Roberts, was at last gaining the upper hand over the Boers, the crowds at Epsom were in a jingoistic mood, and they broke into 'God Save the Queen'. A few days later, Richard Marsh received a cheque from the Prince of Wales for £1,000 for 'the splendid way in which you have trained Diamond Jubilee for the Derby and his other races'.[3] The Prince also gave Lord Marcus Beresford £1,000 for Bert Jones; he was directed to invest it in the City and for some years only to allow the young jockey the interest.

In Diamond Jubilee's next race, the Princess of Wales's Stakes at Newmarket's July Meeting, he was set to give 19 lbs to the Oaks runner-up, Merry Gal; the task proved insurmountable and the filly won by four lengths. Diamond Jubilee had no difficulty in conceding 10 lbs to Chavening in his next race, the Eclipse Stakes at Sandown, when Simon Dale could only finish a distant fourth. He next won the St Leger at 7–2 on by a length from Elopement, but not before causing enormous problems for both Marsh and

Jones. He reverted to his most devilish and intractable behaviour; every time Marsh tried to saddle him the colt stood bolt upright on his hind legs, and it took nearly twenty minutes to get the saddle on him. He refused to be mounted by Jones, who eventually took him unawares and jumped on to his back. Diamond Jubilee reared up, but Jones, with the skill of an acrobat, managed to get his feet into the irons and stay on board. At the starting-post the horse continued to rear up on his hind legs and was in a thoroughly wild mood. By winning the St Leger Diamond Jubilee entered the ranks of the illustrious few who have won the Triple Crown, but it was the last race he was ever to win. Without doubt thereafter his vile temper interfered with his true ability as a racehorse.

In his final race as a three-year-old Diamond Jubilee was unplaced to Disguise II in the Jockey Club Stakes. Although this result was disappointing, the Triple Crown winner was the major contributor in making the Prince the leading owner in 1900 with winnings of £29,585. Before his first run in 1901, Diamond Jubilee showed his ill-temper by biting off the thumb of the lad who was saddling him. He was not completely disgraced in the race, finishing second by half a length to the much improved Epsom Lad. In the Eclipse Stakes Diamond Jubilee finished a close fourth to Epsom Lad. In his final race he was third to the three-year-old Pietermaritzburg and Epsom Lad. All through the season (in which he ran in the colours of the Duke of Devonshire as the Court was in mourning for Queen Victoria) he had been becoming more and more difficult, and eventually Marsh dared not go near him in his box for fear of being savaged. He was retired to stud at Sandringham at a fee of 300 gns; the boy who did him at Egerton went with him to make him more amenable. In 1906 he was sold to an Argentine breeder for £30,000; he did very well there as a stallion, dying at the age of twenty-six. Although a colt of outstanding merit when he consented to show it, Marsh considered him about 14 lbs inferior to his brother Persimmon. Beresford thought that the only time he showed what he was really capable of was when he won the 2,000 Guineas.

The crop of foals bred by the Prince of Wales in 1898 did not compare with that of the previous year: there were only two winners, Lauzun (St Simon–Merrie Lassie), who won the St James's Palace Stakes at Ascot, and Lord Quex (Sir Hugo–Leveret), one of whose three wins came in the Houghton Stakes. The year's biggest disappointment was Perdita II's loss of her foal by St Simon, but she was covered by him again at Welbeck in 1898. There was only one winner from each of the 1899 and 1900 crops; the best was

Mead (Persimmon–Meadow Chat), who won six races including the Richmond Stakes at Goodwood as a juvenile, the Prince of Wales's Stakes at Ascot in 1903 and the Jockey Club Cup at Newmarket in 1905. He did not make the first four in Rock Sand's Derby, when there were only seven runners, and Marsh considered him some way below Classic form. Mead was exported as a stallion to Chile. Perdita II had only one foal after Diamond Jubilee; Nadejda, a full-sister to the Prince of Wales's two Derby winners, was foaled in 1899, but she was never good enough to run and retired to stud at Sandringham in 1903. After foaling Nadejda the most successful broodmare to grace the paddocks at Sandringham unfortunately died. Some years after the purchase of Perdita II, the Prince of Wales had told John Porter, 'When you bought her you as good as made me a present of a quarter of a million in money.'

Queen Victoria died on 22 January 1901 at Osborne. The Prince of Wales thus ascended the throne at the age of fifty-nine, and let it be known that he wished to have the title of King Edward VII. The coronation took place in Westminster Abbey, amid much public rejoicing, on 9 August. Inside the Abbey there was a special King's box, which some wit had called 'the King's Loose Box', in which were seated the King's special friends, including the actress Sarah Bernhardt, Lady Kilmorey and Edward VII's current favourite, the Hon. Mrs George Keppel. The King had met Alice Keppel, a vivacious and intelligent beauty of twenty-nine, at Sandown in 1898, and their friendship lasted till his death.

By 1902 the number of broodmares at Sandringham had increased to seventeen and there were fifteen horses in training with Marsh. Greater quantity, though, did not mean higher quality. Although Persimmon was already proving himself as a stallion, the winners he was getting were all for other people. It was in 1902 that his filly Sceptre won four of the five Classics; none of the crops of foals bred by the King from 1901 to 1905 included any really high-class horse and the thirteen individual winners foaled in those four years only won twenty races between them. The only one of any note was Chatsworth (Persimmon–Meadow Chat), who won three races including the Newmarket St Leger in 1904.

The standard improved in 1905, the foals bred by the King that spring including Pearl of the Loch (Persimmon–Loch Doon) and Perrier (Persimmon–Amphora). Pearl of the Loch won the July Stakes and Soltikoff Stakes as a two-year-old, but unfortunately failed to train on. Marsh considered Perrier backward, but had sufficient faith in him to introduce him to the racecourse in the

Dewhurst Stakes. To his surprise Perrier ran very well, finishing only two lengths behind Rhodora, who was to win the 1,000 Guineas the following spring. Perrier's first run in 1908 was in the Biennial Stakes at Newmarket's Craven Meeting, which he won by two lengths. He was so full of promise and so highly regarded by Richard Marsh that shortly afterwards Queen Alexandra made a special trip alone to Egerton to see him. He was made favourite for the 2,000 Guineas, but was a very disappointing fifth to the American-bred Norman III. The only excuse that Marsh could offer the King was that perhaps Perrier did not appreciate the very heavy going that afternoon. Objectively, both he and Marcus Beresford realized that the colt was not up to Classic standard. Perrier was allowed to take his chance in the Derby, but he was never a threat to the eccentric Chevalier Ginistrelli's 100–1 outsider Signorinetta. After she had completed a famous double by winning the Oaks two days later, King Edward VII sent for Ginistrelli to congratulate him. When they appeared together outside the Royal Box, the crowd greeted them with tremendous applause and loud cheering. Perrier was not disgraced in his final race in 1908 when runner-up in the St James's Palace Stakes at Ascot. He was subsequently sold to some Frenchmen, who were received by Beresford and Marsh when they came to Egerton to inspect him. Beresford told them that Perrier should have won the Derby; when they inquired why he did not, the King's stud manager, who was never at a loss for words, replied, 'Well, at a most critical point of the race six or seven others passed him and he lost!' Marsh recalled that he said it in such a serious way that they bought the horse. In 1909 and 1910 Perrier won two more races at Newmarket. He was later exported to Argentina, where he was a very successful stallion.

The slight revival in the fortunes of the Royal Stud at Sandringham during these years seemed to gather pace, for among the foals born in 1906 was the filly Princesse des Galles (Gallinule–Ecila). One of the best two-year-olds in training in 1908, she won four of her six races including the Chesterfield Stakes at Newmarket, the New Ham Stakes at Goodwood and the Boscawen Stakes in the autumn. She was also unlucky to be beaten by Attic Salt in the Prince of Wales's Stakes at Goodwood when her jockey rode an ill-judged race. Princesse des Galles showed she had lost none of her ability when runner-up to Electra in the 1,000 Guineas with Perola third, and Richard Marsh was more than confident that she would gain her revenge over Electra in the Oaks; but on her arrival at Epsom she was found to be so badly amiss that he knew her chance was gone even before she arrived at the start. Nevertheless she ran a most courageous race; she held off the challenge of Perola till the final furlong and was only beaten two lengths. Electra, who had started favourite, lost so much ground at the start that it was impossible for her to take a hand in the finish. Princesse des Galles easily won the Coronation Stakes at Ascot, but at Doncaster failed to cope with Electra in the Park Hill Stakes. Unfortunately she was to prove the last foal bred by King Edward VII to play any prominent role in any of the Classics.

Nine of the ten foals bred at the Royal Stud at Sandringham in 1906 were fillies; the exception, Royal Escort (Diamond Jubilee–Ambleside), won a minor race at Sandown in 1909. This unusual preponderance of filly foals, combined with the singular lack of success of the Royal horses in the previous five years, led Lord Marcus Beresford to approach Colonel Hall Walker to see if he would lease the King some colts. Hall Walker, who thought he was the reincarnation of Charles II, was an ardent astrologer, and all important decisions regarding his horses were based on their horoscopes. He had acquired the Tully Stud in Co. Kildare at the beginning of the century, and was leading owner in 1905 and 1907. At the Gimcrack dinner in 1908 Hall Walker explained his reasons for agreeing to lease six colts to the King for their racing career: first, to save Beresford the necessity of buying yearling colts at the sales to compensate for the unbalanced 1906 crop of foals, and secondly, so that the King should enjoy more success than he had done in the previous few years. Among the six colts that arrived at Egerton from Tully in August 1907 was one named Minoru (Cyllene–Mother Siegel). Minoru's victories in the 1909 Greenham Stakes, 2,000 Guineas, Derby, St James's Palace Stakes and Sussex Stakes certainly made up for Edward VII's lack of success as an owner since his accession to the throne. Minoru was the first and only Derby winner to be owned by a reigning sovereign and was universally acclaimed. Nevertheless this triumph was not one that concerns the history of the Royal Studs, as the King was not his breeder. Hall Walker, later created Lord Wavertree, sold all his stock and the Tully Stud to the British government in 1916, when the six stallions and forty-three broodmares became the foundation stock of the National Stud.

The Royal Stud at Sandringham produced no outstanding foals between 1907 and Edward VII's death on 6 May 1910. Of the nine living foals born in 1907, only one, Vain Air (Ayrshire–Vane) managed to win two minor races in 1909. Eight of the twelve foals bred in 1908 won twenty races, but none was of great significance. The most interesting was Witch of the Air (Robert le Diable–Vane), whom Marsh ran in the Spring Two-Year-Old Plate at Kempton Park on Friday 6 May 1910. That morning Marsh had called at Buckingham Palace to enquire from Sir Francis Knollys whether it would not be unwise to run the filly since the King was so seriously ill. Knollys assured him that the King had ordered her to run. When Witch of the Air won, the crowd, knowing the gravity of the King's illness, did not know whether to cheer or be silent. Soon after five o'clock the future George V told his father of Witch of the Air's victory; the news delighted the dying King, who said 'I am very glad.' These were his last words, for soon afterwards he lapsed into a coma and died that night at a quarter to midnight.

The foals that King Edward VII bred at Sandringham in 1909 and 1910 but did not live to see on the race course were nothing exceptional. Pintadeau (Florizel II–Guinea Hen) was the most useful; he won five races for King George V and was fourth to Tagalie in the 1912 Derby. His full-brother, Anmer, the winner of one race, gained notoriety when he was brought down in the 1913 Derby by a militant suffragette, Miss Emily Davison, who died of her injuries four days later. Anmer and his jockey, Herbert Jones, escaped serious injury.

Queen Victoria and Prince Albert would have been surprised by Edward VII's achievements as King. His influence was most marked in foreign affairs. The establishment of the Entente Cordiale between England and its traditional enemy, France, after his state visit there in 1903, was partly the result of his charm and popularity among the French. Throughout his reign he had endeavoured to maintain peace in Europe and was nicknamed in Britain 'Edward the Peacemaker'.

Lord Marcus Beresford wrote a letter to Richard Marsh shortly after Edward VII's death, in which he told the trainer that 'nothing ever pleased him so much as winning a race, and receiving the congratulations of his people afterwards.' The modest ambitions that the King expressed to his friend, Henry Chaplin, three years after founding his stud at Sandringham, had been more than fulfilled by Persimmon's and Diamond Jubilee's Classic triumphs.

12

George V,

1910–36

When Edward VII ascended the throne in 1901, he determined that his heir should not be excluded from the affairs of state as his mother, Queen Victoria, had excluded him. Not merely did he give his son access to all official secrets, but he arranged for their desks to be placed side by side at Windsor. In March of that year the Duke and Duchess of York were sent to open the first Commonwealth Parliament in Melbourne. After visiting Sydney, Brisbane, New Zealand, Tasmania and Perth, the Duke and Duchess sailed to South Africa. The visit was a triumphant success and Lord Kitchener, who met them at Durban, assured them that the Boer War was nearing its end. From South Africa the Duke and Duchess of York sailed to Quebec. In Canada they paid official visits to Montreal, Ottawa, Vancouver and Newfoundland. In November Edward VII created his son Prince of Wales and Earl of Chester to 'mark my appreciation of the admirable manner in which you carried out the duties in the Colonies which I entrusted you with'.[1]

This eight-month trip had a lasting effect on the Prince of Wales. Besides increasing his self-confidence, it gave him a much more realistic grasp of the modern idea of Empire, certainly in relation to the white colonies. The Boer War had destroyed the nineteenth-century illusion that the colonies could be taken for granted. The young democratic governments that he had seen made a distinct impression on him. In the speech given on 5 December at the Guildhall he appealed to his fellow countrymen at home 'to prove the strength of the attachment of the Motherland to her children by sending to them of her best'. He finally warned that the impression which generally seemed to prevail in the countries he had visited was 'that the Old Country must wake up if she intends to maintain her old position of pre-eminence in her Colonial trade against foreign competitors'.

The death of his father, King Edward VII, on 6 May 1910 placed King George V on the throne of Great Britain. In his diary for 6 May the new King wrote, 'At 11.45 beloved Papa passed peacefully away and I have lost my best friend and best of fathers . . . I am heartbroken and overwhelmed with grief, but God will help me in my great responsibilities and darling May will be my comfort as she always has been.'

The following twenty-five years were to bring dramatic social changes and a process of democratization, which many attribute to the First World War. However, the spirit of change was already apparent in the reign of Edward VII, and the War only accelerated its speed. During George V's reign five Emperors, eight Kings and eighteen minor dynasties were overthrown and replaced by republics. It says much for George V's impartiality, straightforwardness and desire to mediate that the British monarchy was able to survive the convulsions that overtook so many other countries. For ordinary British citizens the monarchy under George V came to symbolize their spirit of toleration and compromise and their inherent dislike of extreme doctrine. Its popularity had much to do with the King's gift of conciliation.

On George V's accession there were eighteen broodmares at the Royal Stud at Sandringham and fourteen horses in training with Richard Marsh at Egerton. Soon after the death of Edward VII, General Sir Digton Probyn wrote to Richard Marsh from Buckingham Palace: 'I heartily congratulate you, and our young King also, that he proposes carrying on King Edward's racing establishments at Newmarket and Sandringham, in the same way that his great father did. I am delighted that you and Lord Marcus are "as you were", and poor old Walker too. Good luck to all of you.' Throughout the whole of the 1910 season the Royal horses ran in the colours of the Earl of Derby as the Court was in mourning for Edward VII. The last four crops of foals bred by the late King were moderate, however, and few races – none of any consequence – were won in Lord Derby's colours in 1910 or in the Royal colours in 1911 or 1912.

Only one foal, Flowerjug (Florizel II–Amphora), who failed to win on any of her eight outings, was born at Sandringham in 1910 after the death of Edward VII, so 1911 marks the commencement of George V's career as a breeder. Unfortunately, five of the mares at Sandringham were barren that year and one foal died four days after his birth. Four of the eight foals delivered, who went into training with Marsh, won seven races between them. Sunny Lake (Sundridge–Pearl of the Loch) won three races in 1914, including the Greenham Stakes at Newbury; he was exported to New Zealand in 1915. Breakspear (Spearmint–Guinea Hen) won two races and was quite fancied for the 1914 Derby, for which he started third favourite at 100–8. He caused the start to be delayed for a long time as he was most unruly; deservedly getting away only badly, he was never a threat to Durbar II, who was to become the broodmare sire of the great French sire, Tourbillon.

Fifteen yearlings were born at Sandringham in 1912, though regrettably Sunny Lake's dam Pearl of the Loch was barren to Radium. On 26 January Prim Nun gave birth to her second foal, a bay colt by Cicero who was named Friar Marcus. Prim Nun (Persimmon–Nunsuch) had been bred at Sandringham in 1906, but had failed in all of her four starts in 1908 and 1909. Friar Marcus, a very kind and good-tempered animal, turned out to be the best colt Richard Marsh ever trained for King George V. In Marsh's opinion he was a 'perfect model of what a sprinter should be . . . short-coupled and very strong in the back, quarters and arms. He had a beautiful head and neck, the best of shoulders, while his hocks were all they should be.' On his first appearance on the racecourse in the spring of 1914, Friar Marcus made all the running and won by a length and a half from a field of twenty-four. His next victory came at the Derby meeting at Epsom, but he had to be scratched from his engagements at Ascot as he had become quite ill with the cough and a very high temperature a few days earlier. Although his robust constitution helped him to recover quickly, he was still not himself when Marsh galloped him before the Prince of Wales's Stakes at Goodwood. That, combined with the distance of the race (six furlongs), made Marsh nervous about the outcome. Friar Marcus just lasted home, beating off Snow Marten's challenge by a neck; the merit of that performance was made clear when Snow Marten won the following year's Oaks and was second in the St Leger. Friar Marcus's next victory came in the Rous Memorial Stakes at Newmarket. When he beat his six rivals in the Middle Park Stakes and retired for the season, he had never been beaten. Winners of the Middle Park Stakes at that time were considered as leading contenders for the following year's Classics. Marsh was uncertain about Friar Marcus's Classic potential, harbouring grave doubts about his stamina; he was a tremendously muscular and compact colt, not very tall and lacking in scope. When he only grew a quarter of an inch in the winter – he never reached sixteen hands – Marsh's reservations became stronger. Prior to the 2,000 Guineas the unpleasant fact emerged that Friar Marcus did not even really get a mile. He was not seriously fancied, therefore, for the first Classic of the season, for which he made the running for six and a half furlongs before dropping out of contention behind Pommern.

Realizing that if Friar Marcus were to run over distances too far for him, his speed would be blunted, Marsh and Beresford scratched the beautifully actioned colt from the Derby. The King, who had known that Friar Marcus might not stay even when he was a juvenile, was not too disappointed. Reverting to shorter distances, Friar Marcus proved himself to be a high-class sprinter. He won the Great Eastern Handicap and Queensberry Handicap later in the season, and both the Crawford Handicap and the Chesterfield Handicap at Newmarket in 1916 carrying top weight.

Friar Marcus retired to stud at Sandringham in 1917. The majority of his stock, like himself, were not capable of staying, which almost precluded him from being leading sire. He got a total of 343 winners from 1918 to 1935, and from 1923 to 1933 always figured on the list of the first twenty winning sires. His best progeny were Brown Betty, the winner of the 1933 1,000 Guineas, Lemnarchus, who won the Coventry Stakes in 1930, Beresford, whose six victories included the 1923 Clearwell Stakes, Silver Clover, third in the 1,000 Guineas and the enormously influential mare, Feola, who was second in the 1936 1,000 Guineas and third in the Oaks. Feola also won the Easter Plate at Kempton and Midsummer Stakes at Newmarket in 1936. She became one of the most influential mares that the Royal Stud has ever possessed.

Friar Marcus was to prove, moreover, an even better broodmare sire, and he was leading broodmare sire in 1935. The Aga Khan's 1935 Triple Crown hero, Bahram, was out of the Friar Marcus mare Friar's Daughter, who was successful in her only race. Bahram was unbeaten in nine races at two and three and was placed top of the Free Handicap in 1934 when his five wins included the National Produce Stakes, the Gimcrack Stakes and the Middle Park Stakes. Friar's Daughter was also the dam of Dastur, who was runner-up in the 2,000 Guineas, Derby and St Leger in 1932, when he also won the Sussex Stakes and King Edward VII Stakes. In 1933 Dastur won the Coronation Cup and dead-heated for the Champion Stakes.

Friar Marcus was a great favourite with King George V, who derived great pleasure from showing the horse to friends invited to visit the stables at Egerton. When Friar Marcus was standing at Sandringham the King made a point of visiting him with a bunch of carrots in his box at Wolferton after he had inspected all the mares and youngstock on the Stud.

After 1912 the standard of foals bred by the King at the Royal Stud declined dramatically. From the 1913 and 1914 crops of foals there were only two very moderate winners of one race each in England. The solitary exception was Lucknow (Minoru–Amphora), who ran three times in 1916 and twice in 1917 in England without success. He was then sold and exported to Australia, where he improved greatly and won the Caulfield Cup. The number of mares at the Stud varied between seventeen and twenty from 1915 to 1918, but although the number of winners increased, seven foals bred at Sandringham in 1917 winning twelve minor races, their quality did not improve. Even Polignac, a half-brother to Friar Marcus by Polymelus, could not win in three outings in England, and had to wait till he arrived in India in 1921 before gaining his first success.

The dismal fortunes of the Royal Stud changed for the better in 1919 when two useful colts, Weathervane (Lemberg–Vain Air) and London Cry (Call o'the Wild–Vervaine) were foaled. Weathervane only had one race at two, but on a very wet afternoon in the spring of 1922 at Newbury won the Greenham Stakes in the presence of the King and Queen, who had motored over from Windsor. Weathervane could only finish ninth in the 2,000 Guineas to St Louis and did not win again that season, though he was runner-up in the Jersey Stakes and fourth to Tetrameter in the Stewards' Cup. Although he could not be considered a consistent horse, he had a penchant for Ascot and the next year won the Royal Hunt Cup. In 1924 he again ran very well in the Royal Hunt Cup and was only beaten a neck by Dinkie. He was exported to New Zealand in 1925. London Cry did not run at two, and was still backward as a three-year-old when he ran five times without success, though Marsh had a high enough opinion of him to run him in the Princess of Wales's Stakes at Newmarket on his second outing. He slowly began to improve and was third both in the Gordon Stakes, to the Derby and Eclipse Stakes runner-up, Tamar, and in the Newmarket St Leger. His trainer's patient policy with the immature colt paid off handsomely in 1923 when London Cry won four races, including the Prince Edward Handicap at Manchester. By 1924 he had developed into a fine stayer and took the Goodwood Stakes in the presence of King George V and Queen Mary.

Disappointment returned, however, with the foals bred in 1920, only two of which won three minor races. In 1921 Lord Marcus Beresford bought a colt foal, Knight of the Garter (Son-in-Law–Castelline), since the thirteen broodmares at Sandringham had produced nine fillies and only one colt. Although he was not bred by the King, so much of his early life was passed at Sandringham that some mention of his career seems appropriate. He was to be one of the last purchases for the Royal Stud by Lord Marcus Beresford, as the loyal and long-serving stud manager to two Kings died in December 1922, thus missing Knight of the Garter's winning debut in the Eglinton Stakes at York in May. Marsh thought him a marvellously mature juvenile and fully expected him to win the Coventry Stakes at Ascot, which he did without difficulty. He was a little unlucky, in the opinion of his trainer, to be beaten by Lord Derby's Halcyon in the Richmond Stakes at Goodwood, but then won a good race at Nottingham when he was the last mount in the Royal colours for Bert Jones, without whom Diamond Jubilee would never have won the Triple Crown.

Marsh was delighted with the progress Knight of the Garter made from two to three. As he had a slight suspicion about the colt's stamina, he told his jockey, Wragg, in the 2,000 Guineas to delay making his challenge till close to home. Inexplicably, Wragg allowed him to match strides with the leaders; he was done with at the Bushes and faded to finish seventh behind Diophon. The King, who had been at Newmarket on 7 May to see his horses' work in the morning and the race in the afternoon wrote in his diary: 'I fear he [Knight of the Garter] can't stay a mile in the best company and at that pace. Weathervane was just beaten a neck in the Bretby Handicap. I am not in luck just now.' Trials with the proven stayers London Cry and Bowood over a mile and a half convinced Marsh that Knight of the Garter's form in the Guineas was all wrong and that he would certainly stay the Derby distance. The improvement that Knight of the Garter made in a few weeks positively astonished the Royal trainer, but then on the Thursday prior to the Derby it was discovered that he had developed heel-bug. Despite incessant veterinary attention, Marsh had to convey the sad news to George V that the colt would have to be scratched on the very day he was supposed to leave for Epsom by horse-box. Knight of the Garter was unable to run again that season. He appeared only twice more, once in 1924 and once in 1926, but failed to win; in 1927 he retired to stud in Ireland.

The crop of foals at Sandringham in 1922 were the last to be born during the lifetime of Lord Marcus Beresford. Unfortunately half of the mares were barren that year, and only six of the eight living foals went into training with Richard Marsh. Lord Marcus suggested in a letter to the King that the bay colt foal by Hurry On out of Saint's Mead, who was born on 13 February, should be named Runnymede, 'if Your Majesty approves'. He turned out to be the best of the crop, and gave the King a pleasant surprise when unexpectedly winning the July Stakes on a lovely warm afternoon. In his diary, George V recorded, 'I had not a shilling on him, he is an improving horse so I hope he will win me some more races.' The July Stakes was Runnymede's only win in seven outings at two, but his victories in the Brandon Handicap at Newmarket and Dee Stakes at Chester earned him a place in the 1925 Derby for which he started at 100–6. In the event, however, he failed to make any impression behind Mr H. E. Morris's Manna at Epsom. Although third in the St James's Palace Stakes and Gordon Stakes later that season, Runnymede proved disappointing; failing to win any of his other eighteen races in 1925 or 1926, he was eventually sold and exported to Sweden.

With the retirement of Bert Jones approaching, in the early part of 1922 Lord Marcus Beresford requested the champion jockey, Steve Donoghue, to meet him at St James's Palace. He then asked Donoghue if he would be prepared to ride for the King, adding that George V himself wanted him as the Royal jockey for the approaching season. Donoghue was very flattered, but found himself in a quandary which he forthrightly explained to the Royal racing manager: 'I would love to, my Lord, but His Majesty has very few good horses which would enable me to keep where I want to be, at the top of the list.' Lord Marcus smiled and said that he knew what the jockey had said was true and continued, 'Five of my best mares have just come back from different studs and they are all empty. How am I to breed winners for jockeys like you to ride if my mares return to me empty?' He then gave the example of Prim Nun, the dam of Friar Marcus, who had been covered by The Tetrarch for two consecutive years but had been barren in 1920 and 1921, and Neuve Chapelle, who had returned barren from The Tetrarch in 1922. Donoghue recalled that Beresford was very understanding about his refusal to accept a retainer as the Royal jockey; however, he did promise to ride the King's horses when requested, if he was free. In one race he held a winning chance on one of the King's horses until a young apprentice, unable to control his mount, interfered with him so drastically that the chance of victory was destroyed. Several people afterwards criticized Donoghue for his riding, not having seen the incident, but George V was more observant: when the horse returned to the unsaddling enclosure, he remarked to the jockey, 'It was hard luck, Donoghue. We should have won that race but for the apprentice. Never mind!'

Aloysia (Lemberg–Vervaine) was the only foal bred by the King in 1923 who was able to win a race in the Royal colours; the other winner bred at Sandringham that year, Orange Pip (Kwang-Su–Orangepeel) was sold to Fred Darling as a yearling. Aloysia won two races in 1925, one at Doncaster and then the Queen Mary Stakes at Ascot, but failed to train on and was beaten in her three outings as a three-year-old. She was a failure as a broodmare and was exported to Italy in 1933. One other filly bred by the King in 1923, Sister Stella (Friar Marcus–Etoile), was to have a major influence on the Stud Book, however. She was only in training as a two-year-old, and was a maiden when she was sold by the King. Her great claim to fame as a broodmare was that she was the dam of the Aga Khan's Stardust, who was runner-up to Djebel in the 1940 2,000 Guineas and to Turkhan in the St Leger. Stardust had won the National Breeders' Produce Stakes at Sandown in 1939; at stud he sired the Australian champion Star Kingdom, who became an enormously influential stallion.

The foals bred at the Royal Stud in 1924 were the worst that had been born at Sandringham since its foundation: they produced not a solitary win. After the death of Lord Marcus Beresford, the King had appointed Major F. H. Fetherstonhaugh to succeed him as racing manager and manager of the Royal Stud. His first year as racing manager, 1923, resulted in nineteen victories for King George's horses and prize money of £12,095; this was the most successful season for ten years, with the greatest number of races won in one year by the King. It should be pointed out that eight of these wins were achieved by Weathervane, London Cry and Knight of the Garter, whose victories were worth over £8,000 that season. Credit for the success of the Royal horses in 1923 has sometimes been given to Major Fetherstonhaugh's more realistic approach to the question of where the royal horses should race, as compared to that of Lord Marcus Beresford, who considered it inappropriate for horses carrying the royal colours to run in humble races. Beresford had been in charge of the breeding of London Cry, Weathervane and the other minor winners and had bought Knight of the Garter as a yearling. It is appropriate to point out that George V's horses only won three races worth £3,095 in 1924, including the prize money of £1,790 that the King received from Runnymede's win in the July Stakes. Racing and stud managers can only be judged by the quality of the horses that they have under their care. Certainly Richard Marsh made it a policy to try to win races 'at places like Ascot, Epsom and Goodwood, where their Majesties were most likely to be present' and where 'I knew that I should be giving a deal of genuine pleasure.' No owner–breeder would appreciate his racing manager running his horses at small meetings which he could seldom attend, when they had a chance of winning more prestigious races at the more important tracks.

Major Fetherstonhaugh's appointment may have come about partly through the influence of Lord Wolverton, whose cousin Beatrice was married to the new Royal Stud manager. When George V was staying in his suite of rooms at the Jockey Club for meetings at Newmarket, he frequently took dinner with Lord Wolverton. It appears that the much younger Fetherstonhaugh did not always see eye-to-eye with the King's trainer, Richard Marsh, who was by then seventy-two. In 1924 Lord Lascelles approached the Ellesmere family, from whom Marsh held the lease on Egerton House, to see if he could buy it as the Newmarket residence of his wife (the King's daughter, Princess Mary) and himself. In the autumn of 1924 Richard Marsh received a letter from Sir Frederick Ponsonby, the Keeper of the Privy Purse, in which he said that the King would not expect him to make a fresh start in the event of Egerton House being sold to Lord Lascelles, and added,

> I feel that this is a favourable opportunity for you to consider the advisability of placing your resignation in His Majesty's hands, and as Major Fetherstonhaugh finds that the present arrangement does not work satisfactorily and regards a change as indispensable, the King would look for a younger man to succeed you whose position with regard to Major Fetherston-haugh would of course not be the same as that which by your age, standing and experience you have occupied. These views are entirely held by Lord Lascelles.

His Majesty naturally regrets the necessity for the proposed change. For not only have you been personally associated with all that concerned the King's racing, in which His Majesty has enjoyed the benefit of your advice and knowledge, but it was owing to your skill and experience as a trainer of King Edward's horses that his late Majesty was so successful on the Turf.

Ponsonby concluded his letter by mentioning the loyal trainer's increasing years, and his belief that Marsh would admit to the reasonableness of the suggestion that he should express a wish to retire. Marsh had little option but to follow this advice, and left Egerton House at the end of 1924. He later wondered

if any want of success on the part of the horses owned by his present Majesty was due to my shortcomings. Perhaps I had slipped into that groove which exists for the old-fashioned. History must be left to decide that. But nothing can deprive me of the feeling, deep down within me, that I at all times gave of my best endeavours, mentally and physically, and called upon that knowledge and understanding of the horse in training which long years of experience should have taught me. Had I been a miracle-worker I could not have longed more ardently for those splendid victories that eluded us.

Richard Marsh had always found George V to be a 'most human and kindly man'. When he came to the throne, his trainer was quite surprised that the new King was so keen on racing and breeding, and that his interest was so deep-rooted. Marsh considered George V to be a much better judge of a horse than his father and that he had a far more intimate knowledge of the Thoroughbred breed. An example of his consideration for his horses was the occasion when Marsh remarked to him, 'I am afraid your Majesty will think I am a long time bringing out the two-year-olds.' The King replied, 'Never hurry a horse for me, Marsh. When you tell me it is ready to run I shall be quite satisfied.'

Marsh also recalled that, while George V was delighted when he won, and always expressed his pleasure and satisfaction, he was just as sympathetic when there were disappointments. When Knight of the Garter had to miss the Derby, Marsh received a telegram from the King in reply to one sent from Egerton House for George V's birthday on 3 June. The telegram read:

I sincerely thank you, Mrs Marsh, and all at Egerton House for your good wishes on my birthday, which I much appreciate. I

am so sorry for you that Knight of the Garter cannot run on
Wednesday.
GEORGE R.I.

On another occasion Marsh prepared two horses to run in Ireland
during the King's and Queen's coronation visit there in July 1912.
They both finished second, to the disappointment of both their
trainer and the Irish. George V sent Marsh a message of consolation
saying that, although success would naturally have been very
pleasant, he was not to worry about the defeats.

The new Royal trainer was William Jarvis, the son of Bill
Jarvis, who had trained Cyllene, and brother of Jack Jarvis, Lord
Rosebery's trainer, and Basil Jarvis, who trained Papyrus to win
the 1923 Derby. William Jarvis's wife, Isobel, was the sister of
Frank and Fred Butters, both of whom were to train Derby winners.
William Jarvis had started training at Newmarket in 1911, but
service in the South Notts Hussars and the 23rd Middlesex Regiment in the First World War had meant that he had had to start
again in 1919. The recommendation of Lord Derby's trainer,
George Lambton, was largely responsible for his being offered the
position of trainer to King George V. As Egerton House had been
bought by Lord Lascelles, it was decided that William Jarvis and
his wife would occupy the entrance lodge, which was enlarged to
accommodate them. Among the items installed in the house was
the staircase from the Royal Palace at Newmarket built for King
Charles II, which at the time was being demolished. On the King's
first visit to the house, noticing the staircase he said, 'I wonder
how many times Nell Gwyn climbed these stairs.'

The disastrous year suffered by the Royal Stud in 1924 was
followed by a notably successful one: for the eleven foals bred at
Sandringham in 1925 included the only Classic winner owned and
bred by George V. On 5 April 1925 Stained Glass gave birth to a
bay filly foal by Lord Woolavington's 1922 Derby winner, Captain
Cuttle; she was named Scuttle. The previous summer, after a day's
racing at Goodwood, the King had gone over to Lavington Park
where Lord Woolavington had shown him his stud. In his diary
George V described Hurry On and his son, Captain Cuttle, who
was standing there for his first season, as 'fine horses'. Stained
Glass by Tracery, Scuttle's dam, had been bred at Sandringham in
1917 and was a half-sister to Runnymede. She had two runs in
1919 before she fractured her pelvis in training; luckily it was

possible to save her for the paddocks at the Royal Stud. Scuttle was her third foal.

Scuttle pleased her trainer, William Jarvis, as a juvenile, even if she was inclined to be temperamental. After finishing a promising second in the Queen Mary Stakes at Royal Ascot, she won the FitzWilliam Stakes at Doncaster and the Berkshire Foal Plate at Newbury. She crowned her juvenile campaign by winning the Cheveley Park Stakes at Newmarket and retired for the season as a live hope for the next season's 1,000 Guineas. On her first appearance in 1928 Scuttle carried top weight to victory in the nine-furlong Brandon Handicap at Newmarket's Craven Meeting. George V, who was staying at Newmarket during Guineas week, wrote to Queen Mary on the first day, 'Scuttle is very well and I am in great hopes that she will distinguish herself on Friday, but she has a lot of good ones to beat.'

Her jockey, Joe Childs, who had told William Jarvis's young daughter the day before the 1,000 Guineas that he thought the Royal filly would win, did not have an easy time at the start as Scuttle was exceptionally fractious and badly behaved. The result was that she was poorly away. Childs did not rush her up instantly, however, but riding an excellent race brought the 15–8 favourite to challenge coming out of the Dip. Scuttle had a length to spare over Jurisdiction at the winning-post, with Toboggan six lengths away third. The King had been out riding in the morning with his daughter, Princess Mary, and the Prince of Wales, and they had watched work on the Heath. It was the Prince of Wales's first visit to Newmarket, and later that morning his father showed him his rooms at the Jockey Club. In his diary for 4 May 1928 the King noted that everyone was delighted at Scuttle's victory and that she received a great reception. He then concluded his entry for the day: 'I am very proud to win my first Classic and that I bred her at Sandringham. She is certainly a very game little filly.'

Scuttle started even money favourite for the Oaks, but was easily beaten four lengths by Lord Derby's Toboggan, who had been six lengths behind her at Newmarket. King George wrote in his diary: 'It was a great disappointment to me, there was no excuse; perhaps she didn't like coming down the hill. We returned wiser but certainly poorer.' The two most likely explanations of Scuttle's defeat were first, that she did not truly stay a mile and a half, and secondly, that Toboggan, who was by Hurry On out of a St Simon mare, and was to win the Jockey Club Stakes in the autumn, really needed a test of stamina to bring out her best. Scuttle must have taken more out of herself at Epsom than Lord Derby's filly, for when they met again over a mile in the Coronation Stakes at Royal Ascot, she could only finish third to Toboggan. Scuttle did not distinguish herself in the Falmouth Stakes at Newmarket, but was not disgraced as runner-up in the Nassau Stakes at Goodwood when conceding more than a stone to the winner.

King George V's first Classic winner made a valuable addition to his broodmares at Sandringham. Her first foal, sired by Friar Marcus and born on 1 March 1931, tragically died as a yearling. Her second foal, Fairlead, a filly by Fairway, won three minor races, and her third, Canvas, a filly by Solario, won the Durham Plate at Doncaster in 1936. Scuttle's death foaling her fourth offspring, a colt by Singapore which did not survive, was a tragic blow. Canvas produced six foals between 1938 and 1945 at the Royal Stud before she was sold. Her last foal, the filly Canvas Back, never won, though placed four times as a two-year-old, and was exported to Australia in 1948. There she became a most influential broodmare; her best foal was the champion Australian two-year-old, Kingster. Thus, in spite of her premature death, Scuttle did have a little influence on the Stud Book.

Scuttle's disappointing half-brother, Glastonbury by Friar Marcus, who won one minor race, was one of the three moderate foals born at Sandringham in 1926, who were winners of a race each. The fortunes of the Royal Stud at Sandringham reached their nadir in the years 1927 and 1928, when not one of the foals bred by the King won a single race. Not even Lilibet (Friar Marcus–Vain Air), a bay filly born on 30 May 1928, whom King George V named after the Duke and Duchess of York's two-year-old daughter, Princess Elizabeth, and whom he always referred to in his diary as 'sweet little Lilibet', was able to change the luck of the horses he bred. This period was not a happy time for George V; in November 1928 he succumbed to a long and near-fatal streptococcal infection, which left him an invalid for nearly a year. His convalescence was spent at Bognor, which thereafter attached the suffix 'Regis' to its name. When he arrived back at Windsor on 15 May 1929, he wrote in his diary: 'Very glad to be home again after 13½ weeks at Bognor.' A relapse five days later delayed his full recovery until September. He was not a good patient or convalescent as he hated being confined indoors.

Things improved for the Royal Stud in 1929; three of the eight foals born at Sandringham that year were to win a total of fourteen races. On 11 April a brown colt by Pharos out of Vervaine named

Limelight was foaled; he was thus a half-brother to London Cry and Aloysia. Like London Cry he took some time to come to hand, and it was not until his fifth race, at York in August 1931, that he had his first win. He then won at Doncaster and was third in a nursery handicap at Newmarket. Limelight was not entered for the Classics, but won two races at Newmarket in the spring. He then gained his most important success as a three-year-old when he won the Jersey Stakes at Royal Ascot. The reception that Limelight and the King received in the unsaddling enclosure displayed not merely the crowd's great delight at the Royal victory, but also how popular George V had become among his subjects. Limelight, unfortunately, then broke down in a race at Newmarket's July Meeting; though he recovered sufficiently to go back into training, he was unable to run again that season. The Cambridgeshire weights were published before the Aga Khan's Firdaussi won the St Leger from his owner's better-fancied Dastur; Limelight had to give Firdaussi 2 lb. The handicapper must, therefore, have formed a very high opinion of the Royal colt's victory in the Jersey Stakes.

King George V was present at Newbury when Limelight made his seasonal reappearance in the Newbury Spring Cup in April 1933. At the distance Limelight was faced by a seemingly impenetrable wall of horses, but with great skill his jockey Childs found a passage through and got up virtually on the line to win by a short head from Solenoid. Limelight was a temperamental horse; if permitted to, he would play up. Many of his victories were due to the strong but sympathetic way Childs treated him, which brought out his courage. Nevertheless, he often tried to bite his jockey when dismounting after a race. The Egerton House stable was under a cloud when Limelight next ran at Newmarket – possibly there was a virus in the stable – and he was beaten. Prior to the Hardwicke Stakes at Royal Ascot, Limelight played up at the start, and only Childs's patient handling of him prevented him from refusing to race. Limelight was settled early on, and came to challenge the 1932 Cesarewitch winner, Nitischin, in the straight. A tremendous battle all the way to the winning-post ensued with Limelight bravely running on the stronger to win by a very narrow margin. The crescendo of applause that greeted Limelight in the unsaddling enclosure was even more rapturous than that he had received after the Jersey Stakes in 1932. Limelight next won the Duke of York Stakes at Kempton Park, carrying top weight of 9 st 7 lbs, and giving 2 st 10 lb to the runner-up, Shrewton. His last race before he retired to stand as a stallion at the Royal Stud was in the Cambridgeshire, when he was far from disgraced under another welter burden in finishing fourth to Raymond. Limelight was to remain the only stallion at Sandringham until the middle of the Second World War. Always a great favourite, especially with George V and Princess Elizabeth, he will be remembered for his courageous victories on the racecourse.

The foals bred at the Royal Stud in 1930 were not of such high quality, nor did they win so many races, as those of the previous year. Nevertheless The Abbot (Abbot's Trace–Polish Air) turned out to be a more than useful colt, winning four races including the prestigious Sussex Stakes at Goodwood in 1933. Shortly after that victory he developed a thoroughpin which prevented him running again that season.

Nineteen-thirty-one was not a good year for the Royal Stud at Sandringham. Only one of the ten foals born that year, Shamrock (Abbot's Trace–Shanogue), was able to win a solitary race for his Royal owner – breeder, though Free Pass (Warden of the Marches–Frankly) was to become a good winner abroad after he was sold and exported. His dam Frankly (Franklin–Malva) was a half-sister to the immensely influential stallion Blenheim by Blandford, who won the 1930 Derby. Malva's later foals included King Salmon by Salmon Trout, runner-up to Hyperion in the Derby and winner of the Eclipse Stakes in 1934, and Blenheim's full-brother, His Grace, who dead-heated for the Coronation Cup in 1937. The most perspicacious purchase of Frankly for King George V in 1930 was one of the last important services that Major Fetherstonhaugh performed for the Royal Stud, since he died in July 1931 after holding the position of racing and stud manager to the King for only nine years. His widow, Beatrice, continued to assist and advise her husband's successor, Brigadier Henry A. Tomkinson.

'Mouse' Tomkinson, as he was invariably known, was educated at Eton and Sandhurst before being gazetted as a Second Lieutenant to the Royals in 1901. He fought in both the Boer War and the First World War, and won a DSO and Bar. As a result of the paucity of winners that were being bred at the Royal Stud, Tomkinson began to buy foals and yearlings for the King soon after his appointment. When he bought Slam (Winalot–Skip Bridge) in September 1932 for £1,400, George V wrote to him saying, 'it seems a lot of money, I only hope that he will prove as good as he looks, lucky he came up for sale when the prices were low, as I see the last three days they fetched much more. Hope that Jarvis liked him too.'² After Tomkinson bought another yearling colt, Brief (Foxlaw–Reef) for £500 later that week at the Doncaster Sales, he received another letter from the King at Balmoral; George V hoped that the yearling would turn out well and agreed that Brief would make a better three-year-old than juvenile, but was glad that 'you think the other one ought to win races next year. How would Grand Slam do for the Winalot colt if the name is not already taken?'³ Slam, as he was eventually called, did not live up to his expensive purchase price, and on 13 April 1934, in a letter written from Windsor Castle to Tomkinson, the King remarked, 'Just got your telegram that Slam was again unplaced. I fear he is not much use as a racehorse.'⁴

These letters demonstrate not merely George V's interest in his horses, but his depth of knowledge of both racing and breeding. In another letter to Tomkinson, written on 23 August 1933, he makes remarkably accurate predictions about the yearlings born at the Royal Stud in 1932: 'Thank you for your letter telling me the five colts arrived safely on Monday. I took leave of them on Sunday and agree with Jarvis in thinking that Curraghmore and Firestone are the best. I only hope they do well in training.'⁵ Curraghmore (Friar Marcus–Bayberry) proved the best of that year's foals, winning five races, while Firestone (Hotweed–Sparkling Gem) won two. The victory of Curraghmore on 16 November 1935 at Derby was in fact the last time George V's colours were carried to victory before his death.

Fairey (Fairway–Polish Air), who was foaled in 1933 at Sandringham, was the last good colt bred by King George V. A half-brother to The Abbot, Fairey's three wins included the Waterford Stakes at Ascot; he also ran third in the Eclipse Stakes. Nevertheless only three of the other 1933 foals bred by the Royal Stud managed to win.

The yearling filly, Feola (Friar Marcus–Aloe), whom Tomkinson bought at the Newmarket Sales on 5 July 1934 for 3,000 gns was to be the most important purchase he ever made for George V's stud. She was to transform the fortunes of the Royal Stud in the next thirty years in the same way that Perdita II had done in Edward VII's reign. Feola's dam, Aloe, was a full-sister to Foxlaw, who won the Jockey Club Stakes in 1926 and the Ascot Gold Cup in 1927. Another interesting mare acquired by Tomkinson from her breeder, Captain Charles Moore, in Ireland, was Judith (Colorado–Judea), whose chestnut colt Jubilee by Mr Jinks was to be one of the last two winners bred by George V in 1935, the other being Licence (Foxlaw–Wireless). Jubilee won two races as a two-year-old in 1937, while Licence won one small race in 1939. The previous year he had been the first colt owned by George VI, and the last bred by his father, to run in a Derby. He started a 100–1 outsider, and led the field to the top of the hill, but finished in the ruck behind Bois Roussel. Despite these victories, the Royal Stud's final two crops for King George V were very disappointing, for only three of the 1934 foals turned out to be winners, all of minor races.

On Monday 6 May 1935 King George V and Queen Mary attended a Thanksgiving Service in St Paul's Cathedral to celebrate the Silver Jubilee of his reign. In his diary the King wrote: 'A never to be forgotten day when we celebrated our Silver Jubilee. It was a glorious summer's day: 75 degrees in the shade. The greatest number of people in the streets that I have ever seen in my life. The enthusiasm was indeed most touching.' Each day that week the Royal couple appeared on the floodlit balcony of Buckingham Palace to acknowledge the rapturous cheers of the crowds who had waited all day to see them. George V was genuinely surprised by the extent of his popularity and by the heartfelt affection his people had for him.

The Christmas Broadcasts by George V, which he had made since 1932, certainly brought him closer to his subjects, but the true cause of his popularity was that he had been an excellent King and a shining example to his people. In the Great War he had devoted all his time to the war effort, kept to the rationing regulations and even given up alcohol. When the Irish question was at its most divisive and civil war in the island threatened, his advice to Lloyd George to pursue a policy of moderation and conciliation facilitated the agreements of 1922 and the foundation of the Irish Free State and Ulster Parliament. When the slump hit England in the 1930s, the King gave up part of the income due to him from the Civil List. As early as 1934 the King had foreseen the danger Hitler and the Nazi Party posed to peace, and on 24 April at Windsor Castle had told the German Ambassador that the policies of his country were putting the world in peril, and if the German leaders persisted in them, there was bound to be a war.

All of these attitudes and responses to the problems that had occurred during George V's twenty-five years on the throne had contributed to the respect and affection that his subjects felt for him. What they admired most in their King, however, was his honesty, sense of duty, common sense, truthfulness, tolerance and, above all, the way he had kept the monarchy neutral and apart from the petty squabblings of party politics, divisive class animosities and narrow sectional interests.

George V passed Christmas in 1935 with Queen Mary at his beloved Sandringham. On Sunday 12 January 1936 he went to see the mares and yearlings at the Royal Stud in the afternoon, and three days later, though feeling unwell, he went for a short ride on his white pony in the park. On Friday 17 January, the last entry in his diary read: 'A little snow and wind. Dawson arrived this evening. I saw him and feel rotten.' His condition quickly worsened and at five minutes to midnight on 20 January 1936 he died.

Brigadier Tomkinson later wrote in the Household Brigade magazine about George V's involvement with the Royal Stud:

There is no greater mistake than to imagine that the late King raced only from a sense of duty and did not care for it. On the contrary, he loved a day's racing, particularly at Newmarket, and no owner was keener or took a greater interest in his horses than he did. It was not only in the racing that he took such an interest, but even more so in the breeding and welfare of the young stock. Constantly when in London, he would tell me how anxious he was to get to Sandringham to see the foals that had just arrived, and how the yearlings had done since he was last there. Certainly on his arrival there, his first tour of inspection was to go very carefully all round the stud. His quite remarkable consideration and sympathy for the feelings of all about him extended to his horses as well.

13

George VI,

1936–52

Nineteen-thirty-six was the most difficult year that the British monarchy had faced since the accession of Queen Victoria in 1837. King George V was succeeded by his eldest son, Edward Albert Christian George Andrew Patrick David, Prince of Wales. Born on 23 June 1894 at White Lodge, Richmond Park, and known in the Royal Family as David, on his accession he took the name of King Edward VIII. Since he abdicated less than a year after his father's death, his reign was almost an interregnum. So much has been written about the Abdication that it seems superfluous to add more, except in so far as it, and the period when Edward VIII was on the throne, affected the Royal Studs and Sandringham.

Soon after Edward VII had bought Sandringham, he had ordered the clocks there to be put thirty minutes ahead of the rest of the country. Sandringham Time was introduced first so that the winter evenings were longer, thus allowing more time for shooting, and secondly to try to counteract Queen Alexandra's lack of punctuality. George V had continued this tradition on his Norfolk estate in honour of the memory of his father. Such was Edward VIII's resentment of King George V that, as soon as he became King, he peremptorily sent orders from Buckingham Palace for all the clocks at Sandringham to be put back thirty minutes.

Edward VIII signed the document of Abdication on 10 December 1936. The following evening he broadcast a message of farewell to the nation, the final draft of which Winston Churchill, then out of office, helped him compose. In his first draft Edward VIII had attempted to put all the blame for his departure from the throne on pressure put on him by the Church and the political establishment, and none on himself. His treatment of his brother, the Duke of York, during the Abdication Crisis, was more than a little inconsiderate, for it was not until Monday 7 December that King Edward VIII had the courtesy to inform the Duke of York of his irrevocable decision to abdicate and marry Mrs Simpson. Thus he left his brother, the Duke of York, only three days to prepare himself for the burdens of kingship.

Those connected with the Royal Stud and the estate at Sandringham were not displeased to see Edward VIII, by then Duke of Windsor, leave England on board HMS *Fury* on 12 December 1936 for exile in France. As with all things revered and loved by George V, Sandringham aroused Edward VIII's dislike, even though his grandfather, his father and the rest of his family regarded it as their home. In the middle of 1936 he had put the Sandringham estate on the market, and by December had found a buyer. All that remained to be done in December 1936 was the exchange of contracts; the estate would then have passed to the purchaser, for Sandringham had been left to Edward VIII by his father, and so was his personal property. After his abdication, the Duke of Windsor first tried to insist that he kept it as his home in England, something quite unacceptable in the circumstances, both to King George VI and to his government. When this most unreasonable demand was refused, the Duke of Windsor compelled his brother to buy Sandringham from him out of his personal fortune, which, since George VI had not been Duke of Cornwall or Prince of Wales, was considerably less then than that of his elder brother.

King Edward's plan to sell Sandringham in 1936 caused many changes at the Royal Stud. All twenty broodmares were moved to the Hampton Court Stud, the first time all the Royal mares had been there since the dispersal of Queen Victoria's stud in 1894. The twelve foals born in 1936 also went to Hampton Court, as did two of the yearlings, leaving only twelve yearlings and the stallion Limelight remaining at Sandringham. By early 1937 all the Royal mares, foals and yearlings were in residence at Hampton Court, and only Limelight was still at the Wolferton Stud. In 1938 ten of the mares returned to Wolferton, but six, together with the foals and yearlings, remained at Hampton Court. By 1940 all the broodmares were kept at Sandringham, but the foals and yearlings were still quartered by the Thames. In 1942 the policy was adopted of keeping all the yearlings at Wolferton, with the mares and foals being divided between that stud and the one at Hampton Court.

Many feared that Edward VIII's abdication would bring about the downfall of the monarchy, but they had not counted on all the good qualities that King George VI had inherited from his father: his inherent common sense, his courage in the face of adversity, his sense of duty, his self-discipline learned in his naval training and his desire to emphasize the continuity between his own reign and that of his father, which was reflected in the name that he chose: George VI rather than Albert I. He was greatly helped by the sterling character of his mother, Queen Mary, who was outraged by her eldest son's behaviour, and who gave all her sympathy and support to the new King and Queen, feeling that it was they who were making the sacrifice and not the Duke of Windsor. Before the end of 1936 George VI wrote to Stanley Baldwin, the Prime Minister, 'I am new to the job, but I hope that time will be allowed to me to make amends for what has happened.' In the task that lay ahead, the caring support, guidance and encouragement that Queen Elizabeth gave her husband during the next few months, and indeed, throughout his reign, can never be overvalued. More-over, her charm, spontaneity and courage soon won the hearts of his subjects, even those who had been supporters of the man who had renounced his throne.

King George VI had never seen a state paper in his life before being precipitated on to the throne. Through no fault of his own, he had never been trained to be a monarch. Initially he worried about his capabilities of fulfilling the role thrust upon him and worked very long hours over the contents of the dispatch boxes. It is probably true to say that during the whole course of his reign he never realized what a good King he was, especially when one considers that Great Britain was plunged into the Second World War less than three years after his accession.

Despite the frenetic events of December 1936, the King still had time to let it be known before Christmas that he would continue the Royal Stud and his racing stable. On 28 December he wrote to Brigadier Tomkinson:

My dear Mouse,
    I hope I may call you by this name?
    Many thanks for your letters . . .
    I want to come down to Newmarket one day next month to see Jarvis and the horses when we can meet and have a talk . . . I understand there was a question of selling Limelight. This matter will have to wait until we can talk it over. Also his first foals are 2-year-olds this new year aren't they? We must wait and see if they are going to be of any use. I may have to

sell him as I shall want some cash to make the Stables and Stud square on legal grounds.

I shall certainly take a great interest in Racing, but of course at the moment I know nothing about breeding or anything else so you must teach me.

I am so glad you will go on being my manager, and I hope that we shall have a good season to start off with.

Yours very sincerely, George R. I.

Brigadier Tomkinson was, however, not destined to be the new King's stud manager in the next racing season, because at the young age of fifty-six he died on 20 January 1937.

When George VI became King there were twenty broodmares, fourteen yearlings and thirteen foals in the Royal Stud. There were also nineteen horses in training with Jarvis at Egerton House. Six of the thirteen foals bred by Edward VIII in 1936 won a total of eleven races. The best was Cosmopolitan (Sir Cosmo–Papilla), whose four victories included the Stud Produce Stakes at Newmarket's 1938 July Meeting and the July Handicap the next year over the same course. He also was runner-up to Old Reliance in the Cork and Orrery Stakes at Royal Ascot and was later exported to India. The most noteworthy performances of Edward VIII's horses in training were those of the three-year-old filly Feola. After a lacklustre two-year-old campaign, when the best she managed was one second in six outings, in the Allington Stakes at Newmarket, Feola won the Easter Plate at Kempton Park on her three-year-old debut. She then more than recouped her purchase price of 3,000 gns when a length and a half runner-up to Tideway in the 1,000 Guineas. Ridden again by Freddie Fox, Feola was third to Lovely Rosa in the Oaks and won the Midsummer Stakes over a mile at Newmarket. At the end of the 1936 racing season she was retired to stud and covered the next year by Umidwar.

After the premature death of Brigadier Tomkinson, King George VI appointed Captain Charles Moore to succeed him as manager of the Royal Stud. It was one of the most astute appointments he was to make. Charles Moore, who had served in the Irish Guards from September 1914 until June 1922 and had won a Military Cross in 1916, had over the previous thirty years built up a successful stud from a few mares bought inexpensively at his home at Mooresfort in County Tipperary. One of the best horses he had bred was Zionist, who won the Irish Derby and was runner-up to Manna in the Epsom Derby in 1925 in the colours of the Aga Khan; Moore had sold Zionist's half-sister, Judith, to the Royal Stud in 1934.

In 1937 King George VI's colours were first carried to victory by Jubilee in the Molyneux Stakes on the first day of the Grand National meeting at Liverpool. Jubilee won under John Crouch, a promising young rider who had been appointed Royal jockey in succession to Joe Childs but whose career was cut short by a fatal aeroplane accident in June 1939. The King and Queen did not witness Jubilee's success, but were at Liverpool two days later to see Royal Mail win the Grand National, having spent the previous night at Knowesley as guests of Lord Derby, in whose colours the Royal horses had run for the period of Court mourning. Both George VI and Queen Elizabeth attended the 1937 Derby at Epsom, which was won by Mid-day Sun, and the Oaks won by Exhibitionist, as well as Royal Ascot.

A mere three of the nine foals bred by George VI in 1937 won, and only a total of six races. Great Truth (Bahram–Frankly) won the Whitsuntide Foal Stakes at Manchester while the King and Queen were on their exceptionally successful tour of Canada and the USA in the summer of 1939; in doing so Great Truth became the first of Bahram's progeny to win a race. Great Truth was obviously below par when unplaced to Snowberry in the Queen Mary Stakes at Royal Ascot, because she trounced her rivals in the Fulbourne Stakes at Newmarket in July. She did not train on as a three-year-old and was sold at the 1940 December sales at Newmarket. Later Great Truth was exported to New Zealand where she achieved huge fame as a broodmare, principally as the dam of Summertime, who was champion sire there three times. Another foal bred in 1937, Helios (Hyperion–Foxy Gal), unfortunately broke a leg in training, but was saved and sold to Australia as a stallion. Helios distinguished himself in his stud career and was the leading sire in Australia for the 1948–9 season. On 2,000 Guineas day in 1938, the King had seen his colt Fox-Brush, a half-brother to Helios by Jacopo, start favourite for the Somersham Stakes; but he finished unplaced. He never won and was exported to the West Indies. This was George VI's first visit to the races at Newmarket as reigning Sovereign. He had stayed the night with his sister, the Princess Royal, and Lord Harewood at Egerton House, and the next morning went with them on a tour all round the racecourse: he would never have been content with a superficial knowledge of the track. The tour finished up at the stands, where he was received by the Stewards of the Jockey Club.

By 1938 Captain Moore had cut the number of broodmares in the King's stud to fifteen; of the seven foals born that year only three won five small races between them. The most interesting was Foretaste, Feola's first foal by Umwidwar; she won one race, the City Handicap Plate at Worcester, after she had been sold by the King. She later became the grandam of Lassalle, the winner of the 1973 Ascot Gold Cup and Prix du Cadran. Inevitably the Second World War greatly restricted racing opportunities for the crops born after 1936, especially those from 1937 to 1942, so many of the horses foaled in those years never saw a racecourse.

Only five of the nine foals bred by the King in 1939 went into training with Jarvis in 1941, and from the 1938 crop but one, Starling (Noble Star–Feola), was kept in training. Starling was never destined to win a race, but when she was later exported to Argentina, she became one of the most influential broodmares in the history of the breed in that country. She was the dam of Sideral, who won nine races and became Argentine champion sire, of Sagitaria, who was the leading two-year-old of his generation, and of Sideria, who was champion filly of hers. The sole winner bred by the King in 1939 was Channel Swell (Fairway–Papilla), whose eight wins came after he was sold out of the Royal stable at the end of his juvenile career.

The outbreak of the Second World War was to have a profound effect on the Royal Stud. Captain Charles Moore had realized early in 1937 that many of the broodmares needed to be culled; the war gave him the chance to cut back the number of broodmares to nine in 1941 and eight in 1942. He tried to keep only the best, and those included Feola, Scuttle's daughter, Canvas by Solario, Bread Card (Manna–Book Debt), a half-sister to Pay Up by Fairway, the 1936 2,000 Guineas winner, whose dam Book Debt was a full-sister to the 1927 St Leger, Coronation Stakes and Jockey Club Stakes heroine Book Law, Maiden Fair (Fairway–Maid of Perth), whom he had bought at the December Sales in 1939, and Judith, destined to be the ancestress of Dunfermline. At the same time Moore realized that it would take time for these mares to produce the winners he wanted for the King. He therefore reinstituted the policy of his predecessor Lord Marcus Beresford and arranged to lease some horses for their racing careers, on this occasion from the National Stud, though as earlier the yearlings came from the Tully Stud. These leased horses, which Charles Moore mischievously named 'The Hirelings', went into training with the brilliant trainer Fred Darling at Beckhampton. The leased yearlings that arrived at

Darling's yard in 1940 included Big Game (Bahram–Myrobella) and Sun Chariot (Hyperion–Clarence).

Five of the nine foals bred by the King in 1940 went into training with Jarvis at Egerton House, but only two were to win any races, Open Warfare (Umwidwar–Frankly) and Fisherman's Yarn (Salmon Leap–Idle Jest), who won the minor Soham Handicap at Newmarket in 1945. Although Open Warfare only won two races, the Balsham Stakes in 1942 and the Long Stanton Stakes in 1943, both at Newmarket, by finishing third to Last Sybil in the Cheveley Park Stakes and runner-up in the Upwell Stakes to Ribbon, who was second in the 1,000 Guineas and St Leger to Herringbone and to Why Hurry in the Oaks, she had shown herself to be almost top-class. The King's trainer, Captain Cecil Boyd-Rochfort, had given Open Warfare 'a good sporting chance in the 1,000 Guineas'; she had even looked a possible winner till a furlong out, when her lack of stamina caused her to fade out of contention. She was clearly going to be a valuable addition to the Royal broodmares.

In 1941 six foals were born to the Royal broodmares. The best was Knight's Daughter (Sir Cosmo–Feola), who went into training with the King's new trainer, Captain Cecil Boyd-Rochfort. When a yearling, he described her as a 'grand actioned filly and sure to win races but of rather an evil disposition'. She indeed won three races as a two-year-old: the Balsham Stakes, the Lidgate Stakes and the Pampisford Stakes, all at Newmarket, and was then retired to stud. The best of the five foals she got at Sandringham was Love Game by Big Game, the winner of the Kingsclere Stakes. She was sold at the December Sales in 1951 as Captain Moore felt there was more Feola blood coming into the stud, and she had not produced any outstanding foals for the King. The well-known American breeder, A. B. Hancock, bought Knight's Daughter and she was exported to the United States. He mated her in 1953 with Princequillo, who traced back in the male line to Persimmon; in 1954 she foaled the great American champion Round Table, who won forty-three races from sixty-six starts including the Hollywood Gold Cup (twice), the Blue Grass Stakes, the Santa Anita Handicap and the United Nations Handicap (twice), and amassed $1,749,869 in prize money; Round Table also became a leading sire in the United States. Knight's Daughter was also the dam of Monarchy, who won seven races including the Arlington Lassie Stakes. Two of the other 1941 foals were winners: Fair Glint (Hyperion–Maiden Fair) won the Littlebury Nursery Stakes and was only beaten a short head by Effervescence in the Dewhurst Stakes at Newmarket as a juvenile in

1943. Although Fair Glint started as low as 10–1 for Ocean Swell's Derby, he made no show in the Classic, and only won one other race, the Littlewick Green Stakes at Newmarket in 1945.

Six foals bred by the King in 1942 went into training at Boyd-Rochfort's stables at Freemason Lodge in Newmarket. Two of them, Rising Light (Hyperion–Bread Card) and Kingstone (King Salmon–Feola) were to win a total of sixteen races. Captain Moore had bought Rising Light's dam, Bread Card, in 1938. Rising Light was a backward but promising juvenile. He won four races in 1945 as a three-year-old including the Newmarket St Leger and the Burghfield Stakes at Ascot, when he beat Stirling Castle a short head in the presence of the King and his daughter, Princess Elizabeth, who was at Ascot races for the first time; it was also the first occasion she saw the Royal colours carried to victory. George VI had earlier entertained President Truman to lunch at Windsor Castle. The President informed the King of the decision to drop the atomic bomb on Japan; the conversation was dominated by this devastating new weapon and potential peaceful uses of atomic energy. Two days later, on 6 August 1945, the bomb was dropped on Hiroshima, which caused the Japanese to surrender within a week. Notwithstanding this momentous news, in his diary George VI still had place to record: 'My horse Rising Light beat Stirling Castle in a mile and a half race by a short head. It was thrilling for me as I had never seen one of my own horses win before.' Rising Light acquitted himself even better in the St Leger, run at York in 1945, for he ran Chamossaire to two lengths, with Stirling Castle third. As a four-year-old Rising Light won another three times, his most important victory coming in the Jockey Club Stakes. He was also runner-up to Marcel Boussac's 1944 Prix de l'Arc de Triomphe winner, Ardan, in the Coronation Cup and third to the French textile magnate's brilliant stayer, Marsyas, in the Queen Alexandra Stakes. He was syndicated as a stallion and stood at a stud near Newmarket; unfortunately he turned out to be a mediocre sire and was exported to Japan in 1954.

Kingstone, the other outstanding foal bred by King George VI in 1942, won the Gamlingay Stakes as a two-year-old at Newmarket. Boyd-Rochfort placed Kingstone very cleverly to win four staying races in 1945 and another four in 1946, including the Great Yorkshire Stakes. His two best performances, however, were probably when he was runner-up to Marcel Boussac's Marsyas in both the White Rose Stakes at Hurst Park and the Goodwood Cup. He retired as a stallion to the Wolferton Stud, where he remained until the end of 1954. He proved to be as disappointing a sire as Rising Light and eventually left Sandringham to stand in Lancashire; his stock nearly all lacked speed as he had done as a racehorse.

In 1942 the King had his best season as an owner; not with horses he had bred himself at the Royal Stud, but on account of the four Classic victories of Big Game and Sun Chariot, whom he leased from the National Stud. Big Game was unbeaten in his five outings as a juvenile, winning his first three races at Salisbury and then defeating Watling Street in the Coventry Stakes at Newmarket and again in the Champagne Stakes at Newbury. Sun Chariot numbered the Queen Mary Stakes and Middle Park Stakes at Newmarket among her four victorious appearances as a two-year-old. On 12 May 1942 Big Game beat Watling Street four lengths in the 2,000 Guineas and the next day Sun Chariot led throughout the 1,000 Guineas to win by the same distance.

After this memorable Classic double the King and Queen brought their two daughters to Beckhampton to see Big Game and Sun Chariot work. Gordon Richards recalled that the temperamental filly was on her worst behaviour and took him straight into the middle of a ploughed field, went down on her knees and roared like a bull. It was a tremendous struggle to get her finally to do her gallop. Though Sun Chariot was so badly left in the Oaks on 12 June that Richards thought she had lost all chance, such was her brilliance that she threaded her way through the field to win by a length. She was welcomed in the winning enclosure by the King and Queen, for whom an agricultural tour of Cambridgeshire had been arranged to coincide with both the Oaks and the Derby so that they could attend Newmarket on both afternoons. Big Game was odds-on for the Derby, but blew up soon after taking the lead three furlongs out and was not even placed behind Watling Street. The King, in the uniform of a Field Marshal, showed momentary disappointment, but was the first to congratulate Lady Derby on her husband's third success in the race. Gordon Richards was always certain that the King's colt failed through want of stamina, and Big Game redeemed his reputation when he won the mile and a quarter Champion Stakes, the final race of his career. Sun Chariot's last race was in the St Leger on 12 December, when she trounced Watling Street by three lengths. After Gordon Richards had retired, he was to name her as the best filly he ever rode; he regarded Pinza, the Queen's 1953 Derby winner, as the best colt he had ever won on. 'They were both simply terrific, outstanding in every possible way. I still don't know which was the greater.'

He added 'I have no doubt at all that had Sun Chariot run in the Derby, she would have won that just as easily as the St Leger.'

At the end of 1942 the King's trainer, William Jarvis, fell fatally ill and it became necessary to appoint another Royal trainer for the 1943 racing season. The choice was Captain Cecil Boyd-Rochfort, born at Middleton Park, County Westmeath, Ireland in 1887, the youngest boy among the seven children of Major Hamilton Boyd-Rochfort. The Captain's father was one of the largest land-owners in County Westmeath; he had been High Sheriff of the County for several years before his death in 1891, when Cecil Boyd-Rochfort was less than four. He therefore grew up in a world where racehorses and shooting were part of everyday life. He was educated at Eton, where he was further intrigued and fascinated by the Turf, and on leaving there in 1903 determined to make a career in racing. In 1906 he joined Atty Persse as an assistant trainer near Grateley on the Hampshire–Wiltshire borders; two years later he became assistant trainer to Captain R. H. Dewhurst at Bedford Lodge, Newmarket. In 1911 at the age of twenty-four Boyd-Rochfort was appointed racing manager to Sir Ernest Cassel on the recommendation of Lord Durham. Boyd-Rochfort already had a reputation for an extensive knowledge of pedigrees, and in 1912 bought Cassel a yearling named Hapsburg (Desmond–Altesse), who won the Eclipse Stakes and Champion Stakes and was second in the Derby in 1914. This perspicacious purchase established his name among the professionals of the Turf.

In the First World War Cecil Boyd-Rochfort served in the Scots Guards; he was wounded on the Somme in 1916 and won the Croix de Guerre. On his return to England he was appointed English racing manager to the young American millionaire, Marshall Field III, in 1919, a position he was able to take as Cassel was cutting back his stable. Boyd-Rochfort bought a yearling filly for Field in 1919 named Golden Corn who proved the best juvenile of her generation by winning the Champagne Stakes and the Middle Park Stakes. In 1922 Marshall Field decided to have more horses in training, appointed Boyd-Rochfort as his trainer and lent him the money to buy the stables at Freemason Lodge, Newmarket. From that moment on the young trainer never looked back. On a trip to the USA in 1928 Field introduced Boyd-Rochfort to William Woodward, Chairman of the New York Jockey Club, Joseph E. Widener and John Hay Whitney, later the American Ambassador to Britain. So impressed were they by his successes for Marshall Field and his knowledge of racing and breeding that they soon began to send horses to be trained at Freemason Lodge.

Throughout the late 1920s and 1930s Cecil Boyd-Rochfort, who came to be known as 'The Captain' in racing circles, was one of the leading trainers in the country. He won two Classics for William Woodward: the 1933 1,000 Guineas with Brown Betty and the 1936 St Leger with Boswell. He trained three winners of the Eclipse Stakes: Royal Minstrel in 1929, Loaningdale in 1933 and Boswell in 1937, the year he was leading trainer, a feat more than remarkable since none of the Freemason Lodge runners won a Classic that season. He also won the Ascot Gold Cup in consecutive years: with Lady Zia Wernher's Precipitation in 1937 and with Woodward's Flares in 1938, after saddling the runner-up in 1935 with Woodward's Alcazar and in 1936 with his American champion Omaha, who had failed by a short head to beat Lord Derby's Quashed. Considering all these and many other training triumphs, it was hardly surprising that Boyd-Rochfort was appointed Royal trainer at the end of 1942. Captain Charles Moore was an old friend of the Boyd-Rochforts; 'The Captain' had frequently visited Mooresfort to shoot snipe in the winter. Moore never cared much for letter-writing; when he wished to inform Boyd-Rochfort that he had been appointed as the King's new trainer, he discovered that 'The Captain' was travelling to Ireland. On his arrival at Holyhead, a surprised Boyd-Rochfort was told someone wanted him on the telephone; it was Charles Moore with the news of his Royal appointment.

Nineteen-forty-three was a very significant year for King George VI as a breeder. On 3 May Feola gave birth to a bay filly by Hyperion, who was named Hypericum; even as a foal her exceptional qualities showed her to be full of promise. In the autumn of 1944 she went into training at Freemason Lodge, where she quickly gave notice she was temperamental and difficult to train. Although she clearly had plenty of ability, it was necessary for her trainer to place horses on either side of her when cantering or galloping to stop her darting out; Boyd-Rochfort even had to forbid the stable jockey, Douglas Smith, from riding her in her gallops in case he was injured. She was ridden, therefore, in her work from the beginning by Roy Burrows, who had completed his apprenticeship two years earlier. Burrows, who won several races for Cecil Boyd-Rochfort as an apprentice, later recalled that Hypericum was

> a bit scatty. I helped to break her, but she was difficult and temperamental from the start. She did not have much of a mouth

and I used to ride her mostly on a neck-strap, hoping for the best. She would be walking quietly one moment and then almost throwing herself down the next. She kept herself fit with her antics, and most people were windy of her with good reason, but she could really gallop. Funnily enough she was wonderful in her box and a good doer.

Hypericum was odds-on on her debut, the Chesterford Stakes at Newmarket at the end of August, but was narrowly beaten into second place after losing ground at the start. She then won the Swallowfield Stakes at Ascot so impressively that she was allowed to take on the colts in the Middle Park Stakes, in which she finished a creditable runner-up by three quarters of a length to the Aga Khan's good colt Khaled. Khaled was himself runner-up in the 2,000 Guineas and won the St James's Palace Stakes in 1946; he was then exported to the USA where he was an outstanding success as a stallion, siring among others the Kentucky Derby winner Swaps. Hypericum was again odds-on for the Dewhurst Stakes at Newmarket's Houghton meeting, when she was opposed by the grey colt Airborne, who had been bred by her trainer's brother, Colonel Harold Boyd-Rochfort VC, and who was to win the 1946 Derby and St Leger. Hypericum's easy two-length victory was witnessed by Princess Elizabeth, whose party included Lord Porchester, then a young Lieutenant in the Royal Horse Guards.

Both the King and Princess Elizabeth were at Hurst Park on Easter Saturday 1946 to see Hypericum run against the Cheveley Park Stakes winner, Neolight, in the Katheryn Howard Stakes over seven furlongs. Neolight, who had been rated the best two-year-old filly of 1945, beat the King's filly in a canter by four lengths; on the strength of that performance Neolight was odds-on favourite for the 1,000 Guineas while Hypericum was one of the outsiders at 100–6. Freemason Lodge was represented by three fillies in the 1,000 Guineas, the others belonging to Major Harold Cayzer and Lord Portal, but in their final gallop Hypericum had come out just the best.

When Gordon Richards arrived in the paddock, Neolight's trainer, Fred Darling, told him that the filly had gone amiss. Although the blacksmith reported that Hypericum had been 'the devil to plate', she nevertheless arrived in the paddock without incident. Earlier, a fourth Freemason Lodge filly owned by Lady Zia Wernher, who had been an intended runner in the Classic, had got loose and had to be withdrawn at the eleventh hour. The King was represented that afternoon by Princess Elizabeth, who had arrived on the course early with Captain Boyd-Rochfort. Hypericum was drawn number one on the favoured stands side, and she had not played up at all until Captain Allison, the Starter, ordered the runners to line up. With absolutely no warning the King's filly charged the tapes, dislodged her jockey, Douglas Smith, and careered off riderless up the course. She disappeared behind the stands, but fortunately was caught near the car park by the man in charge of the course's fire engine. Grimes, the lad who did her at Freemason Lodge, mounted her and began riding her back to the start. Smith, who had come down the course in an ambulance, met the returning filly, remounted and eventually got her back to where the rest of the field was nervously waiting, cold and stiff.

The race started fourteen minutes late, and Hypericum, who was facing slightly sideways, lost a couple of lengths. Since Smith had decided to ride a waiting race, this was of little consequence. Wayward Belle and Iona made the running on the stands side with Hypericum tucked in behind them; Richards also had Neolight covered up in the middle of the field. Smith made his effort going into the Dip and passed Wayward Belle and Iona as Neolight challenged on the outside. For a brief moment it seemed that the favourite might win, but Hypericum's stamina up the hill proved the stronger and she ran on to win by a length and a half. Her most popular victory was the first Classic that George VI had won with a horse he had bred himself and the first Classic won by a horse bred by the Royal Stud since Scuttle's 1,000 Guineas in 1928.

The King and Queen, Queen Mary and Princess Elizabeth were all present at Epsom to see Hypericum in the Oaks. Given the doubt about Hypericum's stamina, it was rather surprising that Doug Smith immediately disputed the lead with the favourite, Iona, ridden by his brother Eph. At Tattenham Corner the pair were first and second, but early in the straight Hypericum was in distress. She finally finished unplaced behind Steady Aim and Iona. Shortly after the Oaks, Hypericum reared up in her box and injured herself. She did run in the Coronation Stakes at Royal Ascot, but was unplaced to Neolight. She was then retired to the Royal Stud.

The most notable addition to the Royal broodmares at Sandringham in the summer of 1943 was Ste Therese (Santorb–Yser), whom Captain Charles Moore had bought at the Duke of Portland's dispersal sale in July that year. Ste Therese had won five races in 1932 and 1933 and had produced one winner from four foals; her fifth dam was the renowned broodmare Paraffin. Unfortunately her 1944 colt foal by Winterhalter died as a yearling in October 1945. Three of the other four foals bred at the Royal Stud in 1944 won one race each. Although none was anywhere near top-class, Pierette (Mieuxcé–Frivole) ran fifth to Imprudence in the 1947 1,000 Guineas.

Five foals bred by the King at Sandringham in 1945 went into training with Captain Boyd-Rochfort in 1947, but only one, Angelola (Donatello II–Feola) was to win. Canvas Back (William of Valence), who was placed four times as a juvenile, was later to gain great distinction as a broodmare in Australia. Angelola, who was backward as a two-year-old and did not run until she was three, was a big rangy filly lacking both the quality and the speed of her half-sister Hypericum. Angelola made her debut in the Wood Ditton Stakes when she was fifth; she then ran second to Goblet in the Haverhill Stakes at Newmarket at the beginning of May 1948. Ten days later Angelola won the Lingfield Oaks Trial but only narrowly as the firm ground did not suit her. In her next race, the Oaks, she started at 20–1. King George VI had the pleasure of seeing her run an exceptionally fine race in view of her inexperience; always in the leading group she finished runner-up to the Aga Khan's Masaka, who also won the Irish Oaks. Angelola improved steadily as the season progressed, winning the Yorkshire Oaks, the Princess Royal Stakes at Ascot in September and the Newmarket Oaks; in addition she was runner-up to Goblet in the Nassau Stakes at Goodwood when unfavoured by the weights; she only failed when seventh to her stable companion, Black Tarquin, in the St Leger. When she retired to the Royal Stud at the end of the season, Angelola was probably the best staying three-year-old filly in training in the country.

The victory of the Allies over Nazi Germany on 8 May 1945 and the surrender of the Japanese in August offered the prospect of the Royal Stud at Sandringham gradually returning to its pre-war condition. The paddocks at the Sandringham stud were still all being used as farmland, and were to be so for several years, but in 1945 Captain Moore began slowly increasing the number of broodmares towards their former levels; even if the Stud was restricted to using the paddocks at Wolferton, there was still sufficient space at Hampton Court to cope with the extra mares, colts and yearlings. After the war ended Captain Moore also instituted a new policy concerning the foals after they had been weaned: they were now sent either to his own stud at Mooresfort in County Tipperary or to Commander Peter FitzGerald's Mondellihy Stud in County Limerick, the fillies to one and the colts to the other. Since Moore normally spent the winter in Ireland, he had no difficulty in keeping a close eye on these foals, who almost certainly benefited from the complete change of scene in a country famous for the quality of its grass in helping to build up young horses.

On 26 April 1946 Ste Therese foaled a chestnut filly by Hyperion who was named Avila. She was the only one of the five foals bred by the King that year ever to see a racecourse, but she more than compensated for what had been a disappointing number of produce by the quality of her performances. As a two-year-old Avila won the Waterford Stakes at Ascot, was second in the Virginia Water Stakes on the same course and ended her season with an extremely promising second to Pambidian in the Cheveley Park Stakes. She won her first outing as a three-year-old, the Katheryn Howard Stakes at Hurst Park, so easily that Boyd-Rochfort was able to tell the King, 'I really think we have a good chance in the 1,000 Guineas.' George VI, who had been very ill in the autumn of 1948 and was still convalescent, was unable to go to Newmarket for the event; Avila still led the field with a little over a furlong to go, but then faded and finished out of the frame to Musidora. Avila ran creditably but unplaced in the Oaks behind Musidora and Boussac's brilliant but inconsistent filly, Coronation V, who later won the Prix de l'Arc de Triomphe. The King was permitted by his doctors to go to Ascot, on condition that he should remain seated in the Royal Box as much as possible. Avila ran in the Coronation Stakes over the Old Mile course, which is not such a severe test of stamina as the Rowley Mile. Ridden with great finesse and tenderness by Michael Beary, Avila won decisively to the immense delight of the huge crowd. Although she was a small mare, she was to be a valuable addition to the Royal Stud.

At the First October Sales at Newmarket in 1946 Captain Moore bought a chestnut yearling filly named Young Entry. She won four races at two and three, including the Lancashire Oaks, and was runner-up to Vertencia in the Park Hill Stakes. As a broodmare Young Entry was again to underline Moore's excellent judgement in choosing mares and fillies to restock the Royal Stud.

In 1947 eight of the nine foals bred by the King survived and none of the mares was barren. On 4 May Feola gave birth to a bay filly named Above Board by the 1943 Derby winner Straight Deal. Boyd-Rochfort liked her very much in the spring of 1949 when she was a young two-year-old, but she took much longer to mature than he had anticipated. She was second in the Lingfield Oaks Trial but was still immature; she was unplaced in the Oaks and only fifth in the Ribblesdale Stakes at Ascot. Above Board finally won her first race at York, where she proved herself to be a really top-class filly, leading from start to finish in the Yorkshire Oaks. She was fourth in the Park Hill Stakes at Doncaster when unsuited by the dead ground, but ran a fine race when placed in the Princess Royal Stakes at Ascot, despite the weights being against her.

Above Board was set to carry 7 st 12 lbs in the Cesarewitch, and from her running in the Yorkshire Oaks seemed to Boyd-Rochfort to have an outstanding chance. Eph Smith, who had ridden her at York, had told her trainer after her victory that Above Board had exceptional stamina and would go close in the famous autumn handicap, and Boyd-Rochfort had booked him to ride her immediately. Captain Moore, though, was most reluctant to let the filly take part in the handicap, which was always a severe test of stamina; he would have preferred her to run in the Newmarket Oaks. Disputes between the two men, with one vowing never to speak to the other again, were by no means uncommon: they were normally so short-lived that the two would be seen an hour later over a drink, apparently the best of friends. The row about Above Board, however, was not settled until, after much discussion, George VI finally agreed that Boyd-Rochfort could run her in the Cesarewitch. The Royal trainer had never been averse to a tilt at the ring and had had a quite substantial ante-post wager on the filly. Rufus Beasley, who was stable jockey to Freemason Lodge in the 1930s, recalled how 'The Captain' had specially prepared a horse for a coup in the Chesterfield Stakes at Goodwood. To the Irish jockey's great astonishment Boyd-Rochfort himself led his mount from the paddock on to the course, where, in a quiet voice, he told him: 'Remember, Beasley, to look surprised when you have won.' Above Board's six-length victory over her thirty-seven rivals for the Cesarewitch, watched by the King's sister, the Princess Royal, fully vindicated her trainer's choice of engagement. She stayed in training as a four-year-old in 1951, but failed to win again, though she was second to Winston Churchill's Colonist II in the Winston Churchill Stakes and third to him and the 1951 Gold Cup winner, Pan II, in the White Rose Stakes, both run at Hurst Park. Above Board was the last horse trained by Boyd-Rochfort to win an important race for the King.

Feola's 1948 colt by Court Martial, Reprimand, who was sent to Malton to be trained by Captain Charles Elsey, the only colt bred by the King ever to be trained in the north, only managed one win, the Seaboard Stakes at Liverpool on 8 November 1951

– one of the last times George VI's colours were carried to victory. Four of the other eight foals bred by the Royal Stud in 1948 won nineteen races, but none of them was of great significance in England. Sydney Street (Watling Street–Open Warfare) won twice as a two-year-old and was second in the Molecomb Stakes at Goodwood and third in the Convivial Stakes at York; she was then exported to Venezuela, where she won that country's Derby. Her half-sister, Battened Down by Ocean Swell, who was foaled in 1949, won two races in England at two and was exported to Canada, where her three wins included the British Columbia Derby.

Four other winners were bred by the King in 1949. Love Game (Big Game–Knight's Daughter) won the Kingsclere Stakes at Newbury in 1951 and was exported to the United States, where she became a highly successful broodmare: among her five winners was Road House II, winner of eight races and $80,535 and a good sire. Love Game was also the grandam of Turkish Trousers, who won the Hollywood Oaks and was best three-year-old filly in the USA in 1970, and Tell, the winner of the Hollywood Derby and a useful sire. Stream of Light (Borealis–Yeovil) and Choir Boy (Hyperion–Choral) were also good winners bred this year, but their most important successes on the racecourse came after George VI had died.

At the December Sales at Newmarket Captain Moore made another of his inspired purchases for the Royal Stud when he bought the three-year-old filly Malapert (Portlaw–Malatesta) for the paltry sum of 100 gns. She had run only as a juvenile and her best performances had been two seconds in minor races at Newmarket and Pontefract.

On 14 April 1950 Angelola gave birth to her first foal, a chestnut colt by Hyperion with three white socks. A few days later he was inspected by Princess Elizabeth, who chose the name Aureole for him, after the golden disc around the heads of Donatello's marble saints. After he had been weaned, Aureole went to Ireland to the Mondellihy stud. There Commander Peter FitzGerald remembered him as a slightly tricky, highly-strung Hyperion who was very difficult to catch in the paddocks. Aureole was to prove the best colt bred by George VI, but regrettably the King never lived to see his famous victories on the racecourse, which all came after his daughter, Princess Elizabeth, had ascended the throne.

The last crop of foals bred by King George VI, the 1951 crop, contained no great champions. The best of the five winners was Angel Bright (Hyperion–Feola), a full-sister to Angelola, who won one race, the Lingfield Oaks Trial, after finishing second in the Princess Elizabeth Stakes at Epsom. She was, however, not to emulate her sister either on the racecourse or as a broodmare.

The last six years of George VI's reign had not been much easier for him than those of the Second World War. There was no relief from economic crisis or rationing, and in some ways the deprivations and shortages were harder to bear than those of 1939–45. These strains, combined with the King's conscientious sense of duty which led him to overwork, took their toll on his health. On 29 September he was found to have a malignant tumour which necessitated the removal of his left lung.

The King recovered sufficiently to go to Sandringham for Christmas on 21 December. Lighted trees on Wolferton Station greeted the arrival of the biggest gathering of the Royal Family for Christmas at Sandringham since 1938. Sandringham seemed to give the King new life; every day he was out shooting, and when he was examined by the doctors on 29 January 1952 they were more than satisfied by his progress. Two days later Princess Elizabeth and her husband, the Duke of Edinburgh, left London Airport for East Africa on the first leg of their journey to Australia. The King and Queen saw them off at the airport. After taking tea with Queen Mary, they returned to Sandringham. On 5 February the King shot for six hours, bagging nine hares. He, the Queen and Princess Margaret had a quiet dinner, after which the King, worried about his golden retriever who had cut a paw, walked down to the kennels to see him. They retired soon after ten. When his valet, James Macdonald, took him a cup of tea at seven-thirty on the morning of 6 February, he found that the King had died in the night.

George VI had served his country to the limits of his strength through a period of great adversity, both personally at the beginning of his reign, and for the entire country for the majority of it. His unfailing courage, unswerving sense of duty and his modesty at his own achievements had earned his subjects' respect, affection and gratitude. To his eldest daughter, the newly proclaimed Queen Elizabeth II, he left the Royal Stud at Sandringham in potentially the strongest position it had been since the time of Perdita II and Persimmon.

14

Queen Elizabeth II,

1952–60

Princess Elizabeth was unquestionably King George V's favourite granddaughter. When she visited Sandringham, the King would sit next to her at breakfast and talk to her in a most serious fashion. On Sunday afternoons when he visited the Royal Stud, the Princess sometimes would accompany her grandfather and he would point out to her Scuttle and the stallion Limelight. This close relationship between Princess Elizabeth and King George V is one of the remarkable aspects of her early childhood. She cannot fail to have been influenced by his upright attitudes and strict views on how members of the Royal Family should comport themselves, especially as she was never in awe of him like so many of his own children. It is also probable that the seeds of her love of horses, racing and breeding were sown by George V. Her very first pony, a Shetland named Peggy, had been a gift from her grandfather when she was four years old.

Princess Elizabeth also very much enjoyed riding and other country pursuits. She had first been taught to ride by Mr Horace Smith at Holyport. The proximity of his riding school to Royal Lodge meant that regular tuition was possible. Smith called her 'an ideal pupil ... and more than anxious to learn'. She soon became a fine rider, and as she grew older would cross-question Smith about the finer points of feeding, stable management and the training of horses. When she was thirteen she confessed to Horace Smith that if she had not been the heir to the throne, she would like 'to be a lady living in the country, with lots of dogs and horses'.

Three dozen toy horses, which had been given to Princess Elizabeth and her younger sister Princess Margaret, were kept on the top landing of 145 Piccadilly. When the move to Buckingham Palace took place in 1937, all the toy horses came too. They were placed in the corridor outside the children's rooms until after Princess Elizabeth was married. Soon after they arrived at the Palace, the two sisters went to the Royal Mews and asked if they could see the horses. These visits were soon made almost daily when the Royal Family was in residence at Buckingham Palace, and the grooms were closely questioned about the virtues, faults and habits of each of their charges.

During the war there was no bending of regulations for the Royal Family. Rationing was strictly enforced by the King; even the Queen's clothing coupons were the same as those of any other British woman. Baths in the Royal residences had lines painted on them five inches from the bottom to ensure that only the permitted quantity of water was used. The heating systems were turned off in Buckingham Palace and Windsor Castle, and the large, now cold, rooms had only tiny electric fires. The Sandringham estate was transformed: the house closed down, the golf course ploughed up and the paddocks at the Sandringham Stud used for agriculture; only those at Wolferton were retained, for the stallion Limelight and some broodmares. On their visits to Norfolk, the Royal Family stayed at Appleton House, and, to save petrol, the Queen used a pony and trap to go round the estate, with the King and the Princesses following on bicycles.

During the war Princess Elizabeth was permitted to read the King's trainers' reports. When she visited Beckhampton to see Big Game and Sun Chariot gallop, Fred Darling noticed that it was Princess Elizabeth who identified the horses for her father: a very impressed trainer remarked that the Princess must have a natural eye for a horse. During this visit Princess Elizabeth was permitted to run her hand over the 2,000 Guineas winner, Big Game. She later admitted that she did not wash her hands for some considerable time afterwards as she felt it was such a privilege to have touched such a high-class colt. A short while after this trip to Beckhampton, Princess Elizabeth made her first visit to the Hampton Court Stud to see the Royal broodmares and foals. She took especial note of the foal Rising Light, and she took many photographs of him on that and subsequent visits to the Stud in all stages of his early development. Rising Light became one of her favourites and when he raced she was always most anxious to hear the result as soon as possible. Whenever Princess Elizabeth visited the Hampton Court Stud, she always telephoned Captain Moore first to enquire if it was convenient, and always presented herself to him, or in his absence the stud groom, on her arrival. Her questions to the Royal Stud manager were endless, and from his great wealth of knowledge and experience he was able to teach her an enormous amount about broodmares, foals, pedigrees and the management and general running of a stud.

In February 1942 Princess Elizabeth was appointed Colonel of the Grenadier Guards, and on her sixteenth birthday inspected one of the battalions of the regiment with all the attention to detail that characterized her grandfather. In March 1945 the Princess joined the Auxiliary Territorial Service as Subaltern Elizabeth Alexandra Mary Windsor. She was posted to the Mechanical Transport Training Centre near Camberley and learned how to drive three-ton trucks and change their wheels.

On VE Day, 8 May 1945, when Germany surrendered, a huge crowd assembled outside Buckingham Palace. The King, Queen, Winston Churchill, Princess Elizabeth in uniform and Princess Margaret came out on to the balcony seven times to acknowledge the happy and relieved cheers of the crowd. A little after eleven o'clock the Queen allowed her two daughters, accompanied by an escort of Guards officers, to slip out of the Palace and join the quarter of a million people gathered around the Palace.

As the War had progressed Prince Philip of Greece had been a welcome guest at Royal Lodge during his leaves. In August 1946 he proposed to Princess Elizabeth at Balmoral and she accepted. The engagement was officially announced on 10 July 1947, two and a half months after her twenty-first birthday. On the evening of her birthday, Princess Elizabeth broadcast to the Empire from Cape Town: 'I declare before you all that my whole life, whether it be long or short, shall be devoted to your service and the service of our great Imperial Commonwealth to which we all belong . . .'

On 19 November 1947 Lieutenant Philip Mountbatten was created His Royal Highness the Duke of Edinburgh, Earl of Merioneth and Baron Greenwich; he was also invested with the Order of the Garter. The next day he married Princess Elizabeth in Westminster Abbey to great rejoicing in the country. The universal enthusiasm for the wedding, which was both broadcast and tele-vised, emphasized the extent of popular support for the monarchy and affection for the Royal Family.

The King's ill-health meant that more and more public duties devolved on Princess Elizabeth and her husband in the four years and two months that remained of George VI's reign. They were on the first leg of their tour of East Africa when, on 6 February, the Duke of Edinburgh broke the sad news of her father's death to his 26-year-old wife. It was as Queen Elizabeth II that she returned to London the following day.

When Princess Elizabeth was married she received many presents connected with racing, among them a filly foal named Astrakhan (Turkhan–Hastra), a gift from the Aga Khan. In 1949 she registered her racing colours – scarlet, purple hooped sleeves, black cap – for the first time. Unfortunately Astrakhan proved difficult to train, and though she won the Merry Maidens Stakes in the spring of 1950 at Hurst Park, she was retired after trailing in last in the Lingfield Oaks Trial Stakes. On hearing of Astrakhan's training problems, the Aga Khan had insisted on giving Princess Elizabeth another filly, Marsa (Stardust–Bellinzona), but she had even less ability and died in 1951. The Princess owned no other horses that raced on the flat until she ascended the throne. In the summer of 1949 she and her mother bought a steeplechaser named Monaveen; although each had a half-share in the gelding, he raced in Princess Elizabeth's colours. He won four times at Fontwell, Sandown and Hurst Park (twice); he was second in the Grand Sefton Chase at Liverpool, and fifth to Freebooter in the 1950 Grand National, but was killed at Hurst Park on New Year's Day 1951. After the tragic drowning of Lord Mildmay, the friend of the Royal Family who had suggested the purchase of Monaveen, Queen Elizabeth bought his chaser, Manicou, on whom he himself had won six races. Manicou was to run in Queen Elizabeth's colours, blue, buff stripes, black cap, gold tassel, which had been those of the Earls of Strathmore. His three victories for Queen Elizabeth included the prestigious King George VI Stakes at Kempton Park in 1950, but then he broke down and was retired to stud.

After the Queen's accession to the throne in February 1952, she gave up racing under National Hunt Rules, though her mother has continued, with much success and enjoyment. It was quickly announced that Queen Elizabeth II would continue the Royal Stud at Sandringham, whose produce would be trained by Captain Boyd-Rochfort. The horses she leased from the National Stud would be in the care of Noel Murless, who had succeeded Fred Darling when ill-health compelled the great trainer to retire. The Queen's horses ran in the colours of the Duke of Norfolk during the period of Court mourning for King George VI.

In the spring of 1952 the Queen inherited twenty broodmares, seven yearlings and three two-year-old fillies at the Royal Stud at

Sandringham; in addition she had two three-year-olds and four juveniles in training at Freemason Lodge. Both of the three-year-olds were to win famous races. Stream of Light (Borealis–Yeovil) won the Katherine Parr Plate at Hurst Park and the Lancashire Oaks at Manchester, when the Queen's colours were carried to victory for the first time; she also finished third in the Ribblesdale Stakes at Royal Ascot in 1952. Choir Boy (Hyperion–Choral) was Her Majesty's first winner when he took the Wilberton Handicap at Newmarket on 13 May. He later split a pastern and did not race again that season. 'The Captain's' patience with him was well rewarded, for he won the Royal Hunt Cup at Royal Ascot in 1953, thus becoming Queen Elizabeth II's first winner at the Royal meeting. On the previous day the Queen had invested Captain Cecil Boyd-Rochfort as a Commander of the Royal Victorian Order in the Royal Box. Captain Charles Moore had bred Choir Boy's dam, Choral, in Ireland, but after one more victory the colt was sold to Uruguay as a stallion. His form was not good enough to be considered as a sire at the Royal Stud, which had to run on sound business lines. There was never any question of filling the Royal paddocks with pensioners for sentimental reaons.

The most promising of the four two-year-olds bred by her father that the Queen had in training in 1952 was Aureole, who showed tremendous speed in his gallops. He was, however, in common with so many of Hyperion's best progeny, highly-strung, temperamental and difficult to handle. Sometimes he would obstinately refuse to jump off with the other juveniles. When the Queen visited Freemason Lodge in the spring of 1952, Aureole lashed out at her when she offered him an apple. Boyd-Rochfort, nevertheless, had been convinced for some time that the highly-strung stock by Hyperion invariably proved his best; it was merely a question of patient coaxing to make them use their ability to its fullest.

The dislike that Aureole had frequently taken to the starting-gate on the gallops caused the Freemason Lodge team to fear that he might be left at the post on his debut in the Acomb Stakes at York in August 1952. His jockey, Harry Carr, who knew that his mount 'had no badness in him but definitely had a mind of his own', approached the Starter, Alec Marsh, to tell him of his fears that the Queen's colt might be left. Marsh permitted Aureole to walk in from behind and they got away all right; he gradually closed with the leaders and got up close home to beat Brolly. Aureole had but one more race as a two-year-old, in the Middle Park Stakes at Newmarket; this choice illustrated what a high opinion his trainer had of his potential ability. He finished only sixth to Nearula, but was not given a hard race after he was slowly away and it was clear his chance had gone.

At the end of 1952 two new faces appeared at Freemason Lodge: Bruce Hobbs arrived as assistant trainer, and Frank Holmes, who had been travelling head lad to R. A. Jones's Newmarket stable also joined the staff. Soon after his arrival, Holmes, who was an excellent and very patient horseman, was assigned the job of doing Aureole and riding him in his work when Harry Carr was not available. Much credit must be given to Frank Holmes for teaching Aureole how to settle and to relax. The Queen came to Newmarket to see her best three-year-old make his seasonal debut in the 2,000 Guineas, although the stable was not seriously expecting him to win. He acquitted himself well, finishing a highly promising fifth to Nearula, who was trained in Yorkshire by Captain Charles Elsey. Harry Carr later recalled, 'Aureole surprised us by running so well, and, as we came in, I remember saying to Captain Elsey that Nearula would not beat us in the Derby.' Aureole became one of the leading contenders for the Coronation Derby when he trounced his rivals by five lengths in the Lingfield Derby Trial. The horse most likely to be a threat to him in the Derby was Sir Victor Sassoon's Pinza, who had won the Newmarket Stakes very impressively; he was to be the mount of Gordon Richards. The champion jockey, who had just been given a knighthood in the Coronation Honours List, was still seeking that elusive first Derby winner.

Queen Elizabeth II's Coronation took place on Tuesday 2 June 1953 at Westminster Abbey. On that morning, prior to her departure from Buckingham Palace through the enormous cheering crowd, one of her Ladies-in-Waiting asked her if everything was in order, thinking that the Queen might be apprehensive about he long elaborate ceremony. Her Majesty reportedly replied that everything was fine; Boyd-Rochfort had just telephoned to say that Aureole had gone very well in his last work.

In the preliminaries, Aureole played up and began to sweat, especially after a well-wishing racegoer gave him a hefty pat as he left the paddock. But once the race was under way, Harry Carr settled the Queen's colt in the middle of the field on the run up to Tattenham Corner. Coming down the hill Shikampur held a clear lead from Pinza, on whom Richards had found an opening on the inside rails, with Aureole sixth. Two furlongs out Pinza challenged Shikampur and took the lead, still on the bridle. Aureole, who had made steady headway up the middle of the course, looked the only possible danger to Sir Victor Sassoon's colt approaching the final furlong. Pinza's lead was, however, unassailable, and galloping on relentlessly he had four lengths to spare over Aureole at the winning post, with the French colt, Pink Horse, another one and a half lengths away third. Boyd-Rochfort later wrote to William Woodward, 'No excuse. We had a good run all the way. I think a better horse in Pinza beat us.'

A few minutes after the race the Queen sent for Gordon Richards, Sir Victor Sassoon and Norman Bertie, Pinza's trainer, to congratulate them. The famous jockey later recalled, 'There was no disappointment in her face . . . Her Majesty seemed just as delighted with the result of the race as I was.' When the Duke of Edinburgh asked if he was now going to retire, the Queen interposed, 'Of course not! He's going to ride for me in the Derby next year, on Landau.' Landau was one of the colts her Majesty leased from the National Stud; he did run in the 1954 Derby behind Never Say Die, but ridden by W. Snaith as Gordon Richards had not recovered from a bad fall at Salisbury.

In his next two races Aureole was beaten, coming third to the French four-year-olds Argur and Guersant in the Eclipse Stakes, and then second to Pinza again, by three lengths, in the King George VI and Queen Elizabeth Stakes at Ascot. The field at Ascot was of the highest class, however, and Aureole had finished in front of such useful horses as Wilwyn, Nearula, Silnet and Zucchero. Even so, Aureole's excitability was still a source of worry to Boyd-Rochfort. At Goodwood the Queen's trainer and stud manager suggested that Aureole might be treated by Dr Charles Brook, a London neurologist who had developed a method of calming both humans and animals by laying his hands on them and releasing their pent-up nervous tension. He had already successfully used his treatment on temperamental horses that had taken part in the Coronation.

Dr Brook came to Freemason Lodge twice a week in August. Going to Aureole's box, he would place his left hand on the colt's withers and his right one on his girth, resting his head on Aureole's shoulders. He remained in that position for about twenty minutes. Boyd-Rochfort reported to the Queen in Balmoral that the treatment seemed to be working, as the highly-strung colt was eating better and putting on weight. When the news came that Pinza had broken down and been scratched from the St Leger, the way seemed clear for the Royal colt to take the season's final Classic.

The Queen came down from Balmoral to see Aureole run in the St Leger. Aureole was a short-priced favourite at 5–4, but the stable was anxious about him. He had showed all his old obstinacy in his final gallop on the Limekilns, despite Dr Brook's treatment. Landau's victory in the Doncaster Produce Stakes got the afternoon off to a good start for the Queen; unfortunately, Aureole had other ideas. In the parade he began to play up badly, and going down to the start almost pulled Carr's arms out of their sockets. He pulled hard in the race, too, refusing to settle in the early stages; by the two-furlong pole he had exhausted himself and was decisively beaten into third place by Brigadier Wyatt's Premonition and François Dupré's Grand Prix de Paris winner, Northern Light. Boyd-Rochfort was the slightly embarrassed trainer of Premonition, who, although he had been disqualified after winning the Irish Derby and had won the Voltigeur Stakes, had always finished behind Aureole when they had previously met on the racecourse.

With a tarnished reputation to redeem, the Queen's colt ran his last race in 1953 in the Cumberland Lodge Stakes at Ascot; as Harry Carr could not do the weight, his place was taken by Eph Smith. Aureole won the race impressively. Charles Moore noticed that Eph Smith was able to settle the headstrong colt much better than Harry Carr had done at Doncaster, and recommended that Smith should be asked to ride Aureole in all his engagements as a four-year-old; despite opposition from Boyd-Rochfort, who supported his stable-jockey Carr, this advice was accepted once Eph Smith's first retainer, Mr H. J. Joel, gave his permission.

The Queen was still on her Commonwealth tour when Aureole made his seasonal reappearance in the Coronation Stakes at Sandown in April 1954. He was badly crossed early in the straight and nearly brought down; Eph Smith was not hard on him after that incident, but he still managed to finish a length second to Chamier. While in New Zealand the Queen had seen the champion sire, Summertime, at the Ta Rapa Stud; his dam, Great Truth, had been bred at Sandringham in 1937. The Queen was still away when Aureole slaughtered his rivals in the Victor Wild Stakes at Kempton and, although back in England, was prevented by her duties from seeing the reformed four-year-old impressively beat Chatsworth and Nearula in the Coronation Cup at Epsom.

The night before Aureole's next race, the Hardwicke Stakes at Royal Ascot, he was cast in his box; on regaining his feet he knocked his left eye, and when he arrived at Ascot the eye was practically closed. The veterinary surgeon nevertheless passed him fit to run. The Queen told Eph Smith about his mount's state in the paddock; the jockey, who suffered from increasing deafness, replied: 'Then we are both handicapped, Ma'am, I'm afraid. Aureole's half-blind and I'm half-deaf. We are a dilapidated pair.' Aureole had to give 7 lb to Marcel Boussac's very useful Janitor, who may have been unlucky not to have fought out the finish of the 1953 Prix de l'Arc de Triomphe with Premonition, since both suffered such severe interference at a vital stage in the race that their eventual sixth and seventh places were quite remarkable. Aureole put up the most courageous performance of his life in the Hardwicke Stakes. Janitor went a neck up on him inside the final furlong; Smith gave his mount a hard slap with his whip and, responding gamely, Aureole managed to force his head in front again a few yards from the line.

Aureole had his final race in the King George VI and Queen Elizabeth Stakes at Ascot in July 1954. He played up during the parade in front of the stands, so Eph Smith took him down to the start the first of the field. As he arrived there, a racegoer put up his umbrella, so startling Aureole that Smith was thrown. The jockey, who was unhurt, immediately called to his mount and offered him some grass, something he always did after a gallop at Newmarket, and Aureole permitted him to remount. Nevertheless, he must have been upset, because he dug his toes in as the tapes went up and lost all of ten lengths. Fortunately the dead going meant that the early pace was slow, and an unflustered Eph Smith let Aureole slowly make up the lost ground. By the half-way mark he had joined the leaders; he moved into second place entering the straight and went ahead two furlongs out. Aureole was challenged first by Darius, and then by Vamos inside the distance, but he responded gamely to the tap of Smith's whip and held on to win by three quarters of a length. This victory made Aureole the undisputed four-year-old champion of Europe. It was reported that a very excited Queen was seen running to the unsaddling enclosure to greet Aureole as he came into the place reserved for the winner of England's most prestigious weight-for-age race. She certainly arrived in front of Captain Moore.

It had always been intended to retire Aureole to the Royal Stud at Sandringham after the Ascot race. Boyd-Rochfort was never in favour of him running in the Prix de l'Arc de Triomphe after the rough race Premonition had endured in 1953, and an invitation to run in the Washington International was politely declined. His victories helped to make Her Majesty the leading owner and

Captain Boyd-Rochfort the leading trainer of 1954. The Queen's Christmas present to him that year was a lacquered cigarette box inscribed: 'Cecil Boyd-Rochfort, leading trainer, from Elizabeth R, leading winning owner, 1954'. To the end of his life it remained one of his most treasured possessions.

Aureole was sent to stand at the Wolferton Stud in the autumn of 1954, where he came under the control of the stallion man, Ted Grist. He proved easier to handle than had been anticipated, and was never to cause trouble covering his mares. Aureole's four-acre paddock adjoined the railway station at Wolferton; on its western side a magnificent three-sided barn was built as a shelter for him. Grist reported that he was a stickler for routine and disliked anything strange or unusual. When a foot-and-mouth epidemic occurred near Sandringham and disinfected straw was put at the entrance to his paddock, Aureole refused to cross it.

Aureole soon proved to be the most influential stallion to stand at the Royal Stud since Persimmon. His first crop included Saint Crespin, the 1959 winner of the Prix de l'Arc de Triomphe and the Eclipse Stakes, and Piping Rock, who became a very useful sire when exported to Australia. The best of his second crop was St Paddy, who won the 1960 Derby and St Leger and the 1961 Eclipse Stakes and Hardwicke Stakes. Another of the same crop was Sir Winston Churchill's Vienna, who was third in the St Leger and won the Prix d'Harcourt. Vienna achieved fame as a stallion by siring the brilliant 1968 Prix de l'Arc de Triomphe winner, Vaguely Noble, himself the sire of the great racemare Dahlia, Lemhi Gold and Exceller. In 1960 and 1961 Aureole was the leading sire of winners, and he was second in 1965. He sired several other Classic winners: Provoke (St Leger), Aurelius (St Leger), Aurabella (Irish Guinness Oaks) and Paysanne (Prix Vermeille). Other notable horses sired by Aureole included Hopeful Venture (Grand Prix de Saint-Cloud, Hardwicke Stakes), Mirlago (Hardwicke Stakes), Buoy (Princess of Wales's Stakes, Coronation Cup), Saintly Song (Champagne Stakes, St James's Palace Stakes) and Apprentice (Goodwood Cup, Yorkshire Cup). Aureole died at Wolferton in 1974, two years before his great-grandson, Empery by Vaguely Noble, won the Derby. It may be a total coincidence that Aureole, like his great predecessor at the Wolferton Stud, Persimmon, never sired a Classic winner for the Royal Stud.

The seven yearlings that Queen Elizabeth II inherited from her father did not include a champion like Aureole, but five of them won nine races for her. The best was Aureole's full-sister Angel

Bright, who won the Lingfield Oaks Trial and ran second in the Princess Elizabeth Stakes at Epsom. She was soundly beaten in the Oaks by Sun Cap and was regrettably an utter failure in the paddocks.

The eight foals that were born at the Royal Stud in 1952 were the first bred by Queen Elizabeth II; it was quite remarkable that all six who went into training at Freemason Lodge were to win. The best was Sierra Nevada by Djebel, Avila's first foal. Although he did not win at two, his promising second in the Solario Stakes at Sandown boded well for 1955, despite his having no Classic engagements. On his reappearance he won the Blue Riband Stakes at Epsom in April; defeated over a longer distance next time out, he reverted to a mile in the St James's Palace Stakes when he finished a close fourth to Lord Porchester's Tamerlane. In the Queen Elizabeth II Stakes at Ascot in September, Harry Carr made his challenge on Sierra Nevada in the middle of the course. The Royal jockey later said, 'I was cantering one and a half furlongs from home and had the race in my pocket, when I heard a sickening crack. Sierra Nevada had broken a fetlock, but he was so brave he went on trying to gallop before I could pull him up.' Within a few minutes Sierra Nevada had been tragically put down by the racecourse vet.

Sierra Nevada's contemporary, Alexander (Alycidon–Open Warfare), was entered in the Classics as on breeding he should have got a mile and a half. As a juvenile he won the Duke of Edinburgh Stakes at Ascot in the autumn of 1954. The following spring Her Majesty went to see Alexander and her other three-year-olds do their first important work of the year. Alexander made an excellent start to his three-year-old career by beating Our Babu in the 2,000 Guineas Trial Stakes at Kempton. He was very disappointing in the 2,000 Guineas behind Our Babu; possibly he was unsuited by the stiff uphill finish of the Rowley Mile. Alexander was then off the course until Goodwood, having slipped a stifle; in the Sussex Stakes the Queen saw him put up a terrific struggle when only going down by a neck to My Kingdom. Alexander was beaten twice in the autumn at Newmarket and appeared to have lost his enthusiasm for racing, so Bruce Hobbs, Boyd-Rochfort's assistant trainer, put him over some hurdles in the winter, which reawakened his interest. Although he was unplaced in the Victoria Cup at Hurst Park on the Queen's birthday in 1956, Alexander's second to Tudor Jinks in the Jubilee Handicap at Kempton made him one of the leading fancies for the Royal Hunt Cup. His most dangerous rival, Jaspe, ridden by Rae Johnstone, was drawn on the far side of the course and Alexander on the stand side. Carr, who had covered up the Queen's runner for the first six furlongs, as he did best when held up for a late challenge, found himself in front before the furlong pole. Meantime Jaspe was beginning to master his rivals on the far side and launch his challenge. Alexander began to weaken in the last few strides and in a thrilling finish both flashed past the post together. When the Queen asked Carr if he had won, he replied he did not know; Johnstone similarly was uncertain of the result. When, after long deliberation, the Judge announced Alexander had won by half a length, a loud roar of approval went up from the crowd. Carr later remarked, 'My horse hated being in front so long, and was not enjoying himself at the finish.' His task had certainly been made more difficult by his stand-side rivals dropping out so early, but the blinkers that he had worn for the first time that afternoon must have helped him to battle to the line. Alexander was outclassed by Tropique in the Eclipse Stakes and was sold to South Africa as a stallion at the end of the season; he died young as a result of a stud accident.

Corporal (Court Martial–Carmen) was another of the Queen's first crop of foals to distinguish himself on the racecourse. He won four of his eight outings as a two-year-old, including the Newmarket Foal Stakes in October, in which he beat his debutante stable-companion, Lady Zia Wernher's unfancied Meld. It was the sole defeat that brilliant filly was ever to suffer. Corporal also ran second in the Woodcote Stakes at Epsom and in the Windsor Castle Stakes at Royal Ascot. A substantial offer was made for him at the end of 1954 and he was sold to race in California.

Eight of the fourteen foals bred by the Queen in 1953 were successful on the racecourse, and two, Atlas (Djebel–Young Entry) and High Veldt (Hyperion–Open Country), were even better than Alexander and Sierra Nevada. The tiny High Veldt was under fifteen hands as a two-year-old and got himself into such a state before his races that he was scratched from the 2,000 Guineas and Derby. He still won both the Soltykoff Stakes and the Houghton Stakes at Newmarket, and high hopes were held for him when he retired for the season. On his reappearance High Veldt won the 2,000 Guineas Trial Stakes at Kempton, and then took the Thirsk Classic Trial three weeks later. He must have gone close to winning the 2,000 Guineas had he been able to contest it. When he next ran, he finished fourth in the St James's Palace Stakes, but by then a mile was probably too short for him. In his next race High Veldt took on the very best, including Marchese Incisa della Rocchetta's unbeaten champion Ribot, one of the best colts to have raced in Europe this century, and with few peers since the Second World War. Despite a twelve-minute delay at the start, which must have upset the highly-strung High Veldt, the Queen's colt was the only one in the field to look a danger to Ribot two furlongs out, and though the Italian crack drew away from him inside the distance to win comfortably, High Veldt had given him the hardest race of his career. The long-term effects of this very courageous performance left their mark; High Veldt could only finish fifth to Cambremer in the St Leger and was beaten into second place in the Cumberland Lodge Stakes by Sir Winston Churchill's Le Pretendant. Harry Fox, who looked after High Veldt at Freemason Lodge, said later, 'High Veldt never gave me the same feeling again after his race with Ribot . . . I kept on thinking there was something amiss, but we were never able to pin-point anything. I think personally it must have been his heart.' After a very disappointing four-year-old campaign, when the best he could manage was third place in the Coronation Cup and Hardwicke Stakes, High Veldt was exported to South Africa as a stallion; he proved a great success and became leading sire in his new country.

Atlas's dam Young Entry had been bought by Captain Moore for King George VI for 1,800 gns as a yearling at the Newmarket October Sales in 1946. Although Atlas did not win as a juvenile, he showed immense promise when a head runner-up to Dacian in the Dewhurst Stakes. On his reappearance he found the mile of the Blue Riband Stakes at Epsom too sharp, but comfortably won the Dee Stakes from French Beige at Chester. Atlas was outpaced in the early part of the Derby, won by Lavandin, but finished well in the final two furlongs and ran into a respectable fifth place. Since High Veldt was considered superior to Atlas over a mile and a half at home, had he run he was certain to have been concerned in the finish, though Harry Carr did not think he would have beaten Lavandin. Atlas lost his chance by missing the break in the King Edward VII Stakes at Ascot; however, he beat the Ebor Handicap winner, By Thunder, in the Doncaster Cup. Atlas was by no means disgraced by his close third to Kurun in the Jockey Club Stakes at Newmarket, his last race as a three-year-old, and seemed sure to be a major contender for the staying races in 1957. Atlas's four-year-old season, though, proved on balance disappointing: he only won once, the Haydock Park Stakes over two miles in May. He was runner-up in the Chester Cup, a possibly unlucky third to Hornbeam in the Winston Churchill Stakes at Hurst Park, and only fifth to his stable companion, Zarathustra, in the Ascot Gold Cup. After Ascot he was retired and sold to a syndicate to stand at the Hunsley House stud.

The 1954 crop of foals bred by the Queen at the Royal Stud has been one of the most exceptional of her reign. Six of the eight foals that went into training with Captain Boyd-Rochfort won, and four of them succeeded in major races. The best colt, Doutelle by Prince Chevalier, a dark liver chestnut with a pronounced blaze, was Above Board's second foal. He was a small colt who did not act in heavy going. After impressively winning his first race, the Granville Stakes at Ascot in July 1956, he lost the New Ham Foal Stakes by a short head at Goodwood. Both the Gimcrack Stakes and the Royal Lodge Stakes were run in soft going and Doutelle was unplaced; but for the Dewhurst Stakes the going was good, and Doutelle put up a fine performance to run Crepello to three quarters of a length.

Doutelle won the 2,000 Guineas Trial Stakes at Kempton Park on his first appearance in 1957, giving the Queen a hat-trick in the race. As it was felt he would be better suited by distances beyond a mile, he had been scratched from the 2,000 Guineas, and his next race was the Lingfield Derby Trial, which he won by a neck. He thrived after this victory and was considered much better than the other Freemason Lodge runner in the Derby, Mrs Arden Graham's Tempest. According to Harry Carr, the 1957 Derby was the roughest he ever rode in, and Doutelle was right in the middle of the scrimmaging that took place coming down the hill to Tattenham Corner. The Queen's colt, so battered and bruised that he was to be off the racecourse till 12 October, had lost all his chance on his arrival in the straight. Tempest finished fourth, only three and a quarter lengths behind Crepello. Unfortunately the camera patrol did not exist in 1957, and the cut-throat competition between the English and French jockeys, which resulted in the terrible pile-up in Larkspur's 1962 Derby, went on unchecked. What was even sadder was that Doutelle's injuries compelled him to miss the St Leger. On his return he won the Cumberland Lodge Stakes, and the Limekiln Stakes at Newmarket in October when Tempest could only finish third.

Doutelle began his four-year-old campaign with an extremely impressive three-length victory over the St Leger runner-up, Court Harwell. He then proceeded to inflict on Ballymoss the only defeat of his four-year-old season when he beat the future Eclipse, King

George VI and Arc winner a length and a half in the Ormonde Stakes at Chester. Boyd-Rochfort decided to train Doutelle for the Season's Cup races, since he was sure he would stay like his dam, Above Board. In hindsight this policy was probably mistaken, for Doutelle was beaten by Court Harwell in the Winston Churchill Stakes at Hurst Park, by Gladness and Hornbeam in the Ascot Gold Cup, and trailed in last of four behind Gladness in the Goodwood Cup. Each of these defeats can be attributed to lack of stamina. When he reverted to a mile and a half in the King George VI and Queen Elizabeth Stakes at Ascot in July, Doutelle ran a good race to be third to Ballymoss and the Queen's other runner, Almeria, but training him for and running him in the Cup races had blunted his finishing speed. This became more apparent when he finished third in the Cumberland Lodge Stakes to Mon Fetiche at Ascot in October.

Doutelle then retired to the Royal Stud, for the Queen had decided that a stallion should stand at the Sandringham Stud in addition to Aureole at Wolferton. Tragically Doutelle's career as a stallion was short-lived, for he died in 1962. His best produce included Pretendre, who won the King Edward VII Stakes and Dewhurst Stakes, was second in the 1966 Derby and became a very successful sire, Canisbay, the Queen's Eclipse Stakes winner, Dites, the winner of the Cambridgeshire and Amicable, who won the Nell Gwyn Stakes and Oaks Trial Stakes.

The best filly of the 1954 crop was Almeria (Alycidon–Avila), who was very closely inbred to Hyperion as both Avila and Alycidon's dam, Aurora, were by Lord Derby's great stallion. It was almost impossible to fault her conformation, and Boyd-Rochfort often brought his visitors to her box to admire her. Nevertheless, like so many horses with a lot of Hyperion blood, she was highly-strung and had a mind of her own. In her only run as a juvenile, Almeria was a creditable third in the Waterford Maiden Stakes at Ascot. She was third again on her three-year-old debut in the Lingfield Oaks Trial, but after that was unbeaten in her four other races in 1957. She was kept, at Boyd-Rochfort's suggestion, for the Ribblesdale Stakes at Royal Ascot, on the morning of which the Queen came to see her work on the course, as the filly had spent the night at her private stables on the racecourse. Almeria overwhelmed her rivals in the Ribblesdale Stakes, and in the Bentinck Stakes at Goodwood she beat Hindu Festival, the runner-up to Ballymoss in the Irish Derby, despite giving him 2 lb. Almeria proved herself the best filly of her generation when winning the Yorkshire Oaks by six lengths; among her victims was Silken Glider, who had run Carrozza to a short head in the Oaks and then won the Irish equivalent. Carrozza's Oaks victory had been in the Royal colours as she was leased from the National Stud; it was also the first time that Lester Piggott rode a Classic winner for the Queen. Almeria's final victory in 1957 came in the Park Hill Stakes, where she again defeated Silken Glider.

Almeria was retired from training at the end of 1957 and went to the paddocks at Hampton Court. She caused such trouble that Charles Moore persuaded a reluctant Boyd-Rochfort to have her back in training, where she was even more difficult to control than she had been in 1957. After winning the Coombe Stakes at Sandown in May, Almeria was taken to Ascot during Royal Ascot week as Boyd-Rochfort felt a change of scene might improve her obstinate behaviour. All of the Queen's house party at Windsor Castle came to see her work one morning in the course; Almeria, in her most stubborn and contrary mood, refused to start, and it was forty-five minutes before she had completed a circuit of the course. When it was decided that Almeria and Doutelle would both run in the King George VI and Queen Elizabeth Stakes against Ballymoss and the Derby winner Hard Ridden, Carr chose Almeria and Doug Smith Doutelle. It was felt that the best tactics were for both the Royal runners to lead the field, as Doutelle had made all the running when beating Ballymoss at Chester and since Almeria's strongest asset against Ballymoss's finishing burst was her stamina. Unfortunately, Smith was injured in a fall on the Friday at Ascot, and his place on Doutelle was taken by Joe Mercer, who knew neither his chance mount nor the tactical plan agreed on by Boyd-Rochfort and the Queen, who was unwell on the day of the race and so unable to come to Ascot. She was represented by Captain Charles Moore, who either did not know of the proposed tactics or had one of his disagreements with the Royal trainer, for he instructed Joe Mercer to ride a waiting race on Doutelle. Thus Almeria made the running on her own without the help of Doutelle. The pace she set was not strong enough, and Ballymoss was able to come with a wet sail and win by an easy three lengths with Doutelle running on to take third place. Harry Carr was not pleased; as he later remarked, 'If Doutelle had been allowed to help Almeria along as Doug Smith and I planned, I am almost certain I would have beaten Ballymoss. Almeria was in a good humour that day and, apart from Meld, she was the most outstanding filly I rode.'

Almeria's final race was in the Doncaster Cup, in which the Queen's Agreement, who had been acting as her lead horse for two months, was running as a pacemaker. To the consternation of Harry Carr, Almeria refused to pass Agreement in the final furlong although she was going much the best, and the Queen's 25–1 pacemaker beat her 7–4 favourite a neck. After this slightly embarrassing result Almeria was retired to stud.

Agreement (Persian Gulf–Northern Hope) won the Doncaster Cup again the following season and the Chester Cup too, so, although he was definitely inferior to Almeria, he was a useful stayer. He had been prone to savage both horses and men as a three-year-old and had been cut after his victory in the mile Coventry Stakes at Kempton. He won three other races including the Newmarket St Leger. When he retired he was used as a hack by both the Queen and Princess Margaret, and later by the Starter at Ascot.

The other notable foal bred by the Queen in 1954 was Mulberry Harbour (Sicambre–Open Warfare). As a yearling at the Mondellihy Stud one day she had jumped over a five-foot wall and escaped from her paddock. As a half-sister to Alexander high hopes were held of her, but she was unplaced in both the Blue Seal Stakes and Sandwich Stakes as a two-year-old. She had a total loathing of rain, so she was raced with a fringe browband to keep the rain off her face. After winning the Ruth Wood Maiden Stakes at Kempton by an impressive four lengths, she beat Crochet a neck in the Cheshire Oaks. When Crochet won the Lingfield Oaks Trial with Almeria only third, Boyd-Rochfort felt Mulberry Harbour must have a very good chance of defeating the Aga Khan's 1,000 Guineas heroine, Rose Royale II, whom Alec Head trained in France, in the Oaks. Mulberry Harbour started second favourite at 11–4, and carried the first colours of the Queen, whose other runner, Carrozza, trained by Noel Murless, was an outsider at 100–8. Mulberry Harbour was lying second until the straight, when she suddenly compounded and dropped back, finishing a distant ninth. Rose Royale II failed to stay, and Lester Piggott just managed to hold the relentless challenge of the Irish raider Silken Glider by a short head. It was the first Royal victory in a Classic at Epsom since Minoru, another leased horse, had won the 1909 Derby. Mulberry Harbour's condition after the race was so terrible that both Boyd-Rochfort and Bruce Hobbs felt she had been doped. When she finished last but one to the Aga Khan's Toro in the Coronation Stakes at Ascot, a veterinary examination revealed that her heart rate was abnormal. After a long rest Mulberry Harbour won the Newmarket Oaks easily in October, but was a distant last of four to Doutelle in the Limekiln Stakes. She then retired to stud. As dope testing was an infrequent occurrence in 1957, and not nearly as sophisticated as today, it will never be known if Mulberry Harbour's racing career was interfered with in the same fiendish manner as in the notorious case of the 1961 Derby favourite, Pinturischio.

Six of the ten foals bred by the Queen in 1955 became winners, and one, Pall Mall (Palestine–Malapert) was to become the first Classic winner that she had bred. Ironically, after his birth, Captain Moore sold Malapert for 910 gns at the December Sales due to her lack of success as a mare; none of her other four foals had won, although the last, Cheetah, was to win a maiden handicap at Newmarket in October 1957 after she had been sold to Noel Murless. Cheetah later became the grandam of Caergwrle, who won the 1,000 Guineas, and the good miler St Chad.

Pall Mall, a medium-sized chestnut with a long white blaze and three white socks, won the Earlstown Maiden Plate by five lengths on his debut at Haydock in May 1957. As a yearling he had had terrible forelegs, and Boyd-Rochfort was uncertain that he would stand training; he used the same ointment on him, made up by an Australian vet named Macintosh, that he had used to train Black Tarquin, the 1948 St Leger winner, but he did not consider him anything exceptional before his debut. After a particularly good gallop at Newmarket, Pall Mall was sent to run in the New Stakes at Royal Ascot, where the going was hard. That particularly suited Pall Mall, who was straight in front and needed fast ground. The Queen's colt duly won the New Stakes comfortably by a length. He failed to win his next three races, but was not disgraced in defeat, and lost the July Stakes by only three quarters of a length to the Queen Mary Stakes winner Abelia. The soft going in the Gimcrack Stakes was against him, but he still fiished a close third to Pheidippedes. Pall Mall was briefly stopped in his work by leg trouble before the Champagne Stakes at Doncaster, so his short head defeat by Kelly was more than praiseworthy.

On his reappearance in the 2,000 Guineas Trial Stakes at Kempton, which was postponed from the Saturday to Easter Monday on account of the weather, Pall Mall was quite unable to handle the atrocious going and finished fourth to Aggressor. In the Thirsk Classic Trial three weeks later the going was good and Pall Mall had no difficulty in beating Pleiades and Pheidippedes.

Boyd-Rochfort had another runner for the 2,000 Guineas, Captain Harry Guggenheim's Bald Eagle, who had won the Craven Stakes most impressively. In the final gallop before the 2,000 Guineas Bald Eagle seemed to be about a stone in front of Pall Mall, so it was decided that he would be ridden by Harry Carr, while Doug Smith took the mount on the Queen's colt. Smith did not rate his chance very high, feeling the best he could hope for was a place. Pall Mall started at 20–1, while Bald Eagle was clear favourite at 7–4. Bald Eagle played up at the start, was never going well and was beaten by the Bushes. Doug Smith rode a waiting race on Pall Mall, who had been badly drawn on the outside; after four furlongs he was going well, despite being some lengths behind the leaders. He moved into third place behind Major Portion and Nagami at the Bushes, passed Nagami in the Dip, and got the better of Major Portion in the final hundred yards to win by half a length. Unfortunately the Queen, confined to Windsor with a very heavy cold, was unable to witness her first Classic win with a colt of her own breeding, and Pall Mall was welcomed into the winner's enclosure by the Princess Royal. Bald Eagle was to disappoint again in the Derby and St James's Palace Stakes, but proved his class on returning to North America, winning the Washington International in consecutive years.

There was no question of running Pall Mall in the Derby on account of his breeding, so he next ran in the Lockinge Stakes at Newbury when he trounced Pipe of Peace five lengths. In his only other race in 1958, Pall Mall was beaten a length by Major Portion in the Sussex Stakes at Goodwood. Had Mr H. J. Joel's colt, the leading two-year-old of 1957, had a race before the 2,000 Guineas, he might have given Pall Mall a much harder fight.

Pall Mall stayed in training as a four-year-old and won two of his four races. He took the Lockinge Stakes at Newbury for the second consecutive year and won the Midsummer Stakes at Newmarket at the unrewarding odds of 33–1 on. He courageously carried 9 st 7 lbs in the Royal Hunt Cup when second to the useful Faultless Speech, to whom he was conceding 20 lbs. There was no room for Pall Mall to stand at the Royal Stud, so he was sold privately to a syndicate of Irish breeders at the end of 1959. He stood at the Ballkisteen Stud in County Tipperary and was a very successful sire; his best winners included Reform, the winner of the Champion Stakes, Queen Elizabeth II Stakes and St James's Palace Stakes and sire of Polygamy (Oaks Stakes), Catalpa (Ribblesdale Stakes) and Admetus (Prince of Wales's Stakes,

Washington International), and Sallust, the winner of the Sussex Stakes and Prix du Moulin de Longchamp and sire of Tap on Wood (2,000 Guineas, Irish 2,000 Guineas).

Pall Mall's contemporary, Restoration (Persian Gulf–Hypericum) was so difficult to train that the first time he set foot on a racecourse was in the King Edward VII Stakes at Ascot. His two-length victory in such an important race was a truly remarkable feat of training by Boyd-Rochfort. In his second race Restoration was a six-length runner-up to Ballymoss in the Eclipse Stakes; he then ran fourth to Alcide in the St Leger. He was also runner-up in the Hardwicke Stakes and the Jockey Club Stakes in 1959, but never won another race.

The other good foal from the 1955 crop was Miner's Lamp (Signal Light–Young Entry), who had run most promisingly on his debut when runner-up to Pinched in the Royal Lodge Stakes at Ascot. Miner's Lamp was a box-climber; a goat was put in his box to try to calm him, but was quickly removed when the colt started to chew the unfortunate creature. Dr Brook was called once more and his treatment seemed to calm Miner's Lamp down. His effortless victory in the Blue Riband Trial Stakes at Epsom in April made him a possible Derby hope, but soon afterwards he lost condition and was found to be anaemic. He had not fully recovered when beaten in the Newmarket Stakes by Guersillus. After Alcide's rout of his rivals in the Lingfield Derby Trial, Miner's Lamp was relegated to the stable's third string for the Epsom Classic, as Bald Eagle had won the Dante Stakes. Then Alcide was got at by the dopers and was scratched. Miner's Lamp was ridden by Rickaby in the Derby, as Carr was on Bald Eagle, and he ran creditably to dead-heat for sixth place behind Hard Ridden. He next won the Princess of Wales's Stakes by a neck from the very useful four-year-old Primera. Goodwood's Gordon Stakes was Miner's Lamp's next objective, but he broke down so badly that he was forced to retire. He was then sold as a stallion to Japan.

Seven of the fourteen mares covered in 1955 were barren in 1956, but five of the six foals bred by the Queen that went into training at Freemason Lodge won races; the best was Above Suspicion (Court Martial–Above Board). He was a very backward two-year-old, and was unplaced in his three runs in 1958. However, a second in the Newmarket Stakes ensured him a place in the Derby field alongside his much better fancied stable-companion, Sir Humphrey de Trafford's Parthia. Above Suspicion, the mount of Doug Smith, was the pick of the paddock on looks. He had a very bad run coming down the hill, but made up tremendous ground in the straight to finish fifth to Parthia, Captain Boyd-Rochfort's first Derby winner. The Queen was there to congratulate her trainer and the popular owner, whose ill-luck with Alcide the previous year was still in everyone's mind.

Above Suspicion made full use of his maiden allowance when easily winning the St James's Palace Stakes at Royal Ascot, and he then won the Gordon Stakes at Goodwood. The plan to run him in the Champion Stakes was shelved when it was realized he would have to meet Aly Khan's brilliant filly, Petite Etoile. He was to disappoint as a four-year-old, failing to win any of his four races; his two best performances were when finishing third to Petite Etoile and Parthia in the Coronation Cup and third in the Jubilee Handicap at Kempton under top weight. Above Suspicion was then sold as a stallion and stood at the Cloghran Stud in County Dublin, where Blandford had been a sire in the 1930s, but he never remotely emulated his illustrious predecessor's great record at stud.

The only other noteworthy foal bred by the Queen in 1956 was Blue Riband (Blue Peter–Stream of Light), who won three races including the Galtres Stakes at York and the Mornington Stakes at Ascot. She also was fourth in the Park Hill Stakes.

The Royal Stud then went into the doldrums, for no obviously apparent reason. The only foal of any consequence bred by the Queen in 1957 was Optimistic (Never Say Die–Northern Hope), who won three races including the Newbury Autumn Cup in 1961. She was sold as a broodmare to France, and was the dam of St Leonard, who won the Prix Eugene Adam. Nine Royal foals born in 1958 went into training with Boyd-Rochfort; only four won a mere six races. Impudent (Owen Tudor–Saucy Lass) won the Lingfield Oaks Trial, but had only one more race when she was fourth in the Yorkshire Oaks, as she was difficult to keep sound. She was not kept for stud and was sold. Highlight (Borealis–Hypericum) won the Oxted Maiden Stakes at Lingfield and the Ash Maiden Stakes at Kempton in October 1961, after running fourth in the Princess Royal Stakes at Ascot. She had also run in the Oaks, coming almost last to Sweet Solera. Her fame was to come as a broodmare.

The 1959 crop of yearlings was the worst for the Royal Stud since 1944; only three of the nine foals managed to win a total of five races, none of them of great significance. There were again only three winners of nine races from the eight foals bred by the Queen in 1960, but one, Apprentice (Aureole–Young Entry), did have some class. He was third in the Queen's Vase at Royal Ascot in 1963, but broke down badly. He had to be pin-fired, cut and turned out for eighteen months. He returned to the racecourse to run in the Yorkshire Cup, where he was opposed by the 1964 St Leger winner, Indiana. In one of the greatest shocks of the decade, Apprentice, at 33–1, beat Indiana by three quarters of a length. He then threw a splint and did not reappear till the Goodwood Cup. The Queen, who was taking the salute at the Sovereign's Parade at RMC Sandhurst that morning, asked that it should start a quarter of an hour earlier than originally planned, so that she could return to Goodwood, where she had seen Gold Aura win the Goodwood Stakes Handicap the previous day, to be present in time for Apprentice's race. The Royal gelding proved the York result was no fluke; he beat Soderini, the winner of the Hardwicke Stakes, two and a half lengths, with some of the best stayers of the early 1960s, Philemon, Trelawney and Grey of Falloden further in rear.

Gold Aura (Aureole–In Need), another 1960 foal, was also a useful stayer. His four victories, besides the Goodwood Stakes in 1965, included the Great Metropolitan Stakes at Epsom in 1964. The tide of fortune seemed to be turning back in favour of the Royal Stud.

15

Queen Elizabeth II,

1961–73

Captain Charles Moore had been the Royal Stud Manager for twenty-three years in 1960 when he reached the age of eighty. He, more than anyone else, had been responsible for the very high quality of the foals bred by King George VI and Queen Elizabeth II in the late 1940s and 1950s. In 1960 he began the process of handing over the management of the Royal Stud to his deputy since 1957, Brigadier A. D. R. Wingfield, and two years later he retired.

Charles Moore had bought Sacrifice, the foundation mare of his own stud in Ireland, in 1908, so had had more than fifty years of experience in the mating of Thoroughbreds. His objective as Manager of the Royal Studs had been to breed middle-distance three-year-olds for the Classics; in this he had been conspicuously successful. He never advised the Queen to send more than one or two mares a season to sprinting sires, despite his respect for the blood of The Tetrarch. One of the reasons why the Royal Stud went into decline in Moore's last five years as Manager may be because he did not send more of the stoutly bred mares to stallions with some pure speed in their pedigrees.

Noel Murless once described Captain Charles Moore as a genius in all matters relating to racing and breeding. He was a firm believer in a certain amount of inbreeding, especially to the blood of St Simon, Blandford, Gay Crusader and Hyperion, as witnessed by the 3 × 2 inbreeding of Almeria and Highlight. When Moore was planning matings for the mares at Sandringham, or was intending to buy mares or fillies for the Royal Stud, he considered it essential that there should be an outstandingly prepotent stallion or exceptional broodmare in both the top and the bottom half of a horse's pedigree. He also preferred to use proven stallions, though sometimes, as in the case of Rising Light and Keystone, it was not possible. Moore did not always suggest inbreeding, however, as the pedigrees of Aureole and Doutelle illustrate.

Moore was well-known for his wit and charm, and as a raconteur of Irish anecdotes. After his retirement at the end of 1962, his health began to deteriorate. One day in the autumn of 1963 the Queen and the Queen Mother paid him a visit at his grace-and-favour house, The Pavilion, at Hampton Court. He came downstairs in his dressing-gown to welcome the Royal visitors. The Queen asked him how he was feeling. Moore answered: 'Well, Ma'am, I feel rather like a rabbit who has been bolted by a ferret.' Her Majesty was a trifle surprised and said: 'I may have been called many things behind my back, but I have never been called a ferret to my face before!' The Queen wanted to give him a knighthood, but he asked for permission to remain plain Captain Moore. In 1964 Moore returned to Ireland and died at his stud at Mooresfort. His last significant purchase for the Queen had been the yearling filly Amicable (Doutelle–Amy Leigh), acquired at the Newmarket October Sales in 1961. In the season before his death, he had been delighted that Amicable had turned out to be the Queen's best three-year-old that year; she won the Nell Gwyn Stakes and the Oaks Trial Stakes at Lingfield and finished second to Outcrop in the Yorkshire Oaks. He would have been even more pleased at her great success as a broodmare.

This slight upturn in the fortunes of the Royal Stud continued with the crop of foals born in 1961; eight of the eleven two-year-olds that went into training at Freemason Lodge in 1963 won twelve races. Crest of the Wave (Crepello–Mulberry Harbour) won the competitive Glasgow Maiden Stakes at York in May 1964, but found his rivals too strong in the Princess of Wales's Stakes and Cumberland Lodge Stakes. After he had been well beaten in the Hardwicke Stakes at Ascot in 1965, he was sold as a stallion to New Zealand, where he became leading sire.

The best of the 1961 crop was the chestnut colt Canisbay (Doutelle-Stroma). The Queen had visited the Doncaster Sales in September 1956 the morning before she had watched High Veldt run in the St Leger. One of the two yearling fillies she had picked out herself was Stroma (Luminary–Whoa Emma), as she thought they would introduce suitable new blood into the Royal Stud. Stroma, who was bought on her behalf for 1,500 gns, had close connections with the Boyd-Rochfort family, Captain Charles Moore and the Royal Stud. In 1934 Captain Moore sold to the Royal Stud his five-year-old broodmare Judith (Colorado–Judea by Roi Herode), a half-sister to Zionist and Money Maker. Judith's first foal at Sandringham, Jubilee by Mr Jinks, won two races for George VI; her second foal, Judy by Dastur, was placed three times in the Royal colours in 1938, and was then sold as a three-year-old. The purchaser was Captain Cecil Boyd-Rochfort's brother, Harold, who ran the stud at the family home, Middleton Park in County Westmeath. Judy turned out to be a very useful broodmare, producing nine winners including Ready, the grandam of Stroma. Stroma's fifth dam, Judea, who had won the 1918 Irish Oaks, was one of the foals of Captain Moore's foundation mare, Sacrifice, by Symington. Sacrifice's fifth dam, Queen of Prussia by Orlando, had been bred by Queen Victoria at Hampton Court in 1856, sold for 220 gns as a yearling and won four races in Ireland. As Judith produced only two foals for George VI there was none of her blood left at Sandringham in 1956. Another factor that may have influenced the Queen in picking out Stroma was that her 1953 Royal Hunt Cup winner, Choir Boy, came from the same Sacrifice–Judea family, and his dam, Choral, had no mares to carry on her blood at Sandringham. With hindsight the Queen's purchase of Stroma at Doncaster was very astute; the mare's influence was to be felt for the next two decades.

Stroma's quality was not immediately apparent. She was subjected to such a hard race on her debut in the Epsom Stud Produce Stakes on rock-hard going on 23 April 1957, when she was beaten half a length by Butterfly Net, that she was unable to race again that year. The next season Stroma ran five times; on her second outing she was fifth and last in the King's Stand Stakes to Drum Beat, but only a length behind Texana and speedy Abelia, who were second and third. She was made a 2–1 on favourite for the Wood Green Maiden Plate over five furlongs at Alexandra Park a week later, but was a well-beaten runner-up. She was then beaten twenty lengths into third place in the Spring Hall Stakes over the minimum distance at Newmarket in July, and was last to Welsh Abbot in the Singleton Handicap at Goodwood, her final race. There was little in this record to suggest that her second foal, Canisbay, was likely to be anything out of the ordinary.

Canisbay had an accident as a yearling in Ireland, a setback which prevented him running as a juvenile. He began to show promise on the gallops in the spring of 1964 and made his debut in April in the Wood Ditton Stakes at Newmarket, which he won well. He next ran second to Con Brio in the Brighton Derby Trial Stakes, and was due to run in the Dante Stakes at York, when he went lame. He returned to Hampton Court, where it was eventually discovered that a long splinter of wood had entered his near hind foot through the frog. He was not to return to Freemason Lodge until November.

Boyd-Rochfort's stable was laid low by the cough in the spring of 1965, so Canisbay did not run until the Churchill Stakes at Ascot when, considering his long absence, he finished a very respectable third. Boyd-Rochfort, whose stable had only had one winner up to that point in the season, wanted Canisbay to be dropped in class and run in a handicap at Newcastle. The Queen, however, intervened. She had proposed that Stroma be sent to be covered by Doutelle in 1960; Doutelle was by Prince Chevalier and so was Whoa Emma, Stroma's dam. A similar close inbreeding to Hyperion had produced Almeria. She felt that Canisbay might run well in the Eclipse Stakes, and overruled her trainer. Boyd-Rochfort's new stable jockey, Stan Clayton, felt that the Queen was wise to insist that Canisbay run in the Eclipse, as no one knew how good he was; he also considered, after riding him in the Churchill Stakes, that his best trip would probably be ten furlongs.

Canisbay took up the running about two furlongs out; he was challenged by Roan Rocket throughout the final furlong, but running on with the utmost gameness, held on to win by a short head at 20–1. It was the first time a reigning Sovereign had ever won the race; the last Eclipse in which the Royal colours had been carried to victory was the 1900 running, won by Diamond Jubilee for the Prince of Wales. Unfortunately the Queen was not at Sandown that afternoon, as she had public duties to perform in Scotland.

Canisbay did not win again, being well beaten by Oncidium in a two-horse contest at Goodwood, and then by Silly Season in the Champion Stakes. He retired to stud at Sandringham, where he sired Weimar, who won the Gran Premio d'Italia and Gran Premio di Milano in 1971, and the same year's Oaks d'Italia winner, Tingitana. As a result of those victories, a syndicate of Italian breeders headed by Dr Carlo Vittadini bought him to stand in Italy. He was very successful there and headed the list of winning sires; the best of his progeny was Orange Bay, who won the Derby Italiano in 1975, the Hardwicke Stakes, Jockey Club Stakes, Cumberland Lodge Stakes, and was a short head second to The Minstrel in the King George VI and Queen Elizabeth Diamond Stakes.

Unfortunately, the fortunes of the Royal Stud did not continue to improve with the 1962 crop of yearlings. Although eight foals bred by the Queen won fourteen races, none was of great significance; the best, Eucumbene (Sica Boy–Hypericum), whose only victory came in the Strettington Stakes at Goodwood, was second in the Nassau Stakes, to Aunt Edith, and in the Yorkshire Oaks. In 1962 Lord Porchester suggested that the Queen should lease Polhampton Lodge Stud, near Kingsclere, as a place to rest horses out of training. This suggestion was made at the same time as Captain Peter Hastings-Bass, who trained at John Porter's famous Kingsclere stables, was appointed a second trainer for the horses bred by the Queen, who now had twenty-two mares. Sadly, Captain Hastings-Bass was fatally ill with cancer, and trained only one winner for Her Majesty, Planta Genista (Princely Gift–Gallega), who won the Horne Maiden Stakes at Lingfield in April, before he died in June 1964. He was succeeded by his assistant, Ian Balding, who had won a rugby Blue at Cambridge and was a leading amateur jockey; he had won the National Hunt Chase at Cheltenham in 1963 on Time. A short while after Captain Hastings-Bass's death, Balding married his daughter, Emma.

The practice of sending the Queen's yearlings to Ireland had continued throughout the 1960s. The majority, and normally the best, were sent to Captain Peter FitzGerald's stud at Mondellihy, but a few went to Brigadier Wingfield, and the odd one or two to Mooresfort. In 1972 this practice ceased and the Queen bought the Polhampton Lodge Stud, which has proved invaluable as the place where the yearlings are kept.

These changes did not bring immediate success for the Royal Stud's foals. Although eight of the twelve foals bred by the Queen in 1963 which went into training won sixteen races, only two were of any quality. Gaulois (Auriban–Gallega) was set aside for the Goodwood Cup after winning the FitzWilliam Stakes at York in May; his victory at Goodwood was Boyd-Rochfort's final success as a trainer in the long-distance Cup races in which he had had so many notable successes. Castle Yard (St Paddy–Spanish Court) won the valuable Zetland Gold Cup as a five-year-old and was Boyd-Rochfort's last important winner for the Queen.

At the end of 1963 Brigadier Wingfield resigned as manager of the Royal Stud in order to run his own stud at Brownstown, County Meath, Ireland. He was succeeded by Major Richard Shelley, who had been the manager of Lady Zia Wernher's Someries Stud at Newmarket for many years, and thus was very experienced. It was Shelley who finally discovered the cause of Canisbay's lameness as a three-year-old.

The 1964 crop of foals from the Royal Studs was again of poor quality. Although eight of them won ten races, none was of great importance. Again in 1965 foals were mostly very moderate; only five of the fifteen bred by the Queen were successful in a mere eight races. Since Captain Boyd-Rochfort was to retire at the end of the 1968 season, only three 1964 yearlings went into training at Freemason Lodge; six went to Ian Balding at Kingsclere and six went to Major W. R. Hern at West Ilsley. Dick Hern had been private trainer to Major Lionel Holliday at Newmarket up to the end of 1962, and had trained Hethersett, the ill-fated Derby favourite, to win the St Leger in 1961. In 1963 Hern had taken over Jack Colling's stables at West Ilsley, and in 1965 had won the St Leger for Mr J. J. Astor with Provoke. West Ilsley's and Kingsclere's proximity to both London and Windsor made it much easier for the Queen to visit her horses in training during the spring and summer than it had been when they were at Newmarket, as she was seldom at Sandringham during that time of year. The only 1964 foal with any pretensions to class, St Patrick's Blue (St Paddy–Blue Riband) was one of the six two-year-olds who arrived at West Ilsley in 1966; he won four races, including the Cranbourne Chase Stakes at Ascot and the Timeform Gold Trophy at Redcar. He was also unluckily and narrowly beaten in the Northumberland Plate at Newcastle.

Only nine foals bred by the Queen in 1966 went into training at Kingsclere and West Ilsley. Although only four became winners, taking twelve races, Ian Balding soon realized that Magna Carta (Charlottesville–Almeria), a bay with two white feet, had definite potential, although he was very idle at home and would need time. As a yearling and juvenile he was looked after by John Hallum, who was to 'do' Paul Mellon's Mill Reef during all that illustrious champion's time in training. Magna Carta was a late-maturing three-year-old, but won three races that season, the first over two miles at Nottingham and in September the Arran Plate at Ayr. He was clearly going to become a good stayer as a four-year-old.

After finishing a creditable fourth in the Chester Cup and winning a two-mile handicap at Wolverhampton, Magna Carta lined up for his initial summer objective, the Ascot Stakes, with Geoff Lewis in the saddle. Lewis, the Kingsclere stable jockey, had to use all his strength to get the lazy Magna Carta into a challenging position in the straight, and making full use of his finishing speed, took the lead close home. Magna Carta then won the Greenhall Whitley Trophy at Chester and the W. D. and H. O. Wills Trophy at Newcastle. After his narrow defeat in the Goodwood Cup by Parthenon, Geoff Lewis rode a waiting race with him in the Doncaster Cup, when the Royal horse's finishing speed enabled him to defeat his Goodwood conqueror. Early in 1971, a year in which he might well have won the Ascot Gold Cup, Magna Carta got caught up in his haynet and broke his jaw in two places. He was operated on by Professor James Roberts at the Equine Research Centre in Newmarket, but died a few days later as a result of the anaesthetic. It was a tragic blow, and the Queen ordered that haynets were never to be used in her horses' boxes again.

In 1964 it was decided that breeding at the National Stud was to cease and that all its mares and foals would be sold at the Newmarket December Sales. That meant that the Queen would no longer be able to lease horses for their racing careers and have them in training with Noel Murless at Warren Place in Newmarket. One of the last two yearlings to go into training for the Queen from the National Stud was Hopeful Venture (Aureole–White House). Unraced at two, he took the Wood Ditton Stakes on his debut and, a few weeks later, won the Grosvenor Stakes in a canter at Chester. Hopeful Venture avoided a clash in the Derby with H. J. Joel's Royal Palace, acknowledged since his 2,000 Guineas victory as the best colt at Warren Place. Royal Palace won the Derby as expected: the Queen's colt ran instead in the King Edward VII Stakes, which he lost by stumbling on Ascot's final bend. His victories in the Princess of Wales's Stakes and the Oxfordshire Stakes at Newbury showed him to be a top-class horse. He took the place of the *hors de combat* Royal Palace in the St Leger and finished runner-up to the very talented but erratic Ribocco. Hopeful Venture then won the Prix Henry Delamarre at Longchamp decisively from the English filly, In Command; it was the first time the Queen had had a runner in France. Unfortunately the Queen's colt crossed In Command early in the straight, and her jockey, Brian Taylor, objected. The incident had no effect on the result at all, but rules on interference were then very strictly adhered to by the Stewards at Longchamp and Hopeful Venture was disqualified.

In May 1967 Her Majesty had paid a private visit to the studs of Normandy. She saw Right Royal V at Mme Elisabeth Couturie's stud at Le Mesnil, Dan Cupid, Sea Bird's sire, at the Duc d'Audrifret-Pasquier's Château de Sassy, Baldric II at Comte François de Brignac's Haras de Verrerie, Auriban at Marcel Boussac's renowned Haras de Fresnay-le-Buffard, Sicambre at Mme Stern's Haras de Saint-Pair-du-Mont and Exbury at Baron Guy de Rothschild's Haras de Meautry. She also visited Alec Head's Haras de Quesnay. This comprehensive tour of the best studs in France in three days demonstrated once more the Queen's absorbing interest in the breeding of Thoroughbreds.

Hopeful Venture, like his sire Aureole, improved even more as a four-year-old. He defeated the brilliant filly Park Top in the Ormonde Stakes at Chester and was the Queen's only winner at Royal Ascot in 1968 when he easily won the Hardwicke Stakes. On 7 July he beat the best three-year-old in Europe, Vaguely Noble, into third place in the Grand Prix de Saint-Cloud, the sole defeat that brilliant colt ever suffered on the racecourse. He was then retired to stud, having given Noel Murless a very fitting finale as the trainer of the horses the Queen leased from the National Stud.

Nineteen-sixty-seven was a year of notable achievement, when all seven of the foals bred by the Queen which went into training with Ian Balding and Major Hern turned out to be winners. Not all the foals bred at Sandringham in 1967 had been retained by the Queen. Amphora (Ragusa–Amicable), who was sold as a yearling to J. W. Weston-Evans, won two races including the Lancashire Oaks; another, Eucalyptus by Tamerlane, was also sold as a yearling in Dublin at the end of 1968; he won nine races in Ireland including the Ballymoss Stakes.

The best of the foals put into training for the Queen was Charlton (Charlottesville–Ibrox), a big colt with joints that Hern felt were very likely to be a problem. Charlton was given one race at Lingfield as a juvenile, when he ran with promise but returned to West Ilsley with sore shins. He won a maiden race at Newbury in April, and the Queen was at Goodwood to see him win the Predominate Stakes in May, after which he again was sore. Unsuited by the firm going at Ascot when third in the King Edward VII Stakes, Charlton next won the Eglington Stakes at Ayr. As there was a doubt about Nijinsky's stamina in the St Leger, Charlton opposed him at Doncaster, but finished only fourth.

Charlton's first appearance in 1971 was in La Coupe at Long-champ in May, where he found the yielding going he needed. The lack of a previous race may have been the cause of his narrow defeat in the very last strides by High Game and Crucible. He gained prompt compensation a fortnight later, though, when winning the Henry II Stakes at Sandown. On the strength of this performance he was greatly fancied for the Ascot Gold Cup, run in holding conditions; but he failed to quicken in the straight and was well beaten by Rock Roi and Random Shot. He was, however, promoted to third place on Rock Roi's disqualification. The explanation of this relatively poor performance was that Charlton did not stay more than two miles. In July the Queen was at Doncaster to see Charlton win the William Hill Gold Trophy most courageously from Royal

Palace's half-brother, Prince Consort, by a very narrow margin amid roars of approval from the crowd. Charlton's last race was the Ebor Handicap, under top weight: he finished fourth, beaten less than half a length by Knotty Pine. He had looked certain to win when challenging in the final furlong, but had faltered near the line, and it transpired that a tendon had gone. Charlton was sold privately to Mr Alfred Grant to stand at his Gainsborough Lodge Stud near Toowoomba in Queensland, and later moved to another stud in Australia, where he was not unsuccessful as a stallion.

In 1969 increasing ill-health caused Richard Shelley to ask permission to be relieved of his position as manager of the Royal Studs at the end of the year. Since Aureole was drawing to the end of his career as a stallion, the Queen had decided to stand syndicated stallions, in which she had taken a number of shares, in the future. This meant a marked increase in the duties of the Royal Stud Manager, for not merely would he have to look after all the Queen's bloodstock, but he would also have to take charge of the syndicated stallions, the visiting mares – which could number up to 100 in a single year – and all the matters associated with the complex task of managing a top-class sire. It was clearly vital that the new Royal Stud Manager should live in the Sandringham area. It was therefore decided to create two posts: one was to be that of Her Majesty's Racing Manager; the other that of Her Majesty's Stud Manager.

The Queen appointed Lord Porchester as her Racing Manager, and Michael Oswald as her Stud Manager; both appointments came into effect on 1 January 1970. Lord Porchester's duties were to represent Her Majesty at race-meetings, to liaise with her trainers, to take decisions about her bloodstock when she was not in Great Britain, and to give advice on the buying and selling of Thoroughbreds and the mating of the Royal mares. Lord Porchester had been a personal friend of the Queen for very many years; he had also been involved with racing nearly all his life. His father, the Earl of Carnarvon, had bred Blenheim, the 1930 Derby winner, who was such an outstanding sire in both England and the United States. Lord Porchester himself had bred the high-class colt Tamerlane, who had won the New Stakes in 1954 and the St James's Palace Stakes in 1955 at Royal Ascot; he was an unlucky second behind Our Babu in the 2,000 Guineas but was a more than useful stallion. Lord Porchester's home and Highclere Stud was ideally situated for his new appointment due to their proximity to both West Ilsley and Kingsclere.

Michael Oswald's duties as the manager of the Royal Studs

Above: The Queen's horses on the gallops at Newmarket in 1955. From left to right: Belladonna, High Veldt, Kolah, Sierra Nevada, Alexander. Photograph by General Press Photos. Below: The Queen Mother's Isle of Man (W. Smith) in action at Sandown Park in 1979. Photograph by Gerry Cranham.

Above: Almeria (W. H. Carr) trounces her rivals in the 1957 Yorkshire Oaks. Photograph by *Yorkshire Post*.
Below: Doutelle, a successful stallion bred by the Queen. Photograph by R. Anscomb.

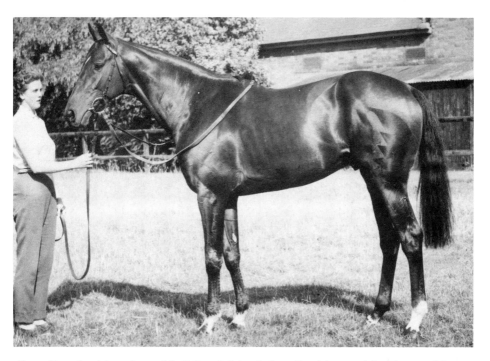

Above: Above Suspicion, winner of the St James's Palace Stakes at Royal Ascot and sire. Photograph by R. Anscomb. Below: Pall Mall (D. Smith) winning the 1958 2,000 Guineas from Major Portion and Nagami at Newmarket in 1958. Photograph by Central Press Photos.

Far Left: Canisbay (S. Clayton) narrowly defeating Roan Rocket in the Eclipse Stakes at Sandown Park in 1965. Photograph by Sport and General. Left: Example (L. Piggott), winner of the Prix Jean de Chaudenay, Saint Cloud, May 1972. Photograph by Agence APRH. Below: Expansive, welcomed by the Queen in the winner's enclosure at Royal Ascot after her victory in the Ribblesdale Stakes, June 1979. Photograph by Gerry Cranham.

Above: The Queen and her Stud Manager Michael Oswald with Highclere after she finished second to Dahlia in the King George VI and Queen Elizabeth Stakes at Ascot, 1974. Photograph by kind permission of HM the Queen. Below: The Queen arriving at Chantilly racecourse with M. Marcel Boussac and the duc de Noailles for the 1974 Prix de Diane won by Highclere. Photograph by Bernard Gourier.

Left: Height of Fashion, bred by the Queen, dam of Nashwan and Unfuwain. Photograph by David Hastings.

Right: Nashwan, winner of the 2,000 Guineas, Derby Stakes, Eclipse Stakes and King George VI and Queen Elizabeth Stakes 1989. Photograph by Gerry Cranham. Below: Height of Fashion (J. Mercer), winning the Hoover Fillies Mile at Ascot, September 1981. Photograph by Selwyn Photos.

Unknown Quantity (J. Velasquez) winning the Arlington Handicap (Grade I) at Arlington Park, Chicago, USA in August 1989. Photograph by Four Footed Photos.

Broodmares visiting Shirley Heights at the Sandringham Stud, May 1986. From left to right: Full Dress (1,000 Guineas), Pawneese (Oaks, Prix de Diane, King George VI and Queen Elizabeth Stakes), HM the Queen holding Dunfermline (Oaks, St. Leger), Time Charter (Oaks, Champion Stakes, Coronation Cup, King George VI and Queen Elizabeth Stakes) Habibti (champion sprinter) and Akiyda (Prix de l'Arc de Triomphe). Photograph by Laurie Morton. Reproduced by kind permission of HM the Queen.

were the overall supervision of the Queen's bloodstock at the Sandringham, Wolferton, Hampton Court and Polhampton Studs, the management of the syndicated stallions that were to stand at Wolferton and Sandringham and to give advice on the mating, buying and culling of mares. Where the mating of broodmares was, and is, concerned, it is important to stress that in the majority of cases it is the Queen herself who plays the principal role, putting up her own ideas to Lord Porchester and Michael Oswald; both gentlemen will then proffer their advice, but the final decision is always Her Majesty's. Michael Oswald hád previously very successfully managed the Lordship and Egerton Studs of Sir Reginald and Lady Macdonald-Buchanan at Newmarket. While there he had been in charge of the management of that great sprinting sire, Abernant; this experience was to prove invaluable when Bustino and Shirley Heights came to stand at Wolferton and Sandringham. Among the foals born at Egerton when Michael Oswald was managing the Egerton Stud was the brilliant Brigadier Gerard.

At the same time Michael Oswald was appointed Racing Manager to the Queen Mother, who has for many years kept five or six mares, divided equally between the Wolferton and Sandringham Studs. Michael Oswald has been responsible not only for their matings, but also for all her bloodstock. Many of the first foals bred by the Queen Mother were by Sir Winston Churchill's very popular stayer Colonist II (Rienzo–Cybele), who retired to stud at Sandringham and was mainly used as a sire of jumpers. Among the best horses the Queen Mother has bred were the full-brothers Inch Arran and Colonius (Colonist II–Queen of the Isle), and their half-brother, Isle of Man by Manicou, each of the three of them winning fourteen races. Her young horses are broken by Captain Charles Radclyffe at Lew in Oxfordshire; her young stock and stores are kept at Lord Townsend's Raynham Hall, about twenty minutes' journey east of Sandringham. In the late 1950s and 1960s her trainer was Peter Cazalet at Fairlawne in Kent; after he died, and since 1973, Fulke Walwyn at Lambourn has trained the Queen Mother's horses.

Only a proportion of the steeplechasers and hurdlers that have run for the Queen Mother since 1949 have been bred by her. Devon Loch, who so tragically lost the Grand National in 1956 by fly-jumping less than fifty yards from the winning-post when in an unassailable lead, had been bought for the Queen Mother five years earlier. When he retired, the Queen Mother loaned him to Noel Murless as a hack. The two best steeplechasers owned, but not bred, by the Queen Mother have been Game Spirit and Special

Cargo. Game Spirit won twenty-one races and finished third to Captain Christy and The Dikler in the 1974 Cheltenham Gold Cup. Special Cargo won the Grand Military Gold Cup at Sandown three times before he retired; but his greatest triumph came when he won the 1984 Whitbread Gold Cup at Sandown in the very last strides from Lettoch and his stable-companion, Diamond Edge, who had been successful in the race in 1979 and 1981. The thrilling finish of this race remains in the memories of steeplechase enthusiasts in the same way as the epic duel between Grundy and Bustino at Ascot is regarded by many supporters of the Flat as the most exciting race they have ever seen. Other notable jumpers that the Queen Mother has owned, but did not breed herself, include Double Star, the winner of twenty-one races, the brilliant two-mile chaser, Black Magic, and The Rip. The Queen Mother's most popular hurdle success was when Tammuz, whom she leased from the Queen, won the Schweppes Gold Trophy Handicap Hurdle in 1975. Other very good hurdlers that the Queen Mother has owned, but did not breed, include Makaldar, the winner of the Victor Ludorum Hurdle at Haydock in 1964, and Sunyboy, who won the Fernbank Hurdle at Ascot.

The Queen Mother has only ever had one horse on the Flat: Bali Ha'i III, who was a gift from New Zealand. He was trained by Captain Boyd-Rochfort and won three races for her, including the Queen Alexandra Stakes at Royal Ascot in 1959. It should be added that the Queen Mother has an enormous interest in Flat racing; she follows the careers of all the foals bred by the Queen extremely closely. One of the foals that the Queen Mother bred, Joliette, was leased by her to the Queen, for whom she won a good race in 1981 when beating Lord Howard de Walden's Strigida, who later won the Ribblesdale Stakes at Royal Ascot.

One other foul bred by the Queen in 1967 is worthy of mention, the filly Strathcona (St Paddy–Stroma). The Queen had felt that Aureole's son, St Paddy, who had won the Derby in 1960, would be a suitable stallion to cover Stroma in 1963; unfortunately Stroma proved barren to him, both in 1964 and after a second attempt the following year. A third covering in 1966 was successful, and on 5 April 1967 Stroma gave birth to a bay filly, named Strathcona. This was the last filly foal Stroma was to produce, for she died at the age of thirteen after foaling a dead colt by Aureole in 1968. Strathcona ran once, unplaced, as a juvenile at Ascot: in her four outings as a three-year-old she won the Bedminster Stakes at Bath over a mile in June, was second in the Durham Stakes at

Newcastle where she refused to exert herself, finished third in the Stewards Stakes at Chester and was well beaten in the Sandleford Priory Stakes at Newbury. After her defeat at Newcastle she was retired to stud at Sandringham.

Nine foals bred by the Queen in 1968 went into training with Hern and Balding; two fillies, Albany (Pall Mall–Almeria) at West Ilsley, and Example (Exbury–Amicable) at Kingsclere, were to prove the best foals to come out of the Royal Studs since Canisbay. Albany, a small, dark chestnut filly, had very thin soles to her feet; when she raced, the blacksmith at West Ilsley fitted her with light steel plates behind and broad aluminium plates in front for protection. Her three runs as a juvenile brought two thirds, in the Elcot Stakes at Newbury and in the Selsey Stakes at Goodwood.

Hern anticipated that Albany was going to be difficult to train in the spring of 1971, since she was coming into season every fortnight. Lord Porchester suggested that she should be covered, a course of action often used to ameliorate the temperament of difficult fillies, and proposed she be sent to Queen's Hussar, who was standing at the Highclere Stud. On the Queen's approval of this suggestion, Albany was duly covered by Queen's Hussar when she was next in season. Within a fortnight she was a changed character, easier to handle and less nervous; she also began to work better. On the morning of her reappearance in the Sandleford Priory Stakes at Newbury, the Queen came to West Ilsley to watch both the first and second lots work on the Summer Gallops; since it was a pleasant May morning, breakfast was taken in the garden of the Herns' house. Before the Queen departed for Newbury, she went to the yard to see Albany boxed-up. Although most of her rivals had both the benefit of a previous race and better form as juveniles, the pregnant Albany won by a length.

As Albany was by the miler Pall Mall, it was uncertain whether she would stay the twelve furlongs of the Oaks. Nevertheless, despite the firm going at Epsom, which she did not like, she finished a good fifth to Altesse Royale, who had earlier won the 1,000 Guineas. Albany was sent to France to contest the Prix de Minerve over ten furlongs at Chantilly on 24 July, the same day as the King George VI and Queen Elizabeth Stakes, so Jimmy Lindley took the mount. The going at Chantilly was soft, which suited Albany, but she was opposed by one of the two best fillies in France, Alec Weisweiller's Cambrizzia, who had run Alec Head's Pistol Packer to a short head in the Prix de Diane in June. Albany put up a tremendous fight against Cambrizzia, and only lost by a neck.

Some idea of the merit of Albany's game performance can be gained by Cambrizzia's later efforts that season: she was runner-up to Pistol Packer in the Prix Vermeille and a very creditable third to Mill Reef and Alec Head's filly in the Prix de l'Arc de Triomphe. Albany's final race, a month later, was at the lovely seaside track of Deauville in Normandy, when she won the Prix de Psyche over ten furlongs against some useful French fillies. She then retired to stud, and on 19 March 1972 gave birth to a bay colt by Queen's Hussar named Allegiance, who never won.

Example, the other good filly of the 1968 crop, was a big chestnut with a white face, who was clearly going to take time to come to maturity. As a yearling she was nervous; she was also slow to develop as a two-year-old, but the Queen told Balding not to be too disturbed by that as the family were slow developers. Example made her debut in the Blue Seal Stakes at Ascot in September, but her preparation had been interrupted by a minor setback and she was unplaced. She then ran a promising fourth in the Radley Maiden Stakes at Newbury.

Example won the Somerset Stakes at Bath in May, and then was runner-up in the Lingfield Oaks Trial to Maina, who ran second to Altesse Royale in the Oaks. She unfortunately pulled a shoulder muscle in the heavy going in the Ribblesdale Stakes and finished last. Two months later she was a close second in the Galtres Stakes at York, and was so clearly returning to her best form that Lord Porchester was able to persuade Lester Piggott to ride her in the Park Hill Stakes. In the paddock, Piggott asked if she had any finishing speed and was told she had. In the race he dropped her out last, came through to challenge two furlongs out and took the lead inside the final furlong to win comfortably. Piggott again had the mount on Example when she ran in the Prix de Royallieu over thirteen furlongs at Longchamp on 10 October, the same day as the Grand Criterium won by Hard to Beat. He dropped her out again in the early part of the race, but came through in the straight to win easily, beating amongst others Pink Pearl, who had been third to Pistol Packer in the Prix Vermeille, and to whom Example had to give weight as a result of her Doncaster victory.

When Lord Porchester and Ian Balding suggested that Example should stay in training as she had been so lightly raced, her Royal owner was a little hesitant, but eventually agreed. After finishing third to Rock Roi in the John Porter Stakes at Newbury in April, when Piggott reported her backward, Example ran in the Prix Jean de Chaudenay at Saint-Cloud in May, when Lord Tryon, Keeper of the Privy Purse, represented the Queen. Piggott again dropped out Example and came with a late challenge to beat Baron Guy de Rothschild's Arlequino a neck, reminding Ian Balding of some of his victories on Petite Etoile. Unfortunately Balding's stable was hit by the virus shortly afterwards, and while Example did race again she never recovered her spring form; she did, however, manage third in the Geoffrey Freer Stakes at Newbury and the Prix de Pomone at Deauville.

In the autumn of 1972 the Queen decided that Nijinsky, who was standing at the Claiborne Stud in Kentucky, should be the first stallion to cover Example. The mare left for Kentucky in October and on 4 May gave birth to a chestnut filly by Nijinsky, later named Pas de Deux. Tragically, during the birth Pas de Deux had put her foot through Example's uterus; the six-year-old mare died from a ruptured colon within a few hours. Michael Oswald immediately arranged through the English National Foaling Bank for a foster-mare to come to Wolferton, and Example's only foal was saved.

Neither the 1969 nor the 1970 crop of foals bred by Her Majesty included any really top-class horses. Alaska Way (Sovereign Path–Kitimat), who won seven races, was the best foal born in 1969. Gloss (Stupendous–Highlight), who was her dam's sixth foal, and the first of any significant merit, was the best of the crop born a year later. Stupendous, an American-bred stallion, was standing at the English National Stud. Gloss won four races and was second in the Queen Anne Stakes at Royal Ascot in 1974, when the first three horses to pass the post were all disqualified, and third to Pitcairn in the Goodwood Mile.

Highlight's first foal, Leading Silk by Counsel, was of little account, and was sold to Robert Sangster, for whom he won a small race in Scotland. Highlight was barren in 1964; her 1965 foal Cullinan by Princely Gift died before he ever ran, and her offspring the next year, Carnival Light by Crepello, did nothing on the race-course and became a country stallion in the south of Ireland. Highlight's 1967 foal, a chestnut filly by Exbury, was sent to Brigadier Wingfield's Brownstown Park Stud in Ireland after she had been weaned together with Strathcona. Wingfield thought Highlight's filly, named Exmoor, the more promising of the two; unfortunately she collapsed and died in her paddock in the summer of 1968, the result, Wingfield thought, of a kick by Strathcona which resulted in a haematoma. In 1968 Highlight produced a bay colt by Tamerlane, Tammuz, who won a maiden race at York in 1971. He then broke down, was pinfired and given to the Queen Mother as a hurdler. In

1975 he won the Schweppes Gold Trophy in February at Newbury. In 1969 Highlight slipped a foal to Baldric II, so by the time Gloss was foaled in 1970, she had not produced any offspring that could be considered anywhere near top-class.

In 1969 Lord Porchester suggested sending Highlight to Queen's Hussar, who was standing at the Highclere Stud. Queen's Hussar had won the Sussex Stakes for the Earl of Carnarvon in 1963, but up to 1969 had only got one good colt, Shiny Tenth, who was to win the 1970 Free Handicap. Both Queen's Hussar's great-grandsire and his grandam were by Fair Trial; furthermore, Fairway, Fair Trial's sire, appeared three times in his first four generations. Highlight was completely devoid of any Fairway or Phalaris blood in her pedigree, so her mating with Queen's Hussar seemed an excellent outcross. Neither Captain Moore nor Captain Boyd-Rochfort had liked the blood of the Phalaris male line, particularly not that of Pharos, whom they thought a common horse, or Fair Trial, who traced back to Americus Girl, a maternal line that had a reputation for producing short runners. As a result there was practically no Fair Trial or Nearco blood in the broodmares at the Royal Stud in 1970.

At the beginning of April 1971 Highlight gave birth to her Queen's Hussar foal, a big bay filly with black points whom the Queen named Highclere. After she had been weaned at Hampton Court, Highclere joined the other Royal yearlings at Polhampton. When she first arrived at West Ilsley, she was so highly-strung, like her grandam Hypericum, that no one wanted to look after her. Finally the only stable-girl employed by Major Hern, Betty Brister, agreed to do so. On account of her size, it was clear to Hern that Highclere could not be hurried and that he had to regard her as a potential three-year-old.

By July 1973 Highclere's trainer considered her his best two-year-old filly: she had a beautiful action and had begun to work extremely well. She made her debut in the Princess Maiden Stakes over six furlongs at Newmarket's July Meeting, and finished a very promising runner-up to Louis Freedman's Polygamy, who had already had a run. Highclere's next race was the Princess Margaret Stakes over six furlongs at Ascot, run on the same day as the King George VI and Queen Elizabeth Stakes was won by another brilliant filly, Dahlia. Highclere was outpaced early on in the race by Celestial Dawn, but finished so well that she was beaten only a head, with Polygamy behind her. Celestial Dawn had previously won the Cherry Hinton Stakes at Newmarket, so Highclere's performance at Ascot was exceptionally encouraging for a filly whose trainer thought she would only reach her true potential the following season.

Highclere had one more outing in 1973, when she was a very unimpressive winner of the Donnington Maiden Stakes at Newbury. A disappointed Major Hern, and his jockey, Joe Mercer, both then felt that she was not up to Classic standard. Lord Porchester was not so despondent, however; he had noticed that the filly had looked about her at Newbury. He also remembered that Queen's Hussar had done exactly the same, and that he was a much better horse when running in blinkers, so he told Hern that Highclere might also need blinkers when she ran in 1974. In addition he noticed that Highclere had done a fast time in the Newbury race, so perhaps her victory was better than it seemed. He suggested to the Queen that Highclere should go back to the Highclere Stud for a couple of months for a change of scene, and Her Majesty agreed to this plan. When the filly returned to West Ilsley, Hern was very impressed with her condition. As she took time to lose her winter coat, Hern decided to run her in the 1,000 Guineas as her first race of the season. He tried her in blinkers on the gallops, and they unquestionably helped her concentration, so it was decided she would wear them at Newmarket. A week before the Guineas, Highclere was given a gallop on Newbury racecourse over seven furlongs, both to reaccustom her to travelling by horsebox and to give her a change of scene.

Although Highclere had beaten the favourite, Polygamy, at Ascot the previous July, she was permitted to start at 12–1: the public seemed to have forgotten that Hern had sent out Brigadier Gerard to win the 2,000 Guineas in 1970 on his first appearance as a three-year-old. Joe Mercer was instructed to keep well in touch with the leaders throughout as the Queen's filly stayed a mile well, and he followed his instructions to the letter. He took the lead two furlongs out, trying to poach as much advantage as possible going down into the Dip. Up the hill Pat Eddery launched a most menacing challenge on Polygamy and the two fillies raced neck and neck for the line. Highclere, with the advantage of the rails, and helped by the blinkers, never veered off a straight line and refused to give in. Neither jockey was certain who had won: the Queen, Lord Porchester, Major Hern and Michael Oswald all felt that Highclere had been just touched off in the final stride. The photograph showed happily that the Royal filly had held on by a very short head. A few minutes later the Queen was able for the first time to welcome a Classic winner she had bred into the unsaddling enclosure herself (a cold had prevented her doing so when Pall Mall had won the 2,000 Guineas) and it was Her Majesty who told the racing journalists that Highclere would not run at Epsom as the course would not suit her, and that she would probably go for the Prix de Diane at Chantilly.

The Queen left Windsor Castle on the morning of the Prix de Diane on a private visit to Chantilly to see Highclere run. Marcel Boussac, the President of the Société d'Encouragement, had invited her to a luncheon party whose guests included the Duc d'Audifret-Pasquier, Jean Romanet, Directeur-Général of the Société d'Encouragement, and the Stewards at Chantilly. A huge bowl of red roses, a welcoming gift to the Queen from the French President, Valéry Giscard d'Estaing, awaited her arrival at Monsieur Boussac's house. The Queen was given a rapturous welcome by the French race-goers, some of whom stood in front of her box with their backs to the track shouting 'Vive La Reine'. The beautiful racecourse, with the Prince of Condé's magnificent château situated beside the back straight and the start of the long turn into the last three furlongs, provided a marvellous setting to the Queen's first visit to a race-meeting at the training centre of France's best Thoroughbreds.

Her Majesty went down to see her filly saddled, when Betty Brister told her that Highclere was in a fiery mood, always a sign that she was on her best form. The two most dangerous rivals she faced were the Prix Saint-Alary winner, Comtesse de Loir, and Hippodamia, who had won the Critérium des Pouliches in 1973 and had been runner-up in the Poule d'Essai des Pouliches and in the Prix Saint-Alary in the spring of 1974. Highclere was always in the leading group, which set a fast pace. Hippodamia took the lead on the final bend into the straight from the Prix de Cleopatre winner, Tropical Cream, with Highclere close up third. In the straight Hippodamia, hugging the rails, had the advantage with Highclere tracking her; Comtesse de Loir, meanwhile, was beginning to make significant progress from the rear. A furlong out a tiring Hippodamia came away from the rails, presenting Joe Mercer with a narrow gap between her and the fence. Mercer asked Highclere for her effort and the response was immediate: Highclere shot through the opening and was clear of her field. Comtesse de Loir tried in vain to get on terms with the Royal filly, but to no avail. Highclere had increased her advantage to two lengths by the winning-post. It had been a superlative performance, her time only a fifth of a second outside the record set by Allez France in 1973.

The Queen was almost mobbed by the enthusiastic crowd as she led in her third Classic winner. Michael Oswald later related, 'I was kissed by several ladies I had never ever met before, and by some Frenchmen as well!' After the weigh-in, the Queen was presented with the Gold Trophy for the winner of the Prix de Diane by Marcel Boussac in the calmer safety of his box. Highclere had become the first filly ever to complete the 1,000 Guineas and Prix de Diane double.

On her return to Windsor, the Queen sent a message to Dick Hern's plane inviting him and Joe Mercer to dinner that evening. It was a family party with the Queen Mother, Prince Philip, Princess Anne, Lord Mountbatten, Lord and Lady Porchester and Michael Oswald. In pride of place on the dining-room table was the Gold Trophy the Queen had received from Marcel Boussac a few hours earlier at Chantilly. Joe Mercer has since described it as 'the greatest day in our lives'.

Highclere regained the 22 lbs she lost on her victorious trip to Chantilly within a week. A little over a month later she took on the best of Europe in the King George VI and Queen Elizabeth Stakes at Ascot, from which Daniel Wildenstein's superb filly, Allez France, was a very late withdrawal. Nelson Bunker Hunt's Dahlia had shown a return to her best form when winning the Grand Prix de Saint-Cloud; she was favourite to win the race for the second consecutive year. Highclere was a long way behind the leaders on the turn into the straight; Piggott on Dahlia tracked the Derby winner, Snow Knight, and the Coronation Cup victor, Buoy, until a furlong and a half out when he let her have her head. Dahlia went into a clear lead. When Highclere eventually got an opening, she finished very strongly to pass Buoy and Snow Knight, and tried bravely but unavailingly to catch Dahlia, who won decisively by two and a half lengths. Marcel Boussac's unlucky Prix du Jockey-Club runner-up Dankaro, who came from even further back, was one length behind Highclere in third, followed by Buoy, Card King and Snow Knight and the Prix du Jockey-Club winner, Caracolero. Given the doubts about Highclere's stamina beforehand, she had run a marvellous race, in addition to beating the winner of the Epsom Derby and the first two in the Prix du Jockey-Club.

When Highclere again met Dahlia and Snow Knight in the Benson and Hedges Gold Cup at York, she ran stones below her best form and finished a distant sixth. It is likely that she had not fully recovered from her hard race at Ascot. In her final race, the

Prix de l'Arc de Triomphe at Longchamp on 6 October 1974, the Queen's exceptional Classic winner had to contend with heavy going and the fact that she had come into season. An incident took place behind the Petit Bois which put paid to her chance: Highclere was just behind the leading group when Paulista crossed to the rails rather sharply and hampered her. Faltering, she was severely buffeted by Sang Bleu, lost at least eight lengths and dropped back to the rear of the field. She never recovered and finished out of the first ten to Allez France, who just held Comtesse de Loir by a head. Nevertheless, up to 1974 Highclere was the best horse ever owned and bred by the Queen.

There was another high-class filly in the same crop of foals as Highclere: Escorial (Royal Palace–Asturia), who went into training with Ian Balding at Kingsclere. Michael Oswald had advised the Queen to send Asturia to Royal Palace as, in addition to Classic victories, he had had both stamina and immense courage as a racehorse. Although he was to prove a disappointment as a stallion, the achievements of first Escorial and then Dunfermline were to show that this advice was not misplaced. On her debut Escorial won the first division of the Donnington Maiden Stakes at Newbury an hour before Highclere won the second. She won the Green Shield Stakes over a mile at Ascot (now better known as the Hoover Fillies' Mile) three weeks later in a very impressive manner; Lester Piggott, who rode her, considered she was a high-class filly, and she became one of the winter favourites for the Oaks. In her first race in 1974, the Pretty Polly Stakes at Newmarket in May, Escorial was a very disappointing third. She redeemed her reputation, however, by winning the Musidora Stakes very easily, despite getting loose earlier in the afternoon when coming across the centre of the course to the saddling boxes. Lester Piggott, who had once more had the ride, afterwards told the Queen that he thought Escorial would have a great chance in the Oaks. It turned out to have been a poor Musidora, however: Escorial ran abysmally at Epsom, failing to come down the hill and finishing a long way behind Polygamy, who was fortunate to win when Dibidale's saddle slipped in the last two furlongs. Piggott had accepted defeat a long way out. Escorial never won again, but she did manage to take second place in the Strensall Stakes at York in August.

The 1972 crop of foals bred by Her Majesty again included a high-class filly, Joking Apart (Jimmy Reppin–Strip the Willow), who won her only outing as a juvenile, the Allington Maiden Plate over six furlongs at Newmarket in October. Joking Apart's dam,

Strip the Willow, was the first produce of a broodmare sent by the Queen to the USA to be covered by an American stallion. Near Miss (Nearco–Beginner's Luck) was sent to Mr Alfred Vanderbilt's Sagamore Farm in 1964 to be covered by Native Dancer, and the offspring of this mating was Strip the Willow. She had ability, but was never placed in five outings and may have been slightly ungenuine, which was why she was sent, on Michael Oswald's advice, to be covered by Jimmy Reppin, a tough colt whose Djebel blood made him an ideal outcross. Other mares that went to the USA in the 1960s were Arbitrate (Arbar–Above Board), who was covered by Kauai King in 1969 and produced Crown Court, the winner of three races, and Guinea Sparrow (Grey Sovereign–Parakeet), whose 1970 foal by Sir Ivor, Golden Ivy, won one race.

From 1972 the Royal broodmares began to go to the Darby Dan Stud Farm of John Galbreath in Lexington, Kentucky. His assistance and great kindness in assisting the Queen and her advisers with her mares in the United States during the 1970s cannot be too strongly emphasized. Among the useful foals who resulted from the matings of the Queen's mares with stallions at Darby Dan were Duke of Normandy (Roberto–Daisy Chain), Gregarious (Graustark–Amicable), Chain of Reasoning (Hail to Reason–Daisy Chain) and Elusive (Little Current–Tartan Pimpernel).

Another American who was immensely helpful to the Royal Stud during the 1970s and 1980s was Mill Reef's owner, Paul Mellon. Mill Reef broke a leg in training on the gallops at Kingsclere in 1972, but fortunately was saved for stud. Mellon, however, did not take his champion back to the USA but most generously stood him at the National Stud so that he might be more easily available as a sire to English breeders. Mellon made sure that the Queen had a nomination to Mill Reef every season from 1974 to 1985; among the good horses sired by him for Her Majesty were English Harbour, Milford, Special Leave and Reflection. The last of these is one of the mares who will be covered by Nashwan in his first covering season in 1990.

Joking Apart was difficult to train as she had knee and shoulder problems as a two-year-old in 1974; it was only in the autumn that she had begun to shine on the gallops. In mid-April 1975 a slightly backward Joking Apart ran third to Carnauba in the Fred Darling Stakes at Newbury on very heavy going. She did a good gallop before the 1,000 Guineas and so was allowed to take her chance at Newmarket. Joe Mercer rode Joking Apart exactly the same way as he had Highclere the previous year, taking the lead going into the Dip. This time, however, the Royal filly tired going up the hill and eventually finished a close third to Nocturnal Spree and Girl Friend, with the unlucky favourite, Rose Bowl, who was baulked at a vital stage, fourth. Joe Mercer felt that she did not quite get a mile, but that over seven furlongs she would have won. Joking Apart next ran, therefore, in the Jersey Stakes at Royal Ascot, where she was opposed by Vincent O'Brien's Gay Fandango, who was still a maiden although he had been fourth to Grundy in the Irish 2,000 Guineas. Unfortunately Joking Apart was twice baulked when coming to challenge Gay Fandango; when she found a passage through, it was too late and she was beaten a head. Joe Mercer apologized after the race, saying that he should have won.

At Newmarket's July Meeting Joking Apart won the Duchess of Montrose Handicap under the welter burden of 9 st 7 lbs. At the start of August she was unplaced in a Deauville sprint over six and a half furlongs in soft going, on which she could not act. In the Hungerford Stakes at Newbury she was kicked at the start, but still ran Court Chad to half a length. Ian Balding considered Joking Apart the most courageous filly he had trained up to then, and felt that she would have been in the highest class if she had been sound.

Highclere's full sister, Light Duty, was also born in 1972. She was an unlucky filly, who only won once, the Twyford Stakes at Newbury by eight lengths as a three-year-old. Her debut in 1974 was planned for the Princess Maiden Stakes at Newmarket, but she was the only one balloted out of the race as there were too many runners. The only suitable race for her was the more competitive St Catherine's Stakes at Newbury one week later, in which, despite stumbling when coming out of the stalls, she was only beaten a short head by a much more experienced rival. Her best performances were in the Ribblesdale Stakes when second to Galina, and in the Yorkshire Oaks when runner-up to May Hill, with the Oaks winner Juliette Marny only fourth.

The crop of foals bred by the Queen in 1973 did not reach the same standard as those of the previous two years. It produced eight winners of eighteen races, but only one was a Group race winner: Gilding (Kauai King–Guinea Sparrow), who won the 1,000 Guineas Trial at Ascot. As a juvenile she had won the Donnington Maiden Stakes at Newbury and finished third in the Argos Fillies Mile at Ascot. Unfortunately she deteriorated after her win at Ascot and never won again.

16

Queen Elizabeth II,

1974–89

Strathcona's first two foals were of little account: the first, Railway Line by Relko, was gelded and still failed to win; the second, Holyroodhouse by Royal Palace, ran twice as a juvenile, was culled and exported to Belgium, where he won five minor races. Strathcona was covered by Royal Palace again in 1973, and the following spring gave birth to a big bay filly foal who was named Dunfermline. She had a rather plain head, but as a yearling at Polhampton walked very well. She also had excellent quarters and plenty of depth, but was a bit back at the knee. Although she had a calm temperament and was very easy to plate, she was a robust filly who needed a strong rider on the gallops.

Prior to Dunfermline's first race, the Catnic Components Plate at Sandown over seven furlongs, Lord Porchester was worried that the firm going might injure her as she had a rather round action and hit the ground hard. In the event, she not merely came out of the race sound, but ran with much promise, finishing third to H. J. Joel's experienced Miss Pinkie. Dunfermline did a good gallop at West Ilsley a week before her next race, the May Hill Stakes at Doncaster on St Leger day. The Queen was present to celebrate the bicentenary of the north's only Classic. Unfortunately Dunfermline sweated a lot in her box going up to Doncaster and was struck into as she came out of the stalls; her performance in the race, finishing a half-length second to the Goodwood winner, Triple First, was all the more meritorious. Two furlongs out, indeed, she had looked the likely winner; Mercer attributed her failure to go through with her challenge to greenness.

Dunfermline's final race as a juvenile was in the Argos Fillies' Mile at Ascot, where she met both Miss Pinkie and Triple First again. The Queen's filly took the lead from Miss Pinkie approaching the final furlong and seemed to have the race won. Lester Piggott, however, launched a renewed challenge on Mr Joel's filly and got up to win, with Triple First in third place. Mercer felt that Dunfermline's defeat was again due to greenness; she had certainly improved since Doncaster, as the reversal of the form with Triple First demonstrated.

Stan Clayton, who had ridden Canisbay to victory in the Eclipse Stakes, had joined Major Hern as an assistant trainer at the end of 1976 from Jack Clayton's yard at Newmarket, where he had occupied the same post. In March 1977 he began to ride Dunfermline in most of her morning work. She had a tendency to hang so she was fitted with an Australian noseband or cheeker instead of an ordinary bridle; a cheeker keeps the bit straight in the mouth and so prevents a horse from hanging. Stan Clayton was confident that Dunfermline would win her first race in 1977, the Pretty Polly Stakes at Newmarket. The new stable jockey, Willie Carson, was not so sure as she had not come in her coat, although she was fit and well. As stamina was her strongest suit, Carson sent Dunfermline into the lead at the Bushes; she struggled initially to overcome Olwyn, but going up the hill lengthened her stride and went away to win by four lengths. The Queen, who had come to Newmarket that afternoon after her Silver Jubilee tour of Australia and New Zealand, came to welcome her filly into the unsaddling enclosure. Carson told her he felt Dunfermline was still green, but that she would act on the Epsom course. It was then decided that her next race would be in the Oaks.

The Queen had been at Epsom to see The Minstrel win a thrilling Derby; she decided not to come to the Oaks, however, as Prince Andrew was returning from Canada that morning, and she had an enormously heavy schedule of Silver Jubilee celebrations in front of her the following week.

Dunfermline had done well since the Pretty Polly Stakes and had not become upset during her trip to Epsom on the morning of the Oaks. The favourite, ridden by Lester Piggott, was Robert Sangster's Durtal, who had won the Cheveley Park Stakes in 1976 and had dead-heated for second place behind Madelia in the Poule d'Essai des Pouliches at Longchamp in April. Durtal sweated up very badly in the paddock and was very worked up when Piggott was taking her past the stands to go to post. Then her saddle slipped after Piggott caught his foot on a post; he was dragged a hundred yards with his other foot caught in the stirrup before getting free, miraculously without serious injury. Durtal, loose and panicking, injured herself so badly that she had to be withdrawn.

Dunfermline settled down in the middle of the field after the start, but at half-way, when she was in about sixth place, she was severely stopped by Geoff Lewis's mount, Brightly, and knocked back almost to the rear of the field of fourteen. As she had only three fillies behind her at the top of Tattenham Corner, Carson had to try to make up the lost ground coming down the hill on the outside. Dunfermline was again checked slightly at Tattenham Corner. She began to move up in the middle of the course and reached the heels of the leaders two furlongs out. She continued to close on the leader, Freeze the Secret, and although she began to hang left towards her principal rival and the rails, Dunfermline collared Freeze the Secret well inside the final furlong to win by three quarters of a length. Carson afterwards commented, 'To overcome all the interference we had in the race and still win was in my view a marvellous performance.'

Dunfermline was welcomed into the famous Epsom winner's circle by a radiantly delighted Queen Mother, who received the winning trophy on the Queen's behalf a few minutes later. The Queen Mother afterwards telephoned the Queen, who had watched the race on television, to congratulate her on not merely owning but also breeding the winner of the Oaks.

Dunfermline's defeat in the Yorkshire Oaks in August when she was only third to Busaca was disappointing, but no blame should be attached to the filly. The race was run at a very slow pace, which did not permit her to use her stamina. As the Park Hill Stakes was likely to be another very slowly run race, the Queen and Lord Porchester decided to take on the unbeaten Alleged in the St Leger instead: a bold move, for after Robert Sangster's colt had trounced the Irish Sweeps Derby third, Classic Example, by seven lengths in the Great Voltigeur Stakes, most people felt he was a certainty for the Doncaster Classic. To make certain that Piggott would not dictate the pace from the front, and to ensure Dunfermline's stamina was fully used, the Queen's Gregarious, who had won the Glasgow Stakes at York and the ATS Trophy Handicap at Newbury, also ran in the St Leger to set a strong pace. Dunfermline worked brilliantly in her final gallop before leaving for Doncaster, and Carson really fancied her chance of upsetting the favourite.

Gregarious, as planned, took the lead from Alleged as soon as the starting gates opened, and set a good but sensible gallop.

Carson had Dunfermline travelling easily in fifth place. As the two leaders approached the final bend into the straight, Carson moved Dunfermline into third place. Once the straight was reached Alleged took the lead, closely tracked on the rails by Dunfermline, whom Carson thought was going just the better. Two furlongs out Piggott kicked for home, but did not shake off the Queen's filly, who challenged and drew level at the furlong pole. Dunfermline edged ahead as Alleged, under extreme pressure from Piggott, came away from the rails. When Carson gave Dunfermline a few strokes with his whip to keep her going, she hung to the left towards Alleged. Dunfermline got the upper hand fifty yards from the line; Carson put his whip down, straightened her and, with hands and heels, rode her out to beat the favourite three quarters of a length. Although the two horses had come very close, Piggott told Carson, as they were pulling up, that there was nothing to worry about and that he would not object. The Stewards nevertheless held an Enquiry into the race, and there was an agonizing wait of fifteen minutes before they announced that the placings remained unaltered.

Dunfermline and Alleged had so outclassed the field that Classic Example, the King Edward VII Stakes winner, was ten lengths behind in third place. Dunfermline's tremendous victory was a first win for the Queen in the St Leger, and the first St Leger for a horse bred at the Royal Studs since La Flèche had won the Doncaster Classic in 1892. Only fifteen fillies have ever completed the Oaks and St Leger double: those who have done it in the last hundred years are Memoir (1890) and La Flèche (1892), both bred by Queen Victoria, Sceptre (1902), Pretty Polly (1904), Sun Chariot (1942), owned but not bred by George VI, Meld (1955), Sun Princess (1983) and Oh So Sharp (1985).

Dunfermline got over her hard race at Doncaster amazingly rapidly; within five days she had regained all the weight she had lost. Unfortunately Gregarious broke down and had to be retired, which was to have a distinct bearing on the result of the Prix de l'Arc de Triomphe. The premier French race was Dunfermline's next objective, despite the fact that she was only just out of season when she did her final gallop one week before her trip to France on Friday 30 September. She travelled well and went straight to the stables at Longchamp.

There was a field of twenty-six for the Prix de l'Arc de Triomphe on 2 October 1977. Many thought Alleged would reverse the St Leger placings over the shorter trip and he was favourite. Other dangerous rivals Dunfermline faced included the Prix du Jockey-Club winner, Crystal Palace, the 1976 St Leger winner, Crow, Balmerino, the champion in Australia and New Zealand in the 1975–6 season, whom John Dunlop trained specially for the race, and whom Lavinia, Duchess of Norfolk, thought was the best horse she had ever seen on the gallops on the Downs near Arundel, Orange Bay, who had run The Minstrel to a short head in the King George VI and Queen Elizabeth Diamond Stakes at Ascot, the Prix Ganay winner, Arctic Tern, and the 1976 Irish Derby winner, Malacate. The only important absentee was Gregarious or another pacemaker for Dunfermline. In such a big field it was natural that Major Hern would assume the race would be run at its normal fast pace, especially as the going was good.

Carson settled Dunfermline in about sixth place as soon as the stalls opened. For the first time for many years there was not the usual blistering gallop from the outset of the race; Yelpana was content to set a leisurely pace to Alleged. None of the jockeys wanted to make the running initially, and before the Petit Bois Piggott had sent Alleged into the lead from Yelpana and Crystal Palace with Dunfermline still sixth. It was clear from this moment that the race was not going to be run to suit Dunfermline, and an error had been made in not having a stable-companion to cut out the running. That Alleged, drawn nineteen, and Crystal Palace, drawn twenty-three, were first and third so early further demonstrated the funereal pace of the first 400 metres. Piggott proceeded to give a masterly display of waiting in front, and, suddenly increasing the leisurely gallop in the straight, managed to steal an unassailable advantage that he held to the line. Dunfermline, who lost a plate early on, found herself pocketed on the rails coming to the final bend behind Yelpana, who was tracking Crystal Palace and Crow. There she remained until a furlong and a half out, when the weakening Yelpana hampered her at the same time as Balmerino launched his challenge on the outside. When Dunfermline recovered, and Carson had extricated her from the pocket inside the final furlong, the Queen's filly began to close rapidly on her rivals and only missed overhauling Crystal Palace by a short neck for third place. The time of the race, which many had expected to break the course record, was nearly two seconds slower than that of Mill Reef in 1970. It was disappointing that the luck of the race did not go Dunfermline's way. We can only speculate whether a pacemaker would have enabled her to repeat her Doncaster victory over Alleged; it was clear that the lack of one made Piggott's task much easier. Dunfermline remained the only horse ever to beat Alleged, who was to win the Prix de l'Arc de Triomphe the following year.

Lord Porchester bought R. D. Hollingsworth's Sea Boat to ensure that Dunfermline had a good gallop in her next race, the Prix Royal-Oak at Longchamp three weeks later. Both had a terrible journey to Longchamp as the aeroplane was delayed; Dunfermline had also gone in her coat. She finished a disappointing third to Rex Magna and the very useful filly Trillion in soft going; her hard race at Longchamp earlier in the month and the fact that she had possibly gone over the top were the likely reasons for her defeat.

Dunfermline's campaign as a four-year-old was short and disappointing. She did not reappear until the Hardwicke Stakes, in which she finished second to the surprise French winner, Montcontour; she was not disgraced as Balmerino was behind her in third place. She then took on the best in Europe in the King George VI and Queen Elizabeth Diamond Stakes. This was a sad occasion, for it was the very last time Marcel Boussac's famous orange colours were to be carried on a racecourse. For several years Boussac's textile empire had been struggling. In order to protect the jobs of his employees he poured his personal fortune into the factories to keep the mills rolling. Shortly after Acamas won the Prix du Jockey-Club in 1978, Marcel Boussac's business affairs were placed in the hands of the Receiver, who ordered all his bloodstock to be sold. It was bought by the Aga Khan with one condition attached, that Acamas should be permitted to run in the famous colours for the last time in Ascot's big race. Marcel Boussac, accompanied by Jean Romanet, the Directeur-Général of the Société d'Encouragement, therefore came to Ascot to see the race. Her Majesty was already standing at the far end of the paddock with her party, and Dunfermline was already walking around, when the two Frenchmen and their connections came into the parade ring and stood under the large oak tree nearest the stands. When the Queen saw him there, she immediately left the group associated with her runner and walked across to greet the old man, who had entertained her so hospitably before Highclere's famous victory at Chantilly. It was an extremely gracious gesture to France's greatest breeder, whose misfortune had been caused by his own loyalty to his workforce.

Sadly Acamas could only finish second to Île de Bourbon, while the Queen's Dunfermline finished out of the first six. It looked as if the time had come to retire her to the paddocks, an impression confirmed a few weeks later in the Geoffrey Freer Stakes at New-bury when she was a well-beaten fourth to the same horse. Like so many great racemares, Dunfermline was difficult to get in foal. She was barren to Nijinsky and Roberto in 1980 and 1981, and to Relkino the next year. Her 1983 foal, Red Shoes by Dance in Time, was placed seven times but never won before she too went to the Royal Stud's paddocks. Neither of Dunfermline's colts, Palais de Danse by Dance in Time and Royal Bank by Mill Reef, had any ability. She was not covered in 1985 and was barren again in 1987, this time to Shirley Heights. In 1988 she foaled a colt by Bellypha: her last produce as she died in January 1989.

The Queen bred two other useful winners in 1974: Circlet (Baldric II–Highlight) and Fife and Drum (Queen's Hussar–Heath-field). Circlet was initially considered a better prospect than Dun-fermline, but she developed a wind problem and had to be hobdayed early in 1976. She won the Blue Seal Stakes at Ascot so convincingly in September 1976 that she was considered to have Classic potential; but when she was a well-beaten second to Lucent in the Lingfield Oaks Trial Stakes, Carson reported that her wind problems had caused her to stop in the final stages. She made no show at Royal Ascot and was retired to stud. Fife and Drum won both his races as a two-year-old, the Washington Singer Stakes at Newbury and Strathclyde Stakes at Ayr, but did not fulfil that promise as a three-year-old.

Four of the 1975 crop of fourteen foals bred by the Queen won Group or Listed Races. Tartan Pimpernel (Blakeney–Strathcona) won the Acomb Stakes impressively by three lengths at York on her second outing. She next ran in the May Hill Stakes, the race immediately following Dunfermline's triumph in the St Leger, and duly completed a double for the Queen. When she was runner-up to Cherry Hinton in the Hoover Fillies' Mile at Ascot in September, there were hopes that she would develop into as good a three-year-old as her half-sister, Dunfermline: but her record the next year was more than a trifle disappointing since she only managed to win the Galtres Stakes at York and finish fourth in the Park Hill Stakes at Doncaster.

English Harbour (Mill Reef–Albany) was trained by Ian Balding and won like a colt with a future when taking the Yattendon Stakes at Newbury in 1977. His victory in the Predominate Stakes at Goodwood earned him a place in Shirley Height's Derby; he was not placed, but was not disgraced either. He was third to Sexton Blake in the Gordon Stakes at Goodwood in July, which showed him to be some way behind the best of his generation. He was later sold as a stallion to New Zealand.

Duke of Normandy (Roberto–Daisy Chain) won the Fenwolf Stakes at the Ascot Heath meeting in June and the Fairhurst Nursery at Newbury in September 1977 as a two-year-old. When he won the Warren Stakes over the Derby course at Epsom in April 1978, it seemed possible that he might develop into quite a high-class colt. As with English Harbour, to whom he was a little inferior, these hopes were to be disappointed, partly as a result of a chipped bone in the knee of one of his forelegs. From his yearling days he had always been prone to injury.

The other foal of the 1975 crop who distinguished himself was Rhyme Royal (Crepello–Lyrical). He was trained by Major Hern at West Ilsley; winning once as a two-year-old in 1977, he improved throughout the following season, taking four races including the Garrowby Stakes at York. Although he always had to concede massive weights to his rivals in handicaps, he won twice more in 1979, when his best performance was to run second to Jellaby in the Brigadier Gerard Stakes at Sandown. His final victory came in 1981 when he was a six-year-old. He was later leased to the Queen Mother, for whom he won over hurdles.

In 1974 Aureole's health had begun to decline rapidly; his fertility rate dropped and he stopped covering mares at the end of June. He developed arthritis in the spine, and in the autumn, after the veterinary surgeon had been consulted, the Queen decided that the kindest thing to do would be to put him down. Ted Grist, who had looked after him so devotedly and loyally since his arrival as a sire at Wolferton, was given a fortnight's holiday, as he did not wish to be present at the death of the stallion for whom he had done so much and whom he had grown to like so deeply. One November morning Aureole was taken to a paddock near his box and given an injection by the vet; he died instantaneously and was buried in the same paddock, where a copper beech marks his grave.

Aureole's death left a vacancy for a stallion at Wolferton. Canisbay had left the Sandringham Stud for Italy at the end of 1972. Ribero, the 1968 Irish Derby and St Leger winner, who was the property of a syndicate, had been standing at the Royal Stud since 1970, but was rather a disappointing sire. When he was sold in 1976 to another stud in Newmarket and later exported to Japan, his best winners had been Ribecourt (Gran Premio d'Italia, Criterium de Saint-Cloud, Prix Kergolay), Riboson (Yorkshire Cup), Riboreen (Lingfield Oaks Trial) and Romper (Blue Riband

Trial Stakes). In 1975 the Queen thought that Bustino (Busted–Ship Yard by Doutelle) might prove a good replacement for Aureole. Although Bustino will be always remembered for his thrilling finish with Grundy in the 1975 King George VI and Queen Elizabeth Diamond Stakes, he had achieved many notable victories before his narrow defeat at Ascot. He had won his only other race in 1975, the Coronation Cup at Epsom, in record time. As a three-year-old he had won the St Leger, the Great Voltigeur Stakes, the Lingfield Derby Trial Stakes and the Classic Trial at Sandown, in the latter two races beating Snow Knight. He had also finished a slightly unlucky fourth to Snow Knight in the Derby and was second to Sagaro in the Grand Prix de Paris. His pedigree bore closer inspection than that of his Ascot conqueror, Grundy, especially its maternal line. The Queen, therefore, took ten shares in the syndicate formed to buy the Busted four-year-old in the summer of 1975. His owner, Lady Beaverbrook, retained the greatest number of shares in the syndicate, and Bustino arrived at the Wolferton Stud late that year.

The 1976 crop of foals bred by the Queen also included four Group or Listed race winners, two colts and two fillies. These four won races of much higher quality than those of the previous year and included the best middle-distance colt the Queen had bred since Canisbay in 1961 and Above Suspicion in 1956: Milford (Mill Reef–Highclere). Milford, a chestnut colt, was Highclere's first foal and he went into training with Major Hern at West Ilsley. It was always likely that he would make a better three-year-old than two-year-old, but he ran with much promise in 1978, finishing runner-up in both the Hyperion Stakes at Ascot and the Houghton Stakes at Newmarket in October.

Milford overwhelmed his opponents in the White Rose Stakes at Ascot on his re-appearance in the spring. He then easily accounted for some moderate rivals in the Lingfield Derby Trial, for which he started 11–4 on favourite. Although he clearly had to be considered a possible Derby winner, it was difficult to weigh up his chance at Epsom accurately, since the horses he had beaten at Ascot and Lingfield were mediocre; there was also a doubt that he would act at Epsom. Furthermore he was only the stable's second string as Sir Michael Sobell's Troy, who had so impressed when winning his trial at Goodwood, was the more fancied and the choice of Willie Carson. In the event Milford lost ground at the start, did not act on the hill down to Tattenham Corner and was never a danger to Troy.

Milford then put up the best performance of his career when he decisively beat M-Lolshan in the Prince of Wales's Stakes at Newmarket in July in record time. He was a slightly disappointing third to Noble Saint and the Queen's Buttress, both of whom received 4 lbs from him, in the Great Voltigeur Stakes at York. He was not considered a high enough calibre colt to stand as a stallion at Sandringham and was sold, first standing at the Bacton Stud in England and later being exported to Japan.

Buttress (Busted–Albany), a chestnut half-brother to English Harbour, also went into training at West Ilsley. He took time to come to hand as a juvenile and ran in one of the big back-end maiden races at Newmarket in October, where he was noted making significant late progress in the final stages. He grew into a useful staying three-year-old and won three races in 1979, when his most important victory came in the Queen's Vase at Ascot. He ran second to Noble Saint in the Great Voltigeur Stakes at York later that year, and was runner-up to the same horse in the Yorkshire Cup the following May. He was also second to Billion in the Henry II Stakes at Sandown and third in the Sagaro Stakes as a four-year-old. If he had possessed a turn of finishing speed, he might have been a very useful stayer, though he, like so many of the Queen's good horses at this time, had had his share of injury problems in training.

Expansive (Exbury–Amicable), a chestnut filly and full-sister to Example, might have been as good as, and possibly even better than her sister, had she not been plagued with problems of soundness. Only enormous patience on the part of Major Hern got her on to a racecourse at all. She ran once in the Chesterton Maiden Stakes over a mile at Newmarket in the autumn of 1978, finishing a creditable third, and on her first race as a three-year-old in May 1979 was second in the Twyford Stakes at Newbury. Considering her inexperience it was an amazing feat of training by Dick Hern to have won a most competitive Ribblesdale Stakes with her at Royal Ascot, when she beat Senorita Pocquito. Her next objective was the Prix Vermeille; unfortunately she fell one morning on the gallops, turning head over heels. As a result of this accident she was taken out of training and retired as a broodmare to the Sandringham Stud.

One other filly from the 1976 crop is worthy of mention, namely Strathspey (Jimmy Reppin–Strip the Willow), who won four races, including the Fern Hill Stakes at Ascot and the Duchess of Montrose Handicap at Newmarket, before being sold in the spring of

1979 to Mrs Henry Chaplin, another patron of her trainer, Ian Balding, and then to Paul Mellon.

After 1976 the Royal Studs ceased to use the Hampton Court Stud for mares and foals and it passed out of their control. The former Crown Equerry, Sir John Miller, took over at Hampton Court; the stud was still used for the carriage horses required on state occasions and for polo ponies, but no longer for Thoroughbreds. The mares that had been at Hampton Court went to the Sandringham Stud, and the weaned foals to Polhampton.

Although two of the 1977 crop of foals bred by Her Majesty won Listed Races, the overall standard was inferior to the previous three years. Deadly Serious (Queen's Hussar–Joking Apart) only ran as a three-year-old; she started five times and won three races, the most important of which was the Galtres Stakes at York. Dukedom (Connaught–Albany) won the White Rose Stakes at Ascot in the early spring and looked to be a good colt in the making, but he ran most disappointingly afterwards and never won another race. He did once show a glimpse of what his true potential might have been when he was runner-up to the lightly raced Fingal's Cave in the Cumberland Lodge Stakes with the hardy Sea Pigeon third.

In 1977 the Queen appointed a third trainer to take some of her horses: William Hastings-Bass, the son of Peter Hastings-Bass, who had trained for her for such a brief time before his untimely death. William Hastings-Bass, who is the brother-in-law of Ian Balding, had served as assistant trainer to Sir Noel Murless and his yard was then at the Marriot Stables at Newmarket. He trained his first winner for Her Majesty when Contralto (Busted–Lyrical) won the Fenwolf Stakes at Ascot in 1978; she later won the Jack Leader Memorial Trophy at Yarmouth.

Six of the foals from the 1978 crop bred by the Queen went into training at West Ilsley, two to Ian Balding and three to Hastings-Bass. By far the best was the bay colt Church Parade (Queen's Hussar–Christchurch), who won two races as a two-year-old, including the Champagne Stakes at Goodwood, and ran third to Gielgud in the Laurent Perrier Champagne Stakes at Doncaster. As a three-year-old he won the High Line Stakes at York and was second in the September Stakes at Kempton Park. He was also third in the normally competitive Prix Eugene Adam at Saint-Cloud in July. On balance he was probably a slight disappointment in 1981. He was later sold as a stallion to New Zealand.

The bay filly Height of Fashion by Bustino was Highclere's

fourth foal; she is unquestionably by far the best foal Highclere has yet produced, besides being the star of the 1979 crop. A big filly like her dam, Height of Fashion's first victory came in the Acomb Stakes at York. Her impressive performance there saw her start 6–4 on favourite for the May Hill Stakes over a mile at Doncaster on the day Cut Above created such a shock by beating Shergar into fourth place in the St Leger. Height of Fashion beat Clare Island in workmanlike rather than spectacular fashion at Doncaster; she may have been still a little green. Her final race as a two-year-old was in the Hoover Fillies' Mile at Ascot; she beat Stratospheric and Zinzara so impressively that afternoon that she was later rated joint top European two-year-old filly by the international panel of handicappers.

Major Hern and Lord Porchester felt that Height of Fashion was too big to act on the course at Epsom, so it was decided in the spring of 1982 that she would not run in the Oaks. She had her first race at Goodwood in the Lupe Stakes in May. It was not a very satisfactory race for the Bustino filly, who had to jump over another runner who had fallen in front of her: still, she eventually won by two lengths from another of the Queen's fillies, Round Tower (High Top–Circlet), who was much inferior to her at home on the gallops. Height of Fashion was favoured by the conditions of her next race, the Princess of Wales's Stakes at Newmarket at the beginning of July. Her most dangerous rival, Ardross, had to give her 26 lb, 6 lb more than the weight-for-age scale and fillies' allowance dictated. Charles St George's very versatile six-year-old had already won four races before he met Height of Fashion at Newmarket: he had beaten Glint of Gold in the Jockey Club Stakes over a mile and a half at Newmarket in April, and then won the Yorkshire Cup, the Henry II Stakes at Sandown and the Ascot Gold Cup, where he easily beat the first two in the Prix du Cadran. He was no match for Height of Fashion, though, that July afternoon; the Queen's filly effortlessly beat the consistent but luckless Amyndas by two lengths with Ardross another four lengths away third, and set a new course record for a mile and a half at the same time, beating the record that the Queen's Milford had set in 1979. On that form the Queen's filly must have gone very close to beating Time Charter and Madam Gay in the Oaks if she had run. Ardross's victory in the Geoffrey Freer Stakes at Newbury, and his magnificent head second to the Aga Khan's Akiyda in the Trusthouse Forte Prix de l'Arc de Triomphe only emphasized the brilliance of Height of Fashion's performance.

The Queen received an offer of more than £1 million for Height of Fashion very soon after her victory in the Princess of Wales's Stakes from Sheikh Hamdan al Maktoum of the Dubai Royal Family. It was an enormous sum to offer for a maiden broodmare in 1982, especially considering that it is never certain that a great racemare will turn into a successful dam of winners, or for that matter ever give birth to any reasonable foals. Highclere still had a long career ahead of her at the Royal Stud; one of her fillies, Burghclere, had been sold in December 1981, but the other, Beacon Hill, was still in the Sandringham paddocks, and on 14 April 1982, Highclere had given birth to another filly foal, Bright Sun by Mill Reef. One other consideration had much bearing on the decision as to whether to sell Height of Fashion. For some time Her Majesty had wanted to buy West Ilsley; to have done so without her being seen to have sold a valuable asset to pay for its purchase was not considered by her advisers to be wise. Height of Fashion was a valuable and visible asset, whose sale would receive wide publicity. It was therefore decided that the huge offer for Height of Fashion should be accepted. The Queen then bought West Ilsley, after which Major Hern was given a seven-year lease terminating at the end of 1989.

When Height of Fashion hit her head on the side of the starting stalls as they opened for the King George VI and Queen Elizabeth Diamond Stakes at Ascot, and was never a factor behind Kalaglow and Assert, the sum paid by the Arab Prince seemed even larger. Her unfortunate experience at Ascot must have affected the filly, as she made no show in her next race and was immediately retired to stud.

Although only four of Height of Fashion's foals have since run, she is undoubtedly the best broodmare ever bred by the Queen, and probably the best in the world at this time. It is certain that she will rank with Perdita II, Quiver, Pocahontas and Feola, some of the outstanding broodmares associated with the Royal Studs. Her first foal, Alwasmi by Northern Dancer, won the John Porter Stakes at Newbury and was second in the Jockey Club Stakes. Her second foal, Unfuwain by Northern Dancer, won the Princess of Wales's Stakes, the Chester Vase and the Warren Stakes in 1988; his best performances, however, were when second to the five-year-old Mtoto in the King George VI and Queen Elizabeth Diamond Stakes at Ascot, and fourth to Tony Bin and Mtoto in the Ciga Prix de l'Arc de Triomphe on going that did not suit him. In both these races he beat all the other three-year-old runners, and he was rated the best colt of his generation. He won the John Porter Stakes and Jockey Club Stakes in the spring of 1989, but firm ground prevented him running again and he was retired to stud.

Height of Fashion's third foal, Nashwan by Blushing Groom, won his only two races as a juvenile, a maiden race at Newbury and a listed race at Ascot. He did such an excellent gallop about three weeks before the 2,000 Guineas that it was decided to let him take his chance in the race, although his objective in the winter had been the Derby. Nashwan won not merely the 2,000 Guineas, but the Derby, the Eclipse Stakes and the King George VI and Queen Elizabeth Diamond Stakes; no colt had previously won these four races in one year. It was decided he would run in the Ciga Prix de l'Arc de Triomphe instead of the St Leger, but unfortunately he was beaten by Golden Pheasant in his preparation race, the Prix de Niel, at Longchamp; possibly he had gone over the top. Nashwan did not contest France's most prestigious race, was scratched from the Champion Stakes on account of a temperature and retired to the Nunnery Stud. It was an immense shame that such a brilliant colt out of a mare bred at the Royal Studs did not run in the Queen's colours and give her a first success in the Derby.

Nashwan's half-brother, Mukddaam by Danzig, showed much promise when winning in the autumn of 1989, and may turn into a Classic contender in 1990. In hindsight the sale of Height of Fashion to Sheikh Hamdan al Maktoum must be regretted, but had she turned out to have been an almost useless broodmare, as has happened before with brilliant fillies, the sale would have been regarded as wise. If success on the racecourse and a classic pedigree were the only criteria needed to produce Classic winners, much of the fascination and all of the uncertainty would go out of breeding Thoroughbreds, and those with the longest pockets would soon dominate racing and breeding, much to the sport's detriment.

One other filly from the 1979 crop of foals bred at the Royal Studs also distinguished herself on the racecourse, Sans Blague (The Minstrel–Joking Apart). She ran three times in 1981 and won the Donnington Stakes (Division II) at Newbury very easily by four lengths. She only ran three times in 1982, but won the Galtres Stakes at York over a mile and a half and was third in the Twickenham Stakes at Kempton.

Height of Fashion was foaled in the same year that Shirley Heights (Mill Reef–Hardiemma by Hardicanute) covered his first mares at the Sandringham Stud. Lord Halifax's colt was the best three-year-old of 1978 winning the Heathorn Stakes, when he gave 10 lbs to Ile de Bourbon, the Dante Stakes, beating the subsequent St Leger winner Julio Mariner, the Derby and the Irish Derby. As a juvenile he won two of his six races, the Royal Lodge Stakes and the Limekilns Stakes. When he was forced to retire through injury after the Irish Derby, the Queen became a major shareholder in the syndicate formed to buy him from the Earl of Halifax, and it was arranged that he should stand at the Sandringham Stud. He has proved an outstanding sire over the last ten years and is, without doubt, the best son of Mill Reef standing at stud at the moment. Not merely did he get the winners of both the Derby (Slip Anchor) and of the Prix du Jockey-Club (Darshaan) in 1985, but also sired the leading two-year-old of 1988, High Estate, and more than twenty other Group and Listed race winners. Furthermore, he is already proving to be a sire of sires; Elegant Air was the leading two-year-old sire in 1989 and Darshaan's filly, Aliysa, won the Oaks that June. Shirley Heights has been one of the success stories of the Royal Stud in the 1980s; much credit for his achievements must be given to the Stud Groom at the Sandringham Stud, Jimmy Scanlan, whose father was also the Stud Groom there before him.

Bustino has also proved a very wise investment for the Queen. He has sired more than twenty-five individual Group or Listed Race winners; in the 1989 Derby he had the distinction of being both the broodmare sire of the winner, Nashwan, and sire of the runner-up, Terimon. Furthermore, in 1989 Bustino was leading broodmare sire in Great Britain. Again, credit for his success as a stallion must be given to Barrie Lister, the Stud Groom at the Wolferton Stud, who had previously been at the Lavington Stud. Bustino and Shirley Heights have averaged an incredibly high 91 per cent fertility rate of mares tested in foal after six weeks, which is, in itself, a testament to the work of Scanlan and Lister. In 1989 Shirley Heights actually achieved a 100 per cent fertility rate, while that of Bustino was 95 per cent.

The foals bred by the Queen in the 1980s have not enjoyed the same success as those of the 1970s or the early and middle 1950s: none the less each crop (with the exception of 1986) has included a winner of a Group or Listed Race. The principal reason for this relative lack of success has been that foals bred in England have faced much stiffer competition than ever before. In the middle 1970s Vincent O'Brien and Robert Sangster began the fashion of buying yearlings with the best Nearco and Northern Dancer blood at the Keeneland Sales in Kentucky and bringing them back to England and Ireland to race. When the Arab princes became deeply involved in racing, and eventually breeding, they followed this example, and were prepared to spend tens of millions of dollars each year to ensure that they obtained the cream of yearlings sold at Keeneland. They too brought them to England to race. The studs in Great Britain of a similar size to that of the Queen, therefore, faced unprecedented competition in the races where their produce had frequently won in the past. It should be added here that all of the Arab princes who started racing and breeding in a very big way in the 1980s – Prince Khalid Abdullah, Sheikh Hamdan al Maktoum, Sheikh Maktoum al Maktoum and Sheikh Mohammed – have all been most supportive of the Royal Studs, especially when the Queen and her racing advisers have wished to buy a share in or nomination to one of their growing band of top-class stallions. The Aga Khan, the most influential breeder in Europe in the 1980s, has also done his utmost to assist the Queen and the Royal Studs. Such encouragement from these principal breeders in the world of racing is much appreciated by the Queen, Lord Carnarvon and Michael Oswald, for in a sporting sense they are all rivals.

Since 1984 the Queen has continued her policy of trying to narrow the disadvantage at which European breeders stand faced with the competition of so many American-bred horses, sending even more of her mares to be covered by some of the best stallions in Kentucky. Round Tower (High Top–Circlet) had produced a colt by John Galbreath's Roberto, Roundlet, at Darby Dan in 1984, and remained in the USA to be covered by Little Current. Three other mares of the Queen's were also sent to the USA at the end of 1984 and were put up at Mill Ridge Stud Farm in Lexington, the property of Alice Chandler, a daughter of Mr Hal Price-Headley, one of the founders of the Keeneland Sales and race-course. In the autumn of 1984 two mares, one of them Christchurch (So Blessed–Highlight) were sent to the Lane's End Stud in Lexington, Kentucky, where Christchurch was covered by Alydar in 1985. In the next three years she was covered by Miswaki, Arctic Tern and Shadeed. Lane's End Stud Farm is owned by the well-known American breeder, Will Farish Jr, who originally came from Houston in Texas, and who also has horses in training with Henry Cecil at Newmarket. The Queen flew out to Kentucky on a private visit in October 1984 and stayed with Will and Sarah Farish at Lane's End. She was accompanied by Lord Porchester, Michael

Oswald, her private secretary, Sir Philip Moore and Lady Angela Oswald as Lady-in-Waiting; it was Lady Angela's great-grandfather, the Marquis of Exeter, who had bought Pocahontas, the dam of Stockwell and King Tom, after the Hampton Court dispersal sale in 1837. While the Queen was in Kentucky in 1984, she visited the Keeneland Sales complex. Since there was no actual sale taking place at the time, the directors arranged a mock auction to be staged, when all the record-breaking sales of recent years were re-enacted. Naturally Her Majesty visited all the major studs in Kentucky during this trip. At Claiborne she saw Nijinsky, Round Table, whose dam Knight's Daughter had been sold out of the Royal Stud, and Secretariat; at Gainesway she inspected Lyphard, Blushing Groom, Riverman and Vaguely Noble, and also renewed acquaintance with the mare she formerly owned, Strathcona. She saw the recently arrived Diesis at Mill Ridge and her own mare, Round Tower, and Roberto at Darby Dan, where she met the doyen of American stud managers, Olin Gentry. Other prominent studs that she visited included Calumet, Spendthrift and the late J. H. Whitney's Greentree.

The Queen has made two more private visits to Kentucky to see her mares and foals since 1984: one in 1986 and another in 1989. After her 1984 visit she went to stay with Lord and Lady Porchester at the latter's ranch in Wyoming, a part of the United States that Her Majesty had never previously visited. During the 1989 trip she saw Highclere's colt foal by Diesis, who impressed all the Royal party with his exceptional good qualities and looks, as well as exciting the admiration of professionals in Lexington. In May 1986 the Queen was the guest of Alec Head and his wife at the Haras de Quesnay; she was thus able to go round the major studs in France for a second time.

Since 1984 the Queen has always had two mares at Lane's End and three at Mill Ridge. The assistance that Her Majesty, Lord Porchester (now, since 1987, Lord Carnarvon) and Michael Oswald have received from both Alice Chandler and Will Farish Jr in all matters pertaining to the mares and foals at these two stud farms can never be overemphasized. Among the mares that have spent one or more covering seasons in Kentucky are Highclere, Dunfermline, Christchurch, Reflection, Beacon Hill and Expansive.

The best foal bred by the Queen in 1980 was Special Leave (Mill Reef–Light Duty). He was exceptionally lucky to be born at all, as Light Duty underwent major surgery for an ulcer in the guttural pouch when she was carrying him: at one point in the operation

Light Duty was considered clinically dead, and those operating were certain the unborn foal would not survive. Special Leave won the Hyperion Stakes at Ascot so impressively that his trainer, Ian Balding, considered he would definitely become a Derby prospect in 1983. He was totally unsuited by the bog-like ground when unplaced in the Guardian Classic Trial at Sandown; indeed, the going was so bad that racing should probably not have taken place. He was being prepared to run in the Derby when he tragically broke a leg in a gallop in May 1983 and had to be put down. Another 1980 foal worthy of mention is Insular (Moulton–Pas de Deux), who won nine races for the Queen and the Imperial Cup Hurdle at Sandown when leased for the winter to the Queen Mother in 1986. In May 1988 the Queen gave him to her trainer, Ian Balding. A few weeks later, ridden by the Princess Royal, Insular won the Queen Mother Cup at York. Castle Rising (Blakeney–Christchurch), who was also foaled in 1980, might have developed into a fine stayer had he not suffered from bad legs. None the less, he was second in the Geoffrey Freer Stakes, third in the Queen's Vase and fourth in the Grand Prix de Paris in 1983. He was bought by the present President of the Turkish Jockey Club, Ozdemir Atman, and stands at his private stud near Izmit on mainland Turkey, about 110 kilometres from Istanbul. Stallions in Turkey cover sometimes as few as ten mares a season; nevertheless Castle Rising's 1987 crop includes the best two-year-old filly in Turkey, who is favourite for the 1990 Turkish 1,000 Guineas.

Elusive (Little Current–Tartan Pimpernel) was the pick of the 1981 crop of foals bred at the Royal Studs. She won the Acomb Stakes at York so well that she was considered a possible Oaks prospect; however, she had problems as a three-year-old, finished unplaced on her sole run that season and was retired to the paddocks at Sandringham.

It was again a filly, Soprano (Kris–Contralto), who was the best of the foals bred by the Queen in 1982. Third in the Virginia Water Stakes at Ascot, her sole outing at two, Soprano developed into a fine miler in 1985. She won the Sefton Stakes at Chester and then the competitive International Stakes at Kempton in the spring. She put up two fine performances when third to the American-bred Al Bahathri and Top Socialite in the Coronation Stakes at Royal Ascot and when second to Ever Genial in the Hungerford Stakes at Newbury. She also won the BBA Atlanta Stakes over a mile at Sandown, was second in the Oak Tree Stakes at Newbury and third in the Kiveton Park Stakes at Doncaster. She then retired to the Sandringham Stud, and is considered one of the best young broodmares in the Queen's possession. Her second foal, Hiawatha's Song by Dancing Brave, is a two-year-old in 1990, and it will be interesting to see how he performs. Her first foal, a filly by Rainbow Quest, will make her debut as a three-year-old this season. Soprano's grandam, Lyrical (Gratitude–Sweet Sonnet) had been bought for the Royal Stud by Michael Oswald in 1971 from Charles Engelhard. She had been bred by the Hon. Mrs George Lambton in 1966 and traced back to that excellent broodmare, Trustful by Bachelor's Double. This is a totally new family for the Royal Stud with a lot more speed in it than some of the more established ones at Sandringham.

Laughter (Shirley Heights–Light Duty) was the pick of the 1983 foals bred at the Royal Studs. She was a good winner of the Houghton Stakes at Newmarket in the autumn of 1985, and high hopes were held of her for the following year's Oaks. She only managed second place in the Lingfield Oaks Trial Stakes, a race that has diminished in status in the last few years, and so was sold to the United States, where she won one more race before being retired as a broodmare.

Yet another filly, Nettle (Kris–Sans Blague), was the best produce of the Royal Stud in 1984. She won two races as a two-year-old in 1986, including the Rochford Thompson Stakes at Newbury; she was also fourth to Invited Guest in the Waterford Candelabra Stakes at Goodwood. Unfortunately she did not train on as a three-year-old and was retired to stud at Sandringham.

The most promising foal of the 1985 crop bred by the Queen was Unknown Quantity (Young Generation–Pas de Deux), who was trained by William Hastings-Bass. He won his only outing as a two-year-old very easily and might have developed into a very useful three-year-old, had he not been struck by a car on his way to the gallops in the spring of 1988. He never fully recovered from this accident in 1988 and his form as a three-year-old was well below his true ability. In the early summer of 1989 he took two very competitive handicaps, first at Lingfield and secondly the Royal Hong Kong Jockey Club Stakes at Sandown on 7 July, when he won in workmanlike fashion from Gulf Pearl and Main Objective. William Hastings-Bass then made the very bold move of sending him to Arlington Park in Chicago to run in the $100,000 Arlington Handicap, a Grade One race. Only the most optimistic expected Unknown Quantity to trouble his main opponents, the

1988 Breeder's Cup winner Great Communicator and Blushing John, who had won the 1988 Poule d'Essai des Poulains before his export to the United States, where he had won several high-class Stakes races. Unknown Quantity started the outsider of the five runners at 10–1, ridden by the Panamanian-born jockey Jorge Velasquez.

The Queen had once before had a runner in the USA, when Landau ran last to Fisherman in the 1954 Washington International Stakes; he had developed a heel infection after his arrival in America. She had never sent one of the horses she had bred herself to run across the Atlantic Ocean, however.

At Arlington Park at the end of August 1989 Her Majesty was represented by Lord Carnarvon. Great Communicator and Blushing John disputed the lead till the final turn into the straight with Unknown Quantity close on their heels on the outside. Blushing John began to fade coming round the bend, and Unknown Quantity moved up to challenge. As the field swung into the straight, Unknown Quantity took the lead and drew two lengths clear of Great Communicator. Frosty the Snowman came to challenge a furlong out, but Unknown Quantity lengthened his stride and won comfortably by three lengths. Jorge Velasquez said after the race that it was 'the greatest day in his racing life'. Although Unknown Quantity was unplaced a fortnight later at Arlington Park, probably suffering from acclimatization problems, he had achieved the first victory for the Queen on American soil against all expectations.

In December 1986 the Queen, on the advice of Lord Porchester, bought the four-year-old sprinter Storm Warning (Tumble Wind–Maggie Mine by Native Prince) as a broodmare in order to inject more speed into the Royal stock. Storm Warning had won four races over five furlongs between 1984 and 1986, including the Group Three Premio Omenoni at San Siro in Italy and the Listed Scarborough Stakes at Doncaster. She had also been third in the 1984 Flying Childers Stakes at Doncaster, third to Never So Bold in the 1985 William Hill Sprint Championship at York, and only beaten a head and a neck by Last Tycoon and Batave in the Prix de Saint-Georges at Longchamp in 1986. Her first foal, a chestnut colt named Mighty Wind by Kris, is a two-year-old in 1990.

The 1986 and 1987 foals bred at Sandringham have yet to produce a Group or Listed winner. Starlet (Teenoso–Pas de Deux), who was unbeaten in two outings as a juvenile in 1988, only ran twice in 1989 as she needed give in the ground. Her promising run in the Manchester November Handicap in the autumn may be a pointer to a Listed race success in 1990. Starlet was the Queen's first runner in 1990; she was also her first horse to take part in a race at Cagnes-sur-Mer in the South of France. Starlet won the mile-and-a-half Prix de Bastia by three lengths on 17 February 1990, and her trainer, William Hastings-Bass, who had saddled twenty-three winners at Cagnes-sur-Mer since 1979, may run her in the Grand Prix du Conseil des Alpes-Maritimes, a Listed race on the same course, on 11 March. Marienski (Nureyev–Highclere), who won his maiden race at Newmarket in the summer, but was found to be coughing after fading into fifth place behind Digression in the Royal Lodge Stakes at Ascot, looks the best prospect of the Queen's three-year-olds in 1990. The 1988 crop of foals, who are in training with Ian Balding and William Hastings-Bass in 1990, is composed of fourteen colts and five fillies, the reverse of the normal ratio during the 1980s. Statistically there must be a greater chance of a potential Derby winner emerging from this crop.

It is to be hoped that the policy of mating the Queen's mares with stallions in Kentucky will revive the fortunes of the Royal Studs to the levels of the 1950s and 1970s. In retrospect, however, there is no question that during the time the Queen has been on the throne, the Royal Studs have enjoyed greater success than at any time since the turn of the century. If that success is to be increased, or even maintained, in the next two decades, much is going to depend on the stallions that must eventually replace Bustino and Shirley Heights. Should the Queen own and breed a Derby winner in the next decade, she will not only fulfil a lifetime ambition, but possibly ensure the success of the Royal Studs for the next quarter of a century.

Notes

The initials R.A. stand for Royal Archives and designate the official and private papers, correspondence and diaries kept in the Round Tower at Windsor Castle. The initials immediately following these (MOH, Z, LB G etc) indicate the series under which the documents have been classified. The figures that follow indicate the number of the file itself and, where needed, the actual number of the document in that file.

Chapter Two: *The Duke of Cumberland's Stud, Windsor Great Park.*
1. R.A., CP Box 70/124.
2. R.A., CP Box 70/132.

Chapter Three: *The Royal Studs of Henry Frederick, Duke of Cumberland, and the Prince of Wales, 1766 to 1799.*
1. R.A., 44022. Quoted Seth-Smith, *Bred for the Purple*, Leslie Frewin, 1969.

Chapter Five: *The Royal Studs of the Prince Regent and King George IV from 1800 to 1830.*
1. R.A., 40449; qu. Seth-Smith, *ibid.*
2. R.A., 25639/131; qu. Seth-Smith, *ibid.*

Chapter Seven: *Dispersal of the Royal Stud at Hampton Court and Interregnum, 1837 to 1850.*
1. R.A., M.P. Box 37/59–61.
2. R.A., MOH LB G 156.

Chapter Eight: *The Royal Stud re-established by Queen Victoria.*
1. R.A., MOH LB H 170.

Chapter Nine: *The Royal Stud at Hampton Court 1868 to 1894.*
1. R.A., MOH LB I 369.
2. R.A., MOH LB I 372.
3. R.A., Z 201 39.
4. R.A., MOH LB K 231.
5. R.A., MOH LB K 232.
6. R.A., MOH LB K 186, 187.
7. R.A., MOH LB K 200.

8. R.A., MOH LB K 219.
9. R.A., MOH 14 162.
10. R.A., MOH 14 163.
11. R.A., MOH 14 163.
12. R.A., Add. A 34/50.
13. R.A., MOH LB L 85.
14. R.A., Z 199/98.
15. R.A., Z 199 Letter 98.

Chapter Ten: *The Foundation of the Royal Stud at Sandringham.*
1. R.A., Queen Victoria's Diary, qu. Magnus, Philip, *King Edward VII*, John Murray, 1964.
2. Lincolnshire Papers; qu. Magnus, Philip, ibid.
3. R.A., George V, AA 15/54; qu. Seth-Smith, Michael, ibid.
4. Quoted, Marchioness of Londonderry, *Henry Chaplin*, Macmillan and Co., 1926, p. 325.
5. Qu. Marchioness of Londonderry, *ibid*, p. 325.

Chapter Eleven: *The Royal Stud at Sandringham 1892 to 1910.*
1. Letter from Lord Marcus Beresford to Richard Marsh, June 24 1896.
2. Qu. Marchioness of Londonderry, *ibid*.

Chapter Twelve: *George V, 1910 to 1936.*
1. R.A., Confidential Register, G.V., O.2570; qu. Nicolson, *Harold*, Constable and Co. Ltd, 1952.
2. R.A., G.V. AA 67/11; qu. Seth-Smith, Michael, *ibid*.
3. R.A., G.V. AA 67/12; qu. Seth-Smith, Michael, *ibid*.
4. R.A., G.V. AA 67/21; qu. Seth-Smith, Michael, *ibid*.
5. R.A., G.V. AA 67/17; qu. Seth-Smith, Michael, *ibid*.

Appendix

PRINCIPAL WINNERS BRED BY THE ROYAL STUDS SINCE 1753.

Abbreviations: F. – filly; C. – colt; B. – bay; Ch. – chestnut; Bl. – black; Br. – brown; Gr. – grey

NOTE: Horses marked with an asterisk before 1850 were probably bred by the Royal Studs but their breeder cannot be conclusively proved owing to inexact records in the first volumes of the General Stud Book.

Year foaled and name	Breeding	Races won
1753	1 winner of 1 race.	
Muley	B. C. Muley Ishmael – Young Ebony by Crab	1
1755	3 winners of 8 races.	
Dapper	Br. C. Cade – Cypron 1750 by Blaze	5
1756	2 winners of 18 races.	
Dorimond	B.C. Dormous – Mare by Whitefoot	13
Dumplin	B.C. Cade – Cypron 1750 by Blaze	5
1758	1 winner of 6 races.	
King Herod	B.C. Tartar – Cypron 1750 by Blaze 1733	6
Eight times Champion Sire.		
1760	3 winners of 27 races.	
Milksop	Bl.C. Crab – Miss Cranbourne 1753 by Godolphin	18
Selim	B.C. Bajazet – Miss Thigh 1750 by Rib	9
1761	2 winners of 2 races.	
1764	2 winners of 28 races.	
Eclipse	Ch.C. Marske – Spiletta 1749 by Regulus 1739 out of Mother Western by Son of Snake	18
Unbeaten. Great Sire.		
Verjuice (aft. Champaigne) B.C. Crab – Regulus Mare 1757		10
Salisbury Silver Bowl.		
1765	2 winners of 15 races.	
Marplot (aft. Hollyhock) B.C. Young Cade – Cypron 1750 by Blaze		12
York Subscription Purse, twice.		
1767	1 winner of 1 race.	
1768	1 winner of 1 race.	
1769	1 winner of 5 races.	
Nancy	B.F. Herod – Young Snip Mare 1762	5

Year foaled and name	Breeding	Races won
1770	1 winner of 3 races.	
1771	1 winner of 5 races.	
Captain Bobadil	Br.C. Posthumus – Whitenose mare	5
1772	3 winners of 13 races.	
Caesar	Ch.C. Marske –Young Cade mare 1762	7
1773	1 winner of 2 races.	
1774	3 winners of 24 races.	
Little Isaac	Ch.C. Sulphur – Caroline 1762 by Snap	10
Pompey	Br.C. Marske – Young Cade mare 1762	10
1775	1 winner of 4 races.	
1776	1 winner of 6 races.	
Crassus	B.C. Eclipse – Young Cade Mare 1762	6
1777	1 winner of 1 race.	
1778	2 winners of 6 races.	
Dido	Ch.F. Eclipse – Miss Rose 1766 by Spectator	5

Second in the Oaks; her full sister, Anna 1782, was dam of the 1799 Oaks winner, Bellina.

Year foaled and name	Breeding	Races won
1780	3 winners of 22 races.	
Chance	B.C. Javelin – Faggergill mare out of mare by Northumberland Golden Arabian	16
Trinidado	B.C. Herod – Blank mare out of mare 1745 by Oroonoko	5
1781	1 winner of 3 races.	
Hardwicke	Br.C. Ancient Pistol – Herod mare out of mare by Bajazet	3
1782	1 winner of 1 race.	
Miss Kitty	B.F. Highflyer – Squirrel mare 1768	—

Third, Oaks Stakes.

Year foaled and name	Breeding	Races won
***Figaro**	B.C. Florizel – Sultana 1765 by Young Cade	1
1783	3 winners of 18 races.	
Mufti	B.C. FitzHerod – Infant mare 1760	14

Craven Stakes, Newmarket, twice.

Year foaled and name	Breeding	Races won
Braganza	Br.C. Justice – Firetail 1772 by Eclipse	1

Fourth, Derby Stakes.

Year foaled and name	Breeding	Races won
1784	4 winners of 29 races.	
Nina	Ch.F. Eclipse – Pomona 1775 by Herod	8
Augusta	Ch.F. Eclipse – Herod mare – Bajazet Mare	—

Second, Oaks Stakes.

Year foaled and name	Breeding	Races won
***Annette**	B.F. Eclipse – Virago 1760 by Snap	5

Oaks Stakes.

Year foaled and name	Breeding	Races won
***Pegasus**	Ch.C. Eclipse – Bosphorus mare	12

Macaroni Stakes, Newmarket.

Year foaled and name	Breeding	Races won
1785	7 winners of 27 races.	
Escape	B.C. Highflyer – Squirrel mare 1768 – mare by Babraham	10
Conflans	Ch.C. Woodpecker – Spectator mare	6

Conflans Stakes, Brighton.

Year foaled and name	Breeding	Races won
Canto Baboo	B.C. Eclipse – Nosegay 1767 by Snap	6
1786	6 winners of 14 races.	
Soujah ul Dowlah	Ch.C. Eclipse – Duchess 1776	—

Fourth, Derby Stakes.

Year foaled and name	Breeding	Races won
Spear	Ch.C. Javelin – Pomona 1775 by Herod	6

Year foaled and name	Breeding	Races won
1787	5 winners of 22 races.	
Chambooe	B.C. Mambrino – Tabitha 1769 by Blank	3
Fourth, Derby Stakes.		
Louisa	B.F. Ancient Pistol – Calash 1775 by Herod	6
*Smoaker	Gr.C. Pilot – Heron 1779 by Herod	9
Conflans Stakes, Brighton.		
1788	2 winners of 8 races.	
St David	Ch.C. Saltram – Herod-mare Bajazet-mare	2
Fourth, Derby Stakes.		
Amelia	B.F. Highflyer – Miss Timms 1767 by Matchem	6
1789	11 winners of 34 races.	
Whiskey	B.C. Saltram – Calash 1775 by Herod	10
Jockey Stakes, 1,400gns Subscription, Newmarket. Leading Sire.		
St George	Gr.C. Anvil – Prophet mare 1777	5
Bolton Stakes, Newmarket.		
1790	4 winners of 23 races.	
Cymbeline	B.C. Anvil – Mrs Siddons 1782 by Garrick	13
July Stakes; Orleans Stakes and Prince's Stakes, Brighton.		
*Mother Bunch	B.F. Mercury – Highflyer mare 1781 – Miranda	7
1791	2 winners of 10 races.	
Eliza	B.F. Highflyer – Augusta 1784 by Eclipse	9
Second, Oaks Stakes.		
1797	1 winner of 1 race.	
1800	1 winner of 6 races.	
Albion	B.C. John Bull – Trumpetta 1789 by Trumpator	6
Pavilion Stakes, Brighton.		
1801	1 winner of 2 races.	
*Lynceus	B.C. Buzzard – Rose 1780 by Sweetbriar	2
1802	6 winners of 23 races.	
Selim	Ch.C. Buzzard – Alexander mare – Highflyer mare	6
Craven Stakes.		
*Barbarossa	B.C. Sir Peter – Mule Spinner 1788	11
Somerset Stakes, Egremont Stakes, Brighton.		
1803	5 winners of 7 races.	
Rosabella	B.F. Whiskey – Diomed mare 1793 out of Harriet by Matchem	2
Third in the Oaks. Dam of 1,000 Guineas winner, Rhoda 1813, by Asparagus.		
1804	7 winners of 21 races.	
Coriolanus	B.C. Gohanna – Skysweeper	1
Pavilion Stakes, Brighton. Third, Derby Stakes.		
Nymphina	B.F. Gouty – Mademoiselle 1789 by Diomed	10
1805	7 winners of 29 races.	
Rubens	Ch.C. Buzzard – Alexander mare – Mare by Highflyer	7
Pavilion Stakes, Brighton; Craven Stakes, Newmarket. Fourth, Derby Stakes. Leading Sire and Broodmare Sire.		
Tumbler	B.C. Trumpator – Walnut mare 1800 out of Mare by Javelin	16
Second in the Ascot Gold Cup. Sent to India.		

Year foaled and name	*Breeding*	*Races won*
Marybella	C.F. Walnut – Maria 1783 by Telemachus	1
	Woodcote Stakes.	
Oberea	Bl.F. Sorcerer – Deceit 1784 by Tandem	1
	Fourth in the Oaks. Sent to Germany in 1816.	
1806	5 winners of 10 races.	
Britannia	Ch.F. Gouty – Lady Mayoress 1796 by Precipitate	3
	Claret Stakes, third in the Ascot Gold Cup.	
1807	4 winners of 10 races.	
Breslaw	Ch.C. Sorcerer – Maria 1783 by Telemachus	4
	Swinley Stakes, Ascot.	
Sagana	B.F. Sorcerer – Woodpecker mare 1798	3
	Swinley Stakes, Ascot; Magna Charta Stakes, Egham.	
Miss Wasp	Br.F. Waxy – Trumpetta 1789 by Trumpator	1
	Dam of 2,000 Guineas winner, Manfred 1814 by Election, and of the St Leger winner, Vespa 1830 by Muley.	
1808	1 winner of 11 races.	
Merry-Go-Round	B.C. Trumpator – Highflyer mare out of Catherine by Young Marske	11
	Pavilion Stakes, Brighton; Port Stakes, Newmarket.	
1809	4 winners of 28 races.	
Pointers	Br.C. Giles – Woodpecker mare 1798 out of Gohanna's dam by Herod	14
	Newmarket Stakes, Wokingham Stakes.	
Venture	B.C. Haphazard – Woodpecker mare 1799 out of Trentham Mare	8
	Gold Cups, Egham and Stockbridge; Oatlands Stakes, Newmarket, twice.	
1810	4 winners of 22 races.	
Aladdin	Ch.C. Giles – Walnut mare 1800 out of mare by Javelin.	15
	Ascot Gold Cup, Wokingham Stakes; second Ascot Gold Cup.	
Miss Whipthong	B.F. Giles – Buzzard mare out of mare by Alexander	3
	2nd Ascot Gold Cup.	
1811	4 winners of 6 races.	
1812	3 winners of 28 races.	
Castanet	B.C. Granicus – Gohanna mare 1807 out of Grey Skim 1793 by Woodpecker	12
	Second 2,000 Guineas. Raced in Ireland in 1817/18. Sent to Russia.	
Scrapall	Ch.C. Granicus – Young Whiskey mare 1808 out of mare by Walnut	10
	Swinley Stakes, Ascot, twice; Oatlands Stakes, Newmarket. Sold to Mr Burgsdorf and sent to Prussia.	
1813	6 winners of 18 races.	
Prince Leopold	B.C. Hedley – Gramarie 1807 by Sorcerer	3
	Derby Stakes, Port Stakes, Newmarket. Died in 1817 after castration.	
Belvoirina	B.F. Stamford – Mercury mare 1790	5
	July Stakes.	
1814	10 winners of 48 races.	
Manfred	B.C. Election – Miss Wasp 1807 by Waxy	8
	2,000 Guineas.	
Vignette	Br.F. Rubens – Sagana 1807 by Sorcerer	3
	Wokingham Stakes twice.	

Year foaled and name	Breeding	Races won
Amabel	B.F. Election – Yong Whiskey mare 1808 out of Walnut mare 1800	7
Second in the Oaks. Sent to India.		
Canvas	Br.F. Rubens – Gohanna mare 1803	10
Leah	Ch.F. Election – Oberea 1805 by Sorcerer	8
Unnamed Filly	B.F. Election – Alexander mare out of mare by Highflyer	1
Third in the Oaks.		
*Gazelle	Br.C. Sorcerer – Jerboa 1803 by Gohanna	7
Newmarket Stakes, Port Stakes, second Ascot Gold Cup, twice. Sent to India.		
1815	5 winners of 8 races.	
Roger Bacon	Ch.C. Sorcerer – Gohanna mare 1807 out of Grey Skim 1793 by Woodpecker	1
Newmarket Stakes. Sent to India in 1821.		
Jereymy Gradus	B.C. Eaton – Buzzard mare out of mare by Alexander	1
Woodcote Stakes.		
1816	6 winners of 41 races.	
Banker	B.C. Smolensko – Quail 1805 by Gohanna	18
Ascot Gold Cup, Claret Stakes, Oatlands Stakes, Newmarket, twice, Swinley Stakes, Ascot; second, Ascot Gold Cup.		
Funny	Ch.F. Seymour or Granicus – Young Whiskey mare 1808 out of Duchess	3
Woodcote Stakes.		
Soota	Bl.C. Election or Seymour – Young Whiskey mare 1808 out of Walnut mare 1800	5
Magna Charta Stakes, Egham.		
Regent	Ch.C. Election – Stamford mare 1805 out of Miss Judy by Alfred	13
Won 10 of his races in Ireland.		
Bella Donna	B.F. Seymour – Gramarie 1807 by Sorcerer	1
	Ch.C. Haphazard – Quiz mare 1808 out of Alexander mare	1
1817	3 winners of 15 races.	
Plumper	Ch.C. Election – Stamford mare 1805 out of Miss Judy by Alfred	8
1818	4 winners of 11 races.	
Gustavus	Gr.C. Election – Lady Grey 1806 by Stamford	7
Derby, Newmarket Stakes, July Stakes. Sent to Prussia March 1836.		
1819	3 winners of 16 races.	
Moses	B.C. Whalebone or Seymour – Gohanna mare 1807 out of Grey Skim 1793 by Woodpecker	5
Derby Stakes.		
Electress	Ch.F. Election – Stamford mare 1805 out of Miss Judy by Alfred	7
Windsor Forest Stakes, Ascot; Oatlands Stakes, Newmarket.		
1820	2 winners of 11 races.	
Premium	Ch.C. Aladdin – Gohanna mare 1807	7
Jane Shore	B.F. Woful – Bella Donna 1816 by Seymour	4
Dam of Derby winner Amato.		

Year foaled and name	Breeding	Races won
1821	6 winners of 28 races.	
Don Carlos	B.C. Election – Miss Wasp 1807 by Waxy	11
	Prendergast Stakes, Newmarket. Exported to India.	
Orion	B.C. Phantom – Hedley mare 1817 out of Gramarie 1807 by Sorcerer	10
	Wokingham Stakes.	
1822	5 winners of 19 races.	
Frogmore	B.C. Phantom – Rubens mare 1814 out of Sir Peter mare	4
	Albany Stakes, Ascot.	
1823	5 winners of 23 races.	
Rachel	B.F. Whalebone – Gohanna mare 1807 out of Grey Skim 1793 by Woodpecker	11
Elizabeth	Ch.F. Rainbow – Belvoirina 1813 by Stamford	6
1824	5 winners of 34 races.	
Maria	B.F. Whalebone – Belvoirina 1813 by Stamford	13
	Windsor Forest Stakes, Swinley Stakes, Ascot; Prendergast Stakes, Newmarket.	
Dandelion	B.C. Merlin – Duchess of York 1817 by Waxy	12
1825	1 winner of 1 race.	
1826	3 winners of 11 races.	
Pauline	B.F. Moses – Quadrille 1815 by Selim	6
	Grand Duke Michael Stakes, Newmarket. Third, 1,000 Guineas.	
1827	4 winners of 18 races.	
Young Orion	B.C. Master Henry – Hedley mare 1817 out of Gramarie 1807 by Sorcerer	1
	Royal Stakes, Ascot.	
Mazeppa	Ch.C. Godolphin – Rubens mare 1814 out of mare by Sir Peter	14
1828	3 winners of 13 races.	
Walter	Br.C. Whalebone – Electress 1819 by Election	10
1829	4 winners of 15 races.	
Posthumus	Br.C. Woful – Posthuma 1819 by Orville	2
	Second in the 2,000 Guineas.	
Landgravine	Br.F. Waterloo or Smolensko – Electress 1819 by Election	3
	Lavant Stakes, Goodwood.	
Corset	Br.F. Whalebone – Sultana 1820 by Selim	9
1830	2 winners of 10 races.	
Shylock	B.C. Waterloo – Gohanna mare 1807 out of Grey Skim 1793 by Woodpecker.	8
	Wokingham Stakes.	
1831	6 winners of 20 races.	
Intriguer	B.C. Reveller – Scandal 1822 by Selim	9
	Magna Charta Stakes, Egham.	
1832	6 winners of 11 races.	
1833	8 winners of 24 races.	
Post Haste	Ch.F. The Colonel – Posthuma 1819 by Orville	7
New Light	B.C. Lamplighter – Elfrida 1827 by Whalebone	6
1834	6 winners of 42 races.	
Caravan	Br.C. Camel – Wings 1822 by The Flyer	19
	Ascot Gold Cup. Second, Derby Stakes. Third, Ascot Gold Cup.	

Year foaled and name	Breeding	Races won
Rat-Trap	Br.C. Bizarre – Young Mouse 1826 by Godolphin	9
	Newmarket Stakes, Port Stakes, Newmarket. Third, St Leger Stakes.	
Benedict	B.C. Peter Lely – Phantasima 1821 by Partisan	3
	Magna Charta Stakes, Egham.	
1835	6 winners of 17 races.	
1836	6 winners of 23 races.	
The Corsair	Br.C. Sir Hercules – Gulnare 1824 by Smolensko	5
	2,000 Guineas.	
Camelino	B.C. Camel – Maria 1824 by Waterloo	8
	Prendergast Stakes, Newmarket.	
Reel	B.F. Camel – La Danseuse 1825 by Blacklock	5
	Clearwell Stakes, Newmarket.	
Prism	Br.F. Camel – Elizabeth 1823 by Rainbow	1
	Dam of Oaks winner Refraction 1842 by Glaucus.	
1837	10 winners of 40 races.	
Monops	Ch.C. Actaeon – Wings 1822 by The Flyer	5
	Wokingham Stakes	
Iris	Ch.F. Cain – Elizabeth 1823 by Rainbow	2
	Woodcote Stakes.	
Spangle	B.F. Croesus – Variella 1829 by Blacklock	2
	Coronation Stakes, Ascot. Third 1,000 Guineas.	
Pocahontas	B.F. Glencoe – Marpessa 1830 by Muley	–
	Dam of Champion Sires Stockwell and King Tom	
Remnant	Ch.F. Cain – Burden 1832 by Camel	9
1851	3 winners of 13 races.	
Spinaway	B.C. Orlando – Distaffina 1845 by Don John	5
	Chesterfield Stakes, Newmarket.	
1852	4 winners of 20 races.	
Redemption	B.F. Orlando – Stamp 1842 by Emilius	17
	Ascot Stakes.	
Cimicina	B.F. Phlegon – The Flea 1846 by Coronation	10
1853	8 winners of 39 races.	
Yellow Jack	Ch.C. Birdcatcher – Jamaica 1841 by Liverpool	1
	Second: Derby Stakes, St Leger, 2,000 Guineas.	
Flyaway	B.F. Orlando – Flight 1846 by Jereed	10
	Chesterfield Stakes, Newmarket.	
Spindle	B.F. Orlando – Distaffina 1845 by Don John	3
	July Stakes.	
Queen's Head	B. F. Bay Middleton – Stamp 1842 by Emilius	2
	Third, 1,000 Guineas.	
Furioso	B.C. Orlando – mare 1837 by Mulatto	14
1854	8 winners of 32 races.	
Imperieuse	B.F. Orlando – Eulogy 1843 by Euclid	6
	1,000 Guineas, St Leger, Lavant Stakes. Dam of Deliane, Prix de Diane 1865.	
Claude Lorraine	Ch.C. Orlando – Sir Hercules mare 1839 out of Electress	2
	Ascot Stakes.	
Spinet	B.F. Orlando – Distaffina 1845 by Don Juan	13
1855	10 winners of 39 races.	
FitzRoland	Ch.C. Orlando – Stamp 1842 by Emilius	3
	2,000 Guineas, St James's Palace Stakes.	

Year foaled and name	Breeding	Races won
Gin	B.C. Orlando – Sir Hercules mare 1839 out of Electress	5
July Stakes.		
Eurydice	B.F. Orlando – Eulogy 1843 by Euclid	3
Cambridgeshire Stakes.		
My Niece	B.F. Cowl – Vanity 1844 by Camel	8
1856	8 winners of 33 races.	
Trumpeter	Ch.C. Orlando – Cavatina 1845 by Redshank	2
Third, Derby Stakes. Sire.		
Old Post	B.C. Bay Middleton – Stamp 1842 by Emilius	14
1857	8 winners of 16 races.	
1858	10 winners of 74 races.	
Diophantus	Ch.C. Orlando – Equation 1839 by Emilius	6
2,000 Guineas, Molecomb Stakes; third, Derby Stakes.		
Walloon	Br.C. The Flying Dutchman – Nina 1846 by Cotherstone	15
Champagne Stakes, St James's Palace Stakes, Wokingham Stakes.		
Imaus	Ch.C. Newminster – Himalaya 1851 by Bay Middleton	6
Newmarket St Leger; fourth, 2,000 Guineas.		
Little Lady	B.F. Orlando – Volley 1845 by Voltaire	16
Dam of 2,000 Guineas winner Camballo. Volley sister to Voltigeur.		
Sherwood	B.C. Barnton – The Arrow 1850 by Slane	11
1859	8 winners of 44 races.	
Imperatrice	B.F. Orlando – Eulogy 1843 by Euclid	4
Park Hill Stakes. Second, Oaks Stakes; third, Yorkshire Oaks.		
Disappointment	B.C. The Flying Dutchman – Distaffina 1845 by Don Juan	10
The Knave	B.C. Orlando – Trickstress 1848 by Sleight of Hand	10
1860	8 winners of 38 races.	
Reviver	B.C. The Cure – mare 1855 by Orlando	9
Neilgherry	B.F. The Cure – Nina 1846 by Cotherstone	8
1861	14 winners of 57 races.	
Cambuscan	Ch.C. Newminster – The Arrow 1850 by Slane	9
July Stakes. Third, St Leger; second, Goodwood Cup.		
Lord Zetland	Br.C. Voltigeur – Lady Gough 1850 by Launcelot	–
Third, Ascot Gold Cup.		
Attraction	B.F. Orlando – Nun Appleton 1845 by Bay Middleton	16
1862	11 winners of 64 races.	
Chattanooga	Ch.C. Orlando – Ayacanora 1854 by Birdcatcher out of Pocahontas 1837 by Glencoe	1
Criterion Stakes.		
The Duke	B.C. Stockwell – Bay Celia 1851 by Orlando	18
Goodwood Cup. Fourth, St Leger, Cambridgeshire Stakes.		
Archimedes	Ch.C. Newminster – Equation 1839 by Emilius	6
Second, 2,000 Guineas; third, St Leger.		
Trapeze	B. or Br.F. Voltigeur – Trickstress 1848 by Sleight of Hand	13
Sister Mary	Br.F. Ellington – Hersey 1842 by Glaucus	7
Princess Dagmar	Br. F. Windhound – Nina 1846 by Cotherstone	7
1863	12 winners of 55 races.	
Goojerat	Ch.C. Stockwell – Lady Gough 1850 by Launcelot	10
Castanet	B. F. Rataplan – Nina 1846 by Cotherstone	9

Year foaled and name	Breeding	Races won
1889	9 winners of 36 races.	
La Flèche	Br.F. St Simon – Quiver 1872 by Toxophilite 1,000 Guineas, Oaks, St Leger, Ascot Gold Cup, Molecomb Stakes, Nassau Stakes, Champagne Stakes, Newmarket Oaks, Cambridgeshire Stakes; second, Derby Stakes	16
Haymaker	B.C. Springfield – Lady Binks 1878 by Adventurer Dee Stakes, Chester.	3
County Council	Ch. C. Isonomy – Lady Peggy 1884 by Hermit Ham Produce Stakes, Goodwood.	1
1890	8 winners of 32 races.	
Best Man	B.C. Ormonde or Melton – Wedlock 1884 by Wenlock July Cup, Queen's Stand Plate, Ascot, Prix du Conseil Municipal, Longchamp.	18
Miss Mildred	B. F. Melton – Merino 1874 by Young Melbourne Dam of 1897 Oaks winner La Roche by St Simon.	1
1891	6 winners of 19 races.	
Florizel II	B.C. St Simon – Perdita II 1881 by Hampton St James's Palace Stakes, Gold Vase, Goodwood Cup, Jockey Club Cup.	11
1892	4 winners of 15 races.	
1893	11 winners of 47 races.	
Persimmon	B.C. St Simon – Perdita II 1881 by Hampton Derby, St Leger, Ascot Gold Cup, Eclipse Stakes, Coventry Stakes, Richmond Stakes, Jockey Club Stakes	7
Thais	Br.F. St Serf – Poetry 1881 by Petrarch One Thousand Guineas	2
Amphora	Ch.F. Amphion – Sierra 1889 by Springfield Gimcrack Stakes, Stewards Cup, Goodwood.	8
1894	5 winners of 6 races.	
Oakdene	B.C. Donovan – Poetry 1881 by Petrarch Criterion Stakes, Newmarket.	2
1895	3 winners of 7 races.	
Mousme	Br.F. St Simon – Fanchette 1880 by Speculum July Stakes.	2
Dunlop	B.C. Ayrshire – Fortuna 1880 by Scottish Chief Third in the Derby	3
1896	1 winner of 3 races.	
Eventail	Ch.F. Ayrshire – Fanchette 1880 by Speculum Acorn Stakes, Epsom, Prince of Wales's Stakes, Goodwood.	3
1897	3 winners of 8 races.	
Diamond Jubilee	B.C. St Simon – Perdita II 1881 by Hampton The Derby, 2,000 Guineas, St Leger, Newmarket Stakes, Eclipse Stakes. Sent to stud in 1902; exported to Argentina in 1906.	6
1898	2 winners of 4 races.	
Lauzun	B.C. St Simon – Merrie Lassie 1884 by Rotherhill St James's Palace Stakes.	1
Lord Quex	B.C. Sir Hugo – Leveret 1891 by Galopin Houghton Stakes.	3
1899	1 winner of 4 races.	
1900	1 winner of 6 races.	
Mead	Ch.C. Persimmon – Meadow Chat 1892 by Minting Richmond Stakes, Prince of Wales's Stakes, Jockey Club Cup. Sent to Chile.	6

Year foaled and name	Breeding	Races won
1901	3 winners of 6 races.	
Chatsworth	B.C. Persimmon – Meadow Chat 1892 by Minting	3
	Newmarket St Leger, Lowther Stakes, Newmarket.	
1902	3 winners of 4 races.	
1903	2 winners of 3 races.	
1904	5 winners of 10 races.	
1905	4 winners of 7 races.	
Pearl of the Loch	Ch.F. Persimmon – Loch Doon 1898 by Bread Knife	2
	July Stakes.	
Perrier	B.C. Persimmon – Amphora 1893 by Amphion	3
	Exported to Argentina. Successful Sire.	
1906	4 winners of 9 races.	
Princesse de Galles	Br. F. Galinule – Ecila 1899 by Persimmon	5
	New Ham Stakes, Goodwood, Coronation Stakes, second in the Oaks.	
1907	1 winner of 2 races.	
1908	7 winners of 21 races.	
1909	4 winners of 9 races.	
1910	2 winners of 2 races.	
1911	4 winners of 7 races.	
Sunny Lake	Ch.C. Sundridge – Pearl of the Loch 1905 by Persimmon	3
	Greenham Stakes. Sent to New Zealand.	
1912	4 winners of 13 races.	
Friar Marcus	Br. C. Cicero – Prim Nun 1906 by Persimmon Middle	
	Middle Park Stakes, Prince of Wales' Stakes, Goodwood.	
	Leading Broodmare Sire.	
1913	1 winner of 1 race.	
1914	1 winner of 1 race.	
1915	3 winners of 6 races.	
1916	3 winners of 7 races.	
1917	7 winners of 12 races.	
1918	3 winners of 13 races.	
1919	4 winners of 14 races.	
Weathervane	B.C. Lemberg – Vain Air 1907 by Ayrshire	2
	Greenham Stakes, Royal Hunt Cup. Sent to New Zealand in 1925.	
London Cry	B.C. Call o'the Wild – Vervaine 1912 by Louviers	5
	Goodwood Stakes, Prince Edward H'cap Manchester.	
1920	2 winners of 3 races.	
1921	4 winners of 8 races.	
1922	3 winners of 6 races.	
Runnymede	B.C. Hurry On – Saints' Mead 1906 by St Simon	3
	July Stakes, Dee Stakes. Sent to Sweden.	
1923	2 winners of 6 races.	
Aloysia	B.F. Lemberg – Vervaine 1912 by Louviers	2
	Queen Mary Stakes.	
1925	4 winners of 9 races.	
Scuttle	B.F. Captain Cuttle – Stained Glass 1917 by Tracery	5
	1,000 Guineas, Cheveley Park Stakes, second in the Oaks.	
1926	3 winners of 3 races.	
1929	3 winners of 14 races.	
Limelight	Br.C. Pharos – Vervaine 1912 by Louviers	8
	Hardwicke Stakes, Jersey Stakes.	

Year foaled and name	Breeding	Races won
1930	3 winners of 6 races.	
The Abbot	Ch.C. Abbots Trace – Polish Air 1923 by Lemberg	4
Sussex Stakes.		
1931	1 winner of 1 race.	
1932	5 winners of 13 races.	
1933	4 winners of 7 races.	
Fairey	B.C. Fairway – Polish Air 1923 by Lemberg	3
Waterford Stakes, Ascot, third in the Eclipse Stakes.		
1934	3 winners of 6 races.	
1935	2 winners of 3 races.	
1936	5 winners of 11 races.	
1937	3 winners of 6 races.	
Great Truth	B.F. Bahram – Frankly 1925 by Franklin	2
Dam of Summertime, 3 times Champion sire in New Zealand.		
Helios	B.C. Hyperion – Foxy Gal 1928 by Sir Gallahad III	–
Broke a leg. Leading Sire in Australia 1948–1949.		
1938	3 winners of 5 races.	
1939	1 winner of 8 races.	
Starling	Br.F. Noble Star – Feola 1933 by Friar Marcus	–
Leading broodmare in South America.		
1940	2 winners of 3 races.	
1941	3 winners of 8 races.	
Knight's Daughter	Br.F. Sir Cosmo – Feola 1933 by Friar Marcus	3
Dam of Round Table.		
Fair Glint	B.C. Hyperion – Maiden Fair 1933 by Hyperion	2
Second in the Dewhurst Stakes.		
1942	2 winners of 16 races.	
Rising Light	B.C. Hyperion – Bread Card 1931 by Manna	7
Newmarket St Leger, Jockey Club Stakes.		
Kingstone	B.C. King Salmon – Feola 1933 by Friar Marcus	9
Great Yorkshire Stakes; sire.		
1943	1 winner of 3 races.	
Hypericum	B.F. Hyperion – Feola 1933 by Friar Marcus	3
1,000 Guineas, Dewhurst Stakes.		
1944	3 winners of 3 races.	
1945	1 winner of 4 races.	
Angelola	B.F. Donatello II – Feola 1933 by Friar Marcus	4
Yorkshire Oaks, Lingfield Oaks Trial Stakes, Princess Royal Stakes.		
Dam of Aureole.		
1946	1 winner of 3 races.	
Avila	Ch.F. Hyperion – Ste. Thérèse 1930 by Santorb	3
Coronation Stakes.		
1947	4 winners of 6 races.	
Above Board	B.F. Straight Deal – Feola 1933 by Friar Marcus	2
Yorkshire Oaks, Cesarewitch Stakes.		
1948	5 winners of 20 races.	
1949	5 winners of 16 races.	
Choir Boy	B.C. Hyperion – Choral 1940 by Caerleon	3
Royal Hunt Cup.		
Battened Down	B.F. Ocean Swell – Open Warfare 1940 by Umidwar	9
British Columbia Derby.		

Year foaled and name	Breeding	Races won
Love Game	B.F. Big Game – Knight's Daughter 1941 by Sir Cosmo Kingsclere Stakes, Newbury.	1
Stream of Light	Ch.F. Borealis – Yeovil 1938 by Pharos Lancashire Oaks.	2
1950	1 winner of 7 races.	
Aureole	Ch.C. Hyperion – Angelola 1945 by Donatello II King George VI and Queen Elizabeth Stakes, Coronation Cup, Dee Stakes, Hardwicke Stakes, Lingfield Derby Trial Stakes, Cumberland Lodge Stakes. Second in the Derby, third in the St Leger. Champion Sire twice.	7
1951	5 winners of 9 races.	
Angel Bright	Ch.F. Hyperion – Angelola 1945 by Donatello II Lingfield Oaks Trial Stakes.	1
1952	6 winners of 11 races.	
Sierra Nevada	Ch.C. Djebel – Avila 1946 by Hyperion Blue Riband Stakes.	1
Alexander	B.C. Alycidon – Open Warfare 1940 by Umidwar Royal Hunt Cup, Duke of Edinburgh Stakes.	3
1953	8 winners of 14 races.	
Atlas	Ch.C. Djebel – Young Entry 1945 by Foxhunter Dee Stakes, Doncaster Cup.	3
High Veldt	Ch.C. Hyperion – Open Country 1946 by Fairway Houghton Stakes, second in the King George VI and the Queen Elizabeth Stakes. Leading Sire in South Africa.	4
1954	7 winners of 24 races.	
Almeria	Ch.F. Alycidon – Avila 1946 by Hyperion Yorkshire Oaks, Ribblesdale Stakes, Park Hill Stakes, Doncaster Cup, second in the King George VI and the Queen Elizabeth Stakes.	5
Doutelle	Ch.C. Prince Chevalier – Above Board 1947 by Straight Deal John Porter Stakes, Ormonde Stakes, third in the King George VI and the Queen Elizabeth Stakes. Successful Sire.	6
Agreement	Ch.C. Persian Gulf – Northern Hope 1948 by Borealis Doncaster Cup (twice), Chester Cup.	7
Mulberry Harbour	B.F. Sicambre – Open Warfare 1940 by Umidwar Cheshire Oaks.	3
1955	6 winners of 15 races.	
Pall Mall	Ch.C. Palestine – Malapert 1946 by Portlaw 2,000 Guineas, Lockinge Stakes, New Stakes. Successful Sire.	7
Miner's Lamp	Ch.C. Signal Light – Young Entry 1945 by Foxhunter Princess of Wales's Stakes, Blue Riband Trial Stakes.	2
Restoration	B.C. Persian Gulf – Hypericum 1943 by Hyperion King Edward VII Stakes.	1
1956	5 winners of 9 races.	
Above Suspicion	B.C. Court Martial – Above Board 1947 by Straight Deal St James's Palace Stakes, Gordon Stakes.	2
Blue Riband	Ch.F. Blue Peter – Stream of Light 1949 by Borealis Galtres Stakes, York.	3
1957	4 winners of 8 races.	
Optimistic	Br.F. Never Say Die – Northern Hope 1948 by Borealis Newbury Autumn Cup.	3

Year foaled and name	Breeding	Races won
1958	4 winners of 6 races.	
Impudent	Br. F. Owen Tudor – Saucy Lass 1948 by Atout Maitre	2
	Lingfield Oaks Trial Stakes.	
Highlight	B.F. Borealis – Hypericum 1943 by Hyperion	2
	Dam of Highclere.	
1959	3 winners of 5 races.	
1960	3 winners of 8 races.	
Apprentice	Ch.C. Aureole – Young Entry 1945 by Foxhunter	2
	Yorkshire Cup, Goodwood Cup.	
1961	8 winners of 12 races.	
Canisbay	Ch.C. Doutelle – Stroma 1955 by Luminary	2
	Eclipse Stakes. Leading Sire in Italy.	
Crest of the Wave	B.C. Crepello – Mulberry Harbour 1954 by Sicambre	1
	Leading Sire in New Zealand.	
1962	8 winners of 14 races.	
1963	8 winners of 16 races.	
Gaulois	B.C. Auriban – Gallega 1957 by Galcador	2
	Goodwood Cup.	
Castle Yard	B.C. St Paddy – Spanish Court 1953 by Court Martial	3
	Zetland Gold Cup.	
1964	8 winners of 10 races.	
1965	5 winners of 8 races.	
1966	3 winners of 11 races.	
Magna Carta	B.C. Charlottesville – Almeria 1954 by Alycidon	8
	Doncaster Cup, Ascot Stakes.	
1967	8 winners of 24 races.	
Charlton	B.C. Charlottesville – Ibrox 1956 by Big Game	5
	Henry II Stakes, William Hill Gold Trophy, Doncaster.	
Eucalyptus	B.C. Tamerlane – Eucumbene 1962 by Sica Boy	6
	Ballymoss Stakes.	
Amphora	Ch.F. Ragusa – Amicable 1960 by Doutelle	2
	Lancashire Oaks.	
Strathcona	B.F. St Paddy – Stroma 1955 by Luminary	1
	Dam of Dunfermline.	
1968	6 winners of 11 races.	
Example	Ch.F. Exbury – Amicable 1960 by Doutelle	4
	Park Hill Stakes, Prix Jean de Chaudenay, Prix de Royallieu.	
Albany	Ch.F. Pall Mall – Almeria 1954 by Alycidon	2
	Sandleford Priory Stakes, Prix de Psyche.	
1969	2 winners of 12 races.	
1970	7 winners of 15 races.	
1971	7 winners of 17 races.	
Highclere	B.F. Queen's Hussar – Highlight 1958 by Borealis	3
	1,000 Guineas, Prix de Diane, second in the King George VI and the Queen Elizabeth Stakes.	
Escorial	Ch.F. Royal Palace – Asturia 1961 by The Phoenix	3
	Musidora Stakes, Green Shield Stakes, Ascot.	
1972	7 winners of 11 races.	
Joking Apart	Ch.F. Jimmy Reppin – Strip the Willow 1965 by Native Dancer	3

Year foaled and name	Breeding	Races won

Strensall Stakes, York, Duchess of Montrose Handicap, Newmarket, Third in the 1,000 Guineas.

1973   8 winners of 18 races.

Gilding   Gr.F. Kauai King – Guinea Sparrow 1960 by Grey Sovereign   2

1,000 Guineas Trial Stakes, Ascot.

1974   10 winners of 16 races.

Dunfermline   B.F. Royal Palace – Strathcona 1967 by St Paddy   3

Oaks, St Leger, Pretty Polly Stakes, fourth in the Prix de l'Arc de Triomphe.

Fife and Drum   B.F. Queen's Hussar – Heathfield 1966 by Hethersett   2

Washington Singer Stakes, Newbury.

Circlet   B.F. Baldric II – Highlight 1958 by Borealis   1

Blue Seal Stakes, Ascot.

1975   11 winners of 35 races.

Rhyme Royal   Ch.C. Crepello – Lyrical 1966 by Gratitude   8

Garrowby Stakes, York.

English Harbour   B.C. Mill Reef – Albany 1968 by Pall Mall   3

Predominate Stakes, Goodwood.

Duke of Normandy   B.C. Roberto – Daisy Chain 1963 by Darius   3

Warren Stakes, Epsom.

Tartan Pimpernel   B.F. Blakeney – Strathcona 1967 by St Paddy   3

May Hill Stakes, Acomb Stakes, York, Galtres Stakes, York.

Zetland   Gr.C. Zeddaan – Mey 1970 by Canisbay   11

1976   11 winners of 23 races.

Milford   Ch.C. Mill Reef – Highclere 1971 by Queen's Hussar   3

Princess of Wales's Stakes, Lingfield Derby Trial Stakes, White Rose Stakes.

Buttress   Ch.C. Busted – Albany 1968 by Pall Mall   3

Queen's Vase, Ascot.

Expansive   Ch.F. Exbury – Amicable 1960 by Doutelle   1

Ribblesdale Stakes.

Strathspey   Ch.F. Jimmy Reppin – Strip the Willow 1965 by Native Dancer   2

Fern Hill Stakes, Ascot, Duchess of Montrose Handicap, Newmarket.

1977   8 winners of 10 races.

Deadly Serious   B.F. Queen's Hussar – Joking Apart 1972 by Jimmy Reppin   3

Galtres Stakes, York.

Dukedom   Ch.C. Connaught – Albany 1968 by Pall Mall   1

White Rose Stakes.

1978   6 winners of 15 races.

Church Parade   B.C. Queen's Hussar – Christchurch 1973 by So Blessed   3

Champagne Stakes, Goodwood, High Line Stakes, York.

1979   9 winners of 18 races.

Height of Fashion   B.F. Bustino – Highclere 1971 by Queen's Hussar   5

Princess of Wales's Stakes, May Hill Stakes, Hoover Fillies Mile, Lupe Stakes, Goodwood, Acomb Stakes, York. Dam of Nashwan and Unfuwain.

Sans Blague   Ch.F. The Minstrel – Joking Apart 1972 by Jimmy Reppin   2

Galtres Stakes, York.

Year foaled and name	*Breeding*	*Races won*
1980	7 winners of 21 races.	
Special Leave	B.C. Mill Reef – Light Duty 1972 by Queen's Hussar	1
Hyperion Stakes, Ascot.		
Insular	B.C. Moulton – Pas de Deux 1974 by Nijinsky	10
1981	5 winners of 12 races.	
Elusive	B.F. Little Current (USA) – Tartan Pimpernel 1975 by Blakeney	1
Acomb Stakes, York.		
1982	8 winners of 17 races.	
Soprano	Ch.F. Kris – Contralto 1976 by Busted	3
BBA Atlanta Stakes, Sandown; International Stakes, Kempton; second, Hungerford Stakes, Newbury; third, Coronation Stakes, Royal Ascot.		
1983	6 winners of 12 races.	
Laughter	B.F. Shirley Heights – Light Duty 1972 by Queen's Hussar	2
Houghton Stakes, Newmarket.		
1984	10 winners of 15 races.	
Nettle	Ch.F. Kris – Sans Blague 1979 by The Minstrel	2
Rochford Thompson Newbury Stakes, Newbury.		
1985	7 winners of 11 races.	
Unknown Quantity	B.C. Young Generation – Pas de Deux 1974 by Nijinsky	4
Arlington Handicap Stakes, Grade One, Chicago, USA.		
Highbrow	B.F. Shirley Heights – Highclere 1971 by Queen's Hussar	1
Second, Ribblesdale Stakes, Royal Ascot.		
1986	8 winners of 15 races.	
Starlet	B.F. Teenoso – Pas de Deux 1974 by Nijinsky	3
Prix de Bastia, Cagnes-sur-Mer.		
1987	4 winners of 5 races.	
Marienski	B.C. Nureyev – Highclere 1971 by Queen's Hussar	1

Results as of 1 March 1990.

BIBLIOGRAPHY

Apperley, C. J., ('Nimrod'), *The Chase, the Road and the Turf*, new ed., Arnold, 1898.

Bagehot, Walter, *The English Constitution*, Chapman and Hall, 1867.

Bland, Ernest (ed.), *Flat Racing since 1900*, Dakers, 1950.

Bobinski, Kazimierz, Zamoyski, S., *Tables of Racehorses*, J. A. Allen, 1953.

Browne, T. H., *History of the English Turf 1904–1930*, 2 vols, Virtue, 1931.

Campbell-Maclachan, Archibald, *William Augustus, Duke of Cumberland*, Harry S. King, 1876.

Cathcart, Helen, *The Queen and the Turf*, Stanley Paul, 1959.

Cecil, David, *Melbourne*, Constable, 1972.

Chifney, Samuel, *Genius Genuine*, published by author, 1804.

Childs, Joe, *My Racing Reminiscences*, Hutchinson, 1952.

Cook, Sir T. A., *A History of the English Turf*, 3 vols, Virtue, 1901.

Cook, Sir T. A., *Eclipse and O'Kelly*, Dutton, 1907.

Crawthorne and Herod, *Royal Ascot*, A. Treheme, 1902.

Cumberland, William Augustus, Duke of, *Historical Memoirs*, E. Weller 1767.

Curling, Bill, *The Captain*, Barrie & Jenkins, 1970.

Curling, Bill, *All the Queen's Horses*, Chatto & Windus, 1978.

Day, Alfred and William, *The Racehorse in Training*, revised ed., Cassell, 1925.

Day, William, *Reminiscences of the Turf*, 2nd ed., Bentley, 1886.

Dixon, H. H. ('The Druid'), *The Post and The Paddock*, 5th ed., Vinton, 1912.

Dixon, W., ('Thormanby'), *Kings of the Turf*, Hutchinson, 1898.

Donoghue, Steve, *Donoghue Up!: the Autobiography of Steve Donoghue*, Collins, 1938.

'The Druid' see Dixon, H. H.

Duff, David, *Elizabeth of Glamis: the Story of the Queen Mother*, Frederick Muller, 1973.

Esher G. C. B., G C V O, Viscount, *The Girlhood of Queen Victoria: a Selection from Her Majesty's Diaries, 1832 to 1840*, John Murray, 1912.

Evelyn, John, *Memoirs of John Evelyn*, ed. W. Bray, 1818.

FitzGerald, Arthur, Seth-Smith, Michael, *History of the Prix de l'Arc de Triomphe 1920 to 1948*, J. A. Allen, 1980.

Fraser, Lady Antonia, ed. *The Lives of the Kings and Queens of England*, Weidenfeld & Nicholson, 1975.

Fulford, Roger, *George IV*, George Duckworth, 1949.

Gore, John, *King George V: a Personal Memoir*, John Murray, 1941.

Greville, Charles, *Memoirs*, ed. Henry Reeve, 5th ed., Longmans Green, 1875.

Hewitt, Abram S., *The Great Breeders and Their Methods*, Thoroughbred Publications Inc., 1982.

Hore, J. P., *History of Newmarket and Annals of the Turf*, 3 vols, Bailey, 1886.

Horse-Racing; its History and Early Records of the Principal and Other Race Meetings, Anon., new ed. J. Roche, 1865.

Jarvis, Sir Jack, *They're Off*, Michael Joseph, 1969.

Kent, John, *Records of Goodwood*, Samson Low, 1896.

Lambton, Anne, Offen, John, *Thoroughbred Style*, Stanley Paul, 1987.

Lambton, Hon. George, *Men and Horses I Have Known*, Thornton Butterworth, 1924.

Lawrence, John, *The Horse, in all his Varieties and Uses*, Arnold, 1829.

Lee, Sir Sidney, *Queen Victoria: a Biography*, Smith, Elder, 1902.

Lehndorff, Count, *Horse-Breeding Recollections*, Cox, 1883.

Leicester, Sir Charles, *Bloodstock Breeding*, new ed., J. A. Allen, 1964.

Londonderry, Marchioness of, *Henry Chaplin: a Memoir*, Macmillan, 1926.

Longrigg, Roger, *The History of Horse Racing*, Macmillan, 1972.

Lonsdale Library, *Flat Racing*, Seeley Service, 1940.

Lyle, R. C., *Royal Newmarket*, Putnam, 1945.

Macey, Alan, *The Romance of the Derby Stakes*, Hutchinson, 1930.

Magnus, Sir Philip, *King Edward VII*, John Murray, 1964.

Markham, Gervase, *How to Chuse, Ride, Trayne and Dyet both Hunting and Running Horses*, 1608.

Markham, Gervase, *Cavalarice or the English Horseman*, 1607.

Marsh, Richard, *A Trainer to Two Kings*, Cassell, 1925.

Middlemas, *The Life and Times of Edward VII*, Weidenfeld & Nicholson, 1972.

Moorhouse, Edward, *The History of the Derby*, 2 vols, Biographical Press, 1908.

Mortimer, Roger, *The Jockey Club*, Cassell, 1958.

Mortimer, Roger, *The Derby Stakes*, Cassell, 1973.

Mortimer, Roger, *Twenty Great Horses*, Cassell, 1967.

Mortimer, Roger, and Willet, Peter, *Great Racehorses of the World*, Michael Joseph, 1969.

Mortimer, Roger, Onslow, Richard, Willett, Peter, *Biographical Encyclopedia of British Racing*, Macdonald and Jane's, 1978.

Muir, J. B., *W. T. Frampton and the "Dragon,"* Sporting Fine Art Gallery, 1895.

Newcastle, William Cavendish, Duke of, *La Methode et Invention Nouvelle de dresser les chevaux*, Anuers, 1657.

Newcastle, William Cavendish, Duke of, *A General System of Horsemanship*, 2 vols, ed. J. Brindley, 1743.

'Nimrod' see Apperley C. J.

Nicholson, Harold, *George V, His Life and Reign*, Constable, 1952.

O'Kelly, Dennis, *Genuine Memoirs of Dennis O'Kelly Esq., commonly called Count O'Kelly*, C. Stalker, 1788.

Onslow, Richard, *The Heath and the Turf: a History of Newmarket*, Arthur Barker Ltd, 1971.

Orton, J. *Turf Annals of York and Doncaster*, 1844.

Palmer, Alan, *George IV*, Weidenfeld & Nicholson, 1972.

Pepys, Samuel, *Diary*, ed. Lord Braybroke, 6th ed., Bohn, 1858.

Pick, William, *Authentic Historical Racing Calendar*, 1786.

Pick, William, *Turf Register and Sportsman and Breeder's Stud Book*, 1803.

Portland, William J.A.C.J. Cavendish-Bentinck, 6th Duke of, *Men, Women and Things*, Faber and Faber, 1937.

Portland, William J. A. C. J. Cavendish-bentinck, 6th Duke of, *Memoirs of Racing and Hunting*, Faber & Faber, 1935.

Prior, C. M., *The Royal Studs of the Sixteenth and Seventeenth Centuries*, Horse and Hound Publications, 1935.

Prior, C. M., *Early Records of the Thoroughbred Horse*, The Sportsman, 1924.

Prior, C. M., *History of the Racing Calendar and Stud Book*, Sporting Life, 1926.

Rice, James, *History of the British Turf*, 2 vols, Samson Low, 1879.

Ridgeway, Professor William, *Origin and Influence of the Thoroughbred Horse*, Cambridge University Press, 1905.

Richards, Sir Gordon, *My Story*, Hodder & Stoughton, 1955.

Robinson, J. R., *Old Q*, Samson Lowe, 1895.

Ruff, William, *Ruff's Guide to the Turf*, 1850 to 1988.

Seth-Smith, Michael, *Bred for the Purple*, Leslie Frewin, 1969.

Seth-Smith, Michael, *International Stallions and Studs*, Foulsham, 1974.

Sewell, J. P. C., *Personal Letters of King Edward VII*, Hutchinson, 1931.

Sievier, R. S., *Autobiography*, The Winning Post, 1906.

Siltzer, Frank, *Newmarket*, Cassell, 1923.

Strutt, Joseph, *Sports and Pastimes of the People of England*, 3rd ed. Thomas Tegg, 1838.

Taunton, Theophilius W., *Famous Racehorses with Portraits, Pedigrees and Principal Performances*, Sampson Lowe, Marston & Co., 1895.

Taunton, Thomas, *Portraits of Celebrated Horses of Past and Present Centuries*, 4 vols, Sampson Lowe, Marston, Searle & Rivington, 1887.

Tesio, Frederico, *Breeding the Racehorse*, tr. Edward Spinola, J. A. Allen, 1958.

'Thormanby' see W. Dixon.

Tisdall, E. E. P., *She Made the World Chaos: the Intimate Story of the Empress Frederick of Prussia*, Stanley Paul, 1940.

Voight, Charles Adolph, *Famous Gentlemen Riders at Home and Abroad*, Hutchinson, 1926.

Watson, A. E. T., *King Edward VII as a Sportsman*, Longmans, 1911.

Weatherby and Sons, *General Stud Book*, 1798 to 1988.

Weatherby and Sons, *Racing Calendar, Races Past and Races to Come*, 1773 to 1988.

Whyte, J. C., *History of the British Turf*, Colburn, 1840.

Willett, Peter, *An Introduction to the Thoroughbred*, Stanley Paul, 1966.

Willett, Peter, *The Thoroughbred*, Weidenfeld & Nicholson, 1970.

Wilson, Julian, Lester Piggott, *A Pictorial Biography*, Macdonald Queen Anne Press, 1985.

Newspapers and periodicals
The Times
St James's Chronicle
Bailey's Magazine
Sporting Review
Sporting Magazine
New Sporting Magazine
Racing Illustrated
British Racehorse

Acknowledgements

I wish first to express my deep gratitude to Her Majesty the Queen, whose gracious permission permitted me to see all the relevant papers at the Royal Stud at Sandringham and those in the Royal Archives at Windsor Castle. Without the unrestricted access that I was given to these papers, this book could never have been written. I would also like to thank Her Majesty the Queen's Librarian, Oliver Everett, and his staff headed by Lady de Bellaigue, for all the assistance that I was given when I visited the Royal Archives, and for the exemplary way in which they unearthed documents that I needed.

The assistance that I have been given by Her Majesty the Queen's Stud Manager, Michael Oswald, since the moment I conceived the idea of writing this book, can never be overstated. His wise advice and suggestions have been invaluable; despite his enormously busy programme, he has always been ready to answer my queries and correct my errors. Furthermore he and his wife, Lady Angela Oswald, have been unstinting in their hospitality during my visits to their house near Sandringham, when they so kindly invited me to stay with them.

During all of the last three years I have been most generously helped by a great many people in my researches. In particular I would like to thank Monsieur Jean Romanet and Monsieur Louis Romanet for permission to see documents and books in the Société d' Encouragement, Monsieur Gerard Monnet and Madame Co-rinne Idris for their help at the Société d' Encouragement, especially in obtaining photographs of Royal winners in France; the Hon. Mrs Jane Roberts and Mrs Prudence Sutcliffe for their assistance in the Print Room at Windsor Castle, Marcus Bishop for his help at Her Majesty the Queen's Collection of paintings at St James's Palace, Miss Biddy Shennan, and David Fuller of Arthur Ackermann's. I would also like to offer a special word of thanks to the staff of the Bodleian Library, Oxford University, especially those in the Upper Reading Room, who dealt with my innumerable requests so efficiently for two years. The advice of my brother-in-law, John Docherty, and his wife, Anne, in the initial stages of this book, especially with regard to the best computer to obtain for storing the research, was much appreciated.

Finally I wish to thank my wife, Rosemary, without whose encouragement, patience, and help this book would never have been written. I also need to ask her forgiveness for being so often totally absent-minded when absorbed in the performances of Royal racehorse running in the last three centuries. Her fortitude was all the greater since, shortly after this book was commenced, she gave birth to our first son, Thomas, and for the last two years has had to take care of him as well as a husband forgetful of everything unconnected with thoroughbreds bred by the Royal Studs.

Charlbury, Oxford.
March 1990.

Index

Only the most influential horses bred by the Royal Studs are listed separately. All other important horses are listed under their royal owners.